AFTER BUDDHISM

RETHINKING THE DHARMA FOR A SECULAR AGE

Stephen Batchelor

Yale UNIVERSITY PRESS/NEW HAVEN & LONDON

Published with assistance from the foundation established in memory of Philip Hamilton McMillan of the Class of 1894, Yale College.

Map by Bill Nelson.

Designed by Mary Valencia.
Set in Scala type by Integrated Publishing Solutions.
Printed in the United States of America.

Library of Congress Control Number: 2015935009
ISBN 978-0-300-20518-3 (cloth : alk. paper)
ISBN 978-0-300-22434-4 (pbk.)

A catalogue record for this book is available from the British Library.

10 9 8 7 6 5 4 3 2 1

For Don Cupitt

The dharma is clearly visible, immediate, inviting, uplifting, to be personally sensed by the wise.

—Gotama, the Buddha (c. 480–c. 400 BCE)

The dharma of the buddhas has no special undertakings. Just act ordinarily, without trying to do anything in particular. Move your bowels, piss, get dressed, eat your rice, and if you get tired, lie down.

—Linji Yixuan (d. 866)

Contents

Preface

This book is an attempt to synthesize an understanding of Buddhism that I have been working toward since my first publication, *Alone with Others,* appeared in 1983. In the intervening thirty years I have published a number of other writings that have branched off in different directions but maintained, at least in the eyes of the author, a steady focus on a single question: What does it mean to practice the dharma of the Buddha in the context of modernity? My most recent publication, the essay "A Secular Buddhism" (2012), can be seen as a preparatory sketch of what I seek to flesh out in this book.

I am indebted to Geshe Tamdrin Rabten for training me in Tibetan Buddhist logic, epistemology, and philosophy, which provided the intellectual foundations for everything I have done since; Satya Narayan Goenka for introducing me to the practice of *vipassanā* and the early Buddhism of the Pali Canon; and Kusan Sunim for instructing me in the practice of Korean Sŏn (Zen), which, together with mindful awareness, continues as the basis for my practice of meditation. While all of these Buddhist traditions have played an important role in my understanding and practice of the dharma, my interpretations of certain Buddhist doctrines may strike some readers as highly unorthodox.

My primary authority for understanding what the Buddha taught is the discourses of the Pali Canon. My inability to read Chinese is the only reason I have not consulted the comparable body of texts preserved in the Āgama literature. The early records of the Sŏn Buddhist tradition, composed during the Tang dynasty of China, likewise serve as an important source for my work. For the later Indian tradition, I have been inspired by the writings of Nāgārjuna and Śāntideva.

I have been influenced in my interpretations of Buddhism by the philosophers Martin Heidegger and Richard Rorty, as well as the Christian theologians Paul Tillich and Don Cupitt. In the field of Buddhist studies, I owe a debt of gratitude to the work of Richard Gombrich, K. R. Norman, Johannes Bronkhorst, and Gregory Schopen. I have been greatly helped in my understanding of the Pali Canon by the translations of Bhikkhu Bodhi, Eugene Watson Burlingame, I. B. Horner, John D. Ireland, Bhikkhu Ñāṇamoli, Caroline Rhys Davids, and Maurice Walshe, as well as by Ñāṇavira Thera's interpretations of some of its key ideas.

Throughout this book I accept Heinz Bechert and Richard Gombrich's dating of the Buddha as c. 480–c. 400 BCE. In moving his dates eighty years nearer to our own time than those accepted by Buddhist tradition, Gotama becomes a contemporary of Socrates rather than Pythagoras, which brings him into closer proximity to the West's own historical self-awareness. I have based the core narrative of the life of Gotama on the account in the Vinaya of the Mūlasarvāstavāda school as preserved in Tibetan and translated by W. Woodville Rockhill in 1884. My previous book *Confession of a Buddhist Atheist* (2010) reconstructed the story of the Buddha's life entirely on the basis of Pali sources. The version presented by Rockhill differs in a number of details, but the story is essentially the same. Since these two textual traditions were preserved at opposite ends of the Indian subcontinent, and since their preservers had no contact with each other for centuries, both texts were presumably based on an earlier version that was probably extant until the time of Emperor Aśoka (304–232 BCE), who was born only a century or so after the death of the Buddha.

As a rule, I give most proper names and Buddhist technical terms in their Pali spelling, unless their provenance is clearly Chinese, Korean, or Tibetan. Since certain well-known terms such as "dharma," "karma" and "nirvana" are now part of the English language, I have left them in their Sanskrit spelling. I have translated *bhikkhu* and *bhikkhuni* as "mendicant" (rather than "monk" and "nun") unless the context requires gender specificity, in which case I leave them in Pali. *Upāsaka* and *upāsika* are translated as "adherent" (rather than "layman" and "laywoman"), and *bhagavant* as "Teacher" (rather than "Blessed One"). I follow H. W. Schumann in spelling the name of the Buddha's clan as "Sakiya" (rather than "Sakya" or "Shakya"). I have left the difficult term *tathāgata* (in most cases more or less synonymous with "buddha") untranslated; I offer an interpretation of it in chapter 5, section 9. The discourse that tradition has titled *Turning the Wheel of Dharma* (*Dhammacakkapavattana Sutta*) I have rendered throughout as *The Four Tasks*. I provide a translation of this and other Pali texts to which I frequently refer in the appendix: "Selected Discourses from the Pali Canon."

I would like to thank the following readers whose comments on the manuscript have contributed to the final form of the work: Darius Cuplinskas, Ann Gleig, Winton Higgins, Bernd Kaponig, Antonia Macaro, Ken McLeod, Stephen Schettini, John Teasdale, Gay Watson, Anne Wiltshire, and Dale Wright. Discussions over the years with my colleagues John Peacock and Marc Akincano Weber have been of great help in clarifying my understanding of early Buddhism. I am most grateful for the support of my agent, Anne Edelstein, as well as my editor, Jennifer Banks, copyeditor Mary Pasti, and the staff at Yale University Press. As always, I am indebted to the unconditional encouragement and tolerance of my wife, Martine. It goes without saying that any errors are my own.

After Buddhism

I

After Buddhism

> So, Bāhiya, should you train yourself: "in the seen, there will be only the seen; in the heard, only the heard; in the sensed, only the sensed; in that of which I am conscious, only that of which I am conscious." This is how you should train.
>
> —UDĀNA

(1)

A well-known story recounts that Gotama—the Buddha—was once staying in Jeta's Grove, his main center near the city of Sāvatthi, capital of the kingdom of Kosala. Many priests, wanderers, and ascetics were living nearby. They are described as people "of various beliefs and opinions, who supported themselves by promoting their different views." The text enumerates the kinds of opinions they taught:

> The world is eternal.
> The world is not eternal.
> The world is finite.
> The world is not finite.
> Body and soul are identical.
> Body and soul are different.
> The *tathāgata* exists after death.

The *tathāgata* does not exist after death.
The *tathāgata* both exists and does not exist after death.
The *tathāgata* neither exists nor does not exist after death.

They took these opinions seriously. "Only this is true," they would insist. "Every other view is false!" As a result, they fell into endless arguments, "wounding each other with verbal darts, saying 'The dharma is like *this!*' 'The dharma is not like *that!*'"[1]

The Buddha commented that such people were blind. "They do not know what is of benefit and what is of harm," he explained. "They do not understand what is and what is not the dharma."[2] He had no interest at all in their propositions. Unconcerned whether such views were true or false, he sought neither to affirm nor to reject them. "A proponent of the dharma," he once observed, "does not dispute with anyone in the world."[3] Whenever a metaphysical claim of this kind was made, Gotama did not react by getting drawn in and taking sides. He remained keenly alert to the complexity of the whole picture without opting for one position over another.

Gotama relates a parable as a commentary on the quarreling priests and ascetics. He tells of a king in Sāvatthi who instructed his servants to gather together all the people of the city who had been blind from birth. He ordered an elephant to be brought before them, then led each blind person to the creature and had him or her touch a different part of the elephant's body. Some rubbed the ears, some felt the trunk, some put their arms around a leg, some stroked the side, and some pulled the tail. He asked: "Now tell me: what is an elephant?" Some said an elephant was "just like a storeroom," some said it was "just like a pillar," and others said it was "just like a broom." They argued—"An elephant is like this! An elephant is not like that!"—until a fight broke out, and they began beating each other with their fists.[4]

The moral of this story is that the dharma cannot be reduced to a set of truth-claims, which will inevitably conflict with other truth-claims. Only by letting go of such views will one be able to understand how dharma practice is not about being "right" or "wrong."

It is notable that the last six of the ten listed views have to do with the possibility (or not) of life after death, which suggests that the topic was much debated. Although the Buddha may have presented his ideas in the context of multiple lifetimes, this oft-repeated passage implies that he did so for cultural and pragmatic reasons alone. "Of that which the wise (*paṇḍitā*) in the world agree upon as not existing," he said, "I too say that it does not exist. And of that which the wise in the world agree upon as existing, I too say that it exists."[5] On such matters, Gotama is content to accept learned consensus. To have affirmed the view that the mind is different from the body and will be reborn after death in another body would have made him no different from those wanderers and ascetics he declared to be blind.

In contrast to those who base their behavior on metaphysical truth-claims, the practitioner of the dharma as Gotama envisioned it takes into account the totality of each situation and responds in accordance with the principles, perspective, and values of the dharma. Since each situation in life is unique, it is impossible to predict in advance exactly how such a person will respond. Instead of asking "What is the 'right' or 'wrong' thing to do?" the practitioner asks, "What is the wisest and most compassionate thing to do?" Many centuries after the Buddha, the Chinese Chan (Zen) patriarch Yunmen (c. 860–949) was asked: "What are the teachings of an entire lifetime?" Yunmen replied: "An appropriate statement."[6] For Yunmen, what counts is whether your words and deeds are an appropriate response to the situation at hand, not whether they accord with an abstract truth.

The dharma is the whole elephant. It is comparable to a complex living organism, each part of which plays a role in animating the mysterious creature that breathes, eats, walks, and sleeps. Dharma practice exposes the limits of human thought and language when we are confronted with the puzzle of being here at all. All people, whether devoutly religious or avowedly secular, share this sense of unknowing, wonder, and perplexity. That is where we all begin.

(2)

As an impressionable nineteen-year-old, I was inducted into an intact medieval Buddhist world that had had little contact with modernity. My Tibetan teachers had been exiled from their homeland for thirteen years and were confident that it would not be long before they returned. I soon found myself involved in far more than a study of the doctrines and practices of Buddhism. I became immersed in a refined culture of awakening, embodied by men and women who had been raised and educated in a world utterly different from the one I knew. My formative years, which would otherwise have been spent in a university in Britain, involved gaining intimate knowledge of and familiarity with the ways these people thought, spoke, and acted. I did not judge them with the detachment of an outside observer. I came to see myself as part of their world. I went native.

Total immersion in a living Buddhist culture allowed me to acquire an intuitive familiarity with a complex worldview worked out and articulated over many centuries. This familiarity provided me with the framework, concepts, and terminology needed to rethink the dharma. I believe that the arguments presented in this book remain entirely true to the logic of the dharma. I seek to torque that logic to bring the dharma into closer alignment with the needs and concerns of people living in modernity. In attempting to come up with a coherent and consistent account of Buddhist thought and practice, my aim is to produce what in Christianity would be called a *systematic theology.* I realize that many Buddhists may find some of what I say heretical. I can sympathize with them—for there is a part of me that also experiences a tremor of unease when I read what I have written.

Throughout my forty years of involvement in the dharma, I have spent a great deal of time pondering and agonizing over Buddhist concepts in order to formulate an understanding of the dharma that is consistent with both core Buddhist teaching and the worldview of modernity. During these years the dharma has slowly broken out of the ghetto of "Oriental religion" and penetrated into the mainstream of contemporary culture. Buddhist imagery, concepts, and terms now crop up in the most unlikely settings: in tattoos and Hollywood movies, in literary novels and slick advertising campaigns. The practice of mindfulness, now widely adopted in health care, business, education, and other fields, has grown from a minority interest among dharma students into a global movement that draws people from all walks of life, most of whom have little interest in the traditional teachings or institutions of Buddhism. What I seek to provide in this book is a philosophical, ethical, historical, and cultural framework for mindfulness and other such practices, which are rooted in the earliest canonical sources but articulated here afresh.

I cannot pretend that my rethinking of the dharma has not been deeply influenced by the culture in which I was raised. As a modern Westerner, I cannot but consider Buddhism as a historically contingent phenomenon that has continually adapted itself to different circumstances. As the product of a Christian culture, I am drawn to recover a thoroughly human Buddha, whose life and deeds tell us as much about the dharma as the written record of what he said does. As someone who identifies with the Protestant movements within Christianity, I am skeptical of the authority and charisma of priests and seek a direct relationship with the dharma through my own study of the original texts. As a European, I am conscious of my indebtedness to the thinkers of ancient Greece who understood philosophy as a practice for the healing and care of the soul.

(3)

From the age of nineteen to the age of twenty-seven, I trained with lamas of the Geluk school of Tibetan Buddhism, who taught me that ultimate truth was an emptiness of something that had never been there in the first place. I have sought to remain true to this idea ever since. I was told that the aim of Buddhist philosophy was to gain knowledge of such emptiness by rational analysis and inference, whereas the goal of Buddhist meditation was to focus on this insight until one achieved an immediate, nonconceptual understanding. This procedure of analysis and meditation was presented as the only way to gain enlightenment about the true nature of reality and thereby liberation from the ignorance that is the root cause of all suffering.

The realization of emptiness begins with an inquiry into what it means to be a self. When you try to get to the essence of a person, whether yourself or someone else, the quest goes on and on. It is not that no one is there—the uncanny sense of someone uniquely alive persists. But you will never arrive at an irreducible core of which you can say: "There! Found you!" In this sense, the self or person is said to be "empty."

To understand the emptiness of a person is to realize that this seemingly irreducible core has never been there in the first place. Tibetan lamas use the technical phrase *rang bzhin gyis grub pa,* usually translated as "inherently existent" or "intrinsically real," to describe what is to be negated. The phrase literally means "existing by virtue of its own face." It implies that no matter where or how probingly you look, you will not find anything in this world that exists self-sufficiently by its own intrinsic nature, in its own right, independent of all else. Why? Because every single thing in this strange world of ours, from an elephant to the tiniest subatomic particle, is contingent on proximate and distant causes, on parts to which it cannot be reduced, and on words and concepts that render it intelligible in a particular human culture.

According to Geluk teaching, the emptiness of inherent existence is a simple negation (*med 'gag*) as opposed to an affirming negation (*ma yin 'gag*). This means that the absence opened up by emptiness does not disclose and thereby affirm a transcendent reality (like God or Pure Consciousness) that was previously obscured by one's egoistic confusion. It simply removes a fiction that was never there. Although human beings seem to be instinctively programmed (no doubt for evolutionary reasons) to see themselves and people they desire or hate as self-sufficiently real, such inherent existence turns out to be a chimera.

I have just summarized the standard understanding of emptiness as it would be taught today by a figure such as the Dalai Lama of Tibet. Rather than using the word "emptiness," other Buddhist teachers might speak of "not-self" (*anattā*), which comes to much the same thing. Appearances, they will claim, are deceptive; unless we dispel the fiction of "self" or "inherent existence" we will never behold the true nature of things.

Yet when we consult the earliest Buddhist discourses, which are found in the Pali Canon and the Chinese Āgamas, we discover that Gotama does not speak about emptiness in this way at all. Reading these earliest texts, I feel as though I am encountering another dialect of the same language: it uses many of the same words but in a curiously different way. The *Shorter Discourse on Emptiness,* for example, begins with the Buddha's attendant Ānanda posing a question:

> "You were once living in Sakiya, sir, among your kinsfolk in the town of Nāgaraka. It was there that I heard you say from your own lips: 'Now I mainly dwell by dwelling in emptiness.' Did I hear that correctly?"
>
> "Yes," replies Gotama. "Then, as now, do I mainly dwell by dwelling in emptiness."[7]

The word that jumps off the page here is "dwell," which translates the Pali *viharati.* The noun form is *vihāra,* "dwelling" or "abode," which has come to mean "monastery"—that is, a dwelling for monks. Yet to "dwell" or "abide" describes a primordial relation to this earth on which we live. Emptiness is first and foremost a condition in which we dwell, abide, and live. Another Pali discourse describes this emptiness as the "abode of a great person."[8] Emptiness thus seems to be a perspective, a sensibility, a way of being in this poignant, contingent world. The "great person" would be one who has cultivated such a sensibility until it has become entirely natural. Rather than being the negation of "self," emptiness discloses the dignity of a person who has realized what it means to be fully human.

Such emptiness is far from being an ultimate truth that needs to be understood through logical inference and then directly realized in a state of nonconceptual meditation. It is a sensibility in which one dwells, not a privileged epistemological object that, through knowing, one gains a cognitive enlightenment.

The *Shorter Discourse on Emptiness* tells the story of a man who was searching for a way to live authentically on earth. Gotama starts his discourse with what is closest to hand: the villa in which he is staying with his mendicants. "In being empty of elephants, cattle, and horses, gold and silver, crowds of women and men," he remarks, "there is just one thing of which this villa is not empty: this group of mendicants." Yet a mendicant who finds this community too noisy and distracting will seek out the solitude of the forest, which is "empty of any awareness of villages or people." Thus the mendicant regards the forest as "empty of what is not there. And of what remains, he knows: 'This is what's here.'"[9] Although the mendicant is no longer upset by the hustle and bustle of the world, he finds himself prone to the anxiety engendered by living in the forest.

To overcome this anxiety, the mendicant enters into progressively refined states of meditative absorption: on the earth's expanse, unlimited space, unlimited consciousness, nothingness, and being-neither-aware-nor-unaware. But at each stage he finds that there is still something within him that gives rise to unease. So he abandons the deep, trance-like states for a "signless concentration of the heart." Even so, he realizes that he is still "prone to the anxiety that comes from having the six sense fields of a living body." Whatever the virtues of his signless concentration, it is nonetheless "compounded and contrived" and therefore "impermanent and subject to ceasing."[10] Only at this point, having exhausted the possibilities of meditating in sylvan solitude, does he realize that all these exercises are ultimately futile because they will come to an end.

He appears to have come full circle. Yet this very insight into impermanence grants him the peace of mind he has been seeking all along. "In knowing and seeing thus," continues Gotama, "his heart is freed from the effluences (*āsava*) of desire, being, and ignorance." But this is not the end of the story. "With none of the anxieties due to those effluences," reflects the mendicant, "I am still prone to the anxiety that comes from having the six sense fields of a living body. This state of awareness is empty of those effluences. What is not empty is this: the six sense fields of a living body."[11]

The *Shorter Discourse on Emptiness* concludes with this insight: to dwell in emptiness means to inhabit fully the embodied space of one's sensory experience, but in a way that is no longer determined by one's habitual reactivity. To dwell in such emptiness does not mean that one will no longer suffer. As long as one has a body and senses, one will be "prone to the anxiety" that comes with being a conscious, feeling creature made of flesh, bones, and blood. And this would have been just as true for Gotama as it is for us today.

Here, emptiness is not a truth—let alone an ultimate truth—that is to be understood correctly as a means to dispel ignorance and thereby attain enlightenment. For Gotama, the point is not to understand emptiness but to *dwell* in it. To dwell in emptiness brings us firmly down to earth and back to our bodies. It is a way of enabling us to open our eyes and see ordinary things as though for the first time. As the Buddha instructed his student Bāhiya, to live in such a way means that "in the seen, there will be only the seen; in the heard, only the heard; in the sensed, only the sensed; in that of which I am conscious, only that of which I am conscious."[12]

How, in the course of Buddhist history, did the concept of emptiness evolve from a way of dwelling on earth unconditioned by reactivity into an ultimate truth to be directly cognized in a nonconceptual state of meditation? This is one of the key questions that I will seek to answer in the rest of this book.

(4)

From the age of twenty-seven to the age of thirty-one, I continued my Buddhist monastic training in a Sŏn (Zen) monastery in South Korea, where the sole meditation practice was to sit facing a wall for ten to twelve hours a day asking oneself: "What is this?"[13] I have been guided by this impossible question ever since. It has led me away from a religious quest for ultimate truth and brought me back to a perplexed encounter with this contingent, poignant, and ambiguous world here and now.

The Sŏn tradition originated in seventh-century Tang China as a reaction against the overly metaphysical concerns of the established Buddhist schools. It sought to recover the simplicity of early Buddhism by following Gotama's example of sitting still beneath a tree in an uncompromising engagement with the primordial questions of what it means to be born, get sick, grow old, and die. The Sŏn masters realized that the very way in which you posed these questions would determine the kind of "enlightenment" you might gain. A famous aphorism encapsulates this realization:

Great doubt—great awakening;
Little doubt—little awakening;
No doubt—no awakening.

The quality of your "doubt"—of the questions you ask—is directly correlated to the quality of your insight. To ask such questions viscerally will engender a correspondingly visceral awakening. To pose them intellectually, with "little doubt," will lead only to intellectual understanding. For those who are not stirred by existential questions at all, awakening is not even conceivable. Sŏn practitioners rejected the metaphysical learning of scholar-monks not because they disagreed with their conclusions but because they disagreed with the way the scholars posed the questions in the first place. To practice Sŏn means to ask these questions with the whole body, with "its 360 bones and joints and the 84,000 pores of one's skin," so that it becomes a "solid lump of doubt." Moreover, the doubt needs to reach a critical mass, "like a red hot iron ball, which you have gulped down and which you try to vomit but cannot."[14]

To sustain this kind of urgent perplexity entails learning how to remain in a balanced, focused, and inquiring frame of mind without succumbing to the seductive lure of "it is this" and "it is not that." To pose a question with sincerity, you need to suspend all expectations as to what the answer might be. You need to rest in a condition of unknowing, vitally alert to the sheer mystery of being alive rather than dead. In this way, you cultivate a middle way between "it is" and "it is not," affirmation and negation, being and nothingness.

To tread this middle way in practice is like walking a tightrope: the path is constantly wobbling and shifting. We inhabit a linguistic realm where we cannot avoid using terms like "is" and "is not," and a moral realm where we are bound to express preferences and make choices. The polarities embedded in human consciousness are useful, if not indispensable, in providing a framework to guide our course through life. They are like the pole carried by the tightrope walker that provides the crucial stability to take the next step. The point, therefore, is not to reject dualities in favor of a hypothetical "non-duality" but to learn to live with them more lightly, fluidly, and ironically. The danger of duality, against which the Buddha warned his followers, does not lie in oppositional thinking itself. Rather, it lies in how we use such thinking to reinforce and justify our egoism, cravings, fears, and hatreds.[15]

(5)

According to one early Buddhist source, the Vinaya of the Mūlasarvāstavāda school, shortly after the awakening Gotama fell seriously ill from eating some overly rich food donated to him by two passing merchants, Tapussa and his younger brother Bhallika. Māra—the demonic personification of death—entreated him to die and thus enter the final nirvana in which he would be finally released from all suffering. But Gotama refused. He declared:

> I will not leave this world until I have men and women mendicants and men and women adherents who are accomplished, trained, skilled, learned, knowers of the dharma, trained in the dharma, walking in the path of the dharma, who will pass on what they have gained from their teacher, teach it, declare it, establish it, expound it, analyse it, make it clear; until they shall be able by means of the dharma to refute false teachings that have arisen, and teach the sublime dharma.[16]

Gotama clearly envisaged a community in which all members—irrespective of their status as men or women, monastics (mendicants) or laity (adherents)—are entirely equal in the training they receive in the dharma, the practices they undertake to master and understand it, and the responsibility they have in communicating its message.

Such an egalitarian community is a far cry from what is normative in many Buddhist traditions in Asia today. Spiritual, moral, and doctrinal authority is generally the preserve of senior monks. Nuns—if they are afforded any recognition or status—play a largely subordinate role. Laypeople, no matter how devout, are often reduced to being providers for the sangha (the word means "community" but has come to refer to monastics alone) and encouraged to accumulate meritorious acts that will enable them to receive ordination in a future life. Not only does this state of affairs contradict and distort what appears to be the Buddha's original intent, but it flies in the face of the values of equality and human dignity that characterize the modern age.

Those who campaign for the restoration of full ordination for women in Buddhism often cite this passage to show that the Buddha intended to establish an order of *bhikkhunis* (nuns) from the very outset of his teaching career.[17] The orthodox view—which seems to have been inserted into the canon by patriarchal hard-liners at a fairly early date—is that the Buddha was initially reluctant to accept women mendicants, gave in to their demands only under pressure from Ānanda, imposed upon them eight "heavy" (*garu*) rules, compared their presence in the community to a "blight" and "disease," and predicted that they would shorten the life of the dharma in the world.[18] What advocates of women's ordination fail to point out, however, is that the same passage endorses an equal role for men and women adherents in the practice and exposition of the dharma.

In keeping with Gotama's initial statement of resolve, I would argue for a complete restoration of equality between mendicants and adherents of both sexes as practitioners and teachers of the dharma. To persist with the inequalities upheld by orthodoxy is unjust and anachronistic. Many of the most effective proponents of the dharma in our time have not been monastics but laypeople, men and women alike, among them such leading figures of Buddhism in twentieth-century Asia as Anagarika Dhammapala (1864–1933), who advocated a "Protestant"-style Buddhist reform in Ceylon; Dr. B. R. Ambedkar (1891–1956), who led mass conversions of former *dalits* (Untouchables) to Buddhism in India; Tsunesaburō Makiguchi (1871–1944) and Jōsei Toda (1900–1958), who established the Sōka Gakkai sect of Buddhism in Japan; Dr. D. T. Suzuki (1870–1966), whose writings introduced Zen and Mahayana Buddhism to the West; and Saya Gyi U Ba Khin (1899–1971), who popularized the practice of *vipassanā* meditation in Burma. As Buddhism has spread through the Western world, many of the most influential teachers and writers have likewise not been ordained monastics but men and women whose authority has lain in their personal integrity and example rather than their ecclesiastical rank.

In today's world, the notion that the ideal to which Buddhists aspire should be that of a celibate monk who embodies the values of fifth century BCE Indian asceticism and adheres to a set of rules determined by the circumstances of that distant place and time is questionable. I have no objection to Buddhist monasticism: for many it might well offer the most appropriate and fulfilling way of practicing the dharma. But if we are to recover the kind of egalitarian community that the Buddha envisioned, practitioners will need to fundamentally reassess the power relations between mendicants and adherents and between men and women.

From a modern perspective, many of the traditional forms of Buddhism inherited from Asia appear to be stagnating. Their initial creativity and imagination have long dissipated, and their practitioners seem primarily intent on preserving time-honored doctrines and practices by endlessly repeating past teachings and instructions. When even a liberal and modernized church such as that of Anglicanism struggles to come to terms with women bishops and homosexual relationships, there seems little prospect that conservative Buddhist institutions will change their patriarchal stances in the foreseeable future. While admiring the work of those who seek to reform Buddhist traditions from within established schools, I suspect that any real change in Buddhist sensibility and identity will take place in the secular rather than the religious sphere.

For this reason, I will focus on the lives of some key followers of the Buddha who did not "leave home for homelessness" to become mendicants but remained fully active in the world. By piecing together the stories of such figures as Mahānāma (Gotama's cousin who became chief of the Buddha's Sakiya clan), Pasenadi (king of Kosala), and Jīvaka (court doctor in Magadha), I will try to restore the sense of a community that was not dominated by detached and saintly monks but embraced those from all walks of life. In a similar vein, I see no need to speculate on the serene perfection of the arahant—the archetypal Buddhist saint. I will concentrate instead on the experience of conversion to the dharma and the ongoing challenge entailed in cultivating a way of life that accords with its values. As we shall see, the Buddha described Mahānāma, Jīvaka, and several other adherents as "seers of the deathless": people who lived their daily lives in the world from the perspective of nirvana.

(6)

The word "religious" is notoriously difficult to define. The term has a long and confusing history, and its meaning has shifted and changed over time.[19] Here I will use it in two related but distinct senses. In the first sense, I understand "religious" to denote our wish to come to terms with or reconcile ourselves to our own birth and death. For many people, religious thoughts and acts are those that engage their deepest, core relationship to the totality of their life and what it means for them. This is what the theologian Paul Tillich called one's "ultimate concern." For Tillich, ultimate concern is the definition of faith, and that about which one is ultimately concerned the definition of God.[20]

In the second sense, I take "religious" to denote whatever formal means are employed—adherence to sacred texts, submission to the authority of monastics and priests, performance of rites and rituals, participation in spiritual retreats—to articulate, frame, and enact ultimate concerns. Secular critics commonly dismiss religious institutions and beliefs as outdated, dogmatic, repressive, and so on, forgetting about the deep human concerns that they were originally created to address. One can be religious in the sense of being motivated by ultimate concerns, without ever engaging in any overtly religious behavior, just as one can be religious in the conventional sense merely out of habit or custom, without being driven by an ultimate concern. Those who describe themselves as "devout atheists" are not entirely joking.

"Secular" is a term that presents as many problems as "religious." The German theologian Dietrich Bonhoeffer, in his final letters from a Nazi prison before he died, foresaw the emergence of a "religionless Christianity," which understands the message of the Gospels to be one of totally embracing the condition of the suffering world and letting go of the superficial consolations of being a devout member of a Christian institution. "We are moving," he wrote, "toward a completely religionless time."[21] From this perspective, too, there seems to be no reason why avowedly "secular" people cannot be deeply "religious" in their ultimate concern to come to terms with their brief and poignant life here and now.

I also use the term "secular" in full consciousness of its etymological roots in the Latin *saeculum*, which means "this age," "this *siècle* (century)," "this generation." If we are secular, then, our primary concerns are those we have about *this* world—about everything that has to do with the quality of the personal, social, and environmental experience of being alive on this planet. A secular approach to Buddhism is thus concerned with how the dharma can enable humans and other living beings to flourish in this biosphere, not in a hypothetical afterlife. Rather than emphasizing personal enlightenment and liberation, it is grounded in a deeply felt concern and compassion for the suffering of all those with whom we share this earth.

Like many who came of age in Europe and North America after the traumas of two world wars, I was raised in a family that had abandoned any affiliation to formal Christianity. I was educated in a rationalist, humanist environment that encouraged me to question and doubt whatever I was told. I find it disturbing when Western converts to Buddhism with a background and upbringing similar to my own uncritically adopt beliefs—in karma and rebirth, for example—that traditional Buddhists simply take for granted. Such reactions as these mark me out as someone who has unashamedly internalized a secular outlook. Whatever form of Buddhism I advocate is bound to bear the imprint of a skeptical, this-worldly approach to the dharma. Such a perspective is in no way preferable or superior to a more traditional outlook—in many ways I envy those who do not have to struggle with orthodox Buddhist beliefs. My approach simply reflects an embedded cultural worldview that I could no more discard than I could willfully cease to comprehend the English language.[22]

Our current use of the terms "religious" and "secular" are determined by the senses they have acquired in modernity. Since they have no equivalents in any of the classical Buddhist languages, we must use them with caution when talking of premodern Buddhism. The same is true of the very word "Buddhism," a term coined by Western scholars in the nineteenth century, which also has no equivalent in Pali, Sanskrit, Chinese, or Tibetan. For this reason, I prefer to use the word "dharma," which I will not translate. At the same time, I cannot pretend that I am not a modern Westerner. I find myself bound to a language that is in many ways inadequate and misleading but, whether I like it or not, happens to be the one we speak.

What sort of Buddhism does a self-declared secular Buddhist like myself advocate? I do not envision a Buddhism that seeks to discard all trace of religiosity, that seeks to arrive at a dharma that is little more than a set of self-help techniques that enable us to operate more calmly and effectively as agents or clients, or both, of capitalist consumerism.[23] We could make the case that the practice of mindfulness, taken out of its original context, reinforces the solipsistic isolation of the self by immunizing practitioners against the unsettling emotions, impulses, anxieties, and doubts that assail our fragile egos. Instead of imagining a dharma that erects even firmer barriers around the alienated self, let us imagine one that works toward a reenchantment of the world. Doing so will require the cultivation of a sensibility to what might be called the "everyday sublime," a theme that will be explored in chapter 9.

I do not see secular Buddhism as the end result of the *secularization* of Buddhism, which renders Buddhist ideas and practices palatable and useful for those who have no interest in committing themselves to the core values of the dharma. The kind of secular Buddhism I envisage would consider those core values to be a necessary framework for humans to flourish and to realize ultimate concerns. I will consider the nature of these values and the ways to internalize and enact them in chapters 2 and 3.

Buddhism today commonly impresses people as a slightly aloof monastic religion committed to training its followers in meditation, morality, and philosophy. Historically, this version of Buddhism is very recent.[24] While it may accord with some of the idealistic representations that Buddhists have preserved of themselves in their textual memory, it ignores the complex relationships that actual Buddhist institutions had with the societies of which they were an integral part. In premodern Asia, the Buddhist *vihāra,* or temple, was a home for those who rejected or fell foul of the norms of society and aspired to cultivate higher values. Depending on the country, it could also be a farm, a granary, a courthouse, a fort, a school, an arts center, a hospital, a bank, an orphanage, a refuge for abandoned animals—as well as a place to perform religious rites (particularly for the deceased) and receive pastoral care. For some, it was also where they might find someone who could instruct them in meditation and philosophy.

One of the consequences of modernization throughout Asia has been to deprive Buddhism of many of its secular functions. While the pace and manner of change vary from country to country, the state has come to assume many of the roles (health care, education, the care of orphans) that was once the preserve of the temples. As a result, monks' and nuns' activities now often tend to focus on pastoral and spiritual matters. With the widespread adoption of mindfulness meditation in counseling and psychotherapy, even these functions are now being coopted by secular bodies.

The shift toward a more secular approach to Buddhism is not new. As Buddhists sought to come to terms with modernity in the past century, a number of secularized variants of traditional forms arose. The worldwide Vipassana community, for example, has its origins in a reform movement among Burmese Buddhists toward the end of the nineteenth century. The aim of the reformers was to affirm an indigenous religious identity capable of standing up to the Christianity and rationalist humanism of the British colonial power. Contemporary Western forms of *vipassanā* meditation spawned the secular mindfulness movement, whose leading teachers are predominantly lay. The

Soka Gakkai, one of the largest global Buddhist movements today, started in Japan in the 1920s as an educational society affiliated with the Nichiren Shoshu school, founded by the thirteenth-century Buddhist reformer Nichiren Daishonin. Since 1992 it has distanced itself from the Nichiren Shoshu priesthood and now operates as a primarily lay movement. In the late 1970s the Kagyu/Rimé lama Chögyam Trungpa explicitly envisioned a secular path of meditation, called Shambhala Training. Although Trungpa conceived of this path as separate from his Buddhist Vajradhatu organization, after his death the two were incorporated into what is now known as Shambhala Buddhism, one of the most active and successful Buddhist movements in the United States.

Despite the secular tone and lay teachers of these movements, all three have an ambivalent relation with the dogmas and hierarchies of the Buddhist institutions from which they originated. Although there may be a reduced public display of overt religiosity in their centers and a deliberate effort by teachers to present the dharma in terms of its psychological and social benefits, little effort has been made to critically reexamine the underlying worldview of Buddhism, in which are still embedded the cosmology and metaphysics of ancient India. To develop an understanding of Buddhism in any of these movements means confronting the traditional doctrines of karma, rebirth, heavens, hells, and supernormal powers.

The secular Buddhism I anticipate would be more radical than any of these secularized Buddhist movements. Its advocates would seek to return to the roots of the tradition and rethink and rearticulate the dharma anew. Just as the term "Tibetan Buddhism" describes the kind of dharma that evolved in Tibet, so, in its broadest sense, would "secular Buddhism" describe the kind of dharma that is evolving in this secular age.

Although many modern Asians are Buddhists who find themselves becoming secularized, I am a secular European finding out what it means to become a Buddhist. We might meet each other on the road, but we are heading in opposite directions. Just as their Buddhism is being challenged by secularity, so my secularity is being challenged by

Buddhism. My concern, therefore, is as much about imagining a Buddhist secularity as about imagining a secular Buddhism. We have seen what can happen to Buddhism when it becomes secularized, but what would happen to a secular perspective inflected by the principles and values of the dharma?

What is taking place between Buddhism and secularity is, at its best, an open-ended dialogue between two partners rather than an attempt by one partner to forcibly impose a viewpoint on the other. In *After Virtue,* the Scottish philosopher Alasdair MacIntyre recognizes that "a living tradition . . . is an historically extended, socially embodied argument, and an argument . . . about the goods which constitute that tradition."[25] Central to such a concept of tradition, he maintains, "is that the past is never something merely to be discarded, but rather that the present is intelligible only as a commentary upon and response to the past, in which the past, if necessary and if possible, is corrected and transcended, yet corrected and transcended in a way that leaves the present open to being in turn corrected and transcended by some yet more adequate future point of view."[26]

(7)

It is all very well for us to aspire to return to the roots of the tradition and rethink and rearticulate the dharma anew, but in practice how is this to be done? I am conscious of the ambitious and potentially arrogant nature of such an endeavor. I am likewise aware of my limited linguistic skills and incomplete knowledge of the vast range of canonical materials on which I could draw. I also acknowledge that much of our historical understanding of early Buddhism is still patchy and speculative. Nonetheless, I believe there is an urgent need for contemporary Buddhist voices to articulate a coherent ethical, contemplative, and philosophical vision of the dharma for our secular age.

The sheer quantity of early Buddhist texts in Pali, Sanskrit, Chinese, and Tibetan is both a blessing and a curse. The very wealth of material raises serious difficulties of interpretation. The early canonical texts are a complex tapestry of linguistic and rhetorical styles, shot through with conflicting ideas, doctrines, and images, all assembled and elaborated orally over about three or four centuries before being committed to writing. Given the [illegible] are we to distinguish betw[illegible]rd as opposed to a well-in[illegible] commentator? We are not yet—[illegible] a point where such questions can be answere[illegible]

As a pr[illegible] just to mine them for sc[illegible]y own birth and death. [illegible]derstanding of their cont[illegible] sometimes anguished c[illegible]at these ancient voices [illegible]ondition as a human ani[illegible]ugh space. In this sense, [illegible] because it is rooted in "[illegible]" [illegible] someone who feels the urgency of such concerns, I am bound, therefore, to risk choices in selecting and interpreting texts now that may or may not turn out to be viable later.

To provide a template for this task of rethinking the dharma, I have found it helpful to distinguish between six broad voices that can be discerned in the early canonical texts:

poetic voices
dramatic voices
skeptical voices
pragmatic voices
dogmatic voices
mythic voices

These voices do not necessarily contradict one another. They may be complementary. But the tone and emphasis of each expresses a distinctive sensibility and outlook.

There is much finely crafted verse in the canon that approaches poetry in its rhythms and imagery, and numerous passages that use dramatic narratives to provide background or to make a moral or doctrinal point. The following verses from the Pali *Chapter of Eights* (*Aṭṭhakavagga*) exemplify a poetic voice that is also skeptical:

> Wrong-minded people do voice opinions
> as do truth-minded people too.
> When an opinion is stated, the sage is not drawn in—
> there's nothing arid about the sage.
>
> Nowhere does a lucid one
> hold contrived views about *it is* or *it is not*.
> How could he succumb to them,
> having let go of illusions and conceit?
>
> The priest without borders
> doesn't seize on what he's known or beheld.
> Not passionate, not dispassionate,
> he doesn't posit anything as ultimate.[27]

In what is considered to be a very early text, we find here a voice that refuses to be drawn into affirming or negating an opinion, into making ontological assertions, or into asserting anything as ultimately true or real. The sage chooses to suspend judgment rather than get involved in disputes.

Such skepticism is challenging. It would require a great deal of discipline and effort to see the world and oneself in this way. Withholding judgment runs counter to how we are conditioned to think and speak. Thinking other than in terms of "it is" and "it is not" goes against the grain of language itself; it is disorienting and confusing. Yet Gotama tells his listeners, in his famous discourse to the Kālāma people, that "it is fitting for you to be perplexed, it is fitting for you to be in doubt."

> Do not go by oral traditions, by lineage of teaching, by hearsay, by a collection of scriptures, by logical reasoning, by inferential reasoning, by reflection on reasons, by the acceptance of a view after pondering it, by the seeming competence of the speaker, or because you think, "That wanderer is my guru."[28]

This skeptical attitude is not an end in itself. Its value lies in opening up opportunities for human flourishing. For Gotama, the problem with holding firmly to an opinion or belief is that those who do so become "entangled in a thicket" or "trapped in a snare" that prevents them from making any movement along the path. The *Kālāma Sutta* continues:

> When you know for yourselves, "These things are blamable; these things are censured by the wise; these things, if undertaken and practised, lead to harm and suffering," then you should let go of them.[29]

The point is to gain practical knowledge that leads to changes in behavior that affect the quality of your life; theoretical knowledge, in contrast, may have little, if any, impact on how you live in the world from day to day. In letting go of self-centered reactivity, a person gradually comes "to dwell pervading the entire world with a mind imbued with loving kindness, compassion, altruistic joy, and equanimity."[30] The transformation involved in the practice of the dharma is as much affective as it is cognitive.

The skeptical voice of the discourses harmonizes with their pragmatic voice. This is nowhere more explicit than in the parable of the arrow. The Buddha tells the story of a man who has been struck by a poisoned arrow and lies bleeding to death on the ground. Before allowing his friends to bring a doctor to remove the arrow, the man insists on knowing the name of the person who shot it, the place where he lives, the complexion of his skin, and so forth, down to such absurd details as the kind of feathers on the arrow shaft: "whether those of a vulture or a crow or a hawk or a peacock or a stork."[31] Gotama compares this man to someone who refuses to practice the dharma until he is given answers to the metaphysical questions listed above: whether the world is beginningless or endless, whether it is finite or infinite, whether the soul and body are the same or different, and whether a *tathāgata* exists or not (or both or neither) after death.

The purpose of the Buddha's teaching is not to resolve doubts about the nature of "reality" by providing answers to such conundrums but to offer a practice that will remove the "arrow" of reactivity, thereby restoring practitioners' health and enabling them to flourish here on earth.

All schools of Buddhism place great emphasis on the importance of practice. Yet most of them have come to rely on a dogmatic rather than a skeptical foundation for that practice. At the risk of making too broad a generalization, let me suggest that religious Buddhists tend to base their practice on *beliefs,* whereas secular Buddhists tend to base their practice on *questions.* If one believes—*pace* the second noble truth of Buddhism, that craving is the origin of suffering—then your practice will be motivated by the intention to overcome craving in order to eliminate suffering. The practice will be the logical consequence of your belief. But if your experience of birth, sickness, aging, and death raises fundamental questions about your existence, then your practice will be driven by the urgent need to come to terms with those questions, irrespective of any theory about where birth, sickness, aging, and death originate. Such a practice is concerned with finding an authentic and autonomous response to the questions that life poses rather than confirming any doctrinal article of faith.

The Sŏn practice of asking "What is this?" entails a radical suspension of judgment about all beliefs—including Buddhist beliefs. Sŏn teachers consistently challenge the student to turn away from abstract speculation and open their eyes to the everyday objects of the world. A student once asked the Chan master Dongshan (807–69): "What is the

Buddha?" Dongshan replied: "Three pounds of flax."[32] A monk asked the teacher Zhaozhou (778–897): "Why did Bodhidharma come from the West?" Zhaozhou answered: "The cypress tree in the courtyard."[33] Rather than offer conventional answers, which would lead to potentially endless disputes, these men pressed their students to consider the far more baffling and urgent questions posed by ordinary things that were right in front of them but overlooked.

Despite the skeptical and pragmatic voices of the Pali Canon, there are also plenty of dogmatic voices. One statement that is often cited in contemporary Buddhist writings is this:

> There is, monks, an Unborn, Unbecome, Unmade, Uncompounded. If there were not this Unborn, Unbecome, Unmade, Uncompounded, then there would be no deliverance here visible from what is born, become, made, compounded. But since there *is* an Unborn, Unbecome, Unmade, Uncompounded, therefore a deliverance is visible from what is born, become, made, compounded.[34]

This ex cathedra declaration of a transcendent reality lying beyond the conditioned world sits uncomfortably with the suspension of judgment and suspicion of ultimacy advocated elsewhere in the same body of texts. I will examine this passage in chapter 5.

Buddhism abounds in dogmatic claims. The four noble truths, the twelve links of dependent origination, the two truths, the end of suffering, not to mention elaborate theories about karma, rebirth, and nonhuman realms of existence—all are presented as self-evident facts revealed through the Buddha's enlightenment and confirmed by his omniscience. We are not called upon to question them but to accept them as unshakable, non-negotiable foundations upon which to build our practice.

The different voices that can be detected in the early Buddhist canon are echoes of the different voices that speak to us in our own minds. There is no need to privilege any one of them. As I read the discourses I find myself drawn by turns to a questioning voice that encourages doubt, to a reasonable voice that instills conviction, to a pragmatic voice that encourages what might actually work. Mythic voices—such as Māra's as he encourages the Buddha to die rather than teach the dharma—occur frequently in the discourses but have grown silent inside our secular souls. Perhaps we no longer hear them because they originate in a long-lost enchanted world where gods and devils alike descended to earth to commune with human beings. Moderns suspect such voices to be either figments of the imagination or signs of incipient madness. Artists might still speak of muses and priests of exorcising the devil, but for many today such references belong to a twilight language of an archaic past.

(8)

While paying heed to the different voices in the canon, I am drawn to the skeptical and pragmatic ones. They stand out as most distinctive and original in Gotama's teaching. Although dogmatic and mythical passages in the canon usually require interpretation, skeptical and pragmatic passages are also generally less ambiguous and more applicable. At the same time, I need to be constantly alert to the danger faced by every interpreter: the danger of unconsciously imposing my own views onto an ancient text and claiming that they were there all along.

My starting point in dealing with dogmatic statements is to bracket off anything attributed to Gotama that could just as well have been said by another wanderer, Jain monk, or brahmin priest of the same period. When he says that a certain action will produce a good or bad result in a future heaven or hell, or when he speaks of bringing to an end the repetitive cycle of rebirth and death in order to attain a final nirvana, I take such utterances to be determined by the common outlook of that time rather than reflecting an intrinsic element of the dharma. I thus give central importance to those teachings in Gotama's dharma that *cannot* be derived from the worldview of fifth century BCE India.

Tentatively, I suggest that bracketing off such metaphysical views leaves us with four central ideas that do not appear to have direct precedents in Indian tradition. I call them the "four *P's*":

the *principle* of conditionality
the *practice* of a fourfold task
the *perspective* of mindful awareness
the *power* of self-reliance

Some time ago I realized that what I found most difficult to accept in Buddhism were those beliefs that it shared with its sister Indian religions, Hinduism and Jainism. In forming the common backdrop to so much of Indian thought, such beliefs cannot be exclusively identified with any one of these in particular. What I struggled with, therefore, was not a uniquely Buddhist teaching but the widespread worldview of ancient India (and beyond) that jarred with the one with which I had been raised. The bracketing off of such beliefs does not, in my opinion, result in a fragmentary and emasculated dharma. Instead, the result is what appears to be an entirely adequate ethical, contemplative, and philosophical framework for leading a flourishing life in *this* world.

In much of the rest of this book I will tease out the implications of these four *P*'s. For now, suffice it to say that I see Gotama's vision to be primarily concerned with these fundamentals:

An understanding of *conditionality* as the context for
A *fourfold task:*

> to comprehend suffering,
> to let go of the arising of reactivity,
> to behold the ceasing of reactivity, and
> to cultivate an eightfold path that is grounded in the perspective of

Mindful awareness and leads one to become
Self-reliant in the practice of the dharma.

Focusing on the dramatic episodes scattered through the canon that recount Gotama's often-fraught dealings with his contemporaries allows his humanity to emerge with more clarity than if we concentrate on abstractions. In every alternate chapter of this book I will pursue this quest for the historical Buddha, but not by focusing exclusively on Gotama; rather, I will tell the stories of five members of his inner circle: Mahānāma (chapter 2), Pasenadi (chapter 4), Sunakkhatta (chapter 6), Jīvaka (chapter 8), and Ānanda (chapter 10). I am as interested in recovering a sense of the Buddha's social world as a sense of his person. Situating him within his relationships with different people makes it possible to construct a multifaceted and nuanced portrait of the man. Three of his close associates (Mahānāma, Pasenadi, and Jīvaka) were adherents rather than mendicants, and one of the mendicants (Sunakkhatta) disrobed. Apart from Ānanda, they have been largely ignored in Buddhist writings.

Forty years ago, the British scholar Trevor Ling argued that what we now know as Buddhism started life as an embryonic civilization or culture that mutated into an organized Indian religion.[35] The project of secular Buddhism builds on this insight. As we seek to articulate a way of practicing the dharma in the context of modernity, we can find vindication in a critical return to canonical sources and the recovery of an understanding of the Buddha's own complex world. One of the core questions that I seek to answer in this book is whether it is still possible to recover the dharma that existed prior to the emergence of Buddhist orthodoxies and then build upon that foundation an adequate ethical, contemplative, and philosophical practice that optimizes human flourishing in a post-credal age. Paradoxically, to imagine what might emerge after Buddhism, we need to go back to the time before Buddhism began.

2

Mahānāma: The Convert

[Mahānāma:] Kapilavatthu is rich and prosperous, populous, crowded, with congested streets. In the evening, when I enter the town after visiting the Teacher or worthy mendicants, I might encounter a runaway elephant or horse, a chariot or cart out of control, a man gone berserk. This disturbs my mindful recollection of the Buddha, dharma, and community. It occurs to me: "If at this moment I should die, what would be my destiny, what would the future hold?"

[Gotama:] Do not fear, Mahānāma! Do not be afraid! Your death will not be a bad one. A noble listener who possesses four things slants, slopes, and leans toward nirvana. What four? Here, Mahānāma, a noble listener has lucid confidence in the Buddha, the dharma, and the community. He possesses the virtues dear to the noble ones. Suppose a tree were leaning toward the east. If it were cut down, in what direction would it fall?

[Mahānāma:] In whatever direction it was leaning, sir.

[Gotama:] So too, Mahānāma, a noble listener who possesses these four things slants, slopes, and leans toward nirvana.

—Sotāpattisaṃyutta

(1)

Gotama's cousin Mahānāma, the chief of Sakiya, is not trampled to death by an elephant, nor run over by a chariot, nor attacked by a madman, as he worries he will be in the passage cited in the epigraph. In the end, to save the citizens of Kapilavatthu from the invading army of King Viḍūḍabha of Kosala, he pleads with the ruler to spare as many of his compatriots who can flee while he remains submerged in water holding his breath. Since Mahānāma was a friend of the king's father, Pasenadi, Viḍūḍabha agrees to the request. "Filled with anguish for his people, Mahānāma went down into the water of a pool. On the edge of the pool grew a sal tree, the branches of which fell into the water; they got entwined in his hair-knot, so that he was pulled under and drowned."[1]

I imagine Mahānāma as a man of small stature dressed in simple white clothes—speckled, perhaps with flecks of mud around the legs—with a mustache, beard, and turban. Even as an important and wealthy person in Sakiya, he would have lived in a house built of wood, plastered with baked mud, and roofed with thatch. He may have described Kapilavatthu as "prosperous" and "populous," but it is hard to know its actual size or population. Its position on the North Road, the trade route that stretched a thousand miles from Magadha, a kingdom south of the Ganges, to Gandhāra, the easternmost satrapy of the Persian Achaemenid empire, in the northwest, might explain how it came to be a busy commercial center. We still do not know exactly where the town of Kapilavatthu was, however. Archaeologists speculate that it may have been near the village of Tilaurakot in southwestern Nepal, but until further excavations are undertaken, the location cannot be confirmed.

Sakiya was situated on the vast alluvial plain that separates the Ganges from the Himalayas. On a clear day a guard on the ramparts of Kapilavatthu would have looked out onto a flat patchwork of fields where rice, millet, mustard seed, and vegetables were cultivated. Be-

yond the fields extended forest, and to the north, visible above the canopy of leaves, hovered a distant line of snowy peaks.

Society in Sakiya consisted of lords (*khattiya*), who composed the ruling class and were the wealthiest landowners, and householders (*gahapati*), including merchants, farmers, and artisans. In addition, there would have been numerous menial laborers, servants, and slaves, whose existence is assumed but not often acknowledged in the canonical texts. On occasion wanderers (*samaṇa*) passed through town and spent the night in groves or parks. These were men and women who had renounced domestic life in search of wisdom and liberation, as a sign of which they shaved their hair and beards, dyed their clothes yellow or ocher, and supported themselves by going from door to door in search of alms.

According to the scholar Johannes Bronkhorst, Sakiya was located in a part of India where the doctrines of Brahmanism, including belief in a creator God and the divinely ordained caste system (*varṇa*), were neither widely known nor accepted.[2] The role of Brahmanism in defining the social and political order did not yet extend to most of the areas where the Buddha lived and worked. It was the dominant culture only in sections of western India, although its influence was already extending eastward along the course of the Ganges River. The pre-Buddhist *Bṛhadāraṇyaka Upaniṣad*, for example, contains dialogues between brahmin sages that it says took place in Videha, to the east of the newly founded city of Benares. Videha was in the Vajjian Confederacy on the northern shore of the Ganges in the Buddha's time.[3] Peripatetic brahmins apparently served as priests and were hired to perform sacrifices and rituals, predict the future, and offer the consolations of spells and magic. Since the Pali discourses also mention "brahmin villages," there may have been small communities in the area that adhered to the principles of the Brahmanic religion.

The ubiquitous use of the phrase "wanderers and brahmins" (*samaṇabrāhmaṇā*) in the Pali discourses suggests that a clear division between these two types of practitioners already existed in the Buddha's time. Although brahmins may not have acquired the prominence and respect for which they aspired, they appear to have established themselves as a distinct community with a strict and exclusive identity. Their lifestyle, customs, and rituals set them apart from the eclectic community of wanderers, which was filled with men and women from all walks of life advocating a wide range of views and engaged in varied styles of practice. While the brahmins insisted on unbroken family lineages—sacred teachings and rites were passed down from father to son over generations—the wanderers were beneficiaries of the surplus wealth and social mobility that characterized the beginnings of the second phase of urbanization in north India. Gotama and his followers formed one of the many *samaṇa* groups.

Around a century after Gotama's death, Megasthenes, a Greek ambassador to Magadha, unhesitatingly employed the terms *brahmanes* and *sramanes* as his starting point for describing the "philosophers" he encountered during his ten years in Pāṭaliputta. He also notes that the brahmins "are best esteemed, for they are more consistent in their opinion."[4] Fifty years later, the Buddhist emperor Aśoka, in his thirteenth rock edict, noted that "there is no country, except among the Greeks, where these two groups, brahmins and wanderers, are not found."[5] Both sources confirm that this twofold division was well established in India by their time. It seems likely, therefore, that brahmins were already making their presence felt in the Buddha's world. Gotama's criticism of their beliefs and social practices was not, however, an attack on a supposed Brahmanic establishment but part of a struggle for philosophical ascendency in which the brahmins were one among many competitors.

By tradition the Sakiyans were sun worshippers. Their folk religion also involved the propitiation and supplication of local spirits (*yakkha*) at moundlike shrines (*cetiya*) and the veneration of trees enclosed by wooden railings.[6] They would have taken for granted the widespread belief in a cycle of rebirth driven by the force of former acts (*karma*), which formed part of the indigenous beliefs of the people in the eastern Gangetic basin. Their notion of rebirth would have been more the intuitive reflex of agriculturalists whose lives were tied to the cycles of rural existence than the kind of elaborate theory found in Jain, Hindu, and Buddhist literature that developed in subsequent centuries. At Mahānāma's time such ideas would have served more as a broad framework that provided a sense of continuity between past and future. The belief might also have encouraged fatalism, causing individuals to feel themselves subject to forces over which they ultimately had no control.

Mahānāma was a cousin of Gotama's on his father's side. Although we do not know their respective ages, they were of the same generation. They would have come from a similar background and quite possibly grew up together. The first we hear of Mahānāma is during the account of the Buddha's flight from Kapilavatthu to become a wandering mendicant. As Gotama was stealthily leaving, "suddenly he came across Mahānāma patrolling the city; but though his cousin begged and cried aloud, telling him of all the sorrow he was bringing to those who loved him, yet he pursued his way."[7]

We have no clear idea of how events unfolded at Kapilavatthu in the wake of Gotama's departure. The texts suggest that a struggle for power ensued, with Mahānāma eventually becoming leader of the Kapilavatthu assembly, the body that governed the affairs of the Sakiyan community. Initially, however, this position was held by another chief, called Bhaddiya, who does not appear to have been part of the Gotama family. It seems that Mahānāma did not make his move for power until after Gotama returned to Sakiya in the sixth year after his awakening and began attracting members of the nobility to his order of mendicants.[8]

A passage in the Pali Vinaya describes how Mahānāma, in collusion with his mother, manipulated this unstable situation to his advantage. Mahānāma's brother was the "delicately nurtured" Anuruddha, who was rich and spoiled, had different homes for each season, and enjoyed spending the Rains being entertained by female lutists. Mahānāma proposed that someone from their branch of the Gotama family join the Buddha's order. Anuruddha refused, saying that the homeless life of a wanderer would be too harsh for him, and insisted that Mahānāma go instead.[9]

"Dear Anuruddha," said Mahānāma. "Let me remind you of what is involved in the household life. First the fields have to be ploughed; then they must be sown; then they must be watered; then the excess water must be drained off; then the fields must be weeded; then you must reap the crop; then you must tie the crop into bundles; then you must thresh the crop; then you must separate the chaff from the grain, collect the grain and bring it indoors. And you must do exactly the same the next year and the one after that. Dear brother, there is no end to this labour. When our fathers and grandfathers passed away, the work still had to go on. Very well. Now that you understand what is involved in the household life, I will go forth from home to homelessness."[10]

Confronted with the prospect of toiling in fields for the rest of his life, Anuruddha changed his mind. Perhaps because he was still below the age of majority, he asked his mother for permission to join the order of mendicants. "You two boys," she replied, "are so very dear to me. If you died, I could not bear being separated from you. So how can I, while you are still alive, allow you to leave me and go forth into homelessness?" Despite this show of maternal affection, she does not appear to have been entirely frank, for she relented and agreed that he could go on one condition: "If, dear Anuruddha, your friend Bhaddiya the Sakiyan chief goes forth from home to homelessness, then I will let you go forth as well."[11]

This Bhaddiya was "ruling over the Sakiyans" and thus stood in the way of whatever political ambitions her other son, Mahānāma, may have had. Initially, Bhaddiya resisted Anuruddha's entreaties to join the order, but he finally agreed to go in a week's time, once he had "handed over his duties to his sons and brothers."[12] It seems likely that Bhaddiya was already under pressure or threat to quit as chief of the Kapilavatthu assembly. Shortly after joining the order, while sitting alone in a forest, another mendicant overheard him say to himself: "O, bliss! O, bliss!" The mendicant assumed that the new recruit was recalling the joys he had once enjoyed as chief of the Sakiyans. But when the Buddha questioned him about his sighs of happiness, Bhaddiya replied: "When I was ruler, there were guards both inside and outside my quarters, both within and outside the town, and in the countryside as well. Yet although well protected, I dwelt anxious, afraid, fearful and alarmed. Now, sitting in a forest at the root of a tree, in an empty place, I am unafraid, unanxious, and unalarmed."[13]

The story breaks off at this point, and we hear no more of Bhaddiya's sons and brothers, whom he supposedly designated to succeed him. From now on, only one person is ever presented as the chief of Sakiya: Mahānāma.

(2)

The *Sekha Sutta* opens by announcing that a new assembly hall had recently been built for the Sakiyans of Kapilavatthu.[14] Following custom, the Sakiyans invited the Buddha to inaugurate the building. He accepted. In preparation, they covered the floor of the hall with carpets, prepared the seats, put out a large water jug, and hung up an oil lamp. When Gotama arrived, he washed his feet, then entered the hall and sat down by the central pillar facing east. His mendicants sat down behind him along the western wall facing east. And the Sakiyans of Kapilavatthu sat by the eastern wall facing west, with the Buddha before them.[15]

This careful description of the seating arrangements shows that the Sakiyans, like other agriculturists the world over, revered the sun. When the Buddha and his mendicants take their seats, they make a point of facing the direction of the rising sun. Indeed, the Sakiyans may have believed they were descended from the sun itself. When, prior to his awakening, Gotama explains his origins to the Magadhan king Bimbisāra, he says: "There is a people, king, living on the flank of the snow ranges, endowed with wealth and energy, belonging to the land of Kosala. They are of the sun-lineage (*adiccagotta*), Sakiyans by birth."[16]

Throughout his life, the Buddha was known as the Friend of the Sun (*adiccamitta*) or Kinsman of the Sun (*adiccabandhu*). He likewise compared any true friend (*kalyāṇamitta*) to the first light at dawn, for in the same way as the dawn is the precursor of the rising sun, a true friend precedes one's cultivation of the noble eightfold path, the route to self-reliance in the practice of the dharma.[17] Through both example and teaching, the true friend encourages the sun to arise in another's life. The sun, in this case, is nirvana, which is beheld as soon as the dark clouds of habitual reactivity are momentarily dispelled from an individual's mind. Such moments open up the possibility of leading a life that is no longer conditioned by impulses of greed, hatred, and confusion.

It was no coincidence that when Mahānāma asked whether he would have a good death, Gotama compared his cousin's destiny to that of a tree leaning to the east. He thereby compared the Sakiyans' traditional object of worship (the sun) with the experiential heart of his own teaching: nirvana. The sun, the radiant source of heat, light, and life itself, becomes a metaphor for nirvana, the radiant source of the eightfold path that enables humans to flourish. He does not reject the animist beliefs of his upbringing but symbolically transforms them. Rather than being a solar cult concerned with the survival of a farming community on the Gangetic plain, his solar dharma becomes a framework of ideas, values, and practices that enables those from all walks of life to flourish as individuals and in communities irrespective of where and when they live and what they do.

As is usual when inaugurating an assembly hall, the Buddha gave a lecture on the dharma to inspire and educate his audience. After a while, though, his back started causing him pain, so he lay down on his robes and slept. It then fell to his attendant Ānanda to continue the discourse, and he "addressed Mahānāma the Sakiyan thus."[18] This is the only place in the discourses where we find a reference to Mahānāma as the ruler of Sakiya. It is possible, therefore, that the new assembly hall was erected to mark the appointment of Mahānāma as chief.

It was all very well for the Sakiyans to build a prestigious new hall in which to meet and conduct their affairs, but what power did Mahānāma, as chief of the assembly, actually possess? "The Sakiyans," according to the discourse *On Origins,* "are vassals of the King of Kosala. They offer him humble service and salute him, rise and do him homage, and pay him fitting service."[19] This subservient role is also implied by the Buddha's comment to King Bimbisāra that he came from the "land of Kosala." Since that exchange dates to the period prior to his awakening, Sakiya must have lost its independence as a self-governing republic by the time of the Buddha's birth. Mahānāma was chief in name only. Within the jurisdiction of Sakiya he would have exercised authority as a magistrate to arbitrate in local disputes, he would have ensured the general peace, and he would have overseen the administration of the town and outlying villages. But he would also have had to raise taxes for a caravan of goods each year to send in tribute to King Pasenadi, his overlord in Sāvatthi, the capital of Kosala.

A proud oligarchic republic, formed from unions of families and clans over generations, whose elders gathered in the assembly hall to conduct the community's affairs, was now not much more than a province within the powerful monarchy of Kosala. The territory of the Sakiyans was squeezed between Kosala proper to the west, the impenetrable Himalayas to the north, and the republic of Mallā to the south. Like Sakiya, Mallā is described as having assembly halls in its main towns of Kusinārā and Pāvā, which Gotama was invited to inaugurate. Yet unlike Sakiya, Mallā is described in the discourses as one of the sixteen great states (*mahājanapada*) of India, and still operated as an independent republic.[20] Mallā must have had a close relationship with Kosala, since, throughout the Buddha's lifetime, Mallān chiefs (Bandhula and then Dīgha Kārāyaṇa) served as commanders in chief of the Kosalan army. It would seem, therefore, that Mallā and Kosala functioned as an alliance, with political leadership given to the Kosalan king and military command given to the Mallāns. The maintenance of such an arrangement depended on strong links of trust between the two states, but they, as we shall see, repeatedly broke.

By becoming chief of the Sakiyans, Mahānāma assumed a position that was still desirable enough for people to fight over but was compromised and weakened by being subordinate to the authority of the Kosalan court. When Mahānāma describes his fear of returning to Kapilavatthu at dusk, he may be expressing more than just concern about running into an untethered horse or belligerent troublemaker. His position was precarious, caught as he was between the forces of nature (horses and elephants, but also droughts and famines), invading armies or roaming militias (chariots), aggressive commerce (carts), and challenges to his authority (violent people). As we have seen, his predecessor, Bhaddiya, likewise confessed to being constantly afraid during his tenure as chief.

Bhaddiya's and Mahānāma's anxieties could be seen as a reflection of the broader uncertainties of their time. They lived during a period in Indian history when rural and agrarian communities that had remained stable for centuries were being replaced by centralized, expanding monarchies with standing armies. The very first cities—such as Sāvatthi, Rājagaha, and Vesālī—were emerging in the eastern Gangetic basin, allowing unprecedented concentrations of people to live, work, and trade together. A cash economy was being introduced, bankers and merchants were amassing fortunes, and luxury goods were being transported up and down thoroughfares such as the North Road. The economic surplus generated by all this activity was able both to support a nonproductive body of homeless wanderers in search of wisdom and to pay the wages of professional soldiers. On a more local scale, Mahānāma would have had to deal with the appetites of his extended family, whetted by the new prosperity and opportunity.

Mahānāma's father was Dronodana, a brother of Suddhodana, the Buddha's father. Although we know nothing about Dronodana, Suddhodana is believed to have ruled the Sakiyan people at least until his son left home at the age of twenty-nine. However, the discourses do not state anywhere that Gotama would automatically have become chief had he remained in Sakiya. Internally, Sakiya still operated as an oligarchy, where elders of the different families decided on who became their leader. It was not a hereditary system, in which the eldest son of the current chief succeeded his father upon the latter's retirement or death. Nonetheless, given Gotama's intelligence and charisma, as well as the account of Mahānāma's attempt to dissuade him from leaving, he would clearly have been a prime contender for the post.

Opposition to Mahānāma's rise to power would likely have come from the family of the Buddha's mother, Māyā, and his aunt (and stepmother) Pajāpatī. According to Pali sources, this branch of the clan was headed by Māyā and Pajāpatī's cantankerous brother Suppabuddha, who was bitterly opposed to Gotama. Suppabuddha was the father of the Buddha's wife, Bhaddakaccānā, whom Gotama left when he became a wanderer. Suppabuddha's animosity may have been driven by Gotama's humiliating abandonment of his daughter. One day Suppabuddha is said to have sat and drunk liquor in an alley in Kapilavatthu in order to block Gotama's way to where he had been invited to eat. A week later, he fell down the stairs of his house in pursuit of an escaping horse and was killed.[21] Although it is hard to know what these fragments of a story mean, they illuminate ongoing conflicts within the Buddha's extended family, which would have added to Mahānāma's woes.[22]

Another episode featuring Mahānāma suggests that Gotama was not always welcome in Kapilavatthu. A discourse tells of how the Buddha returns to his hometown and asks Mahānāma to find a suitable lodging where he could stay the night. Mahānāma was unable to find a room for his cousin and proposed that he stay with a man called Bharaṇḍu the Kālāma, with whom Gotama had studied meditation under the teacher Ālāra Kālāma. The Buddha accepts.

The following morning Mahānāma visits Gotama, who poses a question about the nature of "comprehension" (*pariññā*), a key term that refers to the first of the four tasks in the practice of dharma: comprehending suffering. With Bharaṇḍu sitting at his side, the Buddha explains to Mahānāma that there are three kinds of teachers: some who prescribe comprehension of sensual desire, some who prescribe comprehension of sensual desire and forms, and some who prescribe comprehension of sensual desire, forms, and feelings. He asks Mahānāma whether the goal of these three teachers is the same. But Mahānāma is given no chance to respond. Bharaṇḍu keeps repeating, "Say 'the same,' Mahānāma," while Gotama keeps repeating, "Say 'different,' Mahānāma." It looks as though the two men are teasing or provoking him. We never find out the right answer—assuming there was one. "For it then occurs to Bharaṇḍu: 'the wanderer Gotama has criticized me several times in front of the influential Mahānāma. I had better leave Kapilavatthu.' He then departed and never again returned."[23]

Without any further background, it is difficult to make sense of this story. What is clear is that Bharaṇḍu regards Mahānāma as a powerful figure in Kapilavatthu, someone he cannot afford to cross. By contrast, he calls Gotama merely a "wanderer" and does not appear to hold him in any particular esteem. Perhaps Bharaṇḍu had established himself as a teacher in the town and was acquiring a following. What concerns him is that Gotama's contradictory behavior makes him lose face in the eyes of Mahānāma. He is sufficiently troubled that he leaves town for good. Since the discourse concludes with Bharaṇḍu's departure, we can assume that this was a desirable outcome.

(3)

Mahānāma's duties as chief of Sakiya and his responsibilities as head of the Gotama clan notwithstanding, the discourses consistently portray him as a "stream entrant" (*sotāpanna*). The Buddha's senior disciple Sāriputta explains that the "stream" is a metaphor for the eightfold path and that a person who has entered the stream is one who has made that path his or her own.[24] It is difficult to find an English equivalent for this evocative and core idea. As a metaphor, "to enter a stream" implies that one is no longer trapped in cycles of habitual behavior that lead nowhere but has been released from the grip of those habits to flow freely without impediment. This free flow is experienced as a way of being alive that affirms one's autonomy and integrity. In other words, the path is no longer something Mahānāma believes in or aspires to; it has become his own.

A free-flowing life is contextualized within a framework of commitments and values. Just as a stream is guided along its course to the ocean by the banks between which it flows, so the eightfold path is sustained and directed by "lucid confidence" in the Buddha, the dharma, and the community. This way of life is autonomous in the sense of its no longer being determined by instinctive reactivity—in particular, the impulses of greed, hatred, and confusion. Indeed, the path itself has its source in a person's direct experience of the suspension or absence of these impulses, which is the definition of "nirvana."[25] This does not mean, however, that having once glimpsed nirvana, innate reactivity will never recur. Gotama was not psychologically naive. The experience of nirvana marks a turning point in an individual's life, not a final and immutable goal. After the experience one knows that one is free *not* to act on the impulses that naturally arise in reaction to a given situation. Whether one chooses to act on impulses is another matter. Yet it is precisely this freedom that serves as the wellspring from which the stream of the path begins to flow.

Gotama declares Mahānāma to be one who possesses lucid confidence in the Buddha, the dharma, and the community and whose mind inclines toward nirvana.[26] Mahānāma has seen for himself the possibility of a radically different way of being in this world, a way that is no longer driven by his selfish appetites and fears but springs from conscious choices to think, speak, and act in accordance with the values of the dharma. We might compare his "stream entry" with the experience of undergoing a religious, philosophical, or political conversion. We do not know whether this occurred for him suddenly as a Damascene moment or was the result of gradual reflection. Either way, Mahānāma was "converted" to Gotama's teaching.

Upon becoming a convert Mahānāma entered the noble community (*ariya sangha*) in which he had lucid confidence. Besides homeless mendicants, this community included numerous "men and women adherents (*upāsaka/upāsika*), clothed in white, enjoying sensual pleasures (*kāma*), who carry out the Buddha's instructions, respond to his advice, have gone beyond doubt, become free from perplexity, gained intrepidity, and have become independent of others in the teaching."[27] The noble community was composed, then, of all who had entered the stream of the eightfold path, mendicants and adherents alike.[28]

Besides reorienting his life toward the core values of awakening (embodied by the Buddha), the dharma, and the community, Mahānāma also "possesses the virtues dear to the noble ones."[29] This is the fourth quality ascribed to a stream entrant. It implies that lucid confidence brings with it a degree of *dignity*. To enter the stream of the path is not a purely subjective experience; it ennobles one's character.

That stream entry or conversion was of particular concern to Mahānāma is borne out by a sequence of five discourses, all of which are addressed to him.[30] The first two variously describe the episode where Mahānāma asks the Buddha about his death; the last two deal with the fate of a man called Sarakāni the Sakiyan.

After Sarakāni died, the Buddha declared him to be a stream entrant. A number of Sakiyans were shocked to hear this and complained: "'Wonderful indeed, quite amazing. Now who won't be a stream entrant when the Buddha has declared Sarakāni to be a stream entrant? Sarakāni was too weak for the training; he drank intoxicating drink!'" Sarakāni, it seems, was the local drunk. How, people wondered, could such a person possibly "lean toward nirvana" and be destined for awakening?

Mahānāma goes to Gotama to seek clarification. They meet in a grove of sal trees in Kapilavatthu. The Buddha explains. "If one speaking rightly were to say of anyone, 'He was an adherent who had gone for refuge over a long time to the Buddha, the dharma, and the sangha,' it is of Sarakāni the Sakiyan that one could truly say this."[31] Stream entry, like conversion, is a shift in one's core perspective on life rather than the attainment of a degree of enlightenment or holiness. While it may grant a certain dignity, a relapse into undignified behavior is still possible. Sarakāni, like Mahānāma, may have had his weaknesses, but he should not be judged on those grounds alone. He should be remembered in terms of the heartfelt values—awakening, the dharma, the community—that he sought to embody in his life in spite of repeated failures. The case of Sarakāni illustrates that the noble sangha includes sinners as well as saints. "Even if these great sal trees, Mahānāma, could understand what is well and badly spoken, then I would declare that they too would be stream entrants. How much more so Sarakāni the Sakiyan?"[32]

Conversion appears to have been a divisive topic during the Buddha's lifetime. Those close to Gotama could not agree on what it meant. On another occasion, Mahānāma accompanies a man called Godhā the Sakiyan to ask the Buddha to settle a dispute over what constitutes stream entry. Mahānāma maintained there were four criteria for stream entry, Godhā three. Mahānāma recounts their disagreement, then declares that even if the entire community of mendicants disagreed with something the Buddha said, he would still take the same side as the Buddha. "Please remember me," he concludes, "as one who has such faith in you." Instead of answering their question, Gotama turns to Godhā and asks: "What would you say about Mahānāma when he speaks like that?" The discourse concludes with Godhā's glowing approval of his friend, but I am left with the impression that Gotama was less than happy with the outburst.[33] Since conversion entails "making the path one's own" and becoming "independent of others," such unconditional devotion would seem incongruous and out of place.

This discourse presents Mahānāma as a faithful devotee but also something of a fanatic. For him, authority lies not in the dharma and reasoned reflection and discussion about it with others, which was how Gotama envisioned his teaching being put into practice, but exclusively in the person of the Buddha himself. (Would he, I wonder, have sided with Gotama even if he disagreed with him?) The passage suggests that the community was not always of one mind about everything and that the Buddha was at times content not to impose his view. Such a tolerant approach could have struck Mahānāma as a sign of indecisiveness and weakness, qualities he was struggling to overcome within himself. Living at a time of crisis, he longed for certainty and resolve in his teacher. But desperation easily turns into fanaticism. People adopt inflexible views as a comforting defense mechanism when they find themselves threatened and overwhelmed by forces they cannot control.

(4)

The *Shorter Discourse on the Mass of Suffering* recounts an exchange in Nigrodha's Park outside Kapilavatthu. Mahānāma greets the Buddha, sits to one side, and says:

> I have long understood your dharma as saying: "Greed corrupts the mind, hatred corrupts the mind, delusion corrupts the mind." Yet at times, greedy, hateful, and deluded states overwhelm my mind and stay there. And I wonder: what state (*dhamma*) is still at work within me such that these greedy, hateful, and deluded thoughts keep invading me and won't go away?[34]

The Buddha explains how the "state" that lies at the root of Mahānāma's spiritual anguish is his sensual desire (*kāma*). It is not that Mahānāma fails to understand that sensual desire provides little gratification and often leads to much suffering. On the contrary, he appears to understand this well. But because he has no access to the kind of bliss experienced in deep states of meditative absorption, he remains in thrall to the joys of sensual desire.[35]

Kāma is a very old concept in India. As far back as the Rig Veda (X.129) we find an account of creation that describes how "in the beginning there was sensual desire (*kāma*)," out of which the cosmos and its creatures evolved.[36] In Buddhist cosmology human beings are said to inhabit the world of sensuality (*kāmaloka*), which is ruled by Māra (the "devil"), known as Kāmadeva—the god of sensuality. *Kāma* is closely identified with passion and sexual lust, with the primary, instinctive urge to survive and reproduce. The passage from the *Shorter Discourse on the Mass of Suffering* presents it as more deeply rooted in our neurobiology than the greed, hatred, and confusion that periodically overwhelm us. *Kāma* is what makes greed, hatred, and confusion stick, linger, and fester in our minds.

In addition to the external conflicts that Mahānāma has to deal with in his public role as chief, he also suffers anxiety founded on his heightened awareness of the contradictions within himself. He has dedicated his life to the values taught by his cousin but, despite his best efforts, keeps finding himself invaded by the forces he strives to transcend. He is a tormented man, burdened by his duties to others and troubled by the irrepressible potency of his sensual nature. Although he finds his mind "invaded by thoughts of greed, hatred, and delusion," he is also someone who "slants, slopes, and leans toward nirvana." There is no contradiction here; both conditions can coexist in one person.

Gotama is well aware that people cannot be neatly divided into saints and sinners. In the account of his awakening in *The Noble Quest* he declares that what he has understood is difficult to grasp because it "goes against the stream" (*paṭisotagāmi*).[37] To enter the stream of the eightfold path means to go against the stream of one's reactivity, be that of one's instinctive drives, social conditioning, or psychological inclination. By choosing to think, speak, and act otherwise than as prompted by these habits requires considerable resolve and commitment. For someone like Mahānāma, who is taking his first steps along this new path, it is hardly surprising that he finds himself feeling overwhelmed and battered by the power of those forces that surge within him.

This is understandable. If you start to confront your innate impulsivity instead of following its prompts and letting yourself get carried away, the act of resistance itself seems to intensify the power of the reactions. The ensuing sense of powerlessness and frustration can easily turn into self-loathing. You become furious with yourself, not only for not doing what you want but often for ending up doing the very opposite of what you want. As this self-hatred grows and festers, it can mutate into the wish to harm and punish yourself for your weakness.

While pointing out to Mahānāma the dangers inherent in sensual indulgence, Gotama also warns him against the temptation of self-punishment. He gives the example of some Nigaṇṭhas (Jains) he once observed in Rājagaha who "practiced continual standing and experienced painful, racking, piercing feelings" in the mistaken belief that in this way they would overcome their weakness and thereby find the strength to achieve salvation.[38] The Buddha's vision of liberation, by contrast, entails cultivating a middle way: the individual does not get trapped in either the dead end of sensual indulgence or its opposite, self-punishment.

Mahānāma has no intention of renouncing the world and becoming a mendicant. He is entangled in politics, suffers fear and anxiety, and cannot control his sensual desires. Yet he is also a stream entrant whose mind has "been fortified over a long time by faith, virtue, learning, generosity, and understanding" and inclines toward nirvana.[39] In another passage, he is described as a "householder" who "has found fulfillment in the *tathāgata*, has become a seer of the deathless, and goes about having beheld the deathless."[40] Mahānāma is an eminently worldly figure, a complex flesh-and-blood individual very much like our own conflicted selves.

(5)

Mahānāma, the most prominent adherent of Gotama's teaching in Kapilavatthu, asks the Buddha to explain what it means to be an adherent rather than a mendicant. The answer he receives would still serve to describe adherents in most Buddhist countries today. An adherent is "one who has gone for refuge to the Buddha, the dharma, and the sangha"; an adherent accomplished in virtue is one who "abstains from killing; stealing; sexual abuse; lying; and psycho-active substances that lead to carelessness (*pamāda*)"; an adherent is endowed with "faith in the awakening of the *tathāgata*," "dwells at home with a mind devoid of stinginess, freely generous and open-handed," and "possesses understanding directed to arising and ceasing, which is noble and penetrating."[41]

In most English translations, we find "lay follower" or "layman" rather than "adherent." But "layman" is as problematic a translation of *upāsaka* as "monk" is of *bhikkhu* and "nun" of *bhikkhuni*. In each case we are using a term that implies a formal religious distinction that would not have existed at Mahānāma's time. Such terminology is better suited to a later period in Buddhist history, when mendicants came to live apart in monasteries, functioned as priests, and depended on the laity to provide not only daily almsfood but the upkeep and protection of their institutions.

Literally, *bhikkhu* means "mendicant"; *upāsaka* is derived from the Pali *upāsati*, which means "to sit close by"—hence "adherent." Although adherents provided alms and support for mendicants, it is questionable whether their respective roles mirror those of monastics and laity as we currently understand those terms today. The noble community (*ariya sangha*) that Gotama formed included everyone who had entered the stream of the eightfold path, irrespective of whether that person was a mendicant or an adherent. A mendicant may have undertaken training that entailed full-time dedication to the cultivation of the path, but training and dedication are no guarantee of insight or enlightenment. We find mendicants who abandon training and adherents (like Mahānāma) who, as stream entrants, remain committed to the path and declare unswerving faith in the Buddha.

Because it is widely believed (even by Buddhists) that the Sakiyans of Kapilavatthu lived in a society regulated by the norms of Brahmanism, it is assumed that adherents of the dharma converted from one set of beliefs to another. The new adherents would thus have rejected belief in a creator God and an eternal soul, abandoned any commitment to the caste system, and had no further dealings with brahmin priests. In light of the recent scholarship like Bronkhorst's, this was almost certainly not the case. In becoming an adherent of the dharma, Mahānāma would have consciously adopted, perhaps for the first time, a coherent ethical, contemplative, and philosophical attitude toward his life. Since he would not have ascribed to Brahmanic doctrines, he would have had no need to reject them. Instead, he embraced a perspective on life and the world that transcended the parochial concerns of family and tribe and inspired him to live according to a universal set of values. Because anyone from any background could become an adherent, the community that one entered upon committing oneself to the Buddha, dharma, and sangha potentially included the whole of humanity. In this sense, Gotama's dharma opened the door to an emergent civilization rather than the establishment of a "religion."

(6)

Mahānāma may have struggled with his sensuality and his sexual desire, but he did not treat women as mere objects of his lust. He seems to have respected them and advocated an equal role for them as practitioners of the dharma. When he first heard Gotama teach in Nigrodha's Park, he was so delighted that he went home singing the praises of the Buddha, the dharma, and the sangha. When asked by his wife what he was talking about, he replied: "The arising of the Buddha is fruitful for us. Today the Buddha taught the sort of dharma such that upon hearing it, numerous beings attained great insights." She retorted: "When you say that 'the arising of the Buddha is fruitful for us,' that is true. Yet while it may be fruitful for you, it is not so for us. For the arising of the Buddha in the world is for the sake of men, not women." Mahānāma said: "Dear lady, do not say that. His compassion extends to all beings. You women should also go and listen to the dharma from him in person."[42]

For a woman, going to listen was easier said than done. Suddhodana, Gotama's father, apparently did not allow women to attend his son's discourses in Nigrodha's Park. Finding it difficult to broach this sensitive topic directly with Suddhodana, Mahānāma went instead to Mahāpajāpatī, Suddhodana's wife and Gotama's stepmother. As the chief's strong-willed wife, she persuaded her husband to grant her and other Sakiyan women, including Mahānāma's wife, permission to attend the teachings.

As the scholar Damchö Diana Finnegan points out, such self-confident and affirmative women's voices are rarely heard in the literature of this period in Indian history.[43] Although Sakiya is presented as a patriarchal society ruled by Suddhodana, both he and Mahānāma were swayed in their views by the objections of their wives. Their receptivity suggests that Sakiya was not yet under the dominance of Brahmanic ideology, which assigned every person to a place in the divinely ordained scheme of things. Although the men's flexibility may have been the result of the influence of Gotama's dharma, perhaps Sakiya was not yet affected by the imposition of the strict social norms of Brahmanism.

On another occasion when Gotama was visiting Kapilavatthu, Mahānāma's steward died. The steward was responsible for overseeing the tribal people in the foothills of the Himalayas. In his place Mahānāma appointed a brahmin who had a daughter called Canda (Moon). This girl "grew up to be shrewd and well-bred, and her pretty face gained the hearts of the hill-people."[44] The brahmin soon died—possibly of tuberculosis—having incurred considerable debts in his search for a remedy for his illness. On being told by the hill people of Canda's virtues, Mahānāma agreed to take her into his household as compensation for what her father owed him in uncollected and purloined taxes. In addition to helping Mahānāma's wife in the kitchen, Canda was given the task of making garlands from the garden flowers. So skilled was she at this that Mahānāma gave her the name Mallikā (Garland Girl).

One afternoon, while taking her meal in the garden, she noticed

Gotama pass by on his daily alms round. She was struck by his bearing and appearance but hesitated to offer him food because of her lowly position as a domestic servant. Intuiting her plight, the Buddha held out his bowl to her, and she shared her meal with him while making a prayer that one day she would be lifted out of poverty and servitude. This episode marks, it appears, her becoming an adherent of the dharma. For her prayer to be answered, Gotama would have instructed her to put his teachings into practice, thereby to gain a degree of inner peace and understanding as well as achieve the confidence and commitment needed to rise up in the world.

Some time later, King Pasenadi of Kosala, the overlord of the Sakiyans, rode alone on horseback into Kapilavatthu, having been separated from his entourage during a hunting expedition. Exhausted, he came to Mahānāma's garden and saw Mallikā. He asked her for water to wash his face and to drink, which she provided. He then asked her to massage his feet with a towel, which she did so expertly that he immediately fell into a restful sleep. Worried that the sleeping king would be vulnerable to his enemies, she closed the gate to make sure that no one could see him. So impressed was Pasenadi with Mallikā's gentle touch, intelligence, and thoughtfulness that he asked Mahānāma for permission to take her as his wife. Mahānāma said yes. Although Pasenadi's mother was skeptical of accepting a servant into the royal household at Sāvatthi, she, too, was won over by Mallikā's skills. And when Mallikā gave birth to a son, it was she who insisted on calling the prince Viḍūḍabha, which means "the high born."[45] This was the name of the mythical king whose sons founded the city of Kapilavatthu and sired the Sakiyan clan.[46]

In both of these stories, we find Mahānāma furthering the cause of women: arranging for his wife and others to listen to the dharma and, in spite of Mallikā's humble origins, agreeing that she possessed the qualities to serve as queen of Kosala. In the case of Mallikā, however, he may have misjudged the reaction of his fellow Sakiyans to her union with Pasenadi. When her son Viḍūḍabha comes of age, he, like his father, finds himself on a hunting expedition that takes him to a park near Kapilavatthu. On learning that elephants and horses of the son of Mallikā, the "slave," have trampled the park, the Sakiyans are incensed and prepare to punish the prince for trespassing on their land. Viḍūḍabha chooses to hide rather than face their wrath and leaves a retainer with instructions to tell the Sakiyans that the prince has already left. Unable to punish Viḍūḍabha by cutting off his hands or feet or even killing him, they decide to purify the park of his presence by spreading fresh earth over his footprints, plastering over the walls he has touched, and sprinkling the whole place with scented water, milk, and flowers. When the retainer reports what has happened to Viḍūḍabha, the young prince declares: "Sirs. When my father is dead and I am king, my first act will be to put these Sakiyans to death. Promise me that you will support me in this undertaking."[47]

This, as well as its parallel version in Pali, seems too far-fetched to be treated as history. Since the conclusion of the story turns on fears of the corruption of caste purity, it was almost certainly finalized at a later time, when Buddhists had eventually come to accept the assumptions of a Brahmanic worldview. We need to remember that such a legend would have been used to give moral guidance to the wider populace rather than serve as a training instruction for mendicants. Under these circumstances, it could easily have been embellished and expanded in repeated telling and come to reflect the changing worldview of its narrators.

The primary sources that have come down to us agree on one thing: that toward the end of Gotama's life, Kapilavatthu was invaded and destroyed by the Kosalan army under King Viḍūḍabha. There is no way to know, at this distance in time and with such a paucity of data, the actual reasons why these tragic events occurred.

Possibly the Sakiyans resented King Pasenadi's choice of an outsider—Mallikā—as his queen rather than a noblewoman from the Gotama clan, which would have united clan and royal families through marriage and accorded prestige to the Sakiyans within Kosala. Or perhaps Viḍūḍabha was more offended by the way the Sakiyans regarded his mother than by the way they treated him. Ever since the time of the *Iliad,* nations have employed real or perceived slights to their queens as convenient pretexts for going to war. What seems clear is that the Sakiyans were being punished. Since pride is a trait frequently attributed to them as a people, it is reasonable to consider pride a possible cause of their downfall. Viḍūḍabha could thus be seen as Sakiya's nemesis, the agent of their destruction, who caused them to reap the consequences of their un-Buddhist sin of hubris. In the blunt terms of realpolitik, their destruction translates into the violent suppression of a potentially rebellious minority who threatened the stability and cohesion of the state. As a newly enthroned monarch, Viḍūḍabha may also have wanted to show any other group who had similar aspirations of independence how he would treat them if they sought to rise up against him.

As the troops were preparing to invade, the Buddha is said to have gone to the frontier not far from Kapilavatthu and sat beneath a tree that offered little shade. Viḍūḍabha rode up to him and asked why he did not sit in the shade of a banyan nearby. The Buddha replied: "Do not be concerned, great king. The shade of my kinsmen keeps me cool."[48] Moved by Gotama's compassion for his compatriots, Viḍūḍabha retreated, but eventually the army was ordered to attack. As Buddhist adherents who had vowed not to kill, the Sakiyans put up minimal resistance and retreated to the safety of the walled city of Kapilavatthu, where they waited, "watching from the tops of the ramparts, and sounding their trumpets."[49]

On the advice of his minister, Viḍūḍabha conveyed a message to the Sakiyans: "Although I have no fondness for you, yet I have no hatred either. It is all over, so open up the city gates." Trustingly, the Sakiyans let the king and his army into the city. But as soon as the troops were inside, Viḍūḍabha shouted: "I will shut the Sakiyans' mouths for good, I will exterminate them all!" Then the slaughter began, which, according to Pali sources, "spared not even children at the breast."

On hearing the tumult, Mahānāma ran outside and confronted Viḍūḍabha: "Sir, you came here on a promise; I beseech you to make me another. Spare the people!" Viḍūḍabha replied: "I will not spare your people, but you and your family may leave." It was at this point that Mahānāma said: "Let as many of my people escape as can while I remain submerged in water." Viḍūḍabha agreed, and "filled with anguish for his people," Mahānāma went into the pool, only to drown when his hair was caught on the drooping branches of a sal tree.

In the Pali version of this story, however, Mahānāma untied his long hair, knotted it at one end, inserted his big toes into his hair, then tipped himself into the water.[50] This version confirms what is merely implied in the other account. His death was not the result of his hair becoming accidentally entangled in hanging branches (or, more likely, roots, since sal trees do not have such branches). Instead, this man, who once confessed to the Buddha how afraid he was about his own death, committed suicide. Out of compassion, Mahānāma sacrificed himself so that his people would be saved from the wrath of the soldiers. His leaning forward and toppling into the pond became a physical enactment of his "slanting, sloping, and leaning toward nirvana." He surrendered himself to the radiance of the sun, reflected, perhaps, in the shimmering surface of the water.

3

A Fourfold Task

Whatever is subject to arising is subject to ceasing.

—SACCASAṂYUTTA

This is suffering, this is the arising, this is the ceasing, this is the path: (in each task) there are innumerable nuances, innumerable details, innumerable implications.

—SACCASAṂYUTTA

(1)

At the age of twenty-nine, having just fathered a first son, Gotama left Kapilavatthu and set out on a quest. "Though my mother and father wished otherwise and wept with tearful faces," he recalled, "I shaved off my hair and beard, put on a yellow robe and went forth from the home life into homelessness."[1] His quest was prompted by questions he could no longer ignore:

What is the delight (*assādo*) of life?
What is the tragedy (*ādhinavo*) of life?
What is the emancipation (*nissaraṇa*) of life?[2]

Life as he had known it until then had been "covered with dust," its meaning obscured beneath layers of familiar thoughts and habits of mind, its vitality dulled by everyday comforts and attachments. By contrast, he found that "life gone forth was open wide," exhilarating and rich in possibilities.[3]

According to tradition, it took around six years before he arrived at a satisfying resolution to these questions. What he discovered was not revealed to him in one shattering moment of enlightenment; he did not suddenly realize the nature of Truth or God. He talks of his awakening as a process rather than a state, a story rather than a statement. He describes it in a variety of ways, much as you might recount a journey from different perspectives, each revealing another facet or dimension of the whole experience. In reaching a resolution to his three questions, he recalls realizing that "the happiness and joy that arise conditioned by life, that is the delight of life; that life is impermanent, difficult, and changing, that is the tragedy of life; the removal and abandonment of grasping (*chandarāga*) for life, that is the emancipation of life." Only when this threefold understanding was clear to him could he claim "to have found a peerless awakening in this world."[4]

In *The Noble Quest,* which scholars regard as probably the earliest account of the awakening that has come down to us, Gotama speaks of it as a radical shift in perspective rather than an arrival at a set of answers to existential questions.[5] He describes the shift as leading him to the dharma itself:

> This dharma I have reached is deep, hard to see, difficult to awaken to, quiet and excellent, not confined by thought, subtle, sensed by the wise. But people love their place (*ālaya*): they delight and revel in their place. It is hard for people who love, delight, and revel in their place to see this ground (*ṭhāna*): "because-of-this" conditionality (*idappaccayatā*), conditioned arising (*paṭiccasamuppāda*). And also hard to see

> this ground: the stilling of inclinations, the relinquishing of bases, the fading away of reactivity, desirelessness, ceasing, nirvana.[6]

The dharma Gotama talks of reaching was thus a ground with two dimensions, one that he calls conditioned arising and another that he calls nirvana. These two dimensions are equally fundamental and primordial. Whereas conditioned arising discloses the causal unfolding of life, nirvana discloses the possibility of a life no longer determined by reactivity or habitual inclinations.

This ground might be compared to a clearing in a forest: an opening that is empty of the foliage that both obscures the view and blocks the light. Such a space simultaneously allows a person to see more clearly and move more freely. Its emptiness allows new possibilities of understanding and behavior to emerge.

The identification of the dharma with conditioned arising is stated explicitly by Sāriputta, who quotes the Buddha as saying: "One who sees conditioned arising sees the dharma; and one who sees the dharma, sees conditioned arising."[7] A succinct definition of conditionality is found in a dialogue with a wanderer called Udāyin. Having brushed aside Udāyin's questions about recalling past lives and predicting future lives, Gotama says:

> Let be the past, Udāyin, let be the future. I will show you the dharma: when this is, that comes to be; with the arising of this, that arises. When this is not, that does not come to be; with the ceasing of this, that ceases.[8]

One of the meanings of dharma is "law." Conditioned arising is a way of describing a lawful process of cause and effect. Tempting as it might be to conclude that the Buddha is making a metaphysical claim about causal principles that underpin the workings of the natural world, we need to bear in mind that Gotama's primary concerns are pragmatic. When seeing the dharma you do not behold an abstract principle. You understand how previous choices, acts, and circumstances brought you to your current situation and which present choices and acts might lead to a less restricted and more flourishing future. In this way, Gotama provides the key to knowing past and future lives. The best way to know your past is to examine the quality of your present experience, and the most fruitful way to prepare for the future is to consider the quality of what you think, say, and do in response to situations here and now.

Awareness of conditionality discloses the existential horizons of our time-bound life on earth. To dwell in the present does not mean enclosing yourself in a punctual now, severed from past and future. It means settling in a lucid equanimity that is as open to your personal and communal history as it is open to the projects that can be actualized in whatever time remains before your death. There was one project the Buddha regarded as subsuming all other projects: namely, the project of a finite and temporal self embedded in a finite and temporal world.

A verse from the *Dhammapada* captures this notion:

> Just as a farmer irrigates a field,
> An arrowsmith fashions an arrow,
> And a carpenter shapes a piece of wood,
> So the sage tames his self.[9]

These images are drawn from the life of daily toil in a community of farmers and artisans. The term "self" (*atta*) is employed in an entirely naturalistic sense. It is just another word for a person, an individual. Gotama compares each of us to a barren field that needs watering, the parts of an arrow that need to be assembled, and a rough block of wood that needs to be worked. He conceives of a person as an unfinished project, a work in progress.

Were such a project to be realized, your life would come to fruition just as a field bears a harvest. Such a life would be as focused on its goals as a well-aimed arrow and as valuable to yourself and others as a finely shaped beam or bowl.

Toward the end of his life Gotama would insist that the only true refuges were one's self and the dharma. He includes the self because internalizing the dharma into one's own heart and soul renders a person as autonomous and secure as an island, as radiant and illuminating as a lamp (in Pali *dipa* means both "island" and "lamp"). "There is no other refuge," declared the Buddha, than the integration of the dharma into one's own life.[10] No priest or teacher, no church or temple, no sacred text, is of any help when you are confronting the existential issues of your life and death.

The lawfulness of conditioned arising implies that a life led according to the dharma is a life based on reason. The phrase "when this is, that comes to be" is a claim that when certain conditions prevail in the world, then certain results will follow, but it is also a description of the logical operation "if *p*, then *q*." The dharma that Gotama reached disclosed the possibility of leading a human life according to the norms of reason rather than those of common sense or tradition. The discourses are a showcase for Gotama's skill in dialectical reasoning. His authority is not that of a guru who imposes his views on his followers because of their faith in his enlightenment. He consistently debates with and persuades his interlocutors through the use of reason. Because his concern is to change the way people live, his reason is practical rather than theoretical. He uses reason to help others decide how to think, speak, and act. He has no interest in pursuing an abstract argument to demonstrate a purely theoretical truth. His practical reason is ethical. Its first principle could be stated thus:

> Do no evil,
> Take up what is good,
> Purify the mind—
> This is the teaching of buddhas.[11]

In seeing conditioned arising as a "ground," Gotama implies that insight into conditionality provides "grounds" on which to act. Just as the German *Grund* (ground) means a "reason" for doing something, so does the Pali *ṭhāna* (ground). The dictionary gives the following definition of *ṭhāna:* "ground for assumption, reason, supposition, principle, esp. a sound conclusion, logic, reasonableness."[12] To live a grounded life, therefore, means to live a life founded on practical reason.

As long as people are primarily concerned with their place in the world, the rationale for their behavior will have to do with such things as maintaining their position in society, enhancing their status in the workplace, or improving their handicap at golf. Whether acknowledged or not, these would be the grounds or reasons for why they act in the ways they do. Practitioners of the dharma, by contrast, choose to do things for different reasons. Keenly aware of the new possibilities that keep opening up in a world that is conditional and changing, they seek to realize them in a way that is not predicated on habitual reactivity. Conditionality and nirvana thus become the underlying grounds or reasons for why they do what they do.

We must not forget that the dharma Gotama reached was a *twofold* ground. It includes the "stilling of inclinations" and the "fading away of reactivity," which are synonymous with "nirvana." In one of the *Connected Discourses,* he succinctly defines nirvana as the "ending of desire, ending of hatred, ending of confusion" (*rāgakkhayo dosakkhayo mohakkhayo*).[13] But since nirvana—like the dharma—is also described as "immediate, clearly visible, inviting, uplifting, and personally sensed by the wise," then *khayo* (ending) cannot mean that desire, hatred, and confusion are over for practitioners and will not occur again.[14]

When a wanderer called Sīvaka asked what it meant for the dharma to be "clearly visible" (*sandiṭṭhiko*), Gotama responded by posing another question.

> What do you think, Sīvaka: When there is greed within you, do you know "there's greed within me," and when there is no greed within you, do you know "there's no greed within me"?
>
> Yes.
>
> With hatred, confusion, and those qualities of mind associated with greed, hatred, and confusion: When they are

within you, do you know they are present? And when they are not within you, do you know they are absent?

Yes.

It is in this way, Sīvaka, that the dharma is clearly visible, immediate, inviting, uplifting, to be personally sensed by the wise.[15]

By demonstrating to a non-Buddhist wanderer how the dharma is clearly visible whenever greed, hatred, and confusion are not active in his mind, Gotama shows that nirvana is not something realized only by devout Buddhists who have spent long years meditating in solitude. His awakening revealed to him that nirvana is immediately present right here and now as a ground on which to live one's life in this world. As he told the brahmin Jāṇussoṇī, a person who has let go of reactivity "neither plans for his own harm, nor for the harm of others, nor for the harm of both; and he does not experience in his mind suffering and grief. In this way, brahmin, nirvana is clearly visible."[16]

Nirvana can be compared to the sudden opening up of a space within one's experience when one's innate inclinations die down and reactivity fades away. One glimpses in such moments how one is free to act in a way that is not determined by reactivity, thereby enabling the use of practical reason to decide on another kind of future. But these moments of nirvanic emptiness are liable to vanish just as abruptly as they appear.

Gotama's awakening led him to see both what enabled and what inhibited human flourishing. Cultivating a clear vision of one's mortality and conditionality, committing oneself to a path of practical reason, and aspiring to respond to life in ways not determined by reactivity are how he saw a life grounded in dharma. But he also recognized that to see things in this way "is hard for people who love, delight, and revel in their place." As long as individuals remain preoccupied with place (*ālaya*), they will be blinded to their ground (*ṭhāna*). Although Gotama declared that such a ground was clearly visible, he acknowledged that it was "hard to see" (*dudaso*).

Since the terms *ālaya* (place) and *ṭhāna* (ground) have similar meanings in Pali, Gotama may be engaging in wordplay. What people assume to be their ground, he suggests, turns out not to be a ground at all but merely a temporary place to which they cling in the futile hope of finding existential security in a profoundly insecure world.

The places to which I belong are manifold: a race, a gender, an ethnicity, a culture, a nation, a city, town, or village, a social position, an employment, a political party, a religion (or lack thereof), not to mention a psychological and emotional identity as "me." At different times I catch myself delighting and reveling in all of these things. Here I am: a white European male from Scotland, living in a village near Bordeaux, a middle-class intellectual, a writer and teacher liberal and green in politics, a secular Buddhist who spends a lot of time narrating, editing, and worrying about the story of me in my head.

It is impossible *not* to consider oneself in such terms. The Buddha may have no longer delighted and reveled in his place, but for as long as he lived he belonged to the solar lineage, was a subject of King Pasenadi of Kosala, the father of his son (Rāhula), a nobleman from the town of Kapilavatthu, a cousin of the Sakiyan chief, Mahānāma. And since he continued to inhabit the same body, nervous system, and brain with which he was born, I can see no reason why his primary intuitive sense of being the person he was would have changed significantly either.

To "leave home for homelessness" to become a wandering mendicant therefore means to relinquish a particular way of relating to one's home or place rather than actually repudiating them. How many idealistic young men (like my younger self) have left behind their family and homeland in a grand display of renunciation to become a monk in a foreign land only to find that they have transferred all their delight and reveling in a place to something more exotic? To detest one place only to delight in another does not, from Gotama's point of view, solve anything. Without a genuine change of heart in one's core relationship to life itself, pursuing a "spiritual" vocation will be a waste of time.

Whatever comfort and security may be gained by identifying with a place are achieved at the cost of alienating oneself from one's ground. A place is seductive because it provides relative permanence and reliability in an impermanent and unreliable world. My sense of having a place reassures me about who I am, which is constantly affirmed both by the ongoing monologue in my head and by the way others address and treat me. Only when one's place is threatened—by the failure of a marriage, the loss of a job, the occupation of one's homeland, a crisis of faith, the breakdown of one's health, a psychological collapse—does one realize how fragile and tentative it is. At such moments one may be overwhelmed by a glimpse into the fascinating and terrifying abyss of one's ground.

Gotama describes conditioned arising, nirvana, and the dharma as things he sees (*dasati*), shows (*deseti*), and makes visible. His awakening was not achieved by gaining privileged knowledge of an ultimate truth but by seeing himself and his world in a radically different way. The existential shift he underwent might be understood perceptually as a gestalt switch, as when one suddenly sees two faces in profile rather than a vase or, in Ludwig Wittgenstein's example, a rabbit instead of a duck.[17] Place and ground are not separate states but two different ways of configuring the same life. I can configure myself as a person assured of his identity and place who unhesitatingly follows the bidding of his habitual reactions, or I can configure myself as a person balanced on a shifting, changing ground who aspires to respond to the unique demands of each situation unconditioned by reactivity. The challenge of practicing the dharma is to discover how to establish the optimal conditions under which a human life can flourish from its ground.

(2)

Gotama described the shift from place to ground that constituted his awakening as *paṭisotagāmi*, "going against the stream."[18] The experience of such a displacement in one's existential center of gravity would be akin to that of swimming downstream, turning around, and swimming upstream instead. Rather than being buoyed along by the current of the river, the person struggles to make any headway at all. By glancing at the trees along the riverbank, she realizes that despite her additional efforts, she is making negative progress. And instead of being swept forward by the river at the same rate as the flotsam bobbing on its surface, she now finds herself constantly impacted by wavelets, branches, and other detritus.

To go against the stream is to find yourself going against the cumulative force of innate reactivity. Mythically, this force is described as the "army of Māra," which is composed of "sensual desire; discontent; hunger and thirst; craving; sloth and torpor; fear; doubt; hypocrisy and obstinacy; gain, renown, honour and ill-gotten fame; and the extolling of oneself and disparaging of others."[19] Today we would understand these forces as part of the legacy of biological evolution, the embedded instincts and drives that enabled our ancestors to succeed in the competition for scarce resources and survive. They are summarized in the canon as the "three fires" of "greed, hatred, and confusion" or the "effluences" (*āsava*) of "sensual desire, being, opinion, and ignorance."

Gotama's awakening is said to have involved the "stilling" and "fading away" of these reactive forces and drives. But if such instincts are neurobiological functions of our organism, it is difficult to understand how they can be systematically overcome—"cut off like a palm stump," as many discourses claim, "never to arise again." Although Buddhist orthodoxy insists that these forces and drives have been eliminated in arahants and buddhas, another, less prominent thread in the canon offers a more intelligible account of the ceasing of reactivity.

Not only did the dharma that Gotama reached go against the stream, but it showed him a way of remaining calm and lucid as the stream rushed and roared about him. A short text in the *Sutta-Nipāta* portrays Gotama addressing his mythical nemesis Māra with a statement of resolve:

> That army of yours, which the world together with the gods cannot overcome, I shall destroy with understanding (*paññā*) as if (smashing) an unfired pot with a pebble. Having brought my thoughts under control, and established mindfulness, I shall wander from country to country, training many followers.[20]

This passage acknowledges that Māra's army cannot be defeated by conventional or even divine powers. The Buddha is fully aware that these forces cannot be excised by performing a kind of spiritual lobotomy. The key to overcoming Māra lies in the use of one's intelligence: the ability one has to change how one thinks and imagines. If we represent Māra's forces as an invading army, then we are liable to see ourselves as vulnerable and defenseless. But if we imagine them as unfired pots, we picture ourselves in a different way. Instead of being cowering wimps, we could be transformed into people with a well-honed skill in throwing stones.

The psychology that underpins this metaphor goes to the heart of Gotama's vision of human capability. By learning how to stabilize attention and dwell in a lucid space of non-reactive awareness, we gain the freedom to see the forces of Māra as thoughts, feelings, emotions, beliefs, and stories that naturally arise because of the impact of the environment on the senses of a conscious creature. From that perspective we see a cascading array of transient, impersonal events that—provided we do not energize them by identifying with them—will fade away as soon as their charge is exhausted. They are not overcome by destruction; rather, we must understand how they arise and play themselves out. The dharma, therefore, involves bringing one's wayward thoughts under control, establishing mindfulness and concentration, then setting out to realize one's goals in the world.

Another metaphor at the conclusion of the same text makes this point even more forcefully. Humiliated by the Buddha, Māra slinks off and muses about his failure. He compares himself to a crow hovering over a lump on the ground, thinking it might be a succulent piece of food. But by pecking at the lump the bird discovers that it is a stone. The crow flies away in disgust. "Like a crow attacking a rock and becoming despondent," says Māra to himself, "I attack Gotama and despair."[21]

Māra, the personification of reactivity, is conquered not by eliminating every last reaction from one's mind but by finding a way to become impervious to his attacks. We acquire freedom from reactivity yet without the reactivity ceasing to occur. If we observe these impulses and do not feed them, they will die down over time and diminish in frequency. But, as this text makes clear, Gotama continued to be subject to Māra's attacks even after his awakening. As long as we are embodied in flesh, nerves, and blood, reactivity will be part and parcel of what it entails to be human.

I doubt that the Buddha used the same word *sota* (stream) in two conflicting senses by accident. Here he says that the practice of dharma "goes against the stream," but as we saw in the previous chapter, he described the practitioner of the dharma as one who "enters the stream." In the first case, *sota* denotes the stream of reactivity; in the second, it refers to the stream of the eightfold path. By combining these two metaphors, we arrive at an image of two streams of water encountering each other head on: the stream of the eightfold path flows into and goes against the stream of reactivity. The result is turbulence.

(3)

At some point, Gotama had to face the challenge of articulating what he had come to understand. Whether we accept the traditional account of the awakening as having occurred in the course of one moonlit night beneath a pipal tree in Uruvelā (Bodh Gaya) or we accept what I think is the more likely course, that it occurred gradually over many years of studying, learning, reflecting, discussing, arguing, and meditating in various groves and cities throughout northern India, in either case he had to make a decision to assume the role of a teacher and cease to think of himself as being on a quest.

At the conclusion of the account of his awakening to a twofold ground in *The Noble Quest,* Gotama reflects: "If I were to teach the dharma and others were not to understand me, that would be tiring and vexing for me. . . . Considering this, my mind inclined to inaction rather than action."[22] This hesitation sounds a jarring note. It also conflicts with the passage from the Mūlasarvāstavāda Vinaya in which, shortly after the awakening, he explicitly declares to Māra his resolve to establish a fourfold assembly of men and women mendicants and men and women adherents to understand, practice, and teach the dharma. Since this episode is referred to in the Pali version of the *Great Discourse on the Passing,* it must originally have been included in that tradition, only to be suppressed in favor of the story preserved in *The Noble Quest.*[23]

In *The Noble Quest,* Gotama's supposed reluctance to teach is a pretext to arouse the god Brahmā Sahampati from his slumber. The Buddha recalls how this god "knew with his mind the thought in my mind," and "just as quickly as a strong man might extend his flexed arm, he vanished in the Brahma-world and appeared before me." Once the deity rearranged his clothing, he commanded: "Let the Teacher reveal the dharma! There are beings with little dust in their eyes who are wasting [away] through not hearing the dharma!"[24]

With the appeal to divine authority, this account provides an egregious example of the Brahmanization of the early Buddhist community. After Gotama's death, in a world where the social and religious norms of Brahmanism had taken root, the fortuitous appearance of Brahmā would have provided a convincing explanation of how Gotama was inspired to address the deluded world and teach the dharma. The Pali commentary to this passage goes further and says that Gotama "wanted Brahmā to entreat him to teach so that beings who venerated Brahmā would recognize the precious value of the dharma and desire to listen to it."[25] Bluntly: the dharma is legitimate because it was sanctioned by God.

Introducing the apparition and the command of a deity means

that the Buddha's subsequent movements follow the script of a divinely inspired scenario; they do not represent a human struggle to articulate the dharma. *The Noble Quest* proceeds to describe Gotama's departure from Uruvelā; his arrival at the Deer Park at Isipatana, near Benares; his meeting with his five former companions in asceticism; his regaining of their confidence; and his repeated declaration "The deathless has been attained!" Any wanderer or brahmin of the day would have understood the utterance as shorthand for having reached one's goal. It says nothing distinctive about what Gotama understood. The text seeks to provide Gotama with legitimacy in a Brahmanized world but avoids mentioning the counterintuitive nature of his awakening. And rather than providing an account of what he taught, the text just says: "I was able to convince the mendicants of the group of five."[26]

Only one detail in this narrative might refer to a historical event. Shortly after setting off for Benares, Gotama encountered a wanderer called Upaka of the fatalist Ājīvaka school. "Your faculties are clear," remarked Upaka. "Your skin is pure and bright. Who is your teacher? Whose dharma do you profess?" In reply, Gotama declared (in a series of bombastic verses) that he had no teacher or counterpart and that no one understood things the way he did. Upaka responded: "'May it be so, friend.' Then, shaking his head, he took a bypath and departed."[27] The episode fails to present Gotama in a wholly positive light, and some of the phrasing is in an archaic form of Pali, which together suggest that such a meeting could have taken place. With its ironic tone, the story mocks charismatic authority. Gotama is left chastened. He had impressed Upaka with his presence but had signally failed to impress him with his words. On opening his mouth, he must have sounded like any guru of his (or our) time: gurus tend to be charismatic individuals whose claim to enlightenment rests merely on their own or their followers' say-so.

In recalling how he "set out to wander by stages to Benares," Gotama describes meeting Upaka on the road between Uruvelā and the town of Gayā. Yet Gayā is twelve miles to the northeast of Uruvelā, while Benares lies one hundred fifty miles almost due west. Why would someone heading for Benares proceed in nearly the opposite direction? And when we recall that Gotama had just been seriously ill from eating rich food, it seems implausible that he would even have undertaken a long journey when the pre-monsoon heat would have been at its peak. As a wanderer, he would have also known full well that as soon as the Rains began, the roads would turn into quagmires. All these considerations raise the question as to whether he went to Benares at all.[28]

From the appearance of Brahmā onward, the episode reads like an attempt to present the Buddha as deferring to the cultural and religious norms of Brahmanism. Not only was Benares believed to be the great holy city of the brahmins, but the five ascetics with whom Gotama early on practiced the principles of ascetism were also said to be brahmins. Yet the oddest feature of the story is that three months later he returned from Benares with sixty converts, ending up at the very place where he had started out, Uruvelā, before heading (again) for Gayā, where, after converting a large number of matted-hair fire worshippers, he delivered the discourse *On Fire* on a hill outside the town. Why would he make a three-hundred-mile detour to the west before resuming his journey to Gayā and then Rājagaha in the east? Here is the reason given in *The Noble Quest:* "with the divine eye, which is purified and surpasses the human, I saw that (the five ascetics) were living in Benares in the Deer Park at Isipatana."[29] For a modern reader, this appeal to clairvoyance to fill an explanatory gap casts further doubt on the credibility of the story.

As the Brahmanization of the Gangetic basin took hold, people came to take the Brahmanic worldview for granted. Even if the journey to Benares and the stay at the Deer Park never took place, it would have made perfect sense to them that the first discourse Gotama gave occurred in a sacred Brahmanic site, was delivered to brahmins, and was founded upon a distinctive claim as to what was true—that is, the four noble truths.

A far more likely scenario is that after his awakening the Buddha chose to spend the Rains with the small community of ascetics with whom he had recently been living across the Nerañjarā River in the nearby hills. It was probably to these men that he delivered what have come down to us as the first two discourses: *The Four Tasks* and *On Not-Self.* In economy of structure and refinement of argument, *The Four Tasks* bears the marks of a text worked and reworked over a long time. The different versions that exist in Pali, Sanskrit, Chinese, and Tibetan suggest that editing continued well after the Buddha's death. Yet since its core message lies at the very heart of Gotama's vision, a simplified form of the discourse—summarized perhaps in the slogan "Whatever is subject to arising is subject to ceasing"—was probably in use as a teaching device from a very early period. We know, for example, that when Gotama and his band of converted fire worshippers reached Rājagaha, Sāriputta is said to have uttered this slogan on gaining his first insight into the dharma.[30]

On the basis of what we know about the awakening from *The Noble Quest,* Gotama's primary challenge as a teacher would have been to translate his vision of the dharma as a twofold ground into the practice of the dharma as a way of life. He had to convert an insight about conditioned arising and nirvana into an ethical, contemplative, and philosophical discipline. He had to shape something that was private, intuitive, and inchoate into a form that was accessible to others, carefully reasoned and pragmatically structured. My hypothesis is that at some point he came to conceive of the twofold ground as a fourfold task.

In classical terminology, the fourfold task is this:

Suffering (*dukkha*) is to be comprehended (*pariññā*).
The arising (*samudaya*) is to be let go of (*pahāna*).
The ceasing (*nirodha*) is to be beheld (*sacchikāta*).
The path (*magga*) is to be cultivated (*bhāvanā*).

In more colloquial language, the task can be summarized as a set of injunctions:

> Embrace life.
> Let go of what arises.
> See its ceasing.
> Act!

(4)

Suffering (*dukkha*) is to be comprehended (*pariññā*).

As the first step in moving from a vision of a twofold ground to the practice of a fourfold task, Gotama encourages comprehension: *pariññā*—literally, "total knowing." The prefix *pari* (total) denotes "around, round about, all round, i.e. completely, altogether."[31] Such knowing is not concerned with the acquisition of knowledge about anything specific but with a holistic comprehension of a situation at a given moment. The task of knowing requires considering one's situation from a range of different angles and perspectives.

Here is the classical definition of the *dukkha* (suffering) to be comprehended:

> Birth is *dukkha,* aging is *dukkha,* sickness is *dukkha,* death is *dukkha,* encountering what is not dear is *dukkha,* separation from what is dear is *dukkha,* not getting what one wants is *dukkha*. In short, these five bundles of clinging are *dukkha.*[32]

Since *pariññā* embraces birth, aging, sickness, and death, it is clearly existential in nature. Those with *pariññā* are fully aware of having been thrown into this world at birth and of being constantly subject to illness and breakdown; they know each breath is potentially the last. Comprehension of suffering is unsentimental and realistic: it recognizes that we keep meeting what we do not like, losing what we cherish, and failing to get what we desire. And it is all-encompassing: it includes every aspect of the sensory world—what we see, hear, smell, taste, and touch—as well as our subjective reception of and response to this world: our feelings, perceptions, inclinations, and consciousness—that is, the "five bundles of clinging."[33]

If, according to the canonical definition, *dukkha* denotes such an extensive range of experience, then "suffering" is an inadequate and misleading translation. When the puzzled Licchavi nobleman Mahāli asked Gotama whether he meant that life was suffering, this was the reply:

> If, Mahāli, forms, feelings, perceptions, inclinations, and consciousness were exclusively suffering (*dukkha*) and pervaded by suffering, but if they were not also pervaded by pleasure (*sukha*), beings would not become enamored of them. But because these things are pleasurable, beings become enamored of them. By being enamored of them, they are captivated by them, and by being captivated by them, they are afflicted.[34]

Mahāli failed to grasp what was different about Gotama's teaching. He assumed, as many would doubtless assume today, that the Buddha was talking from the "enlightened" standpoint of someone who has gained a "correct" understanding of the nature of things. This passage shows that the Buddha had no interest in describing what reality *is*. He is not a metaphysician or an ontologist. He wants people to start paying attention to features of their experience that they habitually overlook or ignore. His reason is entirely pragmatic: by not paying heed to the tragic dimension of life, we become enamored, seduced, and captivated by what is merely agreeable, which leads to cycles of reactive and addictive behavior that keep us trapped, frustrated, and afflicted. Comprehension, by contrast, encompasses the totality of what is happening: it is to embrace a life permeated equally by pain *and* pleasure, suffering *and* joy.

To open one's eyes to the totality of a situation requires suspension of such widespread Buddhist beliefs as "life is suffering" and "craving is the origin of suffering" and openness to the ambiguity, uncanniness, and ineffability of life as it reveals itself and withdraws from moment to moment.

On numerous occasions we find Gotama comparing the practice of the dharma to the skilled activity of a laborer or artisan. We saw how he likened the practitioner to a farmer irrigating a field, a fletcher fashioning an arrow, a carpenter shaping a piece of wood.[35] In another passage, he instructs his followers to develop concentration (*samādhi*), exertion (*paggaha*), and equanimity (*upekkhā*) the way "a goldsmith would prepare a furnace, heat up the crucible, take some gold with tongs, and put it into the crucible. From time to time he would blow on it, from time to time sprinkle water over it, and from time to time just look on."[36] He compares the person who practices mindful breathing to a "skilled wood-turner," who "when making a long turn understands 'I'm making a long turn,' and when making a short turn understands 'I'm making a short turn.'"[37] He likens the meditator who analyzes the elements of his body to a "skilled butcher who has killed a cow and is seated at a crossroads cutting it into pieces."[38] The Buddha admires artisans' mastery of the skills they employ so effortlessly and effectively. To master the dharma likewise requires more than just gaining a theoretical knowledge of its teachings. To practice the dharma requires know-how.

To embrace life with comprehension involves coping. It has more to do with how we get about, deal with conflicts, realize possibilities, and engage with others than with acquiring knowledge of the nature of the mind or reality. Comprehension requires the opposite of aloofness; it requires being embedded in a culture, a language, a society, not to mention a flesh-and-blood body that inhales and exhales, drinks and eats, pisses and shits.

The kind of knowing entailed in *pariññā* may therefore be more akin to *connaître* than to *savoir,* or to *kennen* than to *wissen,* to use French and German comparisons. The knowing of *pariññā* is like the ways in which we know a person, a piece of music, a path, a town. It comes from living or working with someone, spending many seasons in a landscape, or slowly gaining an appreciation of a work of art. To comprehend *dukkha* is to comprehend life intimately and ironically with all its paradoxes and quirks, its horrors and jokes, its sublimity and banality. As we saw in the exchange between the Buddha and Mahānāma at Bharaṇḍu's lodging, comprehension is concerned with sensual desire, the physical world, and feelings.[39] As such, it extends far beyond the parameters of one's skin to include other people, animals, birds, insects, grasses, microorganisms—the entire biosphere.

On one occasion at Sāvatthi, Gotama posed the rhetorical question "And what, *bhikkhus*, is comprehension (*pariññā*)?" to which he replied: "The ending of greed, the ending of hatred, the ending of confusion. That is called 'comprehension.'"[40] Such comprehension is neither inflected nor determined by the habitual reactivity of being greedy, full of hate, or confused. In positive terms, we might describe it as an understanding that is openhearted, clearheaded, compassionate, and equanimous.

We have already seen that the phrase "the ending of greed, the ending of hatred, the ending of confusion" is the definition of nirvana.[41] If "comprehension" and "nirvana" are synonymous, then the four tasks must overlap. If the first task, to comprehend suffering, is equivalent to the ending of greed, hatred, and confusion, how does it differ from the third task, to behold the ceasing (of greed, hatred, confusion)—that is, the achievement of nirvana? The tasks emphasize different facets of a single experience. At times we might focus on comprehending the world in which we are embedded, and at other times we might focus on being aware that comprehension is devoid of attachment, aversion, and vanity. For this reason, I prefer to think of the tasks as combined into a single fourfold task.

(5)

The arising (*samudaya*) is to be let go of (*pahāna*).

We are creatures who react as we come into contact with the world through our senses. If what we meet feels pleasant, we react with attraction; if it feels unpleasant, we react with aversion; and if it feels neither pleasant nor unpleasant, we react with restlessness or boredom. To these reactions we could add guilt, self-doubt, vanity, inadequacy, anxiety, conceit, paranoia, expectation, wishful thinking, and so on. Such reactions are entirely natural. They are neither good nor bad. Strictly speaking, they are not even "ours." They are simply what happens when an organism interacts with its environment. They are *what arises.*

The second facet of the fourfold task is to let go of what arises. This might seem contradictory. If what arises as a reaction to the world is just another natural feature of the world, then surely it falls within the scope of the first facet of the fourfold task as something else to be comprehended and embraced. How, you might reasonably ask, can I embrace *and* let go of a reaction at the same time? Another verse from the *Dhammapada* provides a clue:

> The sage moves through a village
> Just as the bee gathers pollen
> And flies off without harming
> The flower, its color, or fragrance.[42]

The sage acquires what is necessary for survival, yet with a sensitivity of touch that leaves no trail of destruction in its wake. The person who lets go of reactivity does not shun involvement with the world but moves nimbly and lightly through it.

The word I am translating as "reactivity" is *taṇhā,* which literally means "thirst" or "craving." Here is the definition of *taṇhā* found in *The Four Tasks:*

> This is the arising (*samudaya*): it is craving (*taṇhā*), which is repetitive, wallows in attachment and greed, obsessively indulges in this and that: craving for stimulation, craving for existence, craving for nonexistence.[43]

Taṇhā is as complex an idea as *dukkha.* Just as "suffering" fails to convey the full sense of *dukkha,* so too does "craving" fail to convey the full sense of *taṇhā*. If we understand *dukkha* as shorthand for "life," we can think of *taṇhā* as shorthand for the myriad reactions that life provokes in us. In both cases, the terms flag a central feature of what they denote (the tragic in the case of *dukkha;* desire in the case of *taṇhā*), but that one feature is not sufficient to capture the entire spectrum of what is meant by the terms.

Taṇhā, as an element within the classical doctrine of the twelve links of conditionality, is what arises in reaction to the feelings that come from sensory contact with the differentiated world (*nāmarūpa*) of a conscious being. The reactions include hatred and indifference, loathing and boredom, as much as craving and desire. Nor is the arising of *taṇhā* just a series of isolated events; it is a self-reinforcing cycle. A conscious being "wallows" and "indulges" in worries, fears, obsessions, and fantasies. In response to a gnawing sense of lack, *taṇhā* supports a yearning to fill the inner void with ever more intense stimulation. Rooted in feelings of existential incompleteness and inadequacy, it inflates the ego and affirms one's importance in the world. And whenever these strategies fail to deliver, it lapses into a hankering for intoxication, oblivion, and even death.

In describing greed, hatred, and confusion as fires, Gotama is aware of how reactivity flares up whenever a spark ignites it. Once it has flared up, a person tends to believe in and indulge it, thereby fanning the flames. In this way, reactivity both *amplifies* the pain initially experienced and *triggers* proliferating thoughts (*papañca*). The Buddha compared physical pain to being struck by an arrow, which is then unnecessarily amplified by a second arrow of mental disquiet and anguish.[44] In an alternative version of the links of conditionality, he spoke of how feelings of pleasure and pain give rise to perceptions that lead to thoughts that endlessly proliferate.[45]

Gotama recognized that human beings spend an inordinate amount of time absorbed in the amplifications and proliferations of reactivity. He talks of these responses as the "snares" or "fishhooks" of Māra. Once someone has been trapped or snagged, it is difficult, painful, and fruitless to struggle to wrench free, for that struggle is likely to be another variant of the very reactivity being struggled against. It just tightens the grip of the snare or embeds the hook's barb deeper in the flesh. People fail to understand why and how they keep getting "tricked" by the "beautiful and hideous shapes" conjured by Māra.[46] And, failing to understand, they become "like tangled balls of string."[47]

By remaining in thrall to repetitive, obsessive reactions, people also become increasingly vain and self-centered. Such reactivity (*taṇhā*) engenders clinging (*upādāna*) in the traditional twelve-link sequence of conditionality. A text in the *Connected Discourses* offers the account of clinging given to Ānanda that led to his conversion. The speaker is his preceptor, a man called Puṇṇa Mantāniputta.

> It is by clinging, Ānanda, that "I am" occurs, not without clinging. It is by clinging to form, feelings, perceptions, inclinations, and consciousness that "I am" occurs, not without clinging. Suppose a vain young person would examine his face in a mirror or in a bowl filled with pure, clean water: he would look at it with clinging, not without clinging. So, too, it is by clinging to form, feelings, perceptions, inclinations and consciousness that "I am" occurs, not without clinging.[48]

What Puṇṇa describes here is not the everyday sense of "I am" but the obsessive self-regard of the narcissist, the person who sees the world solely in terms of his own desires and fears. Wherever such an egoist looks, she beholds only an image of herself reflected back. In considering others merely as means to realize her own ends, she loses the capacity to empathize, which leads to a spiral of alienation, loneliness, and despair.

Self-centered isolation is a state of inner "aridity" (*khila*). The discourse *On the Aridity of the Heart* presents this aridity as the very opposite of stream entry.[49] People who suffer from it are paralyzed by their doubts about their teacher (*satthar*), the dharma, and the community (i.e., their core values) and feel anger and displeasure with their companions. Whereas someone who has embarked on the eightfold path is said to have entered a stream (an unambiguous metaphor of a flourishing life), someone who remains entangled in reactivity is said to experience a barrenness where nothing grows. In the *Connected Discourses*, a short text presents aridity as threefold: "the aridity of greed, the aridity of hatred, and the aridity of confusion." Using the terminology of the fourfold task, it explains how the eightfold path needs to be *cultivated* in order to *comprehend* and *let go* of all three.[50] Since the ending of this reactive triad is both comprehension and nirvana, as Gotama defines them, the discourse implies that a life grounded in a nirvanic embrace of *dukkha* is no longer arid but has become abundant.

I constantly need to remind myself that the language of the discourses does not take for granted, as later Buddhist thinkers and we moderns do, a self-evident split between an experiencing subject and an objective world. Gotama did not parse human experience in this way. For practical purposes (as in his instructions on mindfulness) he may distinguish between "inner" and "outer" foci of attention, but terms such as "subject" and "object" do not occur in the discourses. We should not assume, therefore, that reactivity or aridity are psychological phenomena that refer only to our interior life. At the risk of reading too much into a prefix, let me point out that the word *samudaya* (arising) could be literally translated as "co-arising," while its Tibetan equivalent *kun 'byung* literally means "all-arising." Both terms suggest that when a reactive pattern such as hatred arises, it simultaneously triggers an emotion of rage that surges through the organism and configures the world to present itself as intrinsically hateful and fearful.

We tend to regard the appearance of such a fearful world as a projection of our mental state. But this reading of the situation is based on the cultural habit of interpreting experience psychologically. No matter how much we tell ourselves that the fearfulness of the world is just a projection, such reassurance does not significantly alter either how the world appears to us or how we feel about it. From the perspective of a dharma practitioner, the task of "letting go of what arises" entails releasing one's grip on the whole picture: angry-me-facing-hostile-situation. Letting go is not simply a question of breathing deeply to calm my rattled mind; I need to cleanse the doors of my perception. This requires suspending the default habit of seeing the world as being hostile, desirable, or boring. One of the most effective ways of suspending that habit is to train yourself to comprehend the world as an infinitely suffering world.

There is a symbiosis between "comprehending suffering/life" and "letting go of reactivity." The fourfold task entails cultivating an embrace that is also a release. This action is akin to a dance where each partner holds the other so that both can move with optimal freedom and grace. The more we fully understand the precarious and mysterious situation we are in, the more our egocentric reactivity will either die down of its own accord or appear increasingly petty and absurd. And the more we stop believing what our compulsive mental habits keep telling us, the more the world will tend to reveal itself in all its poignancy, tragedy, and sublimity.

Letting go of reactivity is a consequence of comprehending reactivity. In many of the dialogues with Māra, the Buddha concludes by saying, "I know you, Māra," whereupon Māra vanishes. With such comprehension (here explicitly compared to knowing a person) the practitioner sees the tricksterish wiles of reactivity for what they are: the seductive, infantile play of an organism that is primarily—and, for the most part, redundantly—preoccupied with its biological survival. In one exchange, Māra declares to the Buddha: "Life is long; live like a milk-sucking baby!" Gotama retorts: "Life is short; live as though your head were on fire!"[51] This passage highlights how reactivity is an instinctive behavior that will persist as long as we inhabit the body with which we were born. To release oneself from the hold of this behavior requires coming to a mature comprehension of one's mortality, of how each fragile moment rests on the pumping of a muscle and the drawing of a breath.

(6)

The ceasing (*nirodha*) is to be beheld (*sacchikāta*).

The third facet of the fourfold task is to "behold the ceasing" (*nirodhaṃ sacchikaroti*), which is equivalent to becoming aware of nirvana. Here is the classical definition of "ceasing":

> This is the ceasing: the traceless fading away and ceasing of that reactivity (*taṇhā*), the letting go and abandoning of it, freedom and independence from it.[52]

This succinct description allows for nirvana to be understood in one of two senses: either as the ceasing of *taṇhā* or as freedom and independence from *taṇhā*.

The first sense of nirvana is traditionally understood as a quasi-mystical experience in which an accomplished meditator achieves sufficient calm (*samatha*) and insight (*vipassanā*) to bring his reactivity to a complete stop. But this interpretation makes nirvana accessible only to trained meditators, thus conflicting with the account of it as "immediate, clearly visible, inviting, uplifting, and personally sensed by the wise."[53] Moreover, Gotama's conversation with the wanderer Sīvaka implies that one can become aware of nirvana *whenever* greed, hatred, and confusion are momentarily inactive—irrespective of whether one self-identifies as a Buddhist or practices meditation.[54]

For the second sense of nirvana as freedom *from* reactivity, we again need to turn to the dialogues with Māra. Here, one becomes aware of nirvana whenever one understands reactivity for what it is and thereby gains freedom from its control. In this case, the experience of nirvana becomes possible even while in the throes of reactivity itself.

Unless we regard nirvana as clearly visible to ordinary people and accessible to them as a perspective from which they can live their everyday lives, it would be difficult to understand how "beholding cessation" could be an integral part of a fourfold task that is open to all. To *behold* and thus become aware of nirvana means consciously to affirm and valorize those moments when you see for yourself that you are free to think, speak, and act in ways that are not determined by reactivity. Nirvana is a space of moral possibility, the gateway to an ethical life. This "dharma door" (as the Chinese call it) is always open, but is frequently blocked and hidden from view by the chimeras conjured by Māra. To become aware of this "clearing" in the jungle of reactivity and keep it in view is a task every bit as exacting and arduous as those of comprehending *dukkha* and letting go of *taṇhā*.

Nirvana is clearly visible the moment reactivity stops. *Sacchikaroti* (to behold) literally means to "eye" something, "to look for yourself." At the conclusion of *The Four Tasks*, the "dharma eye" of one of the five ascetics, Koṇḍañña, is said to have opened, which led him to utter the phrase "Whatever is subject to arising is subject to ceasing." The opening of the dharma eye is equivalent to stream entry. Koṇḍañña's vision of nirvana came about as soon as he realized that just as reactions arise, so they invariably cease.

A sequence of texts in the *Numerical Discourses* names twenty-one householders and adherents (including Mahānāma, as well as Jīvaka, whom we will meet in chapter 8) who have found fulfillment in the *tathāgata*, have become seers of the deathless, and go about having beheld the deathless. They are said to have achieved this by virtue of embodying six qualities: "lucid confidence" in the Buddha, the dharma, and the community, together with "noble virtue, noble understanding, and noble liberation."[55] "Deathless" (*amata*) is also defined as the "ending of greed, hatred, and confusion," thus making it synonymous with both "nirvana" and "comprehension."[56] This passage affirms how people fully engaged in the world as "seers of the deathless" had not only become aware of nirvana but lived their lives from its perspective.

This text has troubled traditional commentators because it presents householders as having achieved levels of insight and freedom that are usually reserved for arahants, who, according to orthodox belief, have to be celibate mendicants. Yet in terms of historical critical analysis, the difficulty of aligning a canonical text with orthodoxy makes it more likely to have been spoken by the Buddha himself—for the simple reason that it would not have served the interests of orthodoxy to add it later. By singling out these twenty-one relatively obscure figures in this way, we are provided with concrete examples of people who recognized, performed, and accomplished the fourfold task amid the hustle and bustle of everyday life in fifth century BCE India.

"Deathless" (*amata*) is another word for abundant life. If we think of Māra as death (the words *amata* and *māra* are both rooted in the Vedic *mṛ* = death), then to no longer be constrained by his armies is to be freed to live fully. Gotama does not think of the deathless as immortality—as the term is understood in Brahmanism—but as the positive absence of reactivity. Perhaps he is playing on the mythic sense of *amata* (like the Sanskrit *amṛta* and its Greek cognate *ambrosia*) as the divine nectar that grants eternal life.

The person who is aware of the deathless is one who dwells in emptiness. In the *Shorter Discourse on Emptiness,* we learned of a man who retreats to a forest and passes through the entire gamut of deep meditative states only to realize in the end that all such states are conditioned and contrived. "In knowing and seeing thus, his heart was freed from the effluences (*āsava*) of sensual desire, being, and ignorance." This is yet another way of describing nirvana. But that was not the end of the story. "With none of the anxieties due to those effluences," reflected the man, "I am still prone to the amount of anxiety that comes from having the six sense fields of a living body. This state of awareness is empty of those effluences. What is not empty is this: the six sense fields of a living body."[57]

To behold nirvana is to realize that one is not beholden to the prompts of sensual desire, being, and ignorance. Yet the freedom enabled in this non-reactive space does not occur in a vacuum but within the context of "the six sense fields of a living body," which are not empty at all but full of both anxiety and possibility. The challenge of "beholding what ceases" is to learn how to live *in* and *from* the perspective of such emptiness—the "abode," as Gotama put it, "of the great person"—all the while engaging with a world that constantly and unpredictably impacts one's senses, triggering cascades of reactivity.[58]

One of the oldest passages in the canon from the *Chapter of Eights* (*Aṭṭhakavagga*) that was cited above as an example of a skeptical voice says:

> Wrong-minded people do voice opinions
> As do truth-minded people too.
> When an opinion is stated, the sage is not drawn in—
> There's nothing arid about the sage.[59]

The sage (*muni*) is concerned not only with what impacts his physical senses but with words and concepts that impact his mind. He is on guard against seductive ideas, compelling "images" of the world that seem to explain everything, and beliefs that provide heart-warming consolation. The problem with such ideas, images, and beliefs does not lie in whether they are "true" or "false." There is something about the very way in which a concept is structured that limits and imprisons us. "A picture held us captive," said Wittgenstein in his *Philosophical Investigations*. "And we could not get outside it, for it lay in our language and language seemed to repeat it to us inexorably."[60] There is something arid and barren about holding on to any position, even a Buddhist or Wittgensteinian one.

This healthy suspicion of opinion prevents the sage from getting drawn in to agreeing or disagreeing with a stated view. He may consider what was said in terms of its usefulness—whether it is appropriate for dealing with a situation at hand or resolving a specific dilemma—but does not let himself get lured into disputing whether it is true or false in any final, metaphysical sense. The sage has left behind the aridity of "place"; he no longer seeks certainty and finality to bolster the security of his ego. A sage lives from the fertility of a "ground" that responds creatively and spontaneously to the unfolding conditions of life.

(7)

The path (*magga*) is to be cultivated (*bhāvanā*).

Everything we have covered so far—comprehending *dukkha,* letting go of reactivity, and beholding its ceasing—are also aspects of cultivating the path. This further emphasizes how the fourfold task is as much a synergy of interrelated acts as a causal sequence of practices. This path, which Gotama calls a "middle" or "centered" path, outlines a way of life that includes every aspect of a person's humanity. Here is the classical definition:

> And this is the path: the path with eight branches: complete view, complete thought, complete speech, complete action, complete livelihood, complete effort, complete mindfulness, complete concentration.[61]

I translate *sammā* as "complete" rather than as the more usual "right." It is what the term literally means; the phrase *sammā sambuddha,* for example, means a completely awakened one, not a rightly awakened one. "Complete" lacks the moralistic overtones of "right" and suggests how each element of the path can become an integral part of a whole ("integral" is from the Latin *integer* = entire). The eightfold path is a model for a centered life, which is balanced, harmonious, and integrated instead of imbalanced, discordant, and fragmented. It is not a recipe for a pious Buddhist existence in which the practictioner does everything right and gets nothing wrong.

The goal of the fourfold task, I would argue, is to lead an integrated life. It is perhaps for this reason that cultivating the eightfold path is presented as the fourth facet of this task, even though it is already implicit in the other three. Logically, an integrated life is the outcome of having embraced the suffering world, let go of reactivity, and beheld reactivity's ceasing. From this still and empty space one then *responds* with intuitions, thoughts, intentions, words, and acts that are not determined by reactivity. In practice, though, the moment in which reactivity ceases is also the moment that allows a "complete view" (the first branch of the path) to emerge.

I will take the discourse *To Kaccānagotta* as my primary canonical source on a "complete view." It is not at all clear who this Kaccānagotta —"He of the Kaccāna Lineage"—is. Since he addresses the Buddha as *bhante,* we can assume he is a follower. He starts by asking: "You say 'complete view,' 'complete view.' What is this complete view?" Gotama replies:

> By and large, Kaccāna, this world relies on the duality of "it is" and "it is not." But one who sees the arising of the world as it happens with complete understanding has no sense of "it is not" about the world. And one who sees the ceasing of the world as it happens with complete understanding has no sense of "it is" about the world.[62]

This passage utilizes two of the key terms within the fourfold task: "arising" (*samudaya*) and "ceasing" (*nirodha*). Here they refer to the appearance and disappearance of the world (*loka*)—in other words, to the fluid and contingent processes of life itself. Anyone who sees this conditioned arising and ceasing from the perspective of complete understanding (*sammappaññā*) understands how two of the basic terms of language—"it is" (*atthi*) and "it is not" (*natthi*)—are incapable of capturing the ineffable emergence and slippage of life. This understanding refers, I believe, to the ending of "confusion" (*moha*) in the triad of greed, hatred, and confusion. As such, "complete understanding" appears to be yet another synonym for "comprehension" and "nirvana."

To be confused in this sense is to be "bewitched" by the grammar of language, as Wittgenstein puts it. For Gotama, people in the world "rely" on the dualistic formulae of "it is" and "it is not" in order to make sense of their inner and outer worlds. They believe that things either exist or do not exist. Yet when one pays close attention to such phenomena as a thought, the in-breath, a pain in one's knee, or the cypress tree in the courtyard, none of these things can be reductively determined as either "being" or "not being." For they come and go. They shift and change. They slip and slide. They blur into each other. It is impossible to draw a neat line that marks where or when the in-breath, for example, began or stopped. Such distinctions are useful conventions but quite incapable of showing how nature actually works. The bewitchment of *moha* occurs as soon as we unconsciously assent to the view that words such as "I" describe a corresponding thing (me) that exists in a sphere of its own, independently of the language used to denote it.

As habitual users of language, we assume words to be accurate representations of reality. Complete understanding, however, no longer succumbs to the convenience of oppositional thought but is open to the immediacy and potential of what is happening from moment to moment. Training ourselves to pay intimate and embodied attention to the very pulse of life within and around us exposes the limitations of language. Bearing witness to the arising and unfolding of something renders absurd the notion that "it is not." Similarly, contemplation of its fading away and disappearance undermines any notion that "it is."

To sustain such a "complete view" is a challenging task. It would require a great deal of discipline and effort to come to see the world and oneself in this way, which runs counter to how we are conditioned to think and speak. "By and large," continues Gotama in his reply to Kaccāna, "this world is bound to its prejudices and habits." But, he says, someone who has achieved this view "does not get caught up in the habits, fixations, prejudices or biases of the mind. He is not fixated on 'my self.' He does not doubt that when something is occurring, it is occurring, and when it has come to an end, it has come to an end. His knowledge is independent of others. In these respects his view is complete."[63]

Notice that the Buddha differentiates between something "occurring" (*uppajjati*) or "coming to an end" (*nirujjhati*), on the one hand, and its "being" (*atthi*) or "not being" (*natthi*), on the other. He is comfortable with a language of process but rejects the language of ontology.

To say that the eightfold path is to be cultivated (*bhāvanā*) means that it needs to be created and sustained from moment to moment. The path does not stretch out ahead into the distance waiting for you to take a leisurely stroll along it. It requires ongoing care and application. Grounded in as complete a view as possible, practitioners aspire to think, speak, act, and work in ways that respond appropriately to the situations of life in which they find themselves. These are the tasks of converts, stream entrants, those who have made the eightfold path their own. As such, the tasks are expressions of a core commitment to realize the values of awakening, the dharma, and the community in which they have gained "lucid confidence."

Another tradition in the early canon, however, presents conversion, not in terms of the confidence and virtues that are gained, but in terms of the "ties" or "fetters" (*saṃyojana*) that are lost. For the "stream entrant," the stream of life is able to flow freely, no longer blocked or hindered by the ties of vanity (*sakkāyadiṭṭhi*), doubt (*vicikicchā*), and moral rules (*sīlabbata*).[64] Since egotism is foreign to one who "is not fixated on 'my self'," and doubt is in opposition to lucid confidence, it is fairly easy to see how such ties would fall away in those who behold nirvana and are committed to a path of awakening. But how are moral rules to be understood as a tie or fetter?

For one who no longer thinks in terms of "it is" and "it is not," there can be no ontological basis for ethics. A legalistic moral code, by contrast, tends to be based in the assumption that bad actions have a certain intrinsic nature whereas good actions have a quite different nature. Those who are moral, therefore, follow the rules laid out in this code with the complacent assurance of knowing they are "right." But those who have entered the stream of the path have become "independent of others." Not being tied to a code of conduct devised by others, they will respond in unpredictable ways to whatever moral dilemmas they encounter. They will do so with empathy, intelligence, and compassion, not by first checking with a moral rulebook to see what is allowed. They will recognize how each moral dilemma arises out of a unique blend of complex conditions. Their ethics is thus situational rather than legalistic. They are willing to make what they consider to be an appropriate response, fully aware that they might get it wrong and make things worse. They are no longer "tied" by moral rules but have embraced an ethics of care and risk.

(8)

In the discourse *The City*, Gotama invites his listeners to imagine "a man wandering through a forest"

> who sees an ancient path traveled upon by people in the past. He would follow it and would see an ancient city that had been inhabited in the past, with parks, groves, ponds, and ramparts, a delightful place. Then the man would inform the king or a royal minister: "Sir, know that while wandering through the forest I saw an ancient path. I followed it and saw an ancient city. Renovate that city, sir!" Then the king or royal minister would renovate the city, and sometime later it would become successful and prosperous, filled with people, attained to growth and expansion.[65]

He then explains what the parable means. He compares himself to the man in the forest, and the ancient path to the one that was "traveled by the buddhas of the past." "And what is that ancient path?" he asks. "It is just this noble eightfold path, that is: complete view, thought, speech, action, livelihood, effort, mindfulness, and concentration."[66]

Gotama does not see himself as teaching anything new that was the result of his own peculiar insight or genius. In acknowledging the "buddhas of the past" he recognizes that he has seen something both universal and accessible: a fully human way of life grounded in an embrace of *dukkha,* the release of reactivity, and an awareness of its ceasing. And it is not just the path that he has rediscovered. For he followed the path, and it led him to the ruins of an ancient city. What does that ancient city stand for? The text lapses into standardized doctrinal formulae at this point, but the gist of the passage is clear. The city symbolizes a flourishing communal life based on the principle of conditionality as refracted through each facet of the fourfold task.

Rather than a City of God, Gotama imagines a City of Contingency. To build (or rebuild) it, he calls upon the help of "the king or a royal minister" to provide the resources and recruit the labor for the task. The parable shows that Gotama is concerned to establish a form of society. He may see his "assembly" (*parisā*) of adherents and mendicants as offering a model for how such a society might operate, but he needs to co-opt the ruling powers of his day to be able to translate this vision into reality. He does not wish to overthrow or replace the rulers, but to convert them to his vision. He is not advocating revolution but the reform and development of an existing polity. Toward the end of his life he expresses a preference for a republican form of government as a model for his community, but in his numerous dealings with chiefs, assemblies, and kings throughout his lifetime he appears to accept whatever system of government they represent.

If we consider the fourfold task and the parable of the city to represent a sequence of steps, the result would look like this:

comprehending *dukkha* →
letting go of reactivity →
beholding the ceasing of reactivity →
cultivating the eightfold path →
building the city

The tasks describe a causal process that culminates in a form of society. Were we to embrace fully the existential reality of life, that would lead to a letting go of habitual reactivity. Were we to let go of reactivity, that would enable us to see the stopping of reactivity. Were we to stop reacting, that would allow the possibility of a way of life that is not conditioned by reactivity. And were we all to live in such a way, that would open the door to another kind of society.

This, I believe, is how Gotama translated his vision of a twofold ground of conditionality and nirvana into a way of life structured around a fourfold task. Conditionality and nirvana provide the underlying rationale for living in the world in a way that fosters individual integrity and the renewal of community. In comparing the aim of his teaching to the rebuilding of an ancient city, the Buddha presents his goal as something entirely secular. According to Buddhist orthodoxy, following the eightfold path leads to the complete end of suffering by bringing the cycle of death and rebirth to an end. Here, in contrast, following the eightfold path leads to the emergence of a city: a collaborative civic life in *this* world.

4

Pasenadi: The King

King Pasenadi of Kosala knows: "The wanderer Gotama has gone forth from the neighboring clan of the Sakiyans." Now the Sakiyans are vassals of the King of Kosala. They offer him humble service and salute him, rise and do him homage, and pay him fitting service. And just as the Sakiyans offer the king humble service, so likewise does the king offer humble service to the Tathāgata, thinking: "if the wanderer Gotama is well-born, I am ill-born; if the wanderer Gotama is strong, I am weak; if the wanderer Gotama is handsome, I am ugly; if the wanderer Gotama is influential, I am of little influence."

—AGGAÑÑA SUTTA

(1)

Gotama. Ānanda. Mahānāma. Pasenadi. Who are these people? Who *were* they? Do I consider them as historical figures, as men whose hearts beat just as mine does, who trod the earth with gout in their toes or an ache in the hip: fallible, aging creatures, subject to sickness, anguish, and death? Or, in the absence of any hard evidence that they ever existed—no writings, no artifacts fashioned by their hands, no contemporaneous inscriptions in rock, no mention of their existence outside Buddhist sources—do I consider them as mere ciphers who represent general human types: Gotama, the sage; Ānanda, the disciple; Mahānāma, the sensualist; Pasenadi, the ruler? Or does the truth about them lie elsewhere?

Should I treat them as I might characters in a novel? As I read of their deeds and ponder their words, do I willingly suspend my disbelief in their flesh-and-blood existence as the price to pay for them to shed light on features of our shared humanity and to offer guidance on how to flourish in this life now? Is Gotama no more or less real than Don Quixote or Leopold Bloom? As a figure whose existence has been assumed by millions of people over hundreds of years, who embodies what may be deeply held convictions, Buddhists would find this as hard to accept as Christians would of Jesus, Muslims of Muhammad, or Daoists (Taoists) of Zhuangzi. I cannot accept that Gotama was a fiction conjured up by cynical priests to trick me (for my benefit) into believing in him. I need him to be more than a cipher, but I also require him to be more than merely human.

The devil, as is well known, lies in the details. On the basis of sparse evidence, I am seeking to reconstruct the life of the man known as Gotama and the dharma he taught. In both cases, I try imaginatively to re-inhabit the world of fifth century BCE India in order to recover glimpses of the historical Gotama before he mutated into the quasi-divine Buddha, and the core elements of his teaching before they mutated into the various orthodoxies of Buddhism. In both cases, I often focus on dissonant fragments of text that sit uncomfortably in the discourses where they are embedded. Following the criteria of historicity established by biblical scholars, I recognize such difficult and discontinuous passages as more likely to be original than the rest of the canon. Since they conflict with the accepted views of later Buddhist schools, they are less likely to have been added by members of those schools at a later date.

The tensions between Gotama and the Buddha and between the dharma and Buddhism may have started during Gotama's lifetime. The discourses themselves provide ample examples of how Gotama was transformed from a human being into a quasi-deity, and the dharma was transformed from a practical ethics into a metaphysical doctrine. The texts that make up the early canon cannot, therefore, be regarded as sharing an equivalent antiquity, but need to be understood as products of the doctrinal and literary evolution of a tradition that took place over at least three centuries.

(2)

King Pasenadi of Kosala and Kāsi, to give him his full title, was the adherent with whom Gotama is reported to have held the greatest number of dialogues. The third chapter of the *Saṃyutta Nikāya,* consisting of twenty-five discourses, is devoted to their discussions, as are four consecutive discourses in the *Majjhima Nikāya* (nos. 87–90). Yet despite the relative abundance of material, Pasenadi has remained an obscure figure in the history of Buddhism. The king most closely associated with Gotama tends to be Bimbisāra, ruler of Magadha. Yet the only conversations between Gotama and Bimbisāra concern legalistic matters about rules. Nowhere are the two men shown having a discussion about the dharma. Surprisingly, however, Bimbisāra is said to have become a stream entrant on first hearing Gotama teach, while Pasenadi, who spent a considerable amount of time receiving personal instruction, is not said to have made any progress along the path at all.

There is a curious parallel here with Ānanda, Gotama's younger cousin and devoted attendant. Although numerous minor characters are said to have become arahants upon hearing the Buddha speak a single time, Ānanda and Pasenadi, two of his closest confidants, failed to achieve anything comparable after many years of close exposure to his teaching. Ānanda is often praised by Gotama and invited to deliver discourses to the other mendicants, but he never advanced beyond the stage of a stream entrant. What unites Ānanda and Pasenadi is that both were engaged in the affairs of the world: Ānanda as Gotama's attendant for the last twenty-five years of his life, and Pasenadi as ruler of Gotama's homeland of Kosala. Might this taint of worldliness have made the compilers of the canon uncomfortable about including them among the ranks of the spiritually realized? Is it an accident that two of the most fully human characters, about whom we possess many intimate details, are not deemed worthy of sainthood, whereas many others, about whom we know next to nothing, are presented as faceless saints?

Before proceeding with an account of Pasenadi's character and life, let us look at how the Buddha considered the role of kingship, both literally and metaphorically. The *Shorter Discourse to Saccaka* recounts a dialogue with an esteemed Jain teacher in Vesālī called Saccaka. In response to Saccaka's assertion that "this body is my self, feelings are my self, perceptions are my self, inclinations are my self, and consciousness is my self," Gotama asks:

> What do you think, Saccaka? Would a head-anointed king—for example King Pasenadi of Kosala or King Ajātasattu of Magadha—exercise the power in his own realm to execute those who should be executed, to fine those who should be fined, and to banish those who should be banished?[1]

Saccaka replies that since communities (*sangha*) and societies that still function as oligarchic republics, such as those of the Mallāns and Vajjians, have the right to do these things, then "all the more so" should a king such as Pasenadi of Kosala have such power.[2]

The Buddha agrees. He accepts that kings have the right to execute, fine, and banish people. That is what kings (as well as democratically elected leaders) do: their duty is to protect the integrity of the realm from those who seek to undermine it. Not once in the dialogues with Pasenadi does Gotama attempt to dissuade the king from meting out punishment, even when Pasenadi provokes him with accounts of his own violent behavior. Gotama recognizes that even for a king who has declared himself an adherent of the dharma, the virtue of non-violence need not be applied when it comes to the exercise of royal authority. This acknowledgment of an exception raises an awkward question: How would a king or a ruler practice the first training of not taking life? The Buddha's uncritical acceptance of kingly duty could also be used to justify the argument that a follower of the dharma should not question the authority of the state and its institutions.

But non-violence is not the point of the dialogue. The example of a king's right to exercise power in his domain is being used to counter Saccaka's claim that he is identical to his five psychosomatic bundles: form, feelings, perceptions, inclinations, and consciousness. Gotama continues: "What do you think, Saccaka? When you say: 'this body is my self,' do you exercise any such power so that you could say: 'Let my body be like this; let my body not be like this.' When this was said, Saccaka was silent."[3]

We tend to have an overinflated sense of our power over our own bodies and minds. In thinking of our physical and mental constituents as "me" or "mine" we naively assume a sort of kingship over a complex set of transient, unreliable, and impersonal processes. Gotama's reply to Saccaka follows exactly the same reasoning as in *On Not-Self,* believed to be his second teaching.[4] From that discourse it is clear that Gotama is talking about a person's lack of control over the inner workings of the body. It is impossible, he points out, to command the body to be healthy rather than sick, or to order feelings to be pleasant rather than unpleasant. Unlike a king who issues commands to his subjects that he can expect to be obeyed, we find ourselves powerless over our own sensorium—a situation at odds with the deeply rooted intuition that we are in charge of what is going on.

Gotama's notion of kingship is ambivalent. In worldly matters, he recognizes the authority and duties of kings and makes no effort to advise them to act differently. Metaphorically, however, although he recognizes that no one exercises kingship over his own experience, he encourages people to act in ways other than those prompted by their innate reactivity.

The Buddha compares Saccaka to a man in search of heartwood

who takes an axe to the large trunk of a plantain. "Then he would cut it down at the root, cut off the crown, and unroll the leaf-sheaths, but as he went on unrolling them, he would never come to any heartwood at the core." Not only does this analogy expose the hollowness of Saccaka's position, but it reveals the unfindability of a core self within. When one comes to see the body with complete understanding, one realizes how "this is not mine, this I am not, this is not my self." Through such letting go and non-clinging is a person liberated from reactivity to arrive at "unsurpassed vision, treading-of-the-path (*patipada*), and freedom."[5]

That one cannot find a regal self within the elements of one's experience does not imply that there is no self at all and that one is therefore a mindless automaton incapable of making choices and acting upon them. The freedom gained from such insight is the freedom to see things clearly and tread the path of life wisely. By focusing on Gotama's dialogues with others we witness an example of a person speaking and acting from such a liberated perspective. Rather than regard Gotama as a quasi-omniscient clairvoyant, we encounter him engaging in the cut and thrust of ambiguous and unpredictable human interactions.

In the *Connected Discourses to the Kosalan,* we find Pasenadi and Gotama present at what appears to be a religious procession. The king rises from his seat, kneels on the ground before the assembled brahmins and wanderers, and pays them lavish homage. He then returns to Gotama's side and declares: "Now surely these should be included among men in the world who are saints (*arahant*)." Gotama replies: "That is difficult to say."

> It is only by living together with someone that his virtue is known, and that, after a long time, by one who is attentive and wise. It is only by dealing with someone that his honesty is to be known. . . . It is only in (witnessing him) face adversities that his courage is to be known. . . . It is only through discussion with him that his understanding is to be known.[6]

This pragmatic advice not only punctures any idea one might have of Gotama as able magically to read other people's minds but warns against making hastily formed opinions of others based on first impressions. Just because someone has a shaven head, wears robes, and affects an expression of serenity, we cannot assume their true character. Conversely, no matter how "enlightened" someone may be, it takes time, attention, and discernment to take the measure of another person.

But the king is playing a trick on Gotama to test him. He admits to him that all of these men are in fact his spies, who are disguised as wanderers and ascetics.[7] Gotama remains equanimous. He does not criticize the king for trying to mislead him or others by disguising his spies as wanderers. Perhaps he already suspected that Pasenadi had planted spies within his own community of mendicants. If not, he would now. What emerges from this exchange is a glimpse of Gotama's skill in dealing with a fickle and powerful character. He cannot afford to say or do anything that could prompt this key benefactor to withdraw his support, nor can he be seen to be a weak-willed yes-man if he is to maintain the king's respect.

(3)

Pasenadi, like his vassal Mahānāma in Sakiya, is portrayed as a man riven by conflicts between his public duties and his spiritual yearnings. While drawn to the values taught by Gotama, neither man has the intention to retire from politics and dedicate himself to a life of quiet contemplation. Yet each has internalized the dharma to a sufficient degree to be conscious of how his immersion in the affairs of the world seems to stand in the way of his aspiration for awakening. After a period of solitary retreat, Pasenadi shares with Gotama an insight that came to him. "There are few people in the world," he says, "who, when they obtain great wealth, do not become intoxicated and careless, give in to greed for sensual pleasure, and mistreat others." Given the context, it is unlikely that Pasenadi is just making a bland observation about the corrupting influence of money and power. He seems to be describing the kind of uncomfortable self-knowledge gained during a time of quiet reflection. He himself, he realizes, is someone whose position has led to his becoming intoxicated, careless, lustful, and abusive of others. Gotama offers him no consolation. He simply agrees.[8]

This passage acknowledges the power of external conditions to affect one's inner state of mind. However much one may long not to be careless and greedy, the pressure of social circumstance can override one's best intentions and lead to indulgence in behavior that one subsequently regrets. For an intelligent and sensitive man like Pasenadi, we can imagine such awareness leading to feelings of self-loathing and guilt.

In a passage from the discourse *On Beginnings* cited in the epigraph we find Pasenadi comparing himself unfavorably in every possible respect to Gotama.[9] While we might dismiss this as overblown rhetoric, the words are consistent with other accounts of Pasenadi's character. In one passage, we find him with five of his chiefs earnestly discussing which sense organ provides the greatest pleasure.[10] Elsewhere he is described as a glutton. "Unable to shake off the drowsiness occasioned by over-eating, he went to see Gotama and paced back and forth before him with a weary look." When asked what was the matter, he replied that he was always in pain after finishing a meal. Gotama helped him manage his diet so that the king reduced his intake of food, which resulted in his losing weight and gaining an alert mind.[11]

Pasenadi's interest in the dharma may have initially been due to the influence of his wife Mallikā, the daughter of Mahānāma's steward, whom Pasenadi met while on a hunting expedition in Sakiya. After becoming queen, she gave birth to a daughter, Vajirā, and then a son, Viḍūḍabha, who became the heir to the Kosalan throne.

One day, Pasenadi heard of a dispute that had arisen because of something Gotama had said. A certain householder's only son had died. "After his son's death, he had no more desire to work or eat. He kept going to the charnel ground and crying: 'My only child, where are you?'" In desperation, the householder sought counsel from Gotama. Instead of offering consolation, Gotama bluntly told him that he had lost control of his mind, and his faculties were deranged. What could the man expect? It is in the nature of things that "sorrow, lamentation, pain, grief, and despair are born from those who are dear." The householder is shocked by this unsentimental assessment of the human condition. "No," he retorts, "happiness and joy are born from those who are dear!" Disgusted with what Gotama had told him, he stood up and went away.

When Pasenadi recounted this story to Mallikā, she replied that if that was what the Buddha said, then it must be true. Infuriated by her remark, Pasenadi yelled: "No matter what that Gotama says, you applaud it, just like a pupil who blindly agrees with everything his instructor (*acariya*) says. Be off with you!" Pasenadi seems doubly enraged: with Gotama's assertion as well as his wife's uncritical acceptance of it. When he has calmed down and Mallikā has had time to reflect on what she said, she comes to him and gently asks how he would feel if one of his wives or children fell sick or died. She asks how he would feel if Kosala and Kāsi suffered a calamity. In each case, Pasenadi realizes that if anything happened to these people and places he holds dear, it would affect him deeply. "How," he realizes, "could sorrow, lamentation, pain, grief, and despair not arise in me?"[12]

By focusing the king's attention on his own family members and realm, Mallikā enables Gotama's statement to be translated into a series of personal insights for Pasenadi. These flesh and blood examples transform an abstract truth-claim ("sorrow is born from those who are dear") that can be endlessly disputed, into imaginative acts in which Pasenadi embraces the highly specific *dukkha* of his family and his country. Pasenadi's acceptance of the dharma is achieved by coming to terms with his everyday world from a new perspective rather than by assenting to a set of metaphysical propositions.

This interpretation of the text would also imply that the counterclaim—"happiness and joy are born from those who are dear"—could be treated in the same way. If a man insists that "sorrow, grief, and lamentation come from those who are dear," one could counter the assertion by asking how he would feel were his wife, son, or daughter to achieve success or sudden good fortune. Were the person to admit that their good fortune would make him happy and joyful too, one would have demonstrated how those dear to us can be a source of happiness and joy.

This episode from *On Beginnings* illustrates the difference between a dogmatic and a pragmatic approach to understanding truth-claims. An orthodox reading of this text would interpret it as showing that Gotama's statement "sorrow is born from those who are dear" is true but that the opposite view, "happiness and joy are born from those who are dear," is false. As soon as one chooses to believe either proposition, one find oneself with an irresolvable conflict. Yet in contrast to the dogmatist, who sticks to a position and seeks to defend it against all objections, the pragmatist tests its validity by considering it in the light of specific cases.

Concern for what is dear is the topic of another dialogue between Pasenadi and Mallikā, which takes place one morning while the two of them are on the upper terrace of the palace. "Is there anyone," the king asks his wife, "more dear to you than yourself?" Mallikā replies: "There is no one, your majesty, more dear to me than myself." Then she adds: "Is there anyone more dear to you than yourself?" Pasenadi is forced to admit that the same is true for him. The king reports this conversation to Gotama, who confirms Mallikā's point: that wherever you go in this world you will never find anyone who does not consider himself most dear. Then he draws an unexpected conclusion: "Therefore, one who loves himself should not harm others."[13]

There are striking parallels between this dialogue and the following passage in the *Bṛhadāraṇyaka Upaniṣad:* "The self is dearer than a son, dearer than wealth, dearer than everything else, and is innermost. . . . He who considers the self alone as dear, what he holds dear will not perish."[14] Since the *Bṛhadāraṇyaka Upaniṣad* is a pre-Buddhist text, parts of which were composed in neighboring Videha, it is possible that Gotama's reply to Pasenadi is a tacit critique of its doctrine of self. Rather than dismissing the self as an illusion—as some Buddhist orthodoxies might suggest—Gotama fully accepts that everyone holds his or her own self most dear. Yet he draws a radically different conclusion from this observation than the *Upaniṣad* does. While the *Upaniṣad* considers awareness of one's innermost self an intimation of divine immortality, Gotama considers it the foundation of an ethics of non-harming (*ahiṃsa*).

This idea is stated more succinctly in the *Great Chapter* of the *Sutta-Nipāta* (in K. R. Norman's translation):

> "As I [am], so [are] they; as they [are], so [am] I." Comparing himself [with others], he should not kill or cause to kill.[15]

Gotama's ethic of non-harm is founded on one's capacity to empathize with others, to feel their suffering as though it were one's own. Such an ethic would be incoherent if one did not recognize the other as a self, just like one's own self. For one can only truly empathize with other unique persons. To declare one's love for "humanity" or "all sentient beings" is meaningless if not grounded in actual encounters with particular living creatures. Rather than assent to the self's apparent permanence (as does the author of the *Upaniṣad*), Gotama recognizes that each self is entirely contingent on a shifting complex of unrepeatable physical and mental processes. This enhances his vision of the self as temporary, vulnerable, and tragic. The task of comprehending suffering entails empathetically embracing the *dukkha* of the other. And to embrace the other means to know and accept the other fully as a human being. As Śāntideva puts it in the *Bodhicaryāvatāra:*

> When both myself and others
> Are similar in that we wish to be happy,
> What is so special about me?
> Why do I strive for my happiness alone?

And when both myself and others
Are similar in that we do not wish to suffer,
What is so special about me?
Why do I protect myself and not others?[16]

Mallikā provides a rare canonical example of a woman involved in the affairs of the world who actively embodies the values taught by Gotama. As a girl raised among hill people who was reduced to servitude in Mahānāma's household on the death of her father, she has the status of an outsider. A curious episode recorded in the Pali *Dhammapada Commentary* also presents her as a sensualist and trickster who plays erotic games with her husband in the bathhouse.[17] Since she appears only a handful of times, there is insufficient material to allow a fuller understanding of her character. She seems to have died young and suddenly. Pasenadi was with Gotama in Jeta's Grove when a courtier arrived and whispered the news of her death in his ear. "On hearing this, King Pasenadi was pained and saddened, and he sat there with slumping shoulders, facing downward, glum, and speechless."[18]

(4)

On one occasion, Pasenadi asks Gotama: "Is there one thing which secures both kinds of good (*attha*), the good pertaining to this world (*diṭṭhadhammika*) and that pertaining to what follows after death (*samparāyika*)?" "Yes," Gotama replies. "There is such a thing: care (*appamāda*). Just as the footprints of all living beings that walk fit into the footprint of an elephant," he explains, "so care is the one thing which secures both kinds of good."[19]

Gotama's answer identifies the one outstanding virtue that encompasses all others. Elsewhere he says that all skillful states "are rooted and converge in care, and care is considered the chief among them."[20] Another way of phrasing the question would be, "What, in the dharma, constitutes the highest good?" That Gotama regards the highest good to be care is consistent with his famous last words: "Things fall apart; tread the path with care."

Appamāda (care) is a difficult term to translate. More commonly it is rendered as "diligence," "heedfulness," or "vigilance." My choice of "care" was influenced by Martin Heidegger's treatment of care (*Sorge*) in *Being and Time*. In maintaining that "Being-in-the-world is essentially care," Heidegger regards care, like *appamāda,* to be a "primordial structural totality" of existence rather than a discrete attitude of mind.[21] While Heidegger's conception of care is morally neutral, in Buddhism *appamāda* is invariably considered a virtue. In a German translation of Śāntideva's *Bodhicaryāvatāra,* the scholar Ernst Steinkellner renders it *wachsame Sorge*—"wakeful care"—to highlight its role as a key factor in the path to awakening.[22]

All these attempts at translation (including "care") fail to communicate that *appamāda* is a *negative* term like the English "impeccability," which is also a negative (*im/in* = without + *peccare* = sin), although we tend not to notice the negative and consider impeccability a wholly positive attribute. The first *a-* of *appamāda* is also a privative ("not"); *pamāda* means something like "negligence" or "indolence" and is often compared to a state of being befuddled or drunk. This condition of being "intoxicated and careless" was the one Pasenadi identified as an inevitable consequence of possessing power and wealth. It suggests that we spend a great deal of time stumbling about distracted, veering from one thought to the next, forgetting what we had intended to do as soon as a more diverting possibility presents itself.

When rendered as "care," we can understand *appamāda* to include both a vigilant attention (being care-full) and a heartfelt concern for the well-being of oneself and others (being caring), while *pamāda,* its opposite, comes to suggest being both care-less and un-caring. In addition, *appamāda* refers to what we *care about* most deeply, which Buddhists would summarize as the three core values of the Buddha, the dharma, and the sangha. A stream entrant, therefore, is one who cares about awakening, the practice of the dharma, and creating and sustaining community.

The opposite of care—*pamāda*—is also comparable with another key term, *āsava*, which I have translated literally as "effluence." This, too, suggests that no matter how noble our intentions, we have a deep-seated tendency to succumb to unworthy impulses that leak out uncontrollably. There are four *āsava*—sensual desire, being, views, and ignorance—all of which lead to a kind of mental-emotional incontinence. This state is not dissimilar to the Greek *akrasia*. Another negative term, *akrasia* means "without control." In other words, we keep finding ourselves swept away by habitual impulsivity and acting against what we have carefully judged to be our better interest.

"I do not understand what I do," wrote Paul in his *Letter to the Romans*. "For what I want to do I do not, but what I hate to do I do. . . . For I have the desire to do what is good, but I cannot carry it out. For I do not do the good I want to do, but the evil I do not want to do—this I keep on doing."[23] Or, as Śāntideva put it eight centuries later in India: "Although wishing to be rid of misery, people run towards misery itself. Although wishing to have happiness, like an enemy they ignorantly destroy it."[24] For Paul, this inherent tendency is indicative of man's sinfulness. By personifying such behavior in the figure of Māra, who consistently strives to subvert one's better intentions, Buddhist tradition has likewise characterized it as "evil" (*pāpa*).

Care—*appamāda*—thus refers to the very opposite of being indolent, distracted, reactive, muddled, contradictory, fuzzy-minded, and incontinent. In keeping with the Buddhist tendency to describe virtues in negative terms, it suggests that care arises when the general "pamādic" condition of human beings has finally been subdued through ethical commitment, meditation, and understanding. It is thus a careful, lucid, and contained caring for one's own condition as well as that of others.

Care is thus the overarching perspective of one who practices the dharma rather than a discrete mental state. In the *Greater Discourse on the Simile of the Elephant's Footprint,* Sāriputta employs the same metaphor of the elephant's footprint to refer not to care but to the fourfold task, which reinforces the idea that care is the sensibility that guides one's relationship with life as a whole.[25] Care lies at the heart of the four tasks themselves, infusing and motivating us to undertake each one of them. To genuinely care for the world means to embrace its suffering, let go of one's selfish reactivity, behold the ceasing of such reactivity, and cultivate an integrated way of life. Another passage, in the *Numerical Discourses,* compares this kind of caring to the sun in a cloudless autumn sky that "dispels all darkness from space as it shines and beams and radiates."[26]

"Care," says a verse in the *Dhammapada,* "is the path to the deathless; carelessness (*pamāda*) the path to death. The careful/caring do not die; the careless/uncaring are as if already dead."[27] To care, in this sense, is equivalent to treading the path itself. And to tread the path—to enter into and flow as a stream—is what it means to be fully alive, no longer limited or impeded by the forces of stasis and death. To live in such a way is to be conscientious, to be ever alert to the exigencies and challenges that life presents as well as one's own reactions to them. In the language of Buddhist moral psychology, care is that which "cherishes all that is good while guarding the mind against dwelling in afflicted states."[28] Such care comes close to what we would call "conscience."

That care is not a solitary but a social virtue is implied in the next conversation recorded between Pasenadi and Gotama in the *Connected Discourses to the Kosalan.* Once again, Pasenadi comes to Gotama to report an insight he has gained while alone in seclusion. "While the dharma has been well expounded by you," he says, "it has been done so for those with true friends, not for those with false friends."[29] Pasenadi has grasped that a fruitful practice of the path depends on the kind of company one keeps. Rather than being a purely solitary affair that takes place in the privacy of one's innermost feelings and thoughts, it is a public act embedded in relationships with other men and women.

Gotama agrees, recalling an occasion when he was staying in the Sakiyan town of Nāgaraka. "Then Ānanda approached me and declared: 'True friendship, true companionship, true comradeship: this is half of the spiritual life.' I told him: 'Not so, not so, Ānanda! True friendship is the entirety of the spiritual life. For when one has a true friend, one will develop and cultivate the noble eightfold path. . . . ' Therefore, great king, you should train yourself thus: 'I will be one who has such true friends.' And when you have these true friends, you should live in intimate reliance on one thing: care for skilful states."[30]

Care, as this passage suggests, is sustained by the matrix of relationships one cultivates with others who are likewise committed to realizing comparable values in their lives. Care is something one learns by observing the way careful/caring people live. It is not a quality that can be learned from a text on moral psychology or Buddhist ethics but only by living and interacting with human beings who embody it in their speech and acts. And if you, too, live your life in a caring and care-full way, that will have the effect of inspiring others to do likewise. Gotama concludes: "When you, great king, are living with care, the women of your harem, your vassal lords, your soldiers, your subjects in town and countryside will think: 'the king lives with care, in intimate reliance on care. Come now, let us live likewise.'" As a result of such reciprocity, "you yourself, great king, your harem, your treasury and storehouse will be guarded and protected."[31]

If you care for something, you will guard and protect it. Whether the object of your care be a moral virtue, a child, or an endangered species, in each case your care manifests as a yearning to keep it safe and free from harm. Care, in this sense, is equivalent to the principle of non-harm (*ahiṃsa*) that lies at the heart of Buddhist ethics.

(5)

That some of the core values of the dharma—concern for the other as oneself, care, and friendship—are discussed and refined in dialogues with Pasenadi suggests that the king may have been a conversation partner with whom Gotama explored and developed some of his key ethical ideas. We have a sense when reading these texts that the two men knew each other well and were able to speak frankly and honestly on a wide range of topics. As we have seen, it is often Pasenadi who supplies the insight, which Gotama either confirms or summarizes.

One of the longer passages in Pasenadi's own voice concerns his understanding of what it means to be a friend to oneself. As he explains to Gotama,

> Those who live unethically treat themselves as an enemy even though they say, "we regard ourselves as dear." Why? Because they treat themselves as an enemy might act toward an enemy. But those who live ethically treat themselves as dear even though they may say, "we regard ourselves as our enemy." Why? Because they treat themselves as a dear person might act toward one who is dear.[32]

In a subsequent passage, the king offers Gotama another insight along similar lines about the meaning of security:

> Those who live unethically leave themselves unprotected. Even though an army protects them, they are still left unprotected. Why? Because that protection is external, not internal. But those who live ethically, even though no army is there to guard them, still they protect themselves. Why? Because that protection is internal, not external.[33]

In reply to both statements, Gotama confirms what the king has said, and then summarizes the moral of the story in verse.

While the Buddha is generally assumed to be the author of the discourses collected in the canon, on numerous occasions like these he simply witnesses and affirms the words of others—even, as in this case, those of a worldly man who is not even recorded as having become a stream entrant. Thus the "word of the Buddha" (*buddhavacana*) is not equivalent to the word of Gotama. The discourses that make up the different *Nikāyas* are all regarded as *buddhavacana,* but not all of them are spoken by Gotama. The "word of the Buddha," therefore, refers to whatever is well said, to any utterance that accords with and supports the practice of the dharma, irrespective of who utters it.

The dialogues with King Pasenadi allow us a glimpse of Gotama's attitude to economic activity. One day Pasenadi explains to Gotama that a local financier had recently died intestate, so he had to arrange for the transfer of his estate to the palace, as was the law. Yet although the financier was a very rich man, he ate only the poorest-quality food, wore cheap clothing, and was driven about in a dilapidated cart. Rather than praise the financier for leading a simple life, Gotama deplores his behavior. "When an inferior man gains abundant wealth, he does not make himself, his family, his slaves, servants, or employees happy. . . . That wealth, not being used properly, goes to waste, not to utilization."[34] He contrasts this with the behavior of a superior person who uses his wealth by distributing it wisely. This dialogue shows that Gotama saw wealth as something to be skillfully and generously put to good use. Is he condemning only miserliness here? Or is he criticizing the practice of usury, whereby bankers enrich themselves through interest on loans without having to engage in labor? In either case, Gotama appears to regard money as something to be circulated rather than amassed.

While some of Pasenadi's utterances are praised by Gotama, some of his other activities are not. On one occasion the king had ordered a large group of people to be tied up with ropes and chains.[35] On another occasion a great sacrificial altar had been prepared and numerous animals had been led there to be sacrificed.[36] In both instances, when Gotama is told of these things, he criticizes such practices and draws a suitable moral lesson from them, but in neither case does he present his objections to the king himself.

The only time Gotama comes close to criticizing the king directly is in the final section of the *Connected Discourses to the Kosalan.* Pasenadi tells him that he has just been engaged in the kind of violent behavior that is unavoidable for powerful rulers like him.[37] The discourse does not specify what he had just done, but according to the commentary, the king had impaled a band of rebels who had tried to ambush him and usurp the kingdom. The commentator remarks: "The Buddha thought, 'if I reprimand him for such a terrible deed, he will feel too dismayed to associate closely with me. Instead I will instruct him by an indirect method.'" Modern scholars have remarked that this explanation "does not fit well" (Caroline Rhys Davids) and "detracts from the solemn dignity of the Buddha's discourses" (Bhikkhu Bodhi).[38] Such remarks betray a preconceived view of the Buddha as a paragon of unworldly perfection rather than a man who has to consider the consequences his words could have on the survival of his dharma and community in Kosala in the fifth century BCE.

Gotama responds with a parable. He asks Pasenadi to imagine four trustworthy people, one coming to him from the north, one from the south, one from the east, and one from the west, each of whom reports having seen "a great mountain high as the clouds coming this way, crushing all living beings." And "if such a great peril should arise," Gotama asks, "such a terrible destruction of human life, the human state being so difficult to obtain, what should be done?" Pasenadi replies: "What else should be done but to live by the dharma, to live calmly, and to perform skillful and good deeds?" Gotama says: "Your majesty: aging and death are rolling in on you. When aging and death are rolling in on you, what should be done?" Pasenadi remarks that his army would be utterly useless in the battle against aging and death, his counselors would be unable to use subterfuge to deter them, and all the gold bullion in the vaults would be insufficient to buy them off. Only the practice of the dharma would be of any use at such a time.[39]

Gotama's strategy in dealing with Pasenadi is to turn the king's mind away from the immediate crisis at hand and encourage him to recall the frailty of his own condition and his imminent demise. He does not tell the king what to do but reframes the dilemma from a wider, existential perspective. He presents him with a question so that Pasenadi can draw the appropriate conclusion himself. Gotama is concerned to instill within Pasenadi a keen sense of the core values of the dharma, thus providing him with those inner resources that will enable the king to become independent of others in his choices and acts. He wants the king to assume responsibility for his actions and come to his own decisions. It is not his role to instruct him how to act in response to a specific circumstance.

(6)

As comforting as it may be to imagine Gotama as a man far removed from the cares of the world, wandering along the dusty roads of the Gangetic basin accompanied by his saffron-robed mendicants, stopping regularly to deliver inspiring talks on the dharma, and passing much of his time meditating quietly in forests, the story that we can piece together from the canon presents a far more complex picture. Here we have a man who was intimately involved with the most powerful political figures of his time, many of them brutal, unreliable, and unpredictable, who had to be kept sweet so that Gotama could realize his project of "establishing the dharma and the community" in this world. That he succeeded in this delicate balancing act for more than forty years is a tribute to his political instincts and social skills as much as his "enlightenment."

Gotama belonged to a generation of privileged young men who grew up in a world that was being convulsed by change on all fronts: political, social, economic, and religious. In addition to Pasenadi, two of his other peers were Bandhula, son of the chief of Mallā (the oligarchic republic to the south of Sakiya), who became general of Pasenadi's army, and Mahāli, a prince of the Licchavis, the most powerful clan within the Vajjian Confederacy. To prepare themselves for their roles in this newly emerging world, Pasenadi, Bandhula, and Mahāli are said to have studied statecraft and the arts of war together at Taxilā in Gandhāra. Whether Gotama, son of another prominent chief in the area, also studied at Taxilā with them is nowhere mentioned, but it seems a distinct possibility given the social circles in which he would have moved and the ambitions his father would have had for him.[40] Having studied together would also help explain the frank and familiar tone of his dialogues with Pasenadi. Even if he did not actually set foot in Taxilā, he would have absorbed its culture and learning from those (including also Jīvaka, the doctor to the Magadhan court) who were some of his closest supporters.

In the opening dialogue of the *Connected Discourses to the Kosalan,* Gotama warns Pasenadi of the danger posed to rulers by ambitious young princes. In hindsight this can be understood as prophetic. We have already seen that King Viḍūḍabha, the son of Pasenadi and Mallikā, invaded Sakiya toward the end of Gotama's life in order to punish the Sakiyans for not offering him sufficient respect. Yet before Viḍūḍabha could launch this attack, he had to remove his father from power. As an adherent of the dharma "with aging and death rolling in on him," Pasenadi would presumably have been unwilling to unleash his armies on the defenseless relatives of his teacher. In deposing his father Viḍūḍabha did not act alone. He colluded with Dīgha Kārāyaṇa, the Mallān general of Pasenadi's army, who had his own rather different reasons for exacting revenge.

In another of the *Connected Discourses to the Kosalan,* King Pasenadi relates to Gotama having just witnessed the judges of the high court at Sāvatthi "speaking deliberate lies" for their own advantage. To stamp out this corruption, he dismisses them all and appoints "Handsome" to take charge of the judiciary.[41] "Handsome" appears to be the nickname of his friend Bandhula, the Mallān chief and general of the army. The text concludes with an anodyne response from Gotama, who compares the judges to fish that have been trapped in a net and will experience bitter fruit as a result of their misdeeds. We now have to turn to the Pali *Dhammapada Commentary* for an account of the repercussions of Pasenadi's actions.[42]

The dismissed judges spread a rumor that the powerful Bandhula, now in charge of both the army and the judiciary, is preparing a coup with his sons to overthrow Pasenadi. Whether or not this was the case we have no way of knowing, but Pasenadi believes what he hears. He dispatches Bandhula and sons to quell an uprising on the border of the kingdom. On their return to the capital he has them ambushed and butchered to death. Yet when he realizes that he has killed his old friend, he is consumed by remorse, so he spares Bandhula's wife and daughters-in-law and allows them to return to their estates in the Mallān town of Kusinārā. And as a sign of repentance and good faith toward the Mallāns, he makes the fatal decision to appoint Bandhula's nephew Dīgha Kārāyaṇa to replace his uncle as commander of the army.

(7)

The last meeting between Gotama and Pasenadi is movingly described in the discourse *Shrines of the Dharma*. The text describes how the king and his general, Dīgha Kārāyaṇa, were at the Sakiyan town of Nāgaraka. Pasenadi asks Kārāyaṇa to prepare a carriage so that they can go and visit a park.[43] Nāgaraka was a considerable distance from Sāvatthi. Its exact location is unknown, and it is mentioned in the canon only twice, as the place where Gotama told Ānanda that "true friendship is the entirety of the spiritual life"[44] and that "I now mainly dwell by living in emptiness."[45]

What would have brought the king of Kosala and the general of his army to this otherwise obscure place? The text is vague to the point of sounding evasive. It seems as though two of the most powerful men in north India found themselves at a loose end in Nāgaraka one day and decided to kill time by going to a park. When they get there, Pasenadi is reminded of the quiet rural settings where Gotama and his followers retreat for meditation, which prompts him to ask Kārāyaṇa whether he knows where Gotama is staying. The general tells him that he is staying three leagues away in a Sakiyan town called Medaḷumpa. There is enough daylight left to get there.

When they arrive in Medaḷumpa, Pasenadi sees some mendicants walking up and down in a wooded grove and asks them where he might find Gotama. On being told where Gotama is staying, "Pasenadi handed over his sword and turban to Dīgha Kārāyaṇa then and there. Then Dīgha Kārāyaṇa thought: 'So the king is going into secret session now. And I have to wait here alone!'"[46] Ignoring his indignant general, Pasenadi goes quietly up to Gotama's dwelling, enters the porch, clears his throat, and knocks on the door.

This passage is the first and only time in the discourses where Dīgha Kārāyaṇa is mentioned. It reads like a fragment of a larger story that is not being told. Since the discourse subsequently tells us that both Pasenadi and Gotama are eighty years old, we can at least date the episode to the very end of Gotama's life. Once again, we have to turn to the *Dhammapada Commentary* to elucidate the broader context of which this event forms a small but crucial part.[47] From there we learn that Kārāyaṇa has chosen this moment to avenge the murder of his uncle Bandhula. It seems likely, therefore, that the general orchestrated the visit as part of his own plan to topple the king. He not only had prior knowledge of where Gotama was staying but would have known that Pasenadi would hand over his sword and turban—the insignia of royalty—for safekeeping before he went to see Gotama, thus providing the means to crown Prince Viḍūḍabha in his place. His indignation at being excluded from the meeting was feigned, perhaps to throw Pasenadi off the scent should he suspect that anything sinister might be afoot.

Upon entering the dwelling, Pasenadi falls at Gotama's feet and covers them with kisses and caresses. Gotama appears puzzled and asks him why he is honoring him in this way and expressing such friendship. The question prompts a lengthy panegyric from the king, extolling the exceptional qualities of Gotama, his followers, and his teaching.

> Kings quarrel with kings, lords with lords, brahmins with brahmins, householders with householders; mother quar-

> rels with child, child with mother, father with child, child with father; brother quarrels with brother, brother with sister, sister with brother, friend with friend. But here I see mendicants living in concord, with mutual appreciation, without dispute, blending like milk and water, viewing each other with kindly eyes.[48]

A community living in harmony rather than perpetual conflict is a far cry from Pasenadi's world. Then he turns his attention to himself:

> I am able to have executed those who should be executed, to fine those who should be fined, to banish those who should be banished. Yet when I am sitting in council, they break in and interrupt me. Though I ask them not to, they still break in and interrupt me. But here I see mendicants listening to you teach the dharma and there is not even the sound of anyone coughing or clearing his throat.[49]

Are we to take these words as another example of the overwrought praise we often find in the canon, or are they a lament, an extended sigh of relief? Might they provide a glimpse of a ruler who is losing control of his kingdom, an old man being sidelined and mocked by his subjects, a frail king who is aware that his days in power are numbered? Perhaps he is not as naive and manipulable as Dīgha Kārāyaṇa seems to believe. Maybe he realizes that the game is finally up, and he no longer has the will or strength to resist those who seek to replace him.

He concludes: "The Teacher is a lord and I am a lord; the Teacher is a Kosalan and I am a Kosalan; the Teacher is eighty years old and I am eighty years old. Since that is so, I think it proper to do such supreme honor to the Teacher and to show such friendship."[50]

When Pasenadi leaves Gotama's dwelling, he discovers that his general has abandoned him. The mendicants tell him that Dīgha Kārāyaṇa has taken the royal insignia and departed to make Viḍūḍabha king. Pasenadi decides to flee to Rājagaha, the capital of Magadha, for safety. Before he has gone very far, he meets his wife Varshikā, who set out in search of her husband as soon as she learned of the coup. We know virtually nothing about Varshikā. If, as W. Woodville Rockhill speculates, she was the sister of King Bimbisāra who would have been married to Pasenadi as part of a formal alliance between Kosala and Magadha, then she would have been an old woman at this time.[51] It would also help explain the choice of Rājagaha as a destination for exile, since Varshikā would have been Ajātasattu's aunt. The two of them travel alone, a journey of around two hundred miles, in the hope that Ajātasattu, the king of Magadha, will take mercy on them.

This decision was a clear sign of desperation. Ajātasattu was no great friend of Kosala. In the *Connected Discourses to the Kosalan,* Pasenadi and Ajātasattu are twice described as being at war. The battles they fought were inconclusive, with each claiming victory on different occasions.[52] According to Pali sources, Pasenadi subsequently gave his and Mallikā's daughter Vajirā in marriage to Ajātasattu as part of a truce or peace treaty.[53] In this case, he may have set out from Medaḷumpa to Rājagaha with the additional hope that Ajātasattu would be unlikely to refuse sanctuary to his own father-in-law.

When Pasenadi and Varshikā reach Rājagaha, they settle in one of the royal parks. Varshikā goes into the city to inform Ajātasattu of Pasenadi's arrival. At first, Ajātasattu cannot believe that the mighty king of Kosala has managed to find his way into a nearby park unnoticed. Varshikā asks him: "But, sir, where is his army? His son has usurped the throne, and he has come alone here with his handmaid." During the time it takes for Ajātasattu to believe this story and prepare to receive the deposed king, Pasenadi becomes sick and irritated by the delay. Hungry, he wanders into a nearby field. A farmer gives him some turnips, which he devours, leaves and all. This makes him thirsty, so he drinks some water from a pool. "Suddenly his hands stiffened and, seized with cramps in the stomach, he fell in the road and died, suffocated by the dust caused by the wheels of passing vehicles."[54]

5

Letting Go of Truth

I do not say "this is true," which is what fools say to each other. They make out their own way to be true, therefore they regard their opponent as a fool.

—AṬṬHAKAVAGGA

His liberation, founded on truth, is unshakeable. . . . For this, *bhikkhu,* is the supreme noble truth, namely, nirvana, which is undeceptive.

—DHĀTUVIBHANGA SUTTA

(1)

The dharma may have started out as a twofold ground and a fourfold task, but Buddhism ended up with the two truths and four noble truths. You will not find any references in authoritative sources on Buddhism to either a "twofold ground" or a "fourfold task." These are examples of ideas that either failed to take off or were forgotten, suppressed, marginalized, or lost. Sometime during the centuries after Gotama's death, Buddhism seems to have taken a metaphysical turn. By adopting a language of truth, Buddhists moved from an engaged agency with the world to the theorizing stance of a detached subject contemplating epistemic objects.[1] Rather than consider injunctions to guide their ethical actions, they debated the truth of propositions in order to support their beliefs. They shifted, seemingly en masse with little if any resistance, from prescription to description, from pragmatism to ontology, from skepticism to dogmatism.

How and why did this happen? Possibly the tension between tasks and truths began to make itself felt within the community during the Buddha's lifetime. The two canonical passages cited in the epigraphs, for example, illustrate opposing attitudes to the notion of truth. While the first text, from the *Chapter of Eights*, maintains that anyone who claims "this is true" is a fool, the second, from the *Exposition of the Elements*, declares nirvana to be the "supreme noble truth." Which of these are we to take seriously? Since the *Chapter of Eights* is widely accepted as one of the oldest texts in Pali, I will assume that it represents an earlier perspective. Yet from there we move to a discourse bearing the title of a *vibhanga* (exposition, commentary) that replaces the skeptical, ironic tone of the *Chapter of Eights* with the assured certainty of the believer.

Immediately after the *Exposition of the Elements*, we find another discourse in a similar vein entitled *Exposition of the Truths*. This discourse tells how Gotama returns to the Deer Park at Isipatana near Benares, where he supposedly gave his first discourse, with his disciples Sāriputta and Moggallāna. Having praised them as, respectively, the "mother" and the "midwife" of his community, he announces that Sāriputta "is able to announce, teach, describe, establish, reveal, expound, and exhibit the Four Noble Truths."[2] The Buddha then retires, leaving Sāriputta to deliver a talk on this topic. Sāriputta presents the standard definitions of each of the four truths as found in *The Four Tasks* but comes to an abrupt halt. Unlike in *The Four Tasks*, he does not go on to explain that *dukkha* is to be comprehended, reactivity let go of, ceasing beheld, and the path cultivated. The four tasks are omitted altogether.

The discourses themselves allow us to observe how the differences and conflicts within the early community played themselves out. If, as scholars believe, the Pali Canon became "closed" (i.e., no longer incorporated any additional material) about four hundred years after the Buddha's death, then this would serve as a reasonable estimate of how long the struggle for canonical dominance went on. During the same period, Brahmanism established itself as the guiding framework for social, religious, and metaphysical life throughout the Gangetic basin where Gotama had lived and taught. These two developments were, it would seem, closely intertwined. As Brahmanism came to be accepted as normative, elements of its worldview started to be taken for granted even among non-Brahmanic communities. Not only did the brahmins insist on their divinely ordained authority here and now, they also, in Johannes Bronkhorst's telling phrase, "colonized the past."[3] They came to believe their own propaganda that Brahmanism had been the default philosophy and practice of Indians since the dawn of time.

This was the environment in which Buddhism would have mutated from a pragmatic ethical philosophy to an Indian religion that competed with brahmins, Jains, and others for the allegiance and support of powerful, wealthy patrons. To realize their goals each school needed to make a compelling case that its particular version of truth was more credible than that of its competitors. Yet unlike both Brahmanism and Jainism, Gotama had never posited the existence of either a permanent *ātman* or a consciousness that observed and judged the world from an unconditioned standpoint. A transcendental subject provided the "view from nowhere" needed for making metaphysical assertions supposedly describing the nature of reality.[4] To make such truth-claims requires the adoption of a distanced stance. Otherwise, an opponent could dismiss whatever you say as merely the product of your own relativistic point of view. At a certain point, Buddhists must have felt obliged to adopt this rhetoric of truth.

(2)

Apart from occurring in the ubiquitous phrase "four noble truths," the term "truth" (*sacca*) in the Pali discourses predominantly refers to the virtue of being truthful, honest, loyal, and sincere. Truth is seen as an ethical practice rather than a metaphysical claim; it is something to do, not something to believe in, let alone be enlightened about. This usage survives in the Theravāda Buddhist doctrine of the ten "perfections" (*pāramī*), a post-canonical list of the virtues required for awakening. The seventh of these is *sacca pāramī:* the perfection of truth. Likewise, in his second pillar edict, the Buddhist emperor Aśoka offers a succinct definition of what constitutes the dharma: "little evil, much good, kindness, generosity, truth (Maghadi: *sace*), and purity."[5]

Translators today, however, translate *sacca* in these contexts as "truthfulness" rather than "truth." While this choice fits with the general usage of the term "truth" in orthodox Buddhism, it unwittingly exposes how a word that began by denoting the virtue of honesty came to denote something like "reality." We can see how this could happen. A true statement is an accurate representation in words of what is the case in reality—of facts. Over time, it seems that "truth" started being used for the facts themselves, as well as for correct statements about those facts. A statement is "true" because it corresponds with the "truth," and the person who makes such utterances is said to be "truthful."

Such a correspondence theory of truth came to be taken for granted in Buddhist philosophical thought, much as it has been in most Western philosophy. However, pragmatic philosophers such as William James, John Dewey, and Richard Rorty and phenomenologists such as Martin Heidegger and Gianni Vattimo have all challenged this notion of truth. One of the dangers they see in such a view is that it easily gets elevated into a basis for certainties about what constitutes "the Truth." It becomes, for Rorty, "shorthand for something like 'a natural terminus to inquiry, a way things really are, and that understanding what that way is will tell us what to do with ourselves.'"[6] Truth thus assumes qualities of ultimacy and finality, which turns it into a rhetorical weapon in the armory of religious, political, and scientific fundamentalists alike. But philosophers like Rorty "do not think there is such a terminus. We think that inquiry is just another name for problem-solving, and we cannot imagine inquiry into how human beings should live, into what we should make of ourselves, coming to an end. For solutions to old problems will produce fresh problems, and so on forever."[7]

While Rorty's perspective resonates with Gotama's pragmatic emphasis on impermanence, *dukkha,* and not-self as a means to realize the ongoing project of human flourishing, it sits uncomfortably with Buddhist claims to know things "as they really are" as a means of arriving at ultimate truth, knowledge of which will grant one salvation. The Italian philosopher Gianni Vattimo makes a similar point to Rorty: "We don't reach agreement when we have discovered the truth," he observes; "we say we have discovered the truth when we reach agreement." Vattimo elegantly rejects a metaphysics of truth in favor of an ethics of truth, thereby recovering truth as a virtue of spoken language in human interactions. As long as we insist on the default assumption that I am right and you are wrong, we will be unable to relate to one another with complete empathy, generosity, honesty, and tolerance. "It is in this sense," concludes Vattimo, "that when the word 'truth' is uttered, a shadow of violence is cast as well."[8]

So embedded is this usage of "truth" in our language that we generally fail to remark on it. Bhikkhu Bodhi, in the introduction to his translation of the *Saṃyutta Nikāya,* comments that the discourses disclose "the Buddha's radical insights into the nature of reality" and how they are "vitally relevant to meditators bent on arriving at the undeceptive 'knowledge of things as they really are.'"[9] Walpola Rahula, in his famous *What the Buddha Taught,* translates *Dhammacakka* (Wheel of Dharma) as "Wheel of Truth,"[10] while Ajahn Thanissaro, another prolific translator of Pali texts, explains that the dharma is "the truth taught by the Buddha [that] is uncovered gradually through sustained practice."[11] These are examples of a widespread tendency to equate the dharma itself with "truth" even though the discourses themselves do not treat the terms *sacca* and *dhamma* as synonyms. Elsewhere, we find the English "truth" used when the Pali *sacca* is absent. In Bhikkhu Ñāṇamoli and Bhikkhu Bodhi's translation of *The Noble Quest,* we read:

"It is hard for such a generation to see this truth, namely, specific conditionality, dependent origination."[12] Yet the Pali does not say this. The word they translate as "truth" is not *sacca* but *ṭhāna,* which I have translated as "ground." As we saw in chapter 3, *ṭhāna* has a wide range of meanings, but "truth" is not one of them.

(3)

As the concept of truth metamorphosed from a virtue into a synonym for reality, it exerted a deep and lasting influence on how Buddhists came to understand the nature and purpose of their practice. This is particularly evident in the way *The Four Tasks* has come down to us. As we have seen, this discourse presents the fourfold task that lies at the heart of the Buddha's vision: by accomplishing it he claimed to have attained "peerless awakening." As the text of the discourse evolved over time, these four tasks become progressively overlaid with and obscured by the doctrine of four noble truths. Fortunately, a close reading of the text enables us to see how this shift from tasks to truths took place.

These are the lines from *The Four Tasks* that spell out the nature of each task in Bhikkhu Bodhi's translation:

> This noble truth of suffering is to be fully understood. . . .
> This noble truth of the origin of suffering is to be abandoned. . . .
> This noble truth of the cessation of suffering is to be realized. . . .
> This noble truth of the way leading to the cessation of suffering is to be developed.[13]

I have no issue with the translation. This is indeed what the Pali text says. The problem is that none of these four statements can possibly mean what they say.

The first person to spot the incongruity was F. L. Woodward in his 1930 English translation of *The Four Tasks.* He was puzzled by the second statement, "This noble truth of the origin of suffering is to be abandoned," which he translates as: "This arising of Ill is to be put away." Apart from his choice of terminology ("arising" rather than "origin," "Ill" rather than "suffering," "put away" rather than "abandoned"), what is most striking is that he leaves out the phrase "this noble truth." He gives his reasons in a footnote. Having noted that the Burmese editions of the Pali text leave out the word *ariya* (noble) in this passage, he goes on:

> But we must omit *ariya-saccaṃ* (noble truth); otherwise the text would mean "the Ariyan truth about the arising of Ill is to be put away." *Craving* has to be put away. The frame has obscured the picture here.[14]

Woodward's point is simple. What needs to be *abandoned, put away,* or, as I prefer, *let go of* is craving, that is, reactivity (*taṇhā*). I doubt that anyone would question that this is what the text means, but this is not what the text says. The text says that "this noble truth" is to be abandoned. The second noble truth, though, would remain true irrespective of whether one had abandoned craving or not. According to tradition, the arahant has abandoned *taṇhā* for good, but he has not thereby abandoned the second noble truth. With the conviction and authority born from personal experience, the arahant would continue to teach and affirm it on a regular basis. To abandon the second noble truth makes no sense at all.

Despite this observation, which led him to translate the passage according to what it must mean rather than what it says, Woodward failed to notice that exactly the same problem applies to all four noble truths. Take number four: "This noble truth of the way leading to the cessation of suffering is to be developed." (Here is Woodward's translation: "This Ariyan truth about the practice leading to the ceasing of Ill is to be cultivated.") Yet to develop or cultivate a noble truth is just as absurd as to abandon it. Would developing the fourth noble truth make it more noble? Or more true? Or both? Or neither? Again, the text *means* that the "way," the eightfold path, is to be developed but *says* that the noble truth is to be developed.

The reason why this incongruity is less evident with the first task ("This noble truth of suffering is to be fully understood") is because we habitually use the verb "understand" in reference to truth as well as to suffering: "I fully understand the truth of what you say" and "I fully understand the pain you are in." It is also the case with the third task ("This noble truth of the cessation of suffering is to be realized"). We can say "I realized the truth of what you said" as well as "I realized my goal in life." In both cases, the ambiguity of the English words chosen by the translator allows us to ignore the syntactical absurdity of the Pali sentences.

These considerations are not just a semantic game. They have real-life implications. It is not the *noble truth* of suffering that we need to understand but *suffering* itself. It is one thing to understand a truth but something quite different to understand a person's pain and grief. Someone could understand all about the truth of suffering while failing to grasp their own existential plight or empathize with another's anguish. By shifting the emphasis from tasks to truths, the Buddhist tradition begins tacitly privileging abstract knowledge over felt experience. As long as Buddhist teachers persist in employing the language of "noble truths," they unthinkingly endorse the preeminence of doctrinal belief over practical application.

In a 1982 paper, "The Four Noble Truths," the eminent Pali philologist K. R. Norman acknowledges Woodward's "very perspicacious remark" on the second noble truth. He also maintains that Woodward "did not go far enough," since "he should have suggested the removal of the word *ariya-saccaṃ* (noble truth)" from all four statements. On the basis of this and further detailed textual analyses, Norman comes to the startling conclusion that the "earliest form of this discourse did not include the word *ariya-saccaṃ*."[15] This is tantamount to saying that what is widely regarded as the fundamental doctrine of Buddhism was *grafted onto preexistent teachings*. What caught Woodward's eye were the still visible stitchmarks left by those anonymous hands that inexpertly interpolated the phrase "noble truth."

Over time, the doctrine of the four noble truths superseded the teaching of the four tasks. The frame, to follow Woodward's compelling image, came to obscure the picture. The four noble truths came to obscure the fourfold task. We have now reached a point where Buddhism proudly presents its gilded and ornate frame while the picture itself is only dimly recalled.

(4)

The shift from tasks to truths, from know-how to knowledge, entailed distorting some of the earliest texts. If we continue probing the Buddhist doctrine of the four noble truths, further anomalies become apparent. Take the term *samudaya*. Woodward and I translate it as "arising." I. B. Horner translates it as "uprising." Yet the standard translation used by Walpola Rahula, Maurice Walshe, Bhikkhu Bodhi, and others is "origin." At first glance, "origin" seems the right choice. After all, Buddhist orthodoxy based on the four noble truths insists that *taṇhā* (craving/reactivity) is the *origin* of suffering—*dukkha samudaya*. This is understood to mean that craving is the root *cause* of suffering, the condition without which suffering would not occur. Since suffering is defined as birth, aging, sickness, and death— "in short, these five bundles of clinging"—then craving becomes the causal origin of everything that we experience as human beings. From here it logically follows that in order to bring suffering (and, by implication, life) to an end, one must bring the craving that causes it to an end. Only in this way is it possible to end the cycle of endless death and rebirth, all of which will be extinguished in a final nirvana. This, in a nutshell, is the metaphysical foundation of Buddhism.

If Gotama had really wanted to declare that craving is the cause of suffering, why did he not use a term such as *hetu* or *paccaya*, the common Pali words for "cause" or "condition"? The only occasions when *samudaya* is used in a causal sense in the canon appears to be in the expression "craving is the origin of suffering." In other passages the term is used to mean the very opposite. In the discourse *To Lohicca,* for example, the Buddha talks to the brahmin Lohicca about one who "enjoys the fruits and revenues" of a village called Sālavatikā.[16] The Pali word translated as "fruits" is *samudaya*. Such fruits are clearly the *result* of a state of affairs rather than its origin. They are what "arise" as the effect of good stewardship and management.

Likewise, reactivity is what arises when a living, feeling organism comes into contact with its environment. This is confirmed by another classical Buddhist doctrine: the twelve links of conditioned arising. Here reactivity (*taṇhā*) is said to be caused by feeling (*vedanā*), which in turn is said to be caused by contact (*phassa*). These links are pragmatic rather than dogmatic. The point of the doctrine is not to provide a true account of reality but to describe an effective framework for the performance of a task. By noticing how one instinctively reacts to feelings prompted by contact, one is in a better position to let go of such reactivity by seeing it arise and cease instead of getting caught up in it. To successfully perform this task, it is irrelevant whether or not craving is the origin of suffering. One lets go of the reactive cascades of thoughts and emotions that arise in one's mind because they are the principal obstacle to entering the stream of the path. Reactivity is problematic not because it causes suffering—which, of course, it often does—but because it prevents genuine human flourishing.

"Craving is the origin of suffering" is a metaphysical dogma no different in kind to "God created heaven and earth." It claims to state a fundamental truth about the source of all experience, a truth that is impossible either to verify or to falsify. As Buddhism became an Indian religion, this dogma became one of its fundamental tenets.

At the conclusion of *The Four Tasks,* one of the five ascetics, Koṇḍañña, is said to have grasped what the Buddha taught. He articulates his insight by uttering the phrase "Whatever is subject to arising is subject to ceasing." Since Gotama said in the discourse that what ceases (*nirodha*) is reactivity, it is evident that what arises (*samudaya*) must refer to reactivity as well. The third noble truth, however, is called the noble truth of the cessation of *suffering,* while the fourth is called the noble truth that leads to the cessation of *suffering*. The goal of the dharma becomes to achieve the complete cessation of suffering, of birth, sickness, aging, death, instead of the cultivation of an integral way of life. What began as a fourfold task for coming to terms with *dukkha* mutated into a four-part metaphysics for explaining and overcoming *dukkha*. A practice for enabling life to flourish turned into a theory for bringing life to an end.

Here is a hypothesis for how this might have happened. Let us start with the four key terms that underpin both the four tasks and the four truths:

suffering (*dukkha*)
the arising (*samudaya*)
the ceasing (*nirodha*)
the path (*magga*)

This list provides us with an outline of the primary domains of human experience on which Gotama focused his teaching. "Suffering" denotes the totality of our existential condition—birth, sickness, aging, and death—as well as the physical world, one's body, feelings, perceptions, inclinations, and consciousness. "The arising" denotes craving; greed, hatred, and delusion; and the effluences—that is, whatever reactivity is triggered by our contact with the world. "The ceasing" denotes the ending of that reactivity, which is equivalent to nirvana, the deathless, and the unconditioned. And "the path" denotes the eightfold path, which begins with stream entry and extends to all of our ethical, contemplative, and intelligent responses to life. Once defined, each of these four domains becomes the site for specific practices of the dharma.

The next step is to identify the specific practices that need to be applied to each domain. As we saw in chapter 3, these are:

to comprehend *suffering*
to let go of *the arising*
to behold *the ceasing*
to cultivate *the path*

These practices can be thought of as a fourfold task, in which they intersect and mutually support each other, or as a sequence of four tasks, where each practice serves as the precondition for the next as part of an ongoing positive feedback loop.

At some point, though, these four terms began to be employed to develop a theory of how suffering comes about and how to overcome it. They thus became:

suffering
the arising of suffering
the ceasing of suffering
the path that leads to the ceasing of suffering

Although initially "suffering" was just one term among four, now it came to qualify and define each of the other terms. This change gave rise to two problems. The first, as we saw, entailed giving a causal sense to the word *samudaya* (the arising). The second was to introduce a disparity into the classical definitions of the four noble truths as found in *The Four Tasks.*

In that text and throughout the canon, the first, second, and fourth truths are invariably defined by providing a paraphrase. Thus "suffering" means birth, sickness, aging, death, and so forth; "the arising of suffering" means craving/reactivity in its various guises; and the "path that leads to the ceasing of suffering" means the path with eight branches. But when we come to the third truth, "the ceasing of suffering," such a paraphrase is not given. Instead, we are informed that it is "the traceless fading away and ceasing of that reactivity (*taṇhā*), the letting go and abandoning of it, freedom and independence from it." Since we have already been told that "suffering" is shorthand for the totality of the existential condition of everything from birth to death, we should expect a definition of its ceasing to explain what it is like for that existential condition to have ceased. Yet the text only describes what the ceasing of reactivity is like.

We know that numerous people from all walks of life at Gotama's time not only beheld the ceasing of reactivity but lived their lives from that perspective. Their experience cannot, therefore, have been that of the ceasing of *suffering,* the ceasing of the totality of their existential condition, for the simple reason that they were all still very much alive. The Buddha himself complains of physical ailments, the frustration of having to run an organization, the discomforts of old age, and the pain of dying. As long as we have a physical body, we will experience suffering. We might temporarily avoid such pains and frustrations by entering into meditative absorption—as Gotama says he did in order to cope with his last illness—but once we emerge from such a state, we return to this imperfect world with all its irritations and discomforts.

What Buddhists trumpet as the "end of suffering" cannot therefore mean what it says. Not only does it make little sense, the discourses themselves clearly state that it means the end of reactivity. To let go of reactivity and behold its ceasing is certainly no easy task, but at least it is something to which we can aspire, whereas the end of the suffering will remain a pipe dream for as long as we are pulsating, breathing, ingesting, digesting, defecating bodies.

The incongruous definition of the "ceasing of suffering" again points to the presence of anonymous hands tampering with the early teachings. As a crucial move in the transformation of tasks into truths, it would seem that the term "suffering" was appended as a qualifier to the other three terms ("arising," "ceasing," and "path"). All that remained was to add the stirring title "noble truth" for us to end up with this list:

the noble truth of *suffering*
the noble truth of *the arising* of suffering
the noble truth of *the ceasing* of suffering
the noble truth of *the path* that leads to the ceasing of suffering

Although the four tasks are still retained in the text of *The Four Tasks,* they have become syntactically absurd appendages to the four truths. By the time we get to Sāriputta's *Exposition of the Truths*—dating, according to the canon, to the Buddha's lifetime—they have been dispensed with altogether.[17]

(5)

In taking a metaphysical turn toward truth, Buddhists shifted away from an emphasis on know-how to an emphasis on knowledge. They became increasingly concerned with attaining a state of mind that could allow them to gain infallible knowledge of truth or reality.

One of the first moves in this process was to impute omniscience to the Buddha. Not only did Gotama deny possessing such a quality himself, but he ridiculed his contemporary Nātaputta (Mahāvīra) for claiming to have it. Those who declared him to be omniscient, he says, "misrepresent me with what is untrue and contrary to fact."[18] Nonetheless, the same discourse has him admit to possessing three types of knowledge (*tevijja*): (1) recollection of manifold past lives, (2) the divine eye that sees beings pass away and be reborn according to their acts, and (3) direct knowledge of the destruction of the effluences. Together, these may not amount to full-blown omniscience, but such types of knowledge (especially the first two) are far more than anything an ordinary mortal might possess. Whether we take this passage literally or interpret it symbolically, in both cases we let ourselves be guided by the assumption that what was distinctive about the Buddha was the privileged knowledge he gained about the way things really are.

As I see it, what distinguished Gotama was the manner in which he saw the world as a site for the performance of a set of tasks, and the self as a task in progress. He encouraged his followers to engage in this work in order to transform both the world and the self. He did not stand out among his peers because his knowledge of reality was somehow more accurate or superior to theirs. Yet as soon as awakening began to be conceived in terms of gaining a special kind of knowledge about truth, it was perhaps inevitable that a cognitive hierarchy, extending from ignorance to omniscience, would emerge. The doctrine of the threefold knowledge might well have been a first step in this direction. Much of the later history of Buddhist epistemology, philosophy, and metaphysics is taken up with discussions about such topics as *pramāṇa* (valid cognition), *anumana* (logical inference), and *yogipratyakṣa* (yogic perception), terms that are foreign to the discourses. Without demeaning the richness of philosophical and other insights gained by such developments, I suspect that they were achieved at the cost of losing sight of the skeptical and ethical pragmatism of Gotama's dharma.

It would be beyond the scope of this book (and the competence of its author) to provide a comprehensive account of all the historical, cultural, and philosophical reasons as to why and how Buddhist thought evolved in the ways that it did. Instead, let me focus on the introduction of one other doctrine that, like the four noble truths, became a fatal fork in the road for the Buddhist tradition. This is the doctrine of the two truths: ultimate truth (*paramattha sacca;* Sanskrit: *paramārtha satya*) and conventional truth (*sammuti sacca;* Sanskrit: *samvṛti satya*). The germ of this idea may have originated in the Buddha's vision of a twofold ground, that is, conditioned arising and nirvana. As we have seen in the epigraph, the *Dhātuvibhanga Sutta* calls nirvana the "supreme noble truth" (*parama ariyasacca*).[19] In three other instances we also find the term "supreme truth" (*parama sacca*) used to denote what the practitioner finally comes to "behold bodily" and "penetrate with understanding."[20] In Pali "supreme" (*parama*) is etymologically close to "ultimate" (*paramattha;* literally: "supreme meaning"). Nowhere, however, do we find conditioned arising referred to as a conventional truth.

Simply stated, the two truths doctrine is a way of distinguishing between the conventional truths of everyday life that we need in order to function as social and moral agents and the ultimate truth. By gaining direct, nonconceptual insight of the latter we achieve the liberating knowledge that frees us from suffering and rebirth. There are differing Buddhist interpretations as to what constitutes the higher or ultimate truth, but for the Madhyamaka school in which I was trained, the term refers exclusively to the emptiness of inherent existence. Such emptiness is constantly and irreducibly true; everything else in one's experience is at best only conventionally true.

The present Dalai Lama of Tibet was once asked what advice he would give to a newcomer who wanted to understand the meaning of Buddhism. Would he encourage that person to consider what it means to take refuge in the Buddha, dharma, and sangha? Or would he advise them to study the four noble truths? In reply, the Dalai Lama suggested that "for many in the West today, the Two Truths—conventional truth and ultimate truth—is the best place to start."[21] The Dalai Lama does not provide any reasons for his suggestion. Possibly he thought that this doctrine would appeal to the rational, scientific mind of an educated Westerner. Or his recommendation might simply reflect his personal conviction. The centrality of this doctrine is, after all, emphasized by one of the greatest of Buddhist thinkers, Nāgārjuna, who insists that "those who do not understand the division into Two Truths cannot understand the profound sense of the Buddha's teaching."[22]

The Theravāda tradition, whose teachings are based on the Pali Canon, sets forth a similar view. The late British scholar Maurice Walshe declares, in the introduction to his translation of the *Long Discourses* (*Dīgha Nikāya*):

> An important and often overlooked aspect of the Buddhist teaching concerns the levels of truth, failure to appreciate which has led to many errors. Very often the Buddha talks in the Suttas in terms of conventional or relative truth (*sammuti-* or *vohāra-sacca*), according to which people and things exist just as they appear to the naïve understanding. Elsewhere, however, when addressing an audience capable of appreciating his meaning, he speaks in terms of ultimate truth (*paramattha-sacca*).[23]

In reading Walshe's text, we could easily get the impression that the Buddha himself spoke of these two truths in his discourses. Yet nowhere, not even once, will we find a mention of either *sammuti-sacca* or *paramattha-sacca* in any of the hundreds of discourses attributed to Gotama in the Pali Canon. It is not just that Gotama failed to use that particular terminology; he simply did not think along such lines. As soon as "truth" is parsed in this twofold manner, it becomes difficult to resist slipping into an ontological mindset. "Ultimate truth" becomes a signifier of what *really is,* whereas "conventional truth" signifies merely what people agree upon as true and useful.

What may be the earliest mention of the two truths is found in *Points of Controversy* (*Kathāvatthu*), a polemical Buddhist treatise compiled in the centuries after Gotama's death. The Buddha, the author declares:

> spoke two truths, conventional and ultimate—one does not come across a third; a conventional statement is true because of convention and an ultimate statement is true because (it discloses) the real characteristics of things.[24]

To claim that "ultimate statements" describe the way things really are as opposed to how they conventionally appear is ontology. Yet the Buddha to whom I am drawn in the early discourses is not an ontologist. He has no interest in providing an accurate and final description of the nature of "truth" or "reality." He warns repeatedly of the dangers of getting sidetracked by metaphysical speculation of any kind, of being caught in what he calls "thickets of opinion."

As for what Gotama thinks of those who talk about the "supreme" (*parama*), we only have to turn to the *Chapter of Eights,* the text cited earlier as an example of a skeptical voice in the early canon:

> The priest without borders
> doesn't seize on what he's known or beheld.
> Not passionate, not dispassionate,
> he doesn't posit anything as supreme.
> One who dwells in "supreme" views
> and presents them as final
> will declare all other views "inferior"—
> he has not overcome disputes.[25]

On the basis of such verses, it is hard to understand how Gotama's followers would proceed not only to develop a theory of ultimate truth but to turn it into a central pillar of his teachings. Over time, they also ignored the prescient advice not to declare other views "inferior" (*hīna*). Mahāyāna Buddhists came to regard everything taught in the Pali Canon as pertaining to the "inferior vehicle" (Hīnayāna Buddhism).

Once the doctrine of the two truths took hold, the stage was set for Buddhism to develop along the lines on which it has come down to us today. Although Gotama never used the terms *sammuti* and *paramattha,* every subsequent school of Buddhism adopted this way of thinking about truth. So when Walshe announces that "very often the Buddha talks in the Suttas in terms of conventional or relative truth," he is simply expressing his unselfconscious commitment to Theravāda Buddhist orthodoxy. The language of the two truths is likewise so entrenched in the Tibetan and East Asian traditions that it would be highly unlikely for anyone even to think of questioning its legitimacy.

We do not know exactly when, how, or why the Buddhists made the fateful choice of embracing the doctrine of the two truths. But in doing so, they adopted more than a simple theory. The two truths became the spectacles through which Buddhism came to see itself, its teachings, and its institutions. Once their eyes had adjusted to seeing things in this way, Buddhists forgot that they were wearing glasses. The world that appeared through these lenses became so familiar and self-evident that they took it for granted: it was simply the way things were and always had been.

Part of the appeal of the two truths theory is that it seems to make life so much more straightforward and clear-cut. The "enlightened" can now be understood as those who have gained a direct understanding of ultimate truth, whereas the "unenlightened" are those who remain mired in the ambiguous truths of custom and convention. When phrased in this way, the achievement of enlightenment becomes the private affair of a person who has gained a privileged mystical cognition of the Truth with a capital *T.*

To think and speak like this encourages a tendency to conceive of what is real in singular terms—nirvana, the unconditioned, the deathless, emptiness, non-duality, Buddha nature—thereby nudging Buddhism toward an increasingly absolutist stance. In India, the Buddhist ultimate truth eventually became hard to differentiate from the ultimate truth described in the teachings of the monist Advaita Vedānta, founded by the eighth-century Brahmanic reformer and avowed anti-Buddhist Śaṅkarācārya. Indeed, one of the reasons that Indian Buddhists, particularly former brahmins, may have been instinctively drawn to the two truths doctrine is that it mirrored the familiar division between the absolute, singular reality of Brahman (God) and the world of multiplicity, suffering, and illusion (*māyā*). Yet one of the principal reasons Buddhism disappeared from the Indian subcontinent was due to its having become so blurred with devotional, philosophical, and mystical Hinduism that it began to lose its distinctive identity.

The two truths doctrine opened the door not only to ontology (the nature of what is) but also to epistemology (how we know what is) and logic (how we think and speak of what is). Buddhist scholars such as

Vasubandhu, Dignāga, and Dharmakīrti made significant contributions to all these fields in Indian thought, which for centuries engaged the brightest minds across the entire religious spectrum. The apogee and, as it turned out, the final hurrah of Buddhist thought in India took place in the great monastic university of Nālandā, in present-day Bihar. What the Dalai Lama has named the "Nālandā tradition" served as a primary source for the schools of Buddhism that subsequently flourished throughout East and Central Asia. My own training as a young Tibetan Buddhist monk was effectively an updated version of a Nālandā education.

A further advantage of the two truths doctrine lay in its providing Buddhism with a template for ecclesiastical power. Religious authority could now be understood as the privilege of those who had gained personal insight into the nature of ultimate truth. As the understanding of what constituted ultimate truth became subject to increasingly subtle philosophical and epistemological considerations, it could only be conveyed in the sort of highly technical language employed, for example, by Geluk lamas. Ordinary adherents found themselves excluded from participation in this discourse and thereby cut off from the possibility (at least in this life) of gaining the kind of rarefied understanding required to hold authority within the community. Claiming to possess theoretical and experiential insight into ultimate truth, on the other hand, provided legitimacy for those in power. The result is that Buddhist institutions today tend to be dominated by a professional and often deeply conservative clergy, who resist any attempt by the disempowered (particularly women) to challenge their authority.

Another important, though probably unintended, function of the two truths doctrine has been to reinforce and legitimate dualistic ways of thinking, which, in one form or another, keep emerging in human cultures. Examples are:

sacred versus profane
eternal versus transitory

unconditioned versus conditioned
reality versus appearance

Wherever religious or quasi-religious dogma takes root, it seems, people start thinking in terms of a higher, uncorrupted reality in contrast to which they inhabit a lower, corrupted realm. Whether this duality is phrased in terms of creator and creation, or nirvana and *saṃsāra* makes little difference. Once under the sway of such charged oppositional thinking, a person's life becomes neatly divided into a spiritual zone and a worldly zone. The former becomes associated with all that is good, eternal, and true, while the latter tends to be regarded as unworthy, embarrassing, and ephemeral. In the history of Buddhism, this dualism led to a recurrent emphasis on the innate purity of mind as opposed to the defiled, unclean nature of the body.

Buddhist philosophers were aware of the problematic nature of the two truths doctrine, and they struggled to make sense of it in a way that would fit with the rest of their understanding of the dharma. The basic difficulty was to explain how the two truths were related to one another. Some posited that ultimate truth was entirely different from all conventional truths, existing in a transcendent realm of its own. But if this were the case, how could a person in this benighted, relative world have any access to it? (A similar problem in theology concerns how or if one can ever know God.) But if the two truths were not different from each other, what would be the point of distinguishing between them in the first place? (In theology, this leads to pantheism.)

The most famous Buddhist "solution" to this dilemma is found in the Mahāyāna *Heart Sutra*, where the bodhisatta Avalokiteśvara declares to Sāriputta:

> Form is emptiness, and emptiness is form. Form is not other than emptiness, and emptiness is not other than form.

This passage has become one of the most widely quoted and pondered of all Buddhist texts to have been translated into English. For many

Western Buddhists, it might be the only discourse attributed to the Buddha that they have ever read (even though the Buddha sits in deep meditation throughout the sutra and says only, "Well said, well said," at the end). Yet few of those who admire its paradoxical, Zen-like pithiness are aware that it is an attempt to solve an unnecessary problem that was introduced by Buddhism's adoption of the two truths doctrine. The author of the *Heart Sutra* takes it for granted that "emptiness" and "form" denote two fundamental elements or spheres of reality, an assumption quite alien to the early discourses. Avalokiteśvara's task is to explain to the dim-witted Sāriputta how these two spheres can be reconciled with each other. Simply declaring the conventional truths of the world to be identical with the ultimate truth of emptiness does not explain anything. It merely expresses a preference for one dualistic alternative (identity) over its opposite (difference). The vital question of *how* these truths are identical is left hanging.

The solution proffered to this question by my Geluk teachers was more refined. By explaining that the two truths are "naturally one" (*ngo bo gcig*) but "conceptually different" (*ldog pa tha dad*), they sought to steer a middle path between the Scylla of identity and the Charybdis of difference. They are saying that the doctrine of the two truths is an indispensable pedagogic device, but it lacks any epistemic basis in immediate perceptual experience. In other words, it is crucial to conceive of such a distinction for the purposes of liberation, but it is not the sort of distinction (like that between red and white) that can be directly observed by one's senses. Emptiness is that *quality* of form (its absence of inherent existence) that needs to be realized in order to let go of the innate habit of reification. But emptiness is meaningless apart from form. Destroy the form, and you destroy its emptiness of inherent existence.

The Gelukpa also assert that the last cognitive affliction to be overcome before a person attains the omniscient mind of a buddha is the inability to understand how the two truths do not contradict each other. So deeply rooted is the habit of seeing things as inherently existent that only a buddha, they claim, is able "to cognize simultaneously and directly the emptiness of all phenomena and the phenomena themselves."[26] Appealing to the authority of the Buddha's omniscience is no different from claiming that God alone understands such mysteries.

If the Buddhist tradition had not adopted the doctrine of two truths, it is unlikely that any of these problems would have occurred. There would have been no need either for the pronouncements of the *Heart Sutra* or the hairsplitting ruminations of learned *geshés*. The history of Buddhist thought on this topic is succinctly captured in the words of a well-known nursery rhyme:

> Humpty Dumpty sat on a wall.
> Humpty Dumpty had a great fall.
> All the king's horses and all the king's men
> Couldn't put Humpty together again.

Is it still possible to recover a pre-orthodox dharma, one that existed prior to the doctrine of the two truths, and build upon that foundation an adequate ethical, contemplative, and philosophical practice that would optimize human flourishing in a secular age?

(6)

> There is, monks, an Unborn, Unbecome, Unmade, Uncompounded (*ajātaṃ abhūtaṃ akataṃ asaṅkhataṃ*). If there were not this Unborn . . . , then there would be no deliverance here visible from what is born, become, made, compounded. But since there is an Unborn, Unbecome, Unmade, Uncompounded, therefore a deliverance is visible from what is born, become, made, compounded.[27]

Here we have a passage from an indisputably early source that seems to contradict everything that has just been said. It is often cited to show that the Buddha *did* recognize the presence of an ineffable, ultimate reality that exists apart from the conventional world of conditioned, fleeting, and painful events. Another term not mentioned here but widely used as a synonym is *amata,* "the deathless." In other words, the goal of Buddhism, nirvana, is not only to be defined negatively as the ending of the three fires of desire, hatred, and confusion but also to be described as the attainment of something eternal and transcendent—subjectively experienced as the "supreme bliss" (*paramaṃ sukhaṃ*)—that accompanies realization of the deathless.[28] Liberation, in its truest sense, is more than just the inner freedom from reactivity. It is complete emancipation from the conditioned world through direct experience of the Unborn, Unbecome, Unmade, and Uncompounded.

Maurice Walshe, whose translation I have cited, writes that the passage "is perhaps the best answer we can give concerning the Upaniṣadic *Ātman*":

> Buddhism teaches no such thing—nevertheless the above quotation could certainly be applied to the *Ātman* as understood in Vedānta, or indeed to the Christian concept of God. However, to the followers of those faiths it would be an insufficient description, and the additions they would make would for the most part be unacceptable to Buddhists. It can, however, be suggested that this statement represents the fundamental basis of all religions worthy of the name, as well as providing a criterion to distinguish true religion from such surrogates as Marxism, humanism, and the like.[29]

Note the ambivalence in Walshe's remarks concerning the *ātman.* The ringing affirmation that "Buddhism teaches no such thing" is followed by a series of backsliding qualifications that end up not only agreeing that Buddhism shares with Vedānta and Christianity the notion of an ultimate truth that is compatible with their ideas of *ātman* and God but positing further that this is the "fundamental basis" of "true religion." Rather than Buddhism's being the uncomfortable outsider among the world religions because it has no use for God, it can now be redeemed as a true faith alongside the others.

To make his argument seem more credible, Walshe has taken the liberty of introducing into his English translation a distinction that cannot be made in the Pali. There are no capital letters in Pali. To distinguish, as Walshe does, between the "Unborn" (capitalized) and the "born" (uncapitalized) has no philological justification. It presumably reflects his wish to give added ontological gravity to the Unborn, to make it look more like God or the Absolute. Yet all it does is reveal the translator's ideological bias.

Despite the popularity of this famous passage, it occurs only twice in the Pali Canon: in the *Udāna* and in the *Itivuttaka*, two texts found in the miscellany of shorter volumes that make up the *Khuddaka Nikāya*. While this in itself is no reason to doubt its authority, it highlights how a marginal citation (like the "form is emptiness" passage in the *Heart Sutra*) has come to achieve prominence and popularity in the English-speaking Buddhist world. Why are people drawn to such texts in the canon?

I would answer (provisionally): Because many recent converts to Buddhism, despite their ostensible rejection of Judaic or Christian monotheism, no matter how much they (like Maurice Walshe) have pored over classical Buddhist texts, irrespective of how many years they have spent meditating, find it hard to let go of their attachment to God or one of his surrogates, such as the Transcendent, the Absolute, the One, the Non-Dual, Ultimate Truth, and Pure Consciousness.

None of the discourses that describe Gotama's awakening so much as mention an Unborn, Unbecome, Unmade, Uncompounded, let alone that realization of it constituted his awakening. Moreover, the Buddha explicitly declares that what he awoke to was "conditioned arising"—the very opposite of what is Unborn, Unbecome, and so on. And then we have the discourse on "the all" (*Sabbe Sutta*). "Listen, *bhikkhus*," says Gotama,

> I will teach you the all. And what is the all? The eye and forms, the ear and sounds, the nose and smells, the tongue

> and tastes, the body and sensations, the mind and its contents. That is called the all. If anyone should say, "Having rejected this all, I will make known another all," that would be a mere empty boast on his part. If he were questioned, he would not be able to reply and, further, would end up frustrated. Why? Because that all would not be within his domain.[30]

Gotama's "all" is an unsentimental inventory of fleeting, tragic, impersonal experience. A person who claims there is anything more than this "all" would be showing off, making "an empty boast." If the Buddha acknowledges that there is nothing to be found *beyond* this "all," where *within* it can one find an Unborn, Unbecome, Unmade, Uncompounded? There is only one possibility: among the *dhammas* that constitute the contents of mind (*mano*). This category includes anything that can be known subjectively without the mediation of a physical sense organ. As such, it includes feelings, thoughts, concepts, ideas—all the conditions under which mental consciousness (*manoviññāṇa*) occurs. In this case, it is hard to see how an Unborn, Unbecome, Unmade, Uncompounded could be anything more than a concept or idea—that is, the simple negation of born, become, and so on.

But surely the Unborn must be more than just an idea or a negation. Doesn't the passage open with the declaration "*There is* an Unborn, Unbecome, Unmade, Uncompounded"? Maurice Walshe once again appeals to the all-purpose two truths doctrine. "The Unborn," he explains, "does not 'exist' (relatively), but IS."[31] The Unborn now comes very close to something like Being itself (*esse ipsum*), to invoke a phrase that Thomas of Aquinas uses to define God. It also reminds me of Meister Eckhart's mystical teaching: "There is something in the soul that is so akin to God that it is one with Him. . . . It has nothing in common with anything created"—a statement that would not be out of place in Vedānta either. (Bear in mind that Walshe was also a scholar of medieval German and translated Eckhart's sermons into English.)

As soon as the Unborn—or any ultimate truth—is placed outside the range of ordinary mental cognition (*mano* and *manoviññāṇa*), we are obliged to posit a special kind of non-mundane consciousness that can "know" it.

> For that's where earth, water, fire, and air find no footing,
> There both long and short, small and great, fair and foul—
> There "name-and-form" are wholly destroyed.
> With the cessation of (mundane) consciousness this is all destroyed.[32]

By qualifying the consciousness that ceases as "mundane," the translator tacitly acknowledges the existence of a non-mundane consciousness, which floats free of the everyday sensory experience of "name-and-form." It is hard to see how such "signless, boundless, all-luminous consciousness" is different from the *ātman* of the *Upaniṣads* or Vedānta.

How can a declaration about an Unborn that seems akin to a transcendent God be compatible with Gotama's middle-way approach to teaching the dharma? When asked by Kāccana about the meaning of "complete vision" (*sammā diṭṭhi*), the Buddha replies: "By and large, Kaccāna, this world relies on the duality of 'it is' (*atthī*) and 'it is not' (*natthī*)." He concludes:

> "Everything is (*sabbam-atthī*)," Kaccāna, this is one dead end. "Everything is not (*sabbaṃ natthī*)," this is the other dead end. The Tathāgata reveals the dharma from a middle that avoids both dead ends."[33]

Those who declare that "*there is* an Unborn," and so on, would appear to have fallen prey to the reductive dualism inherent in language, which Gotama warns his followers against. They attribute to the Unborn a reified independent existence as an ultimate truth in sharp contrast to the truths of the changing, suffering world of everyday experience. Such a view would be a clear example of the dead end (*anta*) of eternalism (*sassatavāda*), which the Buddha repeatedly urges his followers to avoid.

(7)

> Monks, there is an unborn, a not-become, a not-made, a not-compounded. Monks, if that unborn, not-become, not-made, not-compounded were not, there would be apparent no escape from this that here is born, become, made, compounded. But since, monks, there is an unborn . . . therefore the escape from this that here is born . . . (and) compounded is apparent.[34]

This is another translation of the same passage, one of the first to appear in English, by F. L. Woodward, the same translator who spotted the incongruity about "noble truth" in *The Four Tasks.* The volume in which it is found includes an introduction by Caroline Rhys Davids, president of the Pali Text Society and doyenne of Pali studies of her day. Yet Rhys Davids has a very different attitude toward this text from Maurice Walshe's. Rather than its presenting "the fundamental basis of all religions worthy of the name," for her the passage promotes a depressingly "monkish" view that "there would be no escape from life, were there not what amounts to no-life." She continues: "I have seen this quoted with approval, yet what poor sort of stuff it is for man's growth and 'uplift'! A very teaching in the Less." She speculates that it might be a "distorted outgrowth" of a verse in the *Upaniṣads,* and cites an example from the *Kaṭha Upaniṣad:*

> When cease the five-sense knowledges,
> together with the mind,
> and intellect (*buddhi*) stirs not—
> that they say is the highest course.

She also notes how this verse mirrors closely the lines from *To Kevaddha* about "all-luminous consciousness."[35]

The English is clumsier in Woodward's translation of 1935, but it does not differ significantly from Walshe's of 1987. Unlike Walshe, Woodward does not capitalize the "Unborn" and the rest. Nor does he italicize the "is" in the line "But since, monks, there is an unborn." And instead of Walshe's: "a deliverance is visible . . . ," he says: "the escape . . . is apparent." Otherwise, the two translators agree on their interpretation of the text.

But why these *four* terms: "unborn, not-become, not-made, not-compounded"? According to the Pali commentary to the passage, the *Udāna-aṭṭhakathā*, they are four different ways of saying the same thing. (It is a common and tiresome feature of Buddhist texts to give long lists of synonyms as qualifications.) They all refer to the "unconditioned" quality of nirvana.

Following John D. Ireland's 1997 rendering of the passage as well as Bhikkhu Bodhi's choice of terminology, I am now going to use "unconditioned" rather than "uncompounded" as a translation of *asaṅkhata. Saṅkhata* (compounded) literally means "made together" or, as we might say idiomatically, "put together." It refers to what has been fabricated, constructed, or put together. And this is what "compounded" means, too: it comes from the Latin *com,* "together," and *ponere,* "to place." While "compounded" works well as a literal translation, it works less well in the context of Buddhist practice. Gotama is looking for a dynamic way of describing how certain conditions give rise to others over time, not a static way of describing how something is compounded at a given moment. A key term in his analysis is *saṅkhāra*—literally, that which "puts together" or "constructs" or "fabricates." Principal among the things that do this "putting together" are desire, hatred, and delusion, along with the words and deeds that they move us to say and do. *Saṅkhāra* are, therefore, the "conditioning factors" that produce the experience of being "conditioned" (*saṅkhata*) by them. The term *saṅkhāra* is notoriously difficult to translate; usually we will find something like "mental formations" (Walshe) or "volitional formations" (Bodhi). My preferred translation, however, is "inclinations."

With this in mind, it is easier to grasp what Gotama means by *asaṅkhata,* "unconditioned." The question that has to be asked is, By what exactly is nirvana *not* conditioned? If you assume the Unconditioned to be another way of talking about the Absolute, it is unlikely that such a question will cross your mind. For absolutes are, by definition, absolute: like God, they neither depend on nor are conditioned by anything else. It would seem obvious that the Unconditioned is simply not conditioned by *anything*—and most certainly not by something within the conditioned world, escape from which, as the text appears to say, is precisely what makes realization of the Unconditioned possible.

Fortunately, Gotama is perfectly clear as to what he means by "unconditioned":

> *Bhikkhus,* I will teach you the unconditioned and the path leading to the unconditioned. Listen to this.
>
> And what, *bhikkhus,* is the unconditioned? An ending of desire, an ending of hatred, an ending of delusion: this is the unconditioned.
>
> And what, *bhikkhus,* is the path leading to the unconditioned? Mindfulness directed to the body: this is called the path leading to the unconditioned.[36]

The unconditioned is an ending of three inclinations (*saṅkhāra*): desire, hatred, and delusion. Note that Gotama does *not* define it as an ending of (or escape from) what is conditioned as such. Instead he points to a possibility that, starting with mindfulness of the body, one can learn to lead one's life *un*-conditioned by desire, hatred, and delusion. In other words, rather than blindly following the inclinations that prompt one to act on one's desires and fears, one trains oneself to dwell in a still and lucid frame of mind that no longer inclines in such ways. In this sense, one might translate *asaṅkhata* as "uninclined" rather than "unconditioned."

Gotama takes a noun, "the unconditioned," and treats it as a verb: "not to be conditioned" by something. He seems acutely aware of the *relational* nature of language. There is no such thing, for example, as freedom per se. There is only freedom *from* constraints, or freedom *to* act in ways that were not possible because of those constraints. Nor is there any awakening per se, but only awakening *from* the "sleep" of delusion, or awakening *to* the presence of others who suffer. And there is no such thing as the unconditioned, only the possibility of not being conditioned *by* something.

Nirvana, therefore, does not refer to the attainment of a transcendent, absolute state apart from the conditions of life but to the possibility of living here and now emancipated from the inclinations of desire, hatred, and delusion. A life *not* conditioned by these instincts and drives would be an enriched one. No longer would one be the victim of paralyzing habits; one would be freed to respond to circumstances in fresh, unimpeded ways.

As we have already seen (in chapter 3), the same Pali phrase *rāgakkhayo dosakkhayo mohakkhayo* (ending of desire, ending of hatred, ending of delusion) that defines the unconditioned (*asaṅkhata*) is also used to define other key terms, including nirvana,[37] the deathless (*amata*),[38] and comprehension (*pariññā*).[39] While it is not surprising to find that "unconditioned" is a synonym for "deathless" and "nirvana," it is less clear how it is synonymous with "comprehension." Here is the text:

> *Bhikkhus,* I will teach you what is to be comprehended and comprehension. Listen to this.
>
> And what is to be comprehended? Form, feeling, perception, inclinations, and consciousness: these are "what are to be comprehended."
>
> And what is comprehension? An ending of desire, an ending of hatred, an ending of delusion: this is "comprehension."[40]

The structure of this passage is identical to the structure of the passage on the unconditioned cited above. If "unconditioned" means not to be conditioned *by* reactivity, then "comprehension" must mean to understand oneself and the world in a way that *is not colored by* reactivity.

"What is to be comprehended" is not the Unconditioned but this conditioned world itself: the immediate experience you are having right now of whatever data are impacting your senses, the feelings evoked by such impact, the perceptual organization of those data, your inclinations to say or do something in response, and your overall consciousness of what is going on. In other words, one seeks to comprehend the five "bundles" that provide the experiential framework for accomplishing the four tasks. But if comprehension (synonymous with the unconditioned) entails a direct insight into the experience of being conditioned, how can it be understood as "deliverance" or "escape" *from* the conditioned?

(8)

> There is, monks, an unborn, not become, not made, uncompounded, and were it not, monks, for this unborn, not become, not made, uncompounded, no escape could be shown here for what is born, has become, is made, is compounded. But because there is, monks, an unborn, not become, not made, uncompounded, therefore an escape can be shown for what is born, has become, is made, is compounded.[41]

Instead of speaking about an escape *from* what is born, become, and conditioned, in this translation published in 1954, the Pali scholar I. B. Horner talks of an escape *for* what is born, has become, and is conditioned. Among all the translators of this passage, she is alone in this. For her the text implies that because there is an unconditioned, this means that an escape or deliverance is possible *for those who are born and conditioned*. By saying "for" instead of "from" she alters the entire meaning of the passage.

By focusing on the term "unconditioned," we have overlooked the term "escape" (Woodward, Horner) or "deliverance" (Walshe). The Pali is *nissaraṇa,* which I will translate as "emancipation." In order to understand how it is being used in the passage, let us recall how it is employed elsewhere in the canon. Once again, here is Gotama's account of the questions that he could no longer ignore and that drove him on his quest:

> While I was still a bodhisatta, it occurred to me: What is the delight of life? What is the tragedy of life? What is the emancipation of life? Then, *bhikkhus,* it occurred to me: The happiness and joy that arise conditioned by life, that is the delight of life; that life is impermanent, difficult, and changing, that is the tragedy of life; the removal and abandonment of grasping for life, that is the emancipation of life.[42]

I am using the word "life"—for which there is no exact Pali equivalent—as shorthand for the six senses and their objects, which Gotama calls "the all." In the text just cited he starts by asking "what is the delight, tragedy, and emancipation of the eye," then repeats the same question and answer for each of the other senses and their objects, ending with *dhamma* (contents of the mind). On each occasion, the words "eye," "ear," "nose," and so forth, are in the genitive case: delight *of* the eye, tragedy *of* the eye, emancipation *of* the eye. It is clear that emancipation (*nissaraṇa*) *of* the eye and the other senses means their emancipation *from* grasping (*chandarāga*)—a term more or less synonymous with "reactivity" (*taṇhā*).

In conclusion Gotama declares: "So long as I did not know the delight, tragedy, and emancipation of life, I did not claim to have found a peerless awakening in this world." Not only does this show that awakening occurs entirely within the context of empirical experience ("the all"), but it shows that awakening consists of a threefold reorientation to experience rather than the attainment of a single privileged insight into an ultimate truth such as the Unconditioned. Moreover, such a reorientation acknowledges that the tragic nature of life does not negate the richness and delight of life. The key to such an awakening lies in emancipating oneself from the pernicious habit of grasping, which turns one's life into a frustrated and pointless struggle to preserve what is delightful while banishing or ignoring what is tragic.

In the Pali of our passage, we find that *saṅkhata* (conditioned) is, just like "eye," "ear," "nose," in the discourse above, also in the genitive case (*saṅkhatassa*). It would therefore seem justified in this instance for I. B. Horner to understand it as "emancipation *of* (i.e., *for*) the conditioned" rather than emancipation *from* the conditioned. So what is it that those who are born and conditioned are emancipated *from*? Given what Gotama understands by "unconditioned," it would seem evident that they are emancipated from reactivity.

Here, then, at last, is my own paraphrased version of the passage:

> It is possible not to be conditioned (by reactivity). Were this not possible, emancipation here for those who are conditioned (by reactivity) would be unintelligible. But since it is possible not to be conditioned (by reactivity), then emancipation of those who are conditioned (by it) is intelligible.

Gotama seems to be saying that the very idea of emancipation here in this world can make sense only if it is possible for people to free themselves from the conditioning power of their desire, hatred, and delusion.

Horner provides an *ethical* rather than a *metaphysical* translation of this passage. She takes it as proposing a radically different way of living in this world, not as offering salvation through gaining access to an unconditioned state beyond this world. Once interpreted ethically, the passage no longer justifies Maurice Walshe's enthusiasm for the eternal or provokes Caroline Rhys Davids's shudder of distaste at its nihilism. Rather, it is a way of affirming that one can live one's life *here* in a way that locates emancipation within the heart of life itself.

This ethical reading shows that there is no need to believe in an absolute state called the "Unconditioned" or the "Unborn." The unconditioned is simply a negation: *not* conditioned. Its place in "the all" is as an object of mind (*dhamma*). It is just an idea—an indispensable one for dharma practice, but an idea nonetheless. It refers to no more than the simple absence—whether momentary or of longer duration—of reactivity in human experience. Such an absence does not reveal some previously concealed Absolute Truth beyond the world. It emancipates one to live in this world unconstrained by such inclinations.

(9)

Rather than insisting on declaring what is true irrespective of any specific context, Gotama is concerned to speak in a way that is true to the needs of the situation at hand. What is remarkable about his style of teaching is that it is more ethical than metaphysical, more pragmatic than dogmatic, more prescriptive than descriptive. These distinctions allow us to make further inferences about how the word "truth"—*sacca*—is employed in the discourses. As already mentioned, apart from its occurrence in the ubiquitous phrase "four noble truths," the predominant use of the term *sacca* is to denote the virtue of being truthful in one's speech. Fleshed out, this use would imply a way of life in which one is true to one's potential, true to one's deepest intuitions, true to one's values, true to one's friends, and—as a Buddhist—true to the rationale (*ṭhāna*) of the dharma. In English, we also find echoes of this usage in expressions such as "twelve men good and true," the classical description of a jury. Being "true" in this sense extends beyond how one expresses oneself in words: it has to do with leading a life of integrity, transparency, and honesty in everything one does, where there is no room for hypocrisy, betrayal, or pretense. And it is such a person who would qualify as a "true friend" (*kalyāṇamitta*): someone who shows by both words and example how to enter the stream of the eightfold path.

In a discourse in the *Aṅguttara Nikāya,* Gotama declares to the *bhikkhus*:

> As the *tathāgata* speaks, so he does; as he does, so he speaks. Since he does as he speaks and speaks as he does, therefore he is called the *tathāgata*.[43]

This passage sheds considerable light on the curious term *tathāgata,* which has long puzzled commentators and translators alike. The term is made up of two parts: *tathā,* which simply means "thus" or "like that" in Pali, and *gata,* which means "gone." Its composition has led to such hyperliteral translations as "one who has gone to suchness." Caroline Rhys Davids interprets it to mean "he who has won through to the truth."[44] In both cases, there is an underlying presumption that the Buddha is to be considered one who has gained privileged access to some higher reality. As Richard Gombrich has pointed out, these readings overdetermine the function of *gata,* "gone," which here simply means "is."[45] *Tathāgata* therefore means "one who is just so." In the light of the passage cited here, this would mean that a *tathāgata* is one who does not dissemble or pretend. The use of the term almost exclusively in reference to the Buddha (or a buddha) implies that not dissembling is one of his defining features. "Since he does as he speaks and speaks as he does," says the text, "*therefore* he is called the *tathāgata.*"

In the *Simile of the Snake,* Gotama uses the term *tathāgata* to refer to any mendicant whose mind is liberated, whose consciousness does not rest on anything: "The *tathāgata,* I say, is untraceable here and now."[46] As we saw in chapter 2, Gotama describes his cousin Mahānāma as a "householder" who "has found fulfillment in the *tathāgata,* has become a seer of the deathless, and goes about having beheld the deathless."[47] In this context, it is questionable that the term *tathāgata* refers to the person Gotama, by having faith in whom Mahānāma had found fulfillment—though one could read the passage that way. It would make more sense here to say that Mahānāma found fulfillment in his own capacity to respond to life from the nirvanic perspective discovered and taught by the Buddha; he thus came to live a life that was true to his deepest values and aspirations.

6

Sunakkhatta: The Traitor

Now on that occasion Sunakkhatta, the Licchavi Son, had recently left the dharma and discipline. He made this statement before the Vesālī assembly:

"The wanderer Gotama does not have any superhuman states, any distinction in knowledge and vision worthy of the noble ones. The wanderer Gotama teaches a dharma hammered out by reasoning, following his own line of enquiry as it occurs to him, and when he teaches the dharma to anyone, it leads when he practises it to the complete end of suffering."

[On hearing of this from Sāriputta, the Buddha replied:]

"Sāriputta, the deluded man Sunakkhatta is angry and his words are spoken out of anger. Thinking to discredit me, he actually praises me; for it is praise of me to say: 'when he teaches the dharma to anyone, it leads when he practises it to the complete end of suffering.'"

—Mahāsīhanāda Sutta

(1)

One of the challenges in recovering a sense of the historical Buddha is to overcome the idealized and archetypal image of Gotama that has been conveyed by Buddhist iconography. According to some of the earliest traditions, he is supposed to have borne thirty-two extraordinary physical marks, including a fleshly protrusion on his head, wheels of a thousand spokes on the soles of his feet, projecting heels, extra-long fingers and toes, and forty even teeth with no spaces between them.[1] Though few today would take this description literally, it continues to haunt the imagination. The canon is ambivalent about his appearance. Sometimes he appears like an ordinary person; on other occasions he is described as a quasi-divine being with barely a trace of humanity. This tension is illustrated in the story of Pukkhusāti.

Pukkhusāti was a nobleman from Taxilā who, on learning of Gotama's teaching, decided to become a follower. He traveled to Rājagaha to meet the famous man. On reaching the Magadhan capital, Pukkhusāti found lodgings in a potter's workshop. Another mendicant arrived and asked Pukkhusāti whether he, too, could stay there. Pukkhusāti welcomed him and invited him to stay. The newcomer prepared a grass mat and spent most of the night seated in meditation.[2]

The next morning the stranger asked Pukkhusāti what dharma he practiced and who had taught him. Pukkhusāti replied that he was a disciple of the wanderer Gotama, whose teachings he followed. On being asked where Gotama lived, Pukkhusāti replied that he lived in the city of Sāvatthi in the north. The stranger then proceeded to deliver a discourse on the elements of existence to Pukkhusāti, at the conclusion of which Pukkhusāti realized that the man must be none other than Gotama himself.[3]

This curious story tells us two things: Gotama looked no different from any other mendicant or wanderer of the day, and he had a sense of humor and enjoyed pulling Pukkhusāti's leg. Yet this humanizing glimpse of Gotama proves to be highly awkward for Buddhist tradition. Presumably to avoid having to suggest that he might have uttered a falsehood in pointlessly asking Pukkhusāti where his teacher lived, the principal commentary on this text (the *Majjhima Nikāya Aṭṭhakathā*) explains that Gotama "saw Pukkhusāti with his clairvoyant knowledge and, recognizing his capacity to attain the paths and fruits, journeyed alone on foot to Rājagaha to meet him."[4] From Sāvatthi to Rājagaha is about two hundred miles.

An even greater problem for the commentator is that Pukkhusāti (and the potter, too) failed to recognize a man who stood out from all others by virtue of his extraordinary thirty-two physical marks. To get round this difficulty, the commentary claims that "by an act of will the Buddha caused his special physical attributes to be concealed, and he appeared just like an ordinary wandering *bhikkhu,*" which, for a contemporary reader, sounds very much like Superman changing back into Clark Kent.[5]

Most Buddhists throughout history have taken for granted that had they seen the Buddha in the flesh, they would have beheld a being endowed with all these marks. By no stretch of the imagination could one consider such a person an ordinary human being. Nor was he exactly a god. At some point, either during or after Gotama's lifetime, the community came to accept a Brahmanic myth—no longer to be found in any extant texts of Hinduism—of a great person who would be recognized by the possession of the specified thirty-two marks. This messianic prophecy foretells of a savior who will appear at a future time to redeem the world through becoming either a mighty "wheel-turning" monarch or a spiritual leader known as a "buddha."

The discourse *To Sela* in the Pali Canon tells how a brahmin called Sela hears of the appearance of such a "great person" and sets out to ascertain whether he possesses the thirty-two marks. On tracking Gotama down, he examines his body but discovers only thirty of the predicted marks. The two that were not visible were his penis enclosed in a sheath and the unusual length of the tongue. So the Buddha "worked a feat of supernatural power that the brahmin Sela saw that the Teacher's penis was enclosed by a sheath." Then Gotama "extruded his tongue, repeatedly touched both ear holes and both nostrils, then covered the whole of his forehead with his tongue."[6]

A modern reader is likely to find this passage either absurd or comical, or both. Yet *To Sela* belongs to the very same body of discourses where we find discussions of lucid ethical guidance, astute psychological insights, and effective contemplative practices that still speak to our condition today. Numerous educated and intelligent readers in the past have regarded this text as just as authoritative as those other discourses we now selectively admire.

That the myth of the great person is a later addition to the canon is implied by the use of the story of Sela to legitimize the position and authority of brahmins. At first sight Gotama seems to emerge triumphant from the encounter. Not only does he demonstrate to Sela that he possesses all the marks, but Sela is so impressed by him that he asks to enter the order as a mendicant, thus renouncing his privileged social status as a brahmin. Not long after, while "dwelling alone, withdrawn, diligent, ardent, and resolute," he becomes an arahant. Implicitly, though, the episode reinforces the authority of Brahmanic beliefs. All of the participants, including Gotama, are shown to accept without question the Brahmanic myth of the great person. Gotama may win this particular battle in the struggle for supremacy between Buddhists and brahmins in India, but in the long run, his community was fatally weakened by its gradual, tacit assent to the norms and values of Brahmanic culture.

Another way to consider this material is to recognize that during the evolution of the canon there would have been at least some who experienced no cognitive or moral dissonance on hearing a particular text. Just as certain people would have had no difficulty in accepting the story of Sela examining Gotama's body for magical marks, others would have had no problem with Gotama appearing as an entirely unremarkable person to Pukkhusāti. The canon is a vast collage of conflicting texts, which, singly or in clusters, were cherished in the memories of different groups of followers. These groups may have lived at different periods of history and in different parts of the Indian subcontinent without knowing anything of one another. At some point, these diverse texts were collated and accepted as canonical. From then on, the reciters (*bhāṇaka*) of the canon would have committed themselves simply to remembering whatever texts they were entrusted with. It would no longer have mattered whether they experienced any cognitive or moral dissonance with particular passages. Their job was to preserve what was handed down; it fell to the commentators to resolve the internal conflicts and contradictions.

(2)

Sunakkhatta, whose life will be told in this chapter, was an idealist who yearned for mystical experiences and metaphysical certainties. Despite his proximity to the Buddha over many years, he failed to grasp what was distinctive and liberating about the dharma.The flesh-and-blood Gotama constantly undermined his unrealistic projections.

Sunakkhatta appears only four times in the discourses of the Pali Canon. On each occasion he is introduced as a "Licchavi son" (*licchaviputta*).[7] If we take "son" in the sense of not only being the progeny of a certain people but embodying their traits and values, then Sunakkhatta may have shared some of the described characteristics of Licchavi youths: "quick-tempered, rough, and greedy fellows; such presents as are sent by the members of their tribe—sugar cane, jujubes, sweet cakes, sweetmeats, etc.—they loot and eat; they slap the women and girls of their tribe on the back."[8] The Licchavis are also portrayed as martial, keen on hunting with bows and arrows, surrounded by yelping hounds. And they had severe moral standards: the assembly is recorded as permitting a husband to kill his wife who had been unfaithful to him.[9]

In other depictions the Licchavis are deeply loyal to one another; they gather in each other's houses to perform ceremonies; they are courteous and generous hosts; they are handsome and colorfully dressed; they are prosperous but live simply, "using blocks of wood as pillows," and are "diligent and ardent in exercise." Yet Gotama warns that they are in danger of succumbing to luxury and becoming dissolute and lazy, which will render them vulnerable to their enemy King Ajātasattu of Magadha.[10] The Licchavis, then, were a proud, independent, and ancient tribe who were showing signs of corruption and degeneration, which perhaps spelled their downfall.

The Licchavis were the dominant clan within the Vajjian Confederacy, which, together with Mallā, was one of the last independent republics of northern India in the fifth century BCE. Rather than a supreme monarch (*mahārājā*), a large assembly of chiefs (*rājās*) governed the confederacy from the city of Vesālī. Throughout Gotama's lifetime the citizens managed to preserve this old form of representative government in spite of being squeezed between the two most powerful kingdoms of the day: Kosala to the north, ruled by Pasenadi, and Magadha, across the Ganges to the south, ruled by Bimbisāra and later by his son, Ajātasattu. The Licchavis' republican form of governance was also the model on which the Buddha established his own community, which he conceived of as being ruled by an impersonal law (the dharma) rather than an elder.

In hindsight, the Licchavis were on the verge of becoming like the Tibetans today: a stateless people with a fierce sense of their own history as an independent nation. At the time, they were eager to avoid the fate already suffered by the Sakiyans, who had also once been an independent republic but were now vassals of the king of Kosala. The might of Magadha was manifest in the fortified city of Pāṭaliputta, visible to the Licchavis across the Ganges. Indeed, the city became the first capital of a unified India less than a century after Gotama's death. But if Magadha was to achieve its imperial ambitions by extending its borders north into the territories of the rival kingdom of Kosala, it would first have to subdue the Licchavi armies that stood in its way. As well as being "deluded," Sunakkhatta could have been desperate and scared when he denounced the wanderer Gotama to the Vesālī assembly.

Although the Buddha counted many prominent Licchavis among his followers, including the chief Mahāli, the general Sīha, and the courtesan Ambapālī, he was not universally respected. His principal rival, the Nigaṇṭha Nātaputta—known today as Mahāvīra, the founder of Jainism—was a native of Vesālī, having been born in the nearby village of Kundala. Though not a Licchavi himself, Nātaputta—the "Nāta son"—belonged to the Nāta tribe within the confederacy. Nigaṇṭha is an epithet meaning "Unbound," used to denote those who followed the teachings and example of the Tirthaṇtaka Pārśva, who had lived around two hundred and fifty years earlier. Nātaputta was revered in Vesālī not only as a son of its soil but also as a formidable ascetic who made a display of not harming even a gnat, a saint who was said to be omniscient, and a teacher who claimed that his lineage went back twenty-two previous Tirthaṇtakas before Pārśva.

The Nigaṇṭhas dismissed Gotama as being "addicted to luxury" and "abiding in delusion"; the Buddha described Nātaputta's doctrines as "ill-proclaimed, unedifyingly displayed, and ineffectual in calming the mind because its proclaimer was not fully awake."[11] Such strong language suggests an intense rivalry between the two men and their followers. The Buddhists accused the Jains of going too far in their practices of self-mortification; the Jains dismissed the Buddhists as being uncommitted to the strenuous task of gaining permanent freedom from the burden of karma that keeps the soul (*jīva*) tied to the round of rebirths (*saṃsāra*). Yet both groups competed for the support of the same body of potential donors and employed similar terminology to persuade people of the validity of their respective doctrines. Both use the terms *buddha, arahant,* and *tathāgata* to refer to the figure of an enlightened person and the terms *nirvāṇa* and *mokṣa* to refer to the goal of the practice. Māra—the "demonic"—is regarded by both as a personification of what is to be overcome on the path to awakening. Although the details differ, both advocate taking "five precepts" and making a commitment to "three jewels." Likewise, both traditions established a "fourfold community" consisting of male and female mendicants and male and female adherents.[12]

The *Shorter Discourse to Saccaka* provides a glimpse of how the rivalry between the two teachers divided the Licchavis. Since Ajātasattu is spoken of as the king of Magadha in this text, the episode recounted must have occurred in the last eight years of Gotama's life. Saccaka, the "Nigaṇṭhas' son," is described as "a debater and a clever speaker regarded by many as a saint," who invites a gathering of Licchavis in the assembly hall to come and witness a debate between him and the wanderer Gotama.[13] The invitation immediately provokes a discussion among those assembled, with some insisting that Saccaka's arguments will prevail, others that the wanderer Gotama will be the victor. When they approach the Buddha seated beneath a tree in the nearby forest, only "some" of the Licchavis pay respect to him before taking their seats.

In a Buddhist text, it is hardly surprising that Gotama then runs circles around Saccaka, but it is striking that at the conclusion of both this and a longer conversation Saccaka does not admit defeat and declare himself a follower of the Buddha, which is a standard outcome of such exchanges.[14] This is in contrast to the outcome with General Sīha, previously a prominent supporter of the Nigaṇṭhas, who converted to the dharma on hearing the Buddha. Presumably to prevent any sectarian resentment over the loss of such a generous benefactor, Gotama only accepts the general as an adherent provided that he continues to provide alms to the Nigaṇṭhas, a condition that further raises him in Sīha's estimation.[15] These episodes suggest that the wanderer Gotama was a divisive figure among the Licchavis of Vesālī even before Sunakkhatta's denunciation, someone who had to tread carefully in order not to offend those who opposed him.

(3)

The passages where Sunakkhatta appears in the canon provide us with just enough information to construct a chronology of his relationship with the Buddha. These episodes offer a consistent portrait of Sunakkhatta as a vacillator and an idealist, someone who, despite his proximity to Gotama, repeatedly fails to understand what is distinctive about what Gotama says.

The discourse *To Sunakkhatta* recounts how the two men meet in Vesālī after Sunakkhatta hears it reported that some of Gotama's mendicants claimed to have attained "final knowledge in the presence of the Teacher." Skeptical of these claims, he goes to Gotama to ask whether this is true or whether those mendicants overestimated themselves. Gotama acknowledges that these mendicants did indeed overestimate themselves and comments that at such times he has to teach the dharma in order to correct them.[16]

The Buddha explains to Sunakkhatta that a person's view of himself is determined by that to which he is dedicated (*ādhimutti*). "If a person is dedicated to worldly things, only talk of that interests him, it is all he thinks and ponders about, and he associates with similar people."[17] As long as a person is "fettered" by his dedication to such things, he will be incapable of taking an interest in anything else and will remain stuck in that frame of mind and that company. Once he becomes disillusioned with mundane affairs, however, the person might dedicate himself to realizing inner states of imperturbability (*āneñja/āṇañja*), in which case he will lose interest in worldly concerns.[18] The process is entirely natural: when one's interests move on from worldly to spiritual matters, one's former concerns, says Gotama, drop away like "yellowing autumn leaves." But simply to shift one's attention from the pleasures of the world to those of meditative absorption is still to be trapped. Even if the person enters such subtle, immaterial states as the "base of nothingness" or the "base of neither perception nor non-perception," he remains fettered by them, which prevents him from dedicating himself to what truly matters for the Buddha: the experience of nirvana.

Neither here nor in other discourses does Gotama explain what he means by "imperturbability." The Pali *āneñja* or *āṇañja* that he employs is rarely used in the canon. In this context, it appears to be a general term for the inner stillness sought by those who seek spiritual well-being as opposed to the turbulent stimulation craved by those in thrall to sensual pleasure. But since Buddhism generally considers inner stillness to be a quality in urgent need of cultivation—complete concentration (*sammā samādhi*) being the final step on the eightfold path—what can he mean here? Without providing any canonical justification, the commentaries explain that "imperturbability" refers to the fourth, fifth, and sixth absorptions (*jhāna*).[19] We have seen in the *Shorter Discourse on Emptiness* that the immaterial absorptions are considered at best a diversion, while in *The Noble Quest* Gotama firmly rejects the last two of them (the base of nothingness and neither-perception-nor-non-perception) for "not leading to peace, awakening, or nirvana."[20] In the discourse *On Fear and Dread*, however, attainment of the fourth absorption is presented as a necessary step on the path to awakening, since it enables the bodhisatta to acquire the supernormal power (*iddhi*) to remember all his past lives.[21]

The presence of such conflicting voices in the canon on the role of the *jhāna*s suggests that the early community was not of one mind on this topic. Given the many passages where the practice of all eight *jhāna*s is considered praiseworthy, it is surprising that here Gotama describes some of them as "fetters," a term usually reserved for vanity, doubt, attachment, pride, and other negative emotions.[22] One way to resolve this conflict is to acknowledge that although the *jhāna*s do not lead to awakening or insight in and of themselves, for those practitioners temperamentally predisposed to concentration they can serve as an effective means of stilling and focusing the mind to enhance their practice of the fourfold task. For others, though, the *jhāna*s are to be avoided if they are likely to foster attachment to and dependence on the ecstatic but disassociated experiences they engender.

In the course of educating Sunakkhatta, Gotama appears to be outlining a path that steers clear of *both* a dedication to sensual indulgence *and* a dedication to *jhāna*s that lead to non-ordinary states of mind. His concern is to focus Sunakkhatta's attention on the ceasing of reactivity, which is nirvana. For in "beholding the deathless" he will be able to enter the stream of the path and thereby flourish as a "healthy" person. Once Sunakkhatta is dedicated to nirvana, he will be interested in that and that alone, and the fetter of the higher *jhānas* will be completely severed.[23]

It is entirely possible that people can deceive themselves about their dedication to nirvana. Gotama recognizes that there may be mendicants who think this way: "Reactivity (*taṇhā*) has been called an arrow by the Wanderer. The poisonous humor of ignorance is spread by desire, greed, and ill-will. That arrow of reactivity has been removed from me, the poison of ignorance expelled. I am one who is completely dedicated to nirvana."[24] Yet such a person may be a fantasist, believing himself to be "enlightened" while continuing to pursue with alacrity his dedication to sensual and mental pleasures, which only feed the desire, greed, and ill-will he believes he has overcome. It would appear (the text does not state this explicitly) that it is such people Gotama had in mind when he spoke of mendicants who "overestimated themselves."

To realize the "freedom from reactivity" that is nirvana is a matter that requires considerable care and attention. The Buddha explains to Sunakkhatta that the practitioner of the dharma is like a man who has been "wounded by a poisoned arrow, and his friends and relatives brought a surgeon, who would cut around the wound with a knife, probe for the arrowhead with a probe, then pull out the arrow and expel the poison."[25] One attains nirvana by removing the arrow of reactivity so that no trace of the poison of ignorance remains in the body. This operation is achieved by applying the "probe" of mindfulness (*sati*) and the "knife" of understanding (*paññā*) as taught by the "surgeon" (the Buddha). No mention is made here of the need to attain imperturbability or practice the immaterial *jhānas* to accomplish this task, but clearly a steady and focused mind will be indispensable in using such surgical instruments effectively.

If the operation fails to remove every last trace of the poison, the doctor has to instruct the patient to take great care in diet and hygiene so that the wound heals and does not get infected. But if the patient ignores these instructions, "the wound would swell, and with its swelling he would incur death or deadly suffering."[26] One may succeed in extracting the arrow of reactivity with mindfulness and understanding and thus momentarily experience nirvana. But without being completely dedicated to nirvana a person may become complacent and careless, which leads once more to indulgence in those habits of mind that lead to an inner "death" and despair. Thus those who have had a taste of nirvana can still be deluding themselves about the nature of their attainment and "overestimate" themselves.

The Buddha goes one step further. Even when the surgeon succeeds in removing every last trace of poison from the wound, the patient is still instructed to "eat only suitable food; do not eat unsuitable food or else the wound may suppurate. From time to time wash the wound and anoint its opening so that pus and blood do not cover it. Do not walk in the wind or sun or dirt may infect the wound."[27] For if the patient fails to take proper care of the wound, it could still get infected and lead to suffering and death. There can be no room for complacency. One's dedication to nirvana needs to be maintained even when reactivity and ignorance have been removed. This implies that even when the arrow and poison are successfully extracted, the patient can nonetheless be left traumatized by the operation. As long as one is still coming to terms with the new perspective on living, one needs to be mindful and attentive and not adopt the consoling idea that being "enlightened" means that no harm can befall one.

At the conclusion of the discourse, we learn that Sunakkhatta was happy with the Buddha's explanation.[28] This may be just a conventional formula, but it nonetheless suggests that unlike Saccaka, Sunakkhatta understood and accepted Gotama's answer to his question. It may well have been a crucial factor in his decision to join the order of mendicants; he may have committed himself with the warning ringing in his ears of the need to be on constant guard against fascination with special states of meditation, spiritual ambition and its attendant inflation, carelessness and complacency, and the ever-present danger of self-deception.

(4)

The next time we hear of Sunakkhatta is from the lips of the Licchavi chief Mahāli. Gotama is again staying in Vesālī, in a solitary meditation retreat, and his attendant is doing his best to prevent visitors from bothering him. Mahāli, together with a large contingent of curious brahmins, finally succeeds in getting an audience by badgering one of the novices. Mahāli explains that he has come to speak to him on behalf of Sunakkhatta, who, a few days before, had told him that although he had trained under the Buddha for three years, he had managed to experience divine visions in his meditation but had yet to hear any divine sounds. "Sir," he asks, "are there any such sounds, which Sunakkhatta cannot hear, or are there not?" Gotama replies (wearily but politely, I imagine) that although there are such sounds that can be heard in meditation, "there are other things, higher and more perfect than these, for the sake of which mendicants lead the spiritual life under me."[29]

Despite everything Gotama told him earlier, Sunakkhatta appears to be obsessed with hearing divine sounds in meditation and frustrated that after three years of practice he has managed only to behold divine visions. Mahāli—and presumably the brahmins with him—likewise seem to believe that the aim of meditation is to experience such non-ordinary states of minds, which, as far as we know, might be nothing more than visual and auditory hallucinations. It is ironic that the Buddha is obliged to leave his meditation retreat to answer their inquiries, but sobering to realize that then, as today, people are irresistibly fascinated with such exotic things.

Sunakkhatta is portrayed as a person who is fixed in his views and stubbornly refuses to change his mind no matter what Gotama says to him. Even while he is serving as the Buddha's attendant—again we do not know for how long or at what age—he is shown to be starry-eyed and susceptible to the appeal of feats of extreme self-punishment—like those of Korakkhattiya, the "dog man," who went around "on all fours, sprawling on the ground, and chewing and eating his food with his mouth alone," and the ascetic Kaḷāramuṭṭhaka, who had made a lifelong vow to "never wear clothes, to remain celibate, to subsist only on alcohol and meat, not touching rice and sour milk, and not to wander beyond the four principal shrines of Vesālī." As soon as Sunakkhatta sees these men, he thinks, "Now that is a real arahant," which leads Gotama to wonder out loud whether his attendant is still a follower of his. Shocked, Sunakkhatta retorts that the Buddha "begrudges others their arahantship."[30]

We do not know how many years Sunakkhatta remained a mendicant. In the end, when he comes to inform Gotama that he has decided to leave the order, the Buddha asks him a series of questions:

> "Did I ever say to you: 'Come, Sunakkhatta, be under my rule?'"
>
> "No, sir."
>
> "Or did you ever say: 'Sir, I will be under your rule?'"
>
> "No, sir."
>
> "So, deluded man, who are you and what are you giving up? Consider how far the fault is yours."
>
> "Well, sir, you have not performed any miracles."
>
> "And did I ever say to you: 'Come under my rule and I will perform miracles for you?'"
>
> "No, sir."
>
> "And did you ever say: 'Sir, I will be under your rule if you will perform miracles for me?'"
>
> "No, sir."
>
> "Then it appears that I made no such promises and you made no such conditions. What do you think? Whether miracles are performed or not, the aim of my teaching the dharma is to lead whoever practices it to the complete end of suffering. So what purpose would the performing of miracles serve?"
>
> "But, sir, you did not make a first beginning known to me."

"And did I ever say: 'Come under my rule and I will make known to you a first beginning?'"

"No, sir."

"So, deluded man, who are you and what are you giving up?"[31]

By providing us with a case study of a person who is drawn to the dharma for all the wrong reasons, Sunakkhatta serves as a rhetorical foil that allows Gotama to state point by point what he is *not* teaching. The Licchavi son is obliged to acknowledge that the reasons he gives for leaving the order have no bearing whatever on why he agreed to join, a step he took entirely of his own volition with all the caveats given to him in the eponymous *To Sunakkhatta*. We are shown a man who, despite his acceptance of the logic of what the Buddha tells him, continues to harbor longings for divine sounds, miracles, and metaphysical pronouncements about the origins of the world.

Sunakkhatta may cut a slightly ridiculous figure, but he embodies proclivities that many of us might share. Indeed, the various forms of Buddhism that we know today have all come to pander to such yearnings in one way or another. Even the discourse cited above which contains the frank and blunt dialogue between Gotama and Sunakkhatta is acutely ambivalent on these issues. Having just dismissed the importance of supernormal powers, the text presents Gotama as one who can predict the future, perform miracles, and explain the first beginning of things. Yet what distinguishes Gotama's teaching so radically from that of his peers is that it is rational, founded on a close observation of human experience, and unsentimental. There is no room for special effects.

Elsewhere, rather than rejecting miracles (*pāṭihāriya*) outright, Gotama appropriates the term for his own ends. He enumerates three kinds of miracle: those of supernormal power (*iddhi*), such as flying, multiplying one's body, walking on water; telepathy (*ādesanā*); and instruction (*anusāsani*). Although he accepts that supernormal powers and telepathy are possible, he concludes: "Seeing the danger of such miracles, I dislike, reject, and despise them."[32] The only "miracle" of which he approves is that of instruction, which simply consists in saying: "Consider it in this way, don't consider it that way, direct your mind this way, not that way, give up this, gain this, and persevere in it."[33] What is truly miraculous is that human beings can learn to think and act differently and thereby transform themselves.

On another occasion Gotama asks a brahmin which of these three miracles is "most excellent and sublime." The brahmin replies:

> As to the miracles of supernormal power and telepathy, only one who performs them will experience their effects; they belong to him alone. These two miracles, Mr. Gotama, appear to me as a conjuror's trick. But as to the miracle of instruction—this, Mr. Gotama, appears to me as the most excellent and sublime among them.

The Buddha praises these "strikingly beneficial words."[34] The true miracle is that instructions have been given that will lead whoever practices them to the experience of nirvana. The rest is just magic.

When Sunakkhatta complains that while he was a mendicant he was not taught a first beginning of the world, he is criticizing the Buddha for not addressing the great metaphysical questions that so often preoccupy those concerned with gaining religious or philosophical certainty. Gotama remains silent on these questions because to comment on them would have no practical relevance to the cultivation of the path he teaches. As we saw in chapter 1, a person who refuses to practice the dharma until he has been given satisfactory answers to such questions is compared to a man wounded by a poisoned arrow who refuses to have it removed until he knows everything about the archer, the bow, the bowstring, and the arrow.[35] The aim of the dharma, as he explained to Sunakkhatta, is to remove the arrow of reactivity with surgical precision in order that one can regain health and lead a full and flourishing life.

In what sounds like a last-ditch attempt to get Sunakkhatta to change his mind, Gotama reminds him that in the past he had spoken highly to the Vajjians of the Buddha, his teaching, and his community. If you leave, he warns, "there will be those who will say: 'Sunakkhatta the Licchavi was unable to lead the spiritual life under the wanderer Gotama, and being thus unable he abandoned the training.'" But Sunakkhatta was unmoved, so he "left this dharma and discipline like one condemned to hell."[36]

(5)

Much of what I have said so far about Mahānāma, Pasenadi, and Sunakkhatta would have been a far more arduous undertaking had it not been for the pioneering work of the Sri Lankan scholar and diplomat G. P. Malalasekera (1899–1973). In particular, his three-volume *Dictionary of Pāli Proper Names,* published in 1938, has been an invaluable resource. This dictionary—today it would be called an encyclopedia—provides an entry for every person, place, and text mentioned in classical Pali literature. In the case of a person, Malalasekera offers an annotated biographical sketch, which enables researchers to locate each canonical passage where he or she appears. This is how he introduces Sunakkhatta:

> A Licchavi prince of Vesālī. He was, at one time, a member of the Order and the personal attendant of the Buddha (*anibaddhaupatthāka*), but later . . . went about defaming the Buddha, saying that he had nothing superhuman and was not distinguished from other men by preaching a saving faith: that the doctrine preached by him did not lead to the destruction of sorrow, etc. Sāriputta, on his alms rounds in Vesālī, heard all this and reported it to the Buddha, who thereupon preached the *Mahāsīhanāda Sutta*.[37]

Despite Malalasekera's erudition, this entry contains a glaring error. For Sunakkhatta did *not* complain that Gotama's teaching fails to "lead to the destruction of sorrow." On the contrary, according to the discourse, Sunakkhatta tells the assembly at Vesālī that the dharma *does* lead to the destruction of sorrow. Had he not said this, the Buddha's reply to Sāriputta—"Thinking to discredit me, [Sunakkhatta] actually praises me; for it is praise of me to say: 'when he teaches the dharma to anyone, it leads when he practises it to the complete end of suffering"—would make no sense.

How could this eminent Pali scholar misread such a straightforward sentence in a language in which he was a renowned authority? The error is unlikely to have been just an oversight or slip of the pen, since he repeats the same mistake in his entry on the *Lomahamsa Jātaka,* a fable in which a character is identified as a former incarnation of Sunakkhatta.

I suspect that Malalasekera was induced to err by common sense. His intuitions as a Buddhist may likewise have led him astray. He could not believe his eyes. To denounce the wanderer Gotama because his dharma when practiced leads to the complete end of suffering would be like vilifying a Christian preacher because his doctrine when practiced leads to the Kingdom of Heaven, or refuting a Marxist because his theory when put into practice leads to a communist utopia. It is hard to imagine anyone, whether in fifth century BCE India or today, who would reject a teaching because it leads to the end of suffering. Such a complaint is absurd. It seems, therefore, that the text of the discourse that has come down to us is corrupt.

To speculate about what the original text might have said cannot, in the absence of any such document, be more than conjecture. But we can be confident that instead of referring to "the complete end of suffering," the discourse must have referred to a goal that Sunakkhatta and his audience would have regarded as unworthy or inadequate and Gotama would have regarded as eminently admirable. What might this reasonably have been?

Given what we have learned about Sunakkhatta, one obvious candidate for such a goal would be the complete end of reactivity (*taṇhā*). After all, this was the main point of *To Sunakkhatta,* where he outlined to the young Licchavi a path that avoided both material indulgence and meditative absorption while leading to the experience of nirvana as the removal of the poisoned arrow of reactivity. Yet despite this explicit injunction to overcome reactivity, Sunakkhatta was unable to relinquish his fascination with divine sounds, miracles, and metaphysics. To reject the Buddha's dharma would have entailed for him the rejection of the end of reactivity as a worthy or adequate goal for human life. Sunakkhatta seems to have aspired for something far more than "just" bringing to an end a certain kind of craving.

This hypothesis finds further support in the definition of "the ceasing of suffering" found in *The Four Tasks,* where we read:

> This is the ceasing of suffering: the traceless fading away and ceasing of that reactivity (*taṇhā*), the letting go and abandoning of it, freedom and independence from it.[38]

We considered the incongruity of this passage in the previous chapter: since suffering is defined in the same discourse as "birth, sickness, aging, and death," then, logically, its cessation should be the ceasing of birth, sickness, aging, and death. But this cannot be so. For whoever "extracts the arrow of reactivity" experiences nirvana itself, which is said to be "immediate, clearly visible, inviting, uplifting, sensed by the wise." Anyone who experiences something that "is immediate and clearly visible" must be alive in a human body and as subject to sickness, aging, and death as everybody else. Thus what is called here "ceasing of suffering" is *not* actually the ceasing of suffering, but the ceasing of *reactivity.*

The Buddha's dictum "I teach suffering and the end of suffering" could thus be rephrased as "I teach suffering and the end of reactivity." Likewise, Sunakkhatta's denunciation would make more sense if it said:

> The wanderer Gotama teaches a dharma hammered out by reasoning, following his own line of enquiry as it occurs to him, and when he teaches the dharma to anyone, it leads when he practises it to the complete end of reactivity.

The phrase "hammered out by reasoning, following his own line of enquiry as it occurs to him" appears in two other discourses, in each case as a pejorative description of a rationalist (*takkī*) or a speculative thinker (*vīmaṃsī*), of whose statements it was said: "Some are well reasoned, and some wrongly reasoned, some are true and some not."[39] Gotama could well have appeared to be a rationalist or speculative thinker to those who judged a teacher in terms of that person's ability to perform miracles and make stirring declarations about the origins of the world. In the end, Sunakkhatta concluded that the Buddha was just a fallible intellectual, still trying to figure things out, who could imagine nothing more exalted or transcendent to aspire for than the ending of reactivity.

(6)

The *Great Discourse on the Lion's Roar,* which opens with Sunakkhatta's denunciation to the Vesālī assembly, concludes with Gotama's lengthy rebuttal of the accusations against him. He starts his defense by addressing Sāriputta. "That deluded man will never infer of me according to the dharma," he says.

> The Teacher enjoys the various kinds of supernormal power: having been one, he becomes many; having been many, he becomes one; he appears and vanishes; he goes unhindered through a wall or mountain as though it were space; he dives in and out of the earth as though it were water; he walks on water without sinking as though it were the earth; seated cross-legged, he travels in space like a bird; with his hand he touches and strokes the sun and the moon.

He then declares that "with the divine ear element the Teacher hears both divine and human sounds," and he "encompasses with his own mind the minds of other beings."[40]

What are we to make of this? The miracles of supernormal power and telepathy, which Gotama elsewhere compared to mere "conjuror's tricks" that he "disliked, rejected, and despised," are now being treated as the necessary accomplishments of a buddha. Likewise, the ability to hear divine sounds, about which he had told Mahāli, "There are other things, higher and more perfect than these, for the sake of which mendicants lead the spiritual life under me," is now presented as a sure sign of his own perfect enlightenment. Which of these two accounts are we to take seriously?

These passages again reveal the presence of conflicting voices in the Pali Canon, each clamoring to be heard. At this distance in time, it may be impossible to know whether they represent contrasting views among the original protagonists or the sectarian opinions of scholar-monks who edited the discourses in the decades following Gotama's death.

Whatever the case, the *Great Discourse on the Lion's Roar* appears to be a clumsy exercise in damage control. That Sunakkhatta's denunciation is remembered at all and retained as the pretext for a defensive, self-justifying discourse in the *Majjhima Nikāya* suggests that it may have come as a serious blow and betrayal to the Buddhist community. For the Licchavis of the assembly to take Sunakkhatta at his word would also imply that he was a person of some standing among them—which would be underscored by the Licchavi chief Mahāli's pestering the Buddha on his behalf. Moreover, for his accusations to be perceived as especially threatening would reinforce the claim that he had been close to the Buddha as his attendant and had gained his trust. Rather than being the "deluded man" who is presented as an object of ridicule, Sunakkhatta seems to have been a mendicant of long standing who had achieved a degree of authority and prestige within the order. Since no other prominent Licchavis are known to have been mendicants, Sunakkhatta might well have been the leading member of his clan to have joined the order and thus served as a crucial link to the network of supporters in Vesālī.

The only hint we have that Sunakkhatta might have at one time been part of the Buddha's inner circle of followers comes from the

Bhūridatta Jātaka (No. 543), a fable about one of the Buddha's previous lives. This long-winded story tells of a lord called Samuddajā who had four sons: Datta, Sudassana, Subhaga, and Arittha. When the *Jātaka* reveals the identity of these four, they turn out to be the Buddha (Datta), his two principal followers, Sāriputta (Sudassana) and Moggallāna (Subhaga), and Sunakkhatta (Arittha). True to form, Arittha (Sunakkhatta) is criticized by his brother Datta (the Buddha) for praising the virtues of the brahmins and emphasizing the importance of performing sacrifices and learning the Vedas.

(7)

One telling detail, which I might have overlooked had G. P. Malalasekera not pointed it out, is that toward the end of the *Great Discourse on the Lion's Roar* the Buddha says: "I am now old, aged, and come to the last stage: my years have turned eighty."[41] This reference to age enables us to locate Sunakkhatta's defection to the final year of Gotama's life. Sunakkhatta would have been denouncing not only a teacher to whom he had been loyal for many years but a frail and elderly man whose world was falling apart.

The five discourses that allow us to reconstruct the chronology of events during this last year reveal that Sunakkhatta's rejection of his teacher was but one element within a far greater tragedy that was threatening to engulf the entire region in war.[42] We have already seen that King Pasenadi of Kosala, after his final meeting with Gotama, realizes that he has been betrayed. The commander of his army has departed with the royal insignia in order to install Prince Viḍūḍabha on the Kosalan throne. Pasenadi flees south into exile, and Viḍūḍabha prepares to attack Sakiya. After failing to dissuade the new king from invading, Gotama, too, is forced to leave Sakiya for the south. Rather than heading for Rājagaha like Pasenadi, Gotama goes to the Vajjian capital of Vesālī, Sunakkhatta's hometown.

Since the Buddha is described as being eighty years old both when he meets Pasenadi for the final time in Sakiya and when Sunakhatta denounces him in Vesālī, these two events must have occurred within a few months of each other. By walking about ten miles a day, it would have taken the old man and his entourage close to a month to cover the two hundred miles that separated Sakiya from Vesālī. The canon does not explain why Gotama headed for the Vajjian Confederacy, but it was probably the first safe haven beyond the borders of Kosala and Mallā.

In all likelihood, Gotama followed the North Road, the main arterial route that connected the two kingdoms of Kosala and Magadha. The first town he would have entered after leaving Sakiya would have been Anupiya, in the republic of Mallā. It was to Anupiya that he first went as a young man of twenty-nine after leaving Sakiya; it was there where he shaved off his hair and beard, took the yellow robe, and embraced the life of a wanderer. Now, fifty-one years later, it is in Anupiya that a renunciant called Bhaggavagotta informs him that "a few days ago Sunakkhatta the Licchavi came to me and said: 'Bhaggava, I have left the Teacher. I am no longer under his rule.'"[43] Since we know that Sunakkhatta had only "recently left the dharma and discipline" when he denounced the wanderer Gotama in Vesālī, it would appear that he, too, was traveling south from Sakiya, ahead of Gotama, when he passed through Anupiya.[44] This sequence is corroborated by the Buddha's telling Bhaggavagotta that Sunakkhatta had also informed him of his decision to leave just "a few days ago."[45]

Such an unusual concentration of coherent factual details points to Sunakkhatta's having been one of the mendicants who was with Gotama in Sakiya before Gotama left. If so, it was in Sakiya where he would have told his teacher that he was leaving him. Why did he make his decision then? Whether Sunakkhatta was actually present at the Sakiyan border when the Buddha tried but failed to dissuade Viḍūḍabha from launching an invasion, he would have followed the events closely as they occurred. The fate of the entire Sakiyan community was at stake. Yet, as we have seen, Gotama failed to perform the miracle that would have turned back the massed soldiers and saved his people from their assault.

While speculative, this scenario explains a great deal. Sunakkhatta left the order in disgust because the Buddha failed to defuse the crisis with Kosala and was forced into a humiliating retreat. Why, Sunakkhatta may have wondered, did he not multiply his bodies in a display of supernormal power before the awestruck troops? Why did he not dive into the earth or fly through space to demonstrate his prowess in miracle making? His failure to resolve the dispute either by diplomacy or by magic revealed him as a thoroughly ordinary and fallible man. So the disappointed Sunakkhatta headed back home to Vesālī, stopping on the way to tell Bhaggavagotta of his decision to leave the order. On reaching his homeland, he spreads the news of the Buddha's defeat and denounces him to the assembly: "The wanderer Gotama doesn't have any superhuman states, any special knowledge or vision worthy of the noble ones. What he teaches is just hammered out by reasoning, following his own line of inquiry as it occurs to him. And all it leads to is the end of reactivity!"

(8)

Instead of finding a safe haven in Vesālī, Gotama arrives in a city where the population is already turning against him. Given the defection of Sunakkhatta, he may well have foreseen that this would happen. We do not know exactly how much time he spends there, but it cannot have been long.

After being denounced at the Vajjian assembly, Gotama continues his journey south, crosses the Ganges, and heads for Rājagaha, the capital city of Magadha. Again, we are not told why. The *Great Discourse on the Passing* opens abruptly with these words: "Once the Teacher was staying at Rājagaha on Vulture's Peak. Now just then King Ajātasattu of Magadha wanted to attack the Vajjians. He said: 'I will strike the Vajjians who are so powerful and strong, I will cut them off and destroy them, I will bring them to ruin and destruction!'"[46] Gotama had left one zone of conflict only to find himself, after a long and arduous journey by foot, in another.

Nor does King Ajātasattu bother to visit the Buddha to explain his plans in person. Instead he sends his chief minister, Brahmin Vassakāra, who climbs up Vulture's Peak to inform Gotama of the king's intentions. In reply, the Buddha turns to his attendant Ānanda, who is fanning him in the pre-monsoon heat, and praises the Vajjians for possessing seven virtues:

They hold regular and frequent meetings as an assembly
They carry out their business together in harmony
They uphold their ancient traditions
They respect, salute, and revere their elders
They do not abduct and rape the women of others
They honour and revere their shrines
They make proper provision for saints (*arahant*s)

But he concludes on a cautionary note. Only as long as they maintain these customs, he explains, "may they be expected to prosper and not decline." The chief minister listens attentively, then concludes that as long as the Vajjians adhere to such principles, they "will never be conquered by force of arms but only by means of propaganda and setting them against each other."[47]

Gotama realizes that he is not particularly welcome in Rājagaha either. The last time he was in the city, King Ajātasattu came in person to Jīvaka's mango grove, where Gotama was staying, to make a tearful confession of his sins.[48] Now, instead of being sought out for consoling or edifying advice, he is being used to gather information for a military campaign against a people who have just turned against him. The king cynically instructs his minister to interrogate him because he believes that "*tathāgata*s never lie."[49] After the Buddha exhorts his remaining followers in Rājagaha to heed the example of the Vajjians by living together in harmony, he once again departs. This time, rather than seeking out a safe haven from the violence that seemed likely to erupt at any moment, he retraces his steps and goes back to Vesālī.

Why would he return to a place where he had just been publicly denounced and was no longer welcome? Why go somewhere that he knew was at risk of being invaded and annihilated? Neither the canon nor the commentaries provide us with any answers to these questions. Yet the Buddha appears assured in his decisions to move from one place to the next. He gives every impression of knowing where he is heading. If Vesālī was on the way to his final destination and could provide lodging for the approaching rainy season, it was perhaps the best option available.

Although the *Great Discourse on the Passing* tells that the Buddha miraculously "vanished from one shore of the Ganges and reappeared with his mendicants on the other shore," it is more likely that the group crossed the river that separates Magadha from the confederacy by boat and landed at the port of Ukkacelā.[50] Here, the Buddha addresses those with him: "This assembly appears empty to me now that Sāriputta and Moggallāna have attained their final nirvana. . . . But can what is born and subject to disintegration not fall apart? That is impossible. It is as if the largest branches would break off a great tree. So too is the great tree of the community of mendicants now that Sāriputta and Moggallāna are gone."[51] In addition to the other hardships, we now learn that during the Buddha's stay in Magadha, his two chief followers have died (Sāriputta of natural causes; Mogallāna was murdered), leaving the community bereft of their example and leadership.

From Ukkacelā the diminished group makes its way to the village of Koṭi, then the brick house at Nādikā, before reaching the outskirts of Vesālī, where they stay at the grove of the courtesan Ambapālī. On hearing of his arrival, some young Licchavis, all wearing clothes and makeup of different colors, mount their chariots and head for the grove. They make an ostentatious invitation to the Buddha to offer him his meal the next day, but he declines, since he has already agreed for Ambapālī to provide for him. The Licchavis snap their fingers in unison, then break into a song with the refrain: "Beaten by the mango woman! Cheated by the mango woman!" (*amba* in Pali means "mango tree"). Then they head back (in high spirits, I imagine) to the city.

There are two slightly different versions of this bizarre episode, one in the *Great Discourse on the Passing*,[52] which I have followed here, and another in the Vinaya.[53] Both texts tell this story in the pious language of the canon with no sense at all of irony or tragedy. Yet here we have a man who in former times would have been greeted by supporters such as the Licchavi chief Mahāli or the general Sīha, both of whom are conspicuous now by their absence. The Buddha neither sets foot in the city nor stays at the "House with the Gabled Roof," his usual base during his visits to the confederacy. We have the impression that his standing has sunk so low that he is not welcome anywhere else but in a mango grove belonging to a courtesan. And when it comes time to start the three-month Rains retreat, he decides to move to the "small village" of Beluva, and tells his mendicants: "You should go anywhere in Vesālī where you have friends or acquaintances or supporters, and spend the Rains there."[54]

All of this is perhaps a way of showing the extent to which the Vajjians are in moral decline. The frivolous, finger-snapping, colorfully costumed Licchavis, the lodging at the courtesan's garden, the lack of anywhere to stay for the Rains: these are hardly ways in which to "respect, salute and revere one's elders" or "make proper provision for saints," two of the seven principles the Buddha said must be honored if the Vajjians were "to prosper and not decline." Such behavior makes a mockery of these virtues.

And as for Sunakkhatta, the Licchavi son, we hear nothing more about him. After denouncing the Buddha to the Vesālī assembly, he disappears from the record.

7

Experience

Were mind and matter me,
I would come and go like them.
If I were something else,
They would say nothing about me.
—NĀGĀRJUNA, *Mūlamadhyamaka-kārikā*

(1)

Not having been raised in a Brahmanic environment, Gotama as a young man was unlikely to have been familiar with any ideas comparable to that of a transcendent God. He would not have internalized the default intuitions of theism. Yet his travels through north India, his discussions and debates with fellow wanderers, and his encounters with prominent teachers would have brought him into contact with such ideas. To present his teaching of a fourfold task, he would have had to articulate a vision of the person and the world that would be conducive to its practice. This project was twofold. He needed to differentiate this vision from that of the Jains and brahmins, which presupposed an eternal soul temporarily imprisoned in a body, while at the same time positing a coherent framework that described the phenomenal reality of human experience without any recourse to such a soul or God.

Gotama is concerned with how a person can flourish within the totality of his or her sensorium, which he calls "the all."[1] As a pragmatist, he has no interest in claiming that "nothing exists outside of experience" or insisting that "God does not exist." These are metaphysical claims, just as indefensible as the metaphysical claims of his opponents. To adopt an atheist position would lay him open to exactly the same charges he makes against those he criticizes. Instead of making a statement about the existence or otherwise of a transcendent consciousness or Divinity, Gotama says that claims to know what is unknowable and see what is unseeable are nonsensical and entirely irrelevant to the task at hand of practicing the dharma.[2]

Dharma practice takes place entirely within this "domain" (*visaya*), which is the realm of human experience, a world intimately tied to the body and the senses. "It is just in this fathom-high mortal frame endowed with perception and mind," says Gotama, "that I make known the world."[3] Elsewhere, he says: "It whirls, it whirls, that is why it's called the world."[4] I have tried to capture the wordplay here. "World" is *loka*, which Gotama connects to the verb *lujjati*, which means to "disintegrate," "break up," or "perish." (In fact, the two words merely sound alike and are not cognates.) *Loka*, for him, does not refer to the world out there that I observe and hear about as a detached spectator but is shorthand for *whatever goes on*. The world is whatever "collapses," "falls apart," or simply "passes." In French, one would say, "*C'est ce qui se passe*": it is what's happening, what's disintegrating on its way to becoming the past. It refers as much to thoughts and feelings that rise up and pass away as to events occurring outside the body.

"The all" (*sabbe*), "domain" (*visaya*), and "world" (*loka*) appear to be synonymous. Together, they imply that human experience is complex, embodied, and transient. To this we can add a further synonym: *dukkha* —"suffering." Life is something we suffer, put up with, bear. For a sentient organism to be born into such a world entails being subject to sickness, aging, and death. *Dukkha* refers not only to explicit pain but to the faint, quivering unease that accompanies happiness. Even as we delight in feeling well, we are aware of the fragility of such a feeling. We are tacitly alert to the sudden stab of physical pain or anguished cry for help that could end it. The very enjoyment of pleasure includes the poignant anticipation of its end. Rather than ignoring these disconcerting facts, we face the challenge of comprehending them.

Dukkha is the tragic dimension of life, implicit in experience because the world is constantly shifting and changing into something else. *Dukkha* is life's minor key, its bittersweet taste, its annoyingly fugitive charm, its fascinating and terrifying sublimity. The origin of *dukkha* lies in the very structure of the world itself, not in an emotion such as craving or an erroneous cognition such as ignorance. A contingent and impermanent world like ours is not the kind of place where we will find enduring happiness. Yet the more we wholeheartedly open ourselves to and embrace this tragic dimension, the more we appreciate the beauty, joy, and enchantment of the world: precisely *because* they are fleeting and destined to vanish.

The whirling disintegration of the world is a failing to be deplored only if we measure the world against the eternity, perfection, and unity of an Absolute. But when God or God's surrogates are outside one's domain, the world is just what it is, neither to be preferred to nor rejected in favor of something else. Instead of grasping hold of the world in order to preserve it from falling apart, or recoiling from it in order to transcend it, someone who practices the dharma embraces the world in order to comprehend it. Such an embrace nurtures a contemplative relation with experience, where attending to what is happening transforms its passing into the fertile nirvanic space from which an unprecedented response to the world's *dukkha* can emerge.

(2)

There is no exact equivalent in Pali or any other classical Buddhist language for "experience," at least in the ways we generally use the term today.[5] In a more technical sense, experience can be thought of as what psychology, physiology, and medicine call the "sensorium," that is, "the total character of the unique and changing sensory environments perceived by individuals."[6] Sensorium cum experience is similar if not identical to what Gotama calls one's "domain," that is, the sense organs and their respective sensory fields.

Dharma practice has to do with coming to terms with experience itself, through cultivating embodied attention, mindfulness, concentration, empathy, and compassion. A central part of this process entails overcoming certain perceptual distortions that lead to patterns of reactivity that block the flow of the stream of the path. Whether such perceptual adjustments thereby disclose an objective "truth" is beside the point. What matters is whether the relinquishing of such perceptions facilitates cultivation of the eightfold path. Experience is constituted out of what appears to us through our senses (including our inner mental sense). It has nothing to do with ontological realities (quantum fluctuations, atoms, subtle consciousness, God) that lie hidden behind what appears to us.

What we might call experience, Gotama calls five "clinging bundles" (*upādāna-khandha*); often translated as "aggregates of clinging." The word *khandha* (bundle) was originally used to refer to the "mass" or "bulk" of something. An elephant's *khandha,* for example, is the bulk of its body. The trunk of a tree is likewise called a *khandha.* The term was also used more metaphorically, as in *aggikhandha,* a "mass of fire," or *udakakhandha,* a "body of water" (a lake or ocean).[7] As a description of experience, *khandha* suggests that we are made up of different "bodies"—a body of physical and material properties, a body of feelings, a body of perceptions, and so on—all of which interact with one another. Were there not the risk of confusing it with the physical body, I would use the word "body" in this sense to translate *khandha.* To avoid this muddle, I have settled for "bundle."

Familiarity with the formulation "five bundles" makes us forget how odd it is. Why five? And why *these* five: form (*rūpa*), feeling (*vedanā*), perception (*saññā*), inclination (*saṅkhāra*), and consciousness (*viññāṇa*)? Why does Gotama say that he could not consider himself to have attained awakening until he "directly knew how the five bundles come about"?[8] Why is someone who "abandons perplexity" about them "known as a 'stream entrant'"?[9] And why do the bundles constitute what needs to be "comprehended" in order to accomplish the first of the four tasks?[10] Equating the five bundles with experience suggests that Gotama's awakening was the result of directly knowing how experience comes about. It implies that a stream entrant is one who is no longer confused by experience, and that one's primary task in practicing the dharma is to comprehend experience.

The doctrine of the five bundles is not an attempt to provide an objective, value-free description of reality. If Gotama's teaching is pragmatic, then his parsing of experience into these five bundles must contribute to realizing the goals of his teaching—as the citations above suggest.

Instead of trying to understand the five bundles as five discrete components of experience, it is more helpful to think of them as an unbroken spectrum of experience, which starts with the physical world (form) and proceeds through feelings, perceptions, and inclinations to consciousness. The bundles are comparable to Martin Heidegger's "being-in-the-world": the immediacy of what is happening prior to any bifurcation into subject and object, mind and matter, or any other categories habitually imposed upon the felt primacy of experience.

A topic upon which Gotama refused to comment was whether body (*sarīra*) and soul (*jīva*) are identical or different. *Sarīra* refers to the inanimate matter of which the body is composed rather than the living and breathing body (*kāya*). The term later came to denote the bones and material relics of deceased monks and saints. *Jīva* (a cognate of the English "quick") is, by contrast, the animating principle that "quickens" dumb matter. While this kind of dualism is in keeping with the Brahmanic view that soul is essentially other than the material world, neither term has a central role in Gotama's lexicon. He refused to get drawn into speculation about the relation between body and soul, nor did he consider such a dualistic distinction a useful starting point for understanding human experience.

Gotama likewise considers consciousness to be inseparable from the rest of the physical, emotional, perceptual, and intentional bundles of which it is an integral part. He makes this point emphatically: "Though someone might say: 'Apart from form, apart from feeling, apart from perception, apart from inclinations, I will make known the coming and going of consciousness, its passing away and rebirth, its growth, increase and expansion'—that is impossible."[11] In contrast to widespread Buddhist beliefs to the contrary, he refuses to grant consciousness any separate or privileged status within experience.

(3)

Given the centrality of the five bundles in Gotama's teaching, it is surprising for a modern reader that the discourses have so little to say about them. The dearth could suggest that the terms were widely used and discussed in the *samaṇa* communities of the time and that an educated audience would need no further clarification of their meaning. One of the few canonical passages to provide definitions of the bundles is found in a discussion in the *Connected Discourses* where the Buddha offers a brief reflection on each one. As we shall see, his aim is to encourage a first-person comprehension of the bundles rather than offer exact definitions of the terms.

"And why do we call it 'form' (*rūpa*)?" he asks? "Because it is deformed (*ruppati*), therefore we call it 'form.' Deformed by cold, by heat, by hunger, by thirst, by contact with flies, mosquitoes, the wind, the sun and snakes, therefore we call it 'form.'"[12] As with his gloss on the term "world" (*loka*), Gotama displays a penchant for etymologically inexact wordplay. Though sounding similar, the verb *ruppati* has nothing to do with the noun *rūpa*. *Ruppati* means "to break, injure or spoil; to be disturbed, stricken, oppressed, or broken." Another way of capturing this wordplay would be to say: "Because it is ruptured, therefore we call it *rūpa*." Gotama highlights the tragic and vulnerable nature of physical existence rather than explaining what matter "is" in an abstract or proto-scientific sense. In keeping with his pragmatic approach, he wants his listeners to contemplate what it feels like to be embodied in a world that constantly intrudes into and threatens their comfort zone.

This passage suggests that *rūpa* refers primarily to the body, but its usage elsewhere shows that it denotes far more than just the physical organism. Unfortunately, we have no single English word that captures its range of meanings. This is not, however, due to the limitations of English. Gotama had a similar problem. The term *rūpa* in Sanskrit or Pali refers to what can be seen with the eyes, to colors and shapes. To translate *rūpa* as "form" fails to capture even this much, since nowadays we do not talk of colors as forms. Neuroscience tells us that colors are not matter, either. And it gets worse. *Rūpa* refers not just to what is visible but to what is audible, smellable, tastable, and tangible too. Gotama borrowed the term *rūpa* from visual experience and employed it to denote everything we see, hear, smell, taste, and touch, as well as our sense organs and bodies. *Rūpa* refers to our physical sensorium in its totality.

From a first-person perspective, the physical sensorium is necessary but not sufficient to account for the experience you and I are having at this moment. For experience always feels a certain way, makes some kind of sense, inclines us to assume a stance toward the world, in ways that are irreducibly and coherently our own. Such is the domain of the mental sense (*mano indriya*) of which Gotama speaks. He is not introducing a spooky, disembodied *jīva* here but simply reporting what it is like to experience anything at all. Whether our feelings, perceptions, and inclinations are identical to the neurological correlates of our *sarīra* is, from a practical point of view, irrelevant.

To explain what "feeling" (*vedanā*) means, the Buddha says: "It feels; that is why we say 'feeling.' What do we feel? We feel pleasure, we feel pain, we feel neither pleasure nor pain."[13] Again he does not get drawn into an abstract discussion about the nature of feeling. He offers an ostensive definition: he points to what his listeners are feeling there and then, as though to say, "You know what it's like to feel something, don't you?" He then indicates that what they are feeling will be either pleasant or painful, or neither. That is all there is to it. *Vedanā* refers to the entire range of possible feelings, with agony at one extreme and ecstasy at the other. A tone or mood is utterly evident yet weirdly ineffable, embedded in the flesh but almost impossible to isolate, let alone define. Yet it is an intrinsic, undeniable feature of our experience at any given moment. It is the silent and truthful answer to the question "How are you feeling right now?" Let your attention rest there, Gotama seems to say, and you will know what it means to feel.

Gotama also offers an ostensive definition of "perception" (*saññā*): "It perceives; that is why we say 'perception.' And what do we perceive? We perceive blue, we perceive yellow, we perceive red, we perceive white."[14] *Saññā,* he suggests, denotes that experience is always differentiated in a comprehensible way. Rather than opening a door into a room and finding myself confronted with a bewildering array of shapes and colors that then have to be identified individually and organized into a coherent whole, I see a table set for dinner, at which sit a group of old friends, who turn their smiling faces to me in welcome and behind whom a bay window opens onto a garden filled with lavender, whose scent is carried into the room by the breeze.

Common sense tells us that the meaning of these things and the identity of the people is conveyed by properties intrinsic to each of them that are somehow conveyed through space to us. But such perceived properties do not exist "out there" in the room—nor does the perceived room itself exist "out there." It is we who have learned to recognize and organize such a complex experience in a way that immediately "makes sense" to us. Similarly, we have learned to construct words and sentences out of black squiggles inscribed on a white ground. Had I never learned to read, I would see only unintelligible marks that make no sense at all. In *An Anthropologist on Mars,* the neurologist Oliver Sacks gives several examples of people born blind whose sight is restored through surgery as adults.[15] When the bandages are removed and they open their eyes, they do not behold the doctors, nurses, and hospital ward but a confusing whirl of meaningless data. It takes years for them to learn, step by step, what all these data "mean." Nor do they ever fully acquire the perceptual skills that those, sighted from birth, take for granted.

Just as *vedanā* discloses how experience feels to us, and *saññā* discloses what it means for us, *saṅkhāra* (inclination) discloses the stance we assume toward it. Experience is made up not only of the impressions and stimuli we receive from the world, which feel a certain way and make sense, but also of the various ways we react and respond to what is happening.

In the Buddha's account of inclinations, however, we run into further semantic difficulties. "Because inclinations (*saṅkhāra*) incline (*abhisaṅkharonti*) what is inclined (*saṅkhataṃ*)," he says, "they are called 'inclinations.'"[16] This makes little sense unless we recall the discussion in chapter 5, where we saw that *saṅkhāra* (inclinations) literally means what "puts together" or "conditions" something else. Inclinations are thus the "conditioning factors" that "condition" what is "conditioned." In this passage, the "conditioned" refers to the totality of one's experience, which Gotama spells out as comprising conditioned forms, conditioned feelings, conditioned perceptions, conditioned inclinations, and conditioned consciousness—the five bundles themselves. If we think of inclinations as patterns of habitual behavior that are repeatedly prompted by encounters with the world, we can see that they are not merely isolated reactions that arise in the privacy of our minds; they color the rest of our experience as well. And since inclinations are said to condition the inclinations, this points to the self-reinforcing and repetitive nature of such reactivity. In other words, the more we react in a particular way, the more we will be inclined to act in that particular way again.

In another discourse, Gotama identifies inclination with intention (*cetanā*).[17] There are, he says, six kinds of intention: those directed to forms, those directed to sounds, those directed to smells, those directed to tastes, those directed to tactile sensations, and those directed to what is occurring in the mind (*dhamma*). Since intention is equated with action (karma), *saṅkhāra* must refer to more than just the organism's inclination to react out of blind habit.[18] The inclination to act extends to our intentions or volitions as moral agents to respond thoughtfully in words or deeds to the world that we encounter. In addition to determining an inner moral stance vis-à-vis the world, our inclination to act simultaneously discloses a world that presents itself as an arena for possible actions. The challenge presented by the fourfold task is to learn how to differentiate between reactivity, in which one blindly follows a familiar impulse, and responsiveness, in which one chooses to act in a way that is *not* conditioned by the impulses of greed, hatred, and confusion.

In two other discourses we find inclinations presented from yet another angle.[19] Neither discourse, however, is spoken by Gotama; one is a discussion between the mendicant Kamabhu and the adherent Citta, and the other a discussion between the *bhikkhuni* Dhammadinnā and the adherent Visākha. In answer to each adherent's question about the nature of inclination, Kamabhu and Dhammadinnā give an identical reply: "There are these three inclinations, friend: bodily inclinations, verbal inclinations and mental inclinations. Breathing-in and breathing-out is the inclination of the body; to think and examine is the inclination of speech; and to feel and perceive is the inclination of the mind."[20] Kamabhu and Dhammadinnā recognize that experience is never passive but always enacted; we are either on the verge of or are already engaged in acts that reach into and affect the world. The primary act of the body is its ceaseless engagement through the breath with its environment. If you hold your breath for a few moments, your body naturally inclines to breathe freely again. Likewise, the endless musing and cogitation of our inner monologue is what inclines us to speak our thoughts out loud. Even our feelings and perceptions, which are usually differentiated from inclinations, are more than just the conditioned content of experience. According to Kamabhu and Dhammadinnā, the mind constantly inclines to feel and perceive in particular ways.

As for consciousness (*viññāṇa*), the fifth of the five bundles, Gotama again offers an ostensive definition: "It knows (*vijānāti*), therefore we call it 'consciousness.' And what do we know? We know: this is sour, this is bitter, this is pungent, this is sweet, this is sharp, this is mild, this is salty, this is bland."[21] Such a definition is hardly illuminating. Not only does it beg the question "What does it mean to know?" but it is difficult to see how consciousness differs in any way from perception ("we perceive blue, we perceive yellow, we perceive red, we perceive white"). Both bundles are described as our way of differentiating one feature of experience from another. We seem to be going round in circles and are left none the wiser about consciousness. Sāriputta, however, seems to be aware of this objection. Toward the end of a dialogue with the intellectual mendicant Mahā Koṭṭhita, he says:

> Feeling, perception, and consciousness, friend—these states are conjoined, not disjoined, and it is impossible to separate each of these states from the others in order to describe the difference between them. For what one feels, that one perceives; and what one perceives, that one knows. That is why these states are conjoined not disjoined.[22]

Experience, therefore, is highly differentiated and, at the same time, seamlessly unified. I can be aware of a nagging pain in the lower back when I lean forward to appreciate the scent of a rose on the table while never losing that warm, satisfied glow of being with chattering and laughing friends I have not seen in years. Yet all these and myriad other details of which I am more or less conscious are bound together in a single whole. As things disappear from my field of vision, the whole doesn't become less; and when something new appears, it doesn't become more. Yet as soon as I isolate one element of the whole to examine and define it, I remove myself from the immediacy of experience itself. The feeling, perception, or inclination that formed an integral part of my experience is stripped out of its living context as though it existed in its own right. Whatever I gain in abstract clarity by this exercise, I lose in sensory presence.

Gotama's love of wordplay and puns suggests that he might not be taking the quest for precise definitions of the five bundles entirely seriously.

(4)

The five-bundle model is only one way Gotama illuminates human experience for the purpose of practicing the fourfold task. A more complex model of experience is found in his presentation of name-form (*nāmarūpa*) and how that is related to consciousness. "And what," he asks, "is *nāmarūpa*?"

> Touch, feeling, perception, intention, attention: this is *nāma* (name). The four great elements and the forms derived from those elements: this is *rūpa* (form). So name and form together are *nāmarūpa*.[23]

Although this analysis covers much of the same ground as the account of the five bundles, nowhere in the discourses does Gotama include consciousness, the fifth bundle, as part of *nāmarūpa*. The omission is not careless. As we shall see, consciousness is not part of *nāmarūpa* because *nāmarūpa* is understood as the necessary condition for consciousness to come about in the first place.

In the passage just cited, *rūpa* is presented through the metaphor of what we "sense" with our bodies, not just with our eyes. Although later schools of Buddhism understood the four great elements (earth, water, fire, air) to be composed of different physical atoms, the discourses never mention atoms. Gotama understands the four elements phenomenologically as the tactile sensations (*phoṭṭhabba*) of heaviness (earth), wetness (water), warmth (fire), and movement (air), which we know firsthand through our embodied experience. The Pali *phoṭṭhabba* is a gerundive of the verb *phusati,* "to touch." Literally, it means "that which is touched." And since *rūpa* extends to whatever "is derived from" these elements (which here would have to include what we see, hear, smell, and taste), this implies that Gotama compares our entire physical sensorium to what we touch with our skin and sense with our bodies as heavy or light, damp or dry, warm or cool, mobile or immobile. The language is metaphorical. "Touch" is being used here, just as "form" is elsewhere, as a *metaphor* for everything we encounter through the physical senses.

However tempting it is to translate *nāmarūpa* as "name *and* form," there is no "and" in the original. As soon as the "and" intervenes, we become prone to thinking that *nāmarūpa* involves two discrete entities that somehow interact with each other, which has led, perhaps, to the common Buddhist misunderstanding of *nāmarūpa* as a synonym for "mind and body."[24] That *nāmarūpa* has nothing to do with "mind" (*citta*) is reinforced by the fact that consciousness (a synonym of *citta*) is never mentioned as part of it. Gotama's contemporaries may have been familiar with the term *nāmarūpa* as referring to the world of multiplicity and variety but they would not have recognized it as referring to a world neatly divided into two components, one material and one mental.[25]

"Touch, feeling, perception, intention, attention," says Gotama: "this is *nāma* (name)."[26] These five "*nāma* factors," as they are called, include three of the five bundles—feeling, perception, and inclination (= intention)—but add two more: touch and attention. "Touch" in Pali is *phassa,* also from the verb *phusati* (to touch) and thus a cognate of *phoṭṭhabba,* "what is touched." (*Phassa* is often translated as "contact.") This cluster of touch words shows that *nāmarūpa* is always a condition of contact, of being-in-touch, which further undermines the dualistic idea of a mind "in here" coming into contact with a physical world "out there." In echoing tactile sensation, touch points to the broader experiential sense of "being in touch with the world" through each of our senses.[27]

"With the arising of touch," says Gotama, "there is the arising of feeling, . . . with the arising of touch, there is the arising of perception, . . . with the arising of touch, there is the arising of inclination."[28] As soon as I come into touch with a situation in the world, it feels a certain way, makes perceptual sense, and inclines me to adopt a stance toward it. Touching an environment (*rūpa*—the first of the five bundles) immediately and simultaneously triggers the bundles of feeling (*vedanā*), perception (*saññā*), and inclination (*saṅkhāra*). However, touch is *not* said to give rise to consciousness (the fifth bundle, *viññāṇa*).

So how does consciousness come about? Gotama explains in the next line: "With the arising of name-form, there is the arising of consciousness."[29] Consciousness emerges out of the entire complex of interactions between an organism and its environment. Consciousness cannot be said to be the exclusive product of either something physical, whether an external sense object or a brain, or something mental, whether a feeling, a perception, or an inclination. Gotama recognizes that consciousness is a seamless whole that is not equivalent to the sum of its parts, much in the same way that a hand as a whole is not reducible to the sum of its fingers, skin, bones, nerves, and muscles. Just as my hand can pick up a glass of water and raise it to my lips (which none of the parts can do on their own), so consciousness has a total, unified awareness of what is happening that none of its constituents (feeling, perception, inclination, etc.) can achieve on their own. To know something (the defining quality of consciousness) differs from merely perceiving something (the quality of perception), because it is a holistic awareness in which all the *nāma* factors of touch, feeling, perception, intention, and attention are integrated. By implication, for Gotama there can be no such thing as "pure" consciousness, an unconditioned or pristine "knowing" that exists independently of the phenomenal world of discrete physical things and mental processes.

"In many discourses," explains Gotama to his disciple Sāti the fisherman's son, who believes in an unconditioned consciousness, "have I not stated consciousness to arise upon conditions, since without a condition there is no arising of consciousness?"[30] He goes on to show how consciousness is determined by the particular conditions that give rise to it. If consciousness is produced by eyes and forms, then it is "visual consciousness"; if it is produced by ears and sounds, then it is "auditory consciousness," and so on. Consciousness is as impermanent, contingent, compounded, and varied as anything else in experience. Open your eyes upon a blue summer sky, and visual consciousness occurs; close your eyes again, and that consciousness is gone. By contrast, we instinctively feel that consciousness lurks as a singular, constant "witness" somewhere in the background, waiting for the opportunity to see, hear, smell, taste, or touch something. As though to dispel this felt-sense of consciousness's priority and privilege, Gotama emphasizes its derivative and mundane nature. He likens it to different kinds of fires. "Just as a fire is reckoned by what it burns—when it depends on logs, it's called a 'log fire,' when it depends on dung, it's called a 'dung fire,' . . . so consciousness too is reckoned by the particular conditions that give rise to it."[31]

Sāriputta, in his dialogue with Mahā Koṭṭhita, also presents consciousness as an emergent property, as something that occurs when the necessary conditions for it are in place. He denies that it is something to be refined or developed through dharma practice. Mahā Koṭṭhita asks him to explain the relation between consciousness (*viññāṇa*) and understanding (*paññā*) or, as it is often translated, wisdom (note that in Pali both terms are rooted in *-ññā,* "to know"). Sāriputta says: "Understanding and consciousness, friend—these states are conjoined not disjoined. You cannot separate one from the other in order to describe the difference between them. For what you understand, you are conscious of; and what you are conscious of, you understand. The difference between them is this: understanding is to be cultivated (*bhāvanā*), consciousness is to be comprehended (*pariññā*)."[32]

Sāriputta recognizes that understanding and consciousness are too fused with one another to be differentiated in order to describe what they *are.* Nonetheless, they can be differentiated pragmatically, that is, in terms of what is to be *done* with them. Consciousness, as one of the five bundles that are shorthand for *dukkha,* is to be comprehended, whereas understanding, as a crucial element of the path, is to be cultivated. By using the language of the fourfold task, Sāriputta refuses to satisfy Mahā Koṭṭhita's metaphysical curiosity and instead encourages him to do two things: *comprehend* his existential condition as a conscious, sentient being rather than ask questions about what consciousness is; and *cultivate* his own understanding rather than inquire into its nature.

Such comprehension involves gaining experiential insight into how consciousness, as a conditioned phenomenon, comes about. Two discourses preserve an identical passage in which Gotama recalls a key moment in his understanding of the origins of consciousness:

> Then, *bhikkhus,* it occurred to me: "By what is consciousness conditioned?" Through embodied attention, there occurred for me a breakthrough in understanding: "When there is name-form, consciousness comes to be; consciousness has name-form as its condition. When consciousness turns back, it goes back no further than name-form."[33]

Contrary both to common sense and received opinion, Gotama sees how the unified experience of consciousness is crystallized out of the complexity and variety of name-form.

But the causality is not quite so straightforward. Gotama rejects a simplistic, one-directional view of causality: of either consciousness causing name-form, or name-form causing consciousness. The same passage concludes with his recognition that the experience of life entails having "consciousness with name-form as its condition, *and* name-form with consciousness as its condition" (my italics).[34] He understands each to be a condition for the other; they are interdependent. Sāriputta tries to explain what this means in another dialogue with Mahā Koṭṭhita. "Well then, friend," he says, "I will make up a simile for you. Just as two sheaves of reeds might stand leaning against each other, likewise, with name-form as condition, consciousness comes to be, and with consciousness as condition, name-form comes to be."[35]

What does it mean, this intricate, tumbling dance of *nāmarūpa* and consciousness? If one partner were to slip and fall, the other would crash to the ground as well. Two sheaves of reeds leaning against each other is a helpful but rather static way of illustrating the endlessly mutating and reconfiguring interplay of form-touch-feeling-perception-intention-attention-consciousness. The key to understanding this synergy of name-form and consciousness is to recall that experience—any experience—is simultaneously unified *and* highly differentiated; it is both a single, coherent whole *and* a mass of whirling, contrasting detail. Just as the complexity of name-form is needed to generate a unified consciousness, so a unified consciousness is needed to bring the complexity of name-form into focus. Name-form without consciousness would be chaos. Consciousness without name-form would be meaningless.

(5)

Gotama describes what enabled his understanding of the interdependence of name-form and consciousness as the practice of "embodied attention" (*yoniso manasikāra*). This statement brings us to the fifth and final *nāma* factor: attention (*manasikāra*). Experience is triggered by finding oneself in *touch* with an environment, which simultaneously prompts *feelings, perceptions,* and *intentions.* But this description is incomplete. Not only does experience feel a certain way, make perceptual sense, and incline one to adopt a stance toward it, but one pays *attention* to what is happening and thinks about it. Such intimate reflections are the "activity of the mind," which is the literal meaning of *manasikāra.* There is a meditative quality to human experience: as conscious beings, we constantly ponder and worry about how we feel, what we perceive, and how we intend to respond to it all.

The discourses talk of two kinds of attention: embodied (*yoniso*) and disembodied (*ayoniso*). To the extent that I am preoccupied with getting through the day without too much hardship or struggle, my attention tends to be disembodied. I do not inquire deeply into why I feel a certain way, I do not question or probe the veracity of my perceptions, I do not submit my intentions to rigorous moral scrutiny. I just muddle along, "eaten up by thoughts," taking whatever appears for granted, indulging in the occasional fantasy, not complaining too loudly, and speaking and acting more out of politeness than conviction.[36]

The practice of dharma starts by paying embodied attention to what is going on. Although *yoniso manasikāra* is usually translated as "wise" or "careful" attention, neither adjective captures the metaphoric richness of *yoni,* which means "womb" or "vagina." The ablative *yoniso,* which means "from the womb," suggests that such attention can be understood as attention that is born from one's belly, attention that is nurturing, caring, and loving, or, as the Pali Text Society's dictionary suggests, attention that "gets down to the origin or foundation" of something.[37] In yet another dialogue, Mahā Koṭṭhita asks Sāriputta what a skillful practitioner should pay embodied attention to. Sāriputta answers that one should "pay embodied attention to the five bundles *as* impermanent, *dukkha,* . . . empty and not-self." Should one cultivate these reflections, "they will lead to dwelling happily in this very life, to mindfulness and awareness."[38] Embodied attention begins when we doubt our perceptions. Instead of habitually regarding ourselves and the world as things that will endure, as essentially satisfactory, as solid and "mine," Sāriputta tells Mahā Koṭṭhita to attend to his experience as fleeting, tragic, empty, and selfless.

Despite abundant evidence to the contrary, human beings tend to perceive themselves and the world as permanent, satisfactory, and as "me" or "mine." These instinctive perceptual habits are traditionally explained as the result of ignorance, craving, and our karmic inheritance. Today we could understand them as the legacy of evolution, as selected behavioral traits that have conferred survival advantages on our ancestors and their kin over long stretches of time. No matter which explanation you prefer, the task of dharma practice remains the same: to pay attention to the very "flesh" of your experience, such that you become viscerally aware of its ephemeral, poignant, empty, and impersonal character. Embodied attention is thus synonymous with comprehending *dukkha,* the first of the four tasks. It is also one of four key conditions (along with association with true friends, listening to the dharma, and following its instructions) needed to enter the stream of the eightfold path, cultivation of which is the fourth task.[39]

(6)

Gotama's analysis of *nāma* as touch, feeling, perception, intention, and attention may have encouraged early Buddhists to think of "name" in terms of mental processes—or simply as a synonym for "mind." The terms all later came to be classified in the *Abhidharma* as "mental events" (*cetasika*), a term that does not occur in the discourses. As a result, the continued use of "name" becomes something of a puzzle. Why are these five functions collectively called "name," when only one of them (perception) has anything remotely to do with naming things?

Two of the principal ways in which one becomes conscious of oneself as a person are through one's "name" and one's "form." If you see an envelope with your name written on it, you feel a pang of recognition and think: "Oh, that's me." If you see your body or face reflected in a mirror, or a photograph or video footage of yourself, you likewise recognize those forms as "me." Buddhist texts do not say so, but name-form seems in some way to be intimately connected to personality and individual identity. To understand how and why this is so, we need to return to the pre-Buddhist *Bṛhadāraṇyaka Upaniṣad.* For here we learn that the singularity of God became "differentiated by name-form, so that one could say: 'He is so-and-so, and has such and such a form.'"[40] For Gotama's contemporaries, *nāmarūpa* would have implied not only a world of multiplicity and variety but also that each individual in the world had a distinct identity as a person.

Although Buddhism says a great deal about the mind, it says hardly anything about the self or person who is conscious, who feels, perceives, intends, attends, and thinks. This is largely, I suspect, because *anattā* is misinterpreted as "no self," which has led to a reluctance to think of the self as anything more than a concept or convention. Embodied attention to the characteristic of *anattā* means that when one examines the five bundles, one finds that they are devoid of any mark or trace of self. Such an analysis has led to the unjustified conclusion that while the bundles themselves possess a degree of realness because the physical and mental processes are observable, the self that "undergoes" them is a fiction, an illusion: it does not really exist. This disjunction is problematic: it is like saying that individual hydrogen and oxygen atoms are real, but the water molecules formed through their combination are illusory. Taking such a stance means that Buddhists have to explain how such a non-existent self can function as a moral agent, capable of making responsible choices with consequences that will determine a person's fate. At this point, the ever-useful two truth doctrine is called upon to resolve the difficulty. We are told that although the self does not exist *ultimately*, it does exist *conventionally*, and that is sufficient for it to operate as a moral agent with motives and goals.

If we think of the dharma as a task-based ethics rather than a truth-based metaphysics, such intellectual gymnastics become unnecessary. In a short discourse that has given rise to much debate, Gotama declares: "I will show you the burden and the carrier of the burden, the burden's addition and the burden's relief."[41] He explains that the burden (*bhāra*) is the five bundles, and the carrier of the burden (*bhārahāra*) is "the person . . . of such and such a name and clan." What is added to the burden (*bhāradāna*) is reactivity/craving (*taṇhā*), and the burden's relief (*bhāranikkhepa*) is the "fading away and ceasing of that reactivity," that is, nirvana. What troubles orthodox Buddhists is that Gotama appears to give equivalent status to the bundles and to the person who "carries" the bundles, thus raising the spectre of an *ātman*-like self existing independently of its attributes. That this is seen as problematic reveals the entrenched ontological mindset of commentators; they seem incapable of taking such a statement as anything other than a claim about the existence of a self. Yet the passage could just as well be read as providing a compelling metaphorical frame for contextualizing a person's performance of the fourfold task.

The five bundles are compared to a burden, to the "cross" we bear, which we suffer through life. The task is to accept and embrace this burden rather than increasing the load by pointlessly adding resentful reactivity. We come to terms with our lot by letting go of such reactivity and settling into the equanimity of nirvana, which both relieves us of unnecessary anguish and allows us the opportunity to cultivate another way of life. Reactivity is revealed as an additional burden that we do not need to carry; the person who lets go of it is thereby transformed.

The person or self spoken of here is not an entity standing apart from life, who carries life's burden as though it is separate from him or her. As we have seen, Gotama compares the process of self-transformation to the farmer's cultivation of a barren field, the arrowsmith's fashioning of an arrow from disparate elements, and the carpenter's carving an object from a block of wood.[42] One's body, feelings, perceptions, inclinations, and consciousness are understood as the raw materials for the practice of the fourfold task. What was felt to be a burden is thereby transformed into the human equivalents of an ample harvest, a well-designed arrow, a wooden utensil or sculpture. Gotama describes the practice of the fourfold task as a process of self-discipline in which one "tames" reactivity. The aim of this process is for a person to flourish rather than remain like a barren field, to become integrated and directed rather than remain fragmented and unfocused, and to become more and more individuated rather than remain unformed.

After Gotama's discourse on the fourfold task, the next thing he is said to have taught his five companions was about "not-self" *(anattā)*. On hearing and understanding this teaching, all five are said to have achieved complete liberation of mind and become arahants. Yet nowhere in this pithy text does Gotama declare that there is no self.

"*Bhikkhus,*" he says. "The body (*rūpa*) is not self. If it were, it would not get sick. You could tell your body: 'be like this' or 'don't be like that.' But because the body is not self, it does get sick. You can't tell it: 'be like this,' or 'don't be like that.'"[43] He points out that the same is true for feelings, perceptions, inclinations, and consciousness. You cannot determine in advance how you will feel, what you will perceive, how you will be inclined to act, or what you will be conscious of. You do not choose to feel happy rather than sad, to perceive a world that delights rather than disturbs you, to always incline to a calm rather than an agitated response, to be unconscious rather than conscious of something distressing. In other words, you are not in charge of what is going on within your own experience.

Experience happens to you. You are thrown into this world at birth, subjected to accidents, infections, cancers, and strokes; if you survive, you will age and decline until one day you exhale your last breath and die. Each of us seeks to mitigate the negatives in life by taking care of our health, keeping fit and active, avoiding dark alleys and war zones, but in the end the grim reaper cuts us down. There is nothing we can do about it. Gotama regards belief in self as the conviction that one is ultimately in control of one's destiny. This could well be a reference to the idea of self as "the ruler within, the immortal," found in the *Bṛhadāraṇyaka Upaniṣad*.[44] Gotama objects to a specific intuition of what the self is. But he does not thereby deny that one leads one's life as a distinct person or self endowed with moral agency.

Gotama made and acted on decisions that made a profound difference in his life. Had he not believed this was possible for others, too, there would have been little point to spending forty-five years encouraging people to pursue a path of moral responsibility, contemplative practice, and philosophical reflection. The self may not be an aloof, independent "ruler" of body and mind, but neither is it an illusory product of impersonal physical and mental forces. Gotama is interested in what people can *do*, not with what they *are*. The task he proposes entails distinguishing between what is to be accepted as the natural condition of life itself (the unfolding of experience) and what is to be let go of (reactivity). We may have no control over the rush of fear prompted by finding a snake under our bed, but we do have the ability to respond to the situation in a way that is not determined by that fear.

But if reactivity is an inclination, and therefore part of the experience over which you have no control, how can you exercise any choice that might make a difference? Or, more simply stated: If everything you experience arises from conditions, how can there be free will? Surely the doctrines of not-self and conditioned arising preclude the possibility of freely chosen agency and present a vision of life that plays itself out according to the blind forces of impersonal causality. These oft-stated objections come from treating the Buddha's teaching as though it were a metaphysics concerned with illuminating the true nature of reality. As soon as we consider it a task-based ethics, however, such objections vanish. The only thing that matters is whether or not you can perform a task. When an inclination to say something cruel occurs, for example, can you resist acting on that impulse? If you can, you have succeeded. Whether your decision to withhold the barbed remark was the result of free will or not is beside the point.

The question of free will versus determinism should perhaps be added to the list of questions about which the Buddha refused to make any comment. Like the others, it has no direct bearing on the practice of the dharma. It is also a peculiarly Western concern; it has never been an issue for Buddhist thinkers. That it is still generating debate today after centuries of discussion strongly suggests that it may never be conclusively resolved.

When the wanderer Vacchagotta asked whether there is a self, Gotama remained silent. After Vacchagotta had gone away, Gotama explained to Ānanda that to have affirmed or denied the existence of self would have led to a metaphysical dead end.[45] We might interpret this post-reflective silence as another way of showing that what matters for him is not what selves *are* but what selves *do*. In his case, he chose to remain silent rather than engage in theoretical speculation.

"So, *bhikkhus*," the Buddha concludes his conversation with his five companions, "any form, feeling, perception, inclination, or consciousness whatever should be seen with complete understanding as it occurs: 'This is not mine, I am not this, this is not my self.'"[46] The liberating insight he proposes is *not* the realization that there is no self but the realization that I am not the same as or reducible to any or all of the five bundles that constitute me. But how, we might ask, is this any different from the *neti, neti* (not this, not this) of the *Bṛhadāraṇyaka Upaniṣad*, where the yogin is taught to disidentify with everything that makes up the world of ordinary experience in order to gain blissful release into the non-dual awareness of God?[47] The answer goes to the core of what distinguishes Gotama's teaching from the received opinion of his contemporaries. For not only are we not identical with what makes up our experience, we are not something different from it either.

Gotama illustrates this identity in a dialogue with the elder monk Anurādha. He asks Anurādha whether he (Anurādha) can see the *Tathāgata* (the Buddha) within each of the five bundles. Anurādha says no. Gotama then asks whether Anurādha can see the *Tathāgata* apart from each of the five bundles. Anurādha replies no. Gotama continues: "What do you think, Anurādha, do you regard form, feeling, perception, inclination and consciousness as the *Tathāgata*?" "No, sir." "So what do you think, do you regard the *Tathāgata* as one who is without form, feeling, perception, inclination and consciousness?" "No, sir." The *Tathāgata*, therefore, "is not apprehended by you as real and actual here in this very life."[48] But such unfindability of self is not an exclusive property of Gotama's. It is equally true of Anurādha, you, and me.

This unfindability of the self in no way entails that the self does not exist and therefore cannot function as a moral agent. All it means is that the self is ambiguous and elusive, incapable of being pinned down and defined. Today we might say that this is because a person is not a static, circumscribed thing but a hub of complex living processes that are continually evolving and changing in vital interactions with the environment.

The ambiguity and elusiveness of self is captured in a verse from Nāgārjuna's *Mūlamadhyamaka-kārikā:*

> If the self were the bundles,
> It would be something that arises and passes away;
> If it were other than the bundles,
> It would not bear their characteristics.[49]

Were I reducible to my body, feelings, perceptions, inclinations, and consciousness, then, since they are constantly changing, I would be constantly changing, too. But that is clearly not the case. Nāgārjuna takes it for granted that to be a self means to have a perspective on experience that remains constant while the feelings, perceptions, and inclinations that make up one's experience arise and pass away. At the same time he recognizes the absurdity of thinking of the self as something different from what makes up its experience. Why? Because the only way "I" or "you" can be known is through our features: our name, our physical appearance, our moods, our thoughts, our acts. Remove these features, and the self to whom they belong vanishes as well.

Ever since I can remember, I have had the undeniable sense that the same "me" has had every one of my experiences. I am intuitively convinced that the one who is writing these words is identical to the one who played with his toys as a child. Yet I also know that this cannot be the case. Physically, mentally, emotionally, I have changed and grown over the years and will continue to do so. Logically, there may be a conflict between my sense of "me" as a constant perspective and my sense of "me" as an unfolding narrative. In practice, however, these two kinds of self coexist perfectly well. I change and evolve from one day to the next, yet, at the same time, as the one who undergoes these changes, I appear not to change at all. Nāgārjuna understands this ambiguity as central to what it means to be a self. By contrast, the assumption in the *Upaniṣads* is that our innate sense of self as a constant perspective or witness reflects a metaphysically real and unconditioned self or consciousness that is identical with God.

For Gotama experience is what matters. Although we seem to observe ourselves from the perspective of a detached witness, we should not be tricked into believing that the witness is therefore more enduring or reliable than anything else. If we do so, we resist "comprehending" the world, secure in the conceit that what we really are has nothing to do with the shifting, tragic lives of ourselves and others. Embracing *dukkha* entails abandoning any ontological commitment to a disembodied self or consciousness that is apart from experience yet magically peers in on it. Whatever survival advantages such a perspective might have provided our ancestors, believing in it as real holds us back from giving ourselves over totally to life. In this sense, embodied attention is an unflinching participation with what is happening now; it is indistinguishable, in the end, from love.

Gotama has no hesitation in using the first person singular or the words *ahaṃ* (I) or *atta* (self) in a completely ordinary and non-problematic way. On recalling his key insight into the relation between name-form and consciousness, he says: "There occurred *for me* (*mayhaṃ*) a breakthrough in understanding."[50] Toward the end of his life he encourages his followers to rely on themselves (*atta*) as their island and refuge.[51] Elsewhere he speaks of a person's identity as a farmer, a craftsman, a merchant, a soldier, and so on, as what is created as the result of the person's choices and acts.[52] One's self is a work in progress, an unfinished project to be realized, not a fiction that needs to be exposed and eradicated. One can think of oneself as an ongoing *practice*. I forge my personality and character out of how I connect with myself and the world, how I feel about things, how I make sense of what appears to me, how I choose to speak and act, how I attend to what is going on.

(7)

As we have seen, Gotama understood awakening as the result of directly knowing how experience comes about; he understood a stream entrant as a person who is no longer confused about experience; and he understood the primary task in practicing the dharma as comprehending experience. To consider awakening in terms of the workings of the five bundles marks a departure from Brahmanic orthodoxy, where the goal of the path is to achieve union with a transcendent and unknowable consciousness or God. If nothing else, Gotama's emphasis on the five bundles points to a practice that from the outset is engaged with the specificity and diversity of the world of human experience rather than seeking an ultimate truth that lies hidden from view.

The key to freeing oneself from the repetitive cycles of reactivity and beholding nirvana is attention (*manasikāra*), the fifth *nāma* factor. When attention becomes embodied through contemplation of the transient, tragic, impersonal, and empty nature of the bundles, our relationship to experience begins to shift in disconcerting ways. The practice of embodied attention challenges our habitual *perceptions* of self and world as permanent, satisfactory, and intrinsically ours. By stabilizing attention through mindfulness and concentration, we begin to see for ourselves how pleasurable and painful *feelings* trigger habitual patterns of reactivity and craving. These two insights not only undermine our *inclinations* to hold on to what we like and to push away what we fear but open up the possibility of thinking, speaking, and acting otherwise.

"Seeing things this way," says Gotama at the conclusion of his discourse on not-self, "the attentive noble disciple disengages from form, disengages from feelings, disengages from perceptions, disengages from inclinations, disengages from consciousness. By disengaging, reactivity fades; non-reactive, he is freed; the knowledge arises: 'I am freed.'"[53] This is the experience of nirvana as "immediate and clearly visible"; it is at this crucial point that one sees for oneself how one is free *not* to react to life but *to* respond to it from a perspective that is no longer conditioned by such inclinations.

Gotama parsed experience into the five bundles for entirely pragmatic reasons. He was not interested in providing a value-free, protoscientific account of the nature of reality. His concern was to offer a paradigm that would optimize the practice of the fourfold task. That parts of his account of human experience may have anticipated certain insights in modern philosophy, psychology, and cognitive science should not mislead us into thinking that he shared the same goals as most contemporary academics, therapists, and researchers. His project was primarily ethical. He sought to establish a pragmatic framework to enable men and women to experience for themselves that they are free not to live according to the instinctive dictates of craving and egotism. This freedom is not an end in itself but a freedom to embark on a way of life in which human beings can flourish.

Consider how Gotama understands the Indian metaphor of rivers losing their identity when they pour into the ocean. The *Muṇḍaka Upaniṣad* says: "As the flowing rivers disappear into the sea, losing their name and form, thus a wise man, freed from name-form, goes to the Divine One."[54] Here the aim of human life is to lose one's identity as a person differentiated by name-form and merge into the transpersonal unity of God. For Gotama, however, the ocean becomes a metaphor for his dharma and the community of those who practice it. "Just as the great rivers on reaching the ocean lose their former names and identities, so also those of the four castes—nobles, brahmins, merchants, and workers—having gone forth from home to homelessness in the dharma and discipline, abandon their former names and identities and are just called 'wanderers, followers of the Sakiyan Son.'"[55] Instead of losing oneself in mystic union with the Absolute, one loses one's class identity in order to practice the dharma as a free, self-creating person.

8

Jīvaka: The Doctor

Suppose a man needing a snake, wandering in search of a snake, saw a large snake and grasped its coils or its tail. It would turn back on him and bite his hand or arm or one of his limbs, and because of that he would come to death or deadly suffering. Why? Because of his wrong grasp of the snake. So too, here some misguided men learn the dharma but having learned the dharma, they do not examine the meaning of the teachings with intelligence, they do not arrive at a reasoned understanding of them. Instead, they learn the dharma only for the sake of criticising others and winning in debates, and they do not experience the good for the sake of which they learned the dharma. These teachings, being wrongly grasped by them, conduce to their harm and suffering for a long time.

—ALAGADDŪPAMA SUTTA

(1)

In the parable of the snake, narrated in the epigraph, Gotama presents his listeners with a stark warning: the dharma he reached through his awakening and then dedicated his life to sharing with others is dangerous, something to be handled with skill and care. Mishandle it, he cautions, and it might destroy you. Not even the dharma possesses an inbuilt safeguard to prevent it from being turned into yet another place in which we can "love, delight, and revel," where once more the contingent and nirvanic ground of our life is obscured.[1]

All too often in the name of Buddhism, people transform the dharma into a belief system, a religious or ethnic identity, a dialectical tool that they employ to secure a place either in their own egoistic scheme of self-appraisal or in the various pecking orders established by society and the world. Far from dwelling in the radiant, open-hearted equanimity that allows them the freedom to risk responding to life unconditioned by reactivity, they prefer to encase themselves in an armor of fixed opinions, where they can feel self-righteous and impervious to criticism.

This, perhaps, is why the dharma is like a poisonous snake. If you seize a cobra by its body or tail rather than carefully gripping it by the back of its neck, it will whip round and sink its fangs into your flesh to inject its venom into your bloodstream. If you treat the dharma as a set of dogmas rather than a liberative practice, it, too, will function as a toxin: it can poison and "kill" you. Metaphorically, a fixed place in which one delights and revels is a stasis comparable to death. By turning the dharma into a static place, it, too, can become a living death rather than a source of life.

(2)

This interpretation of the parable of the snake fails to cast light on its curious opening phrase: "Suppose a man needing a snake, wandering in search of a snake . . ." What sort of person would need and wander in search of a snake? Poisonous snakes are universally feared and shunned. They are to be avoided rather than sought out. If you were to come across a cobra, the natural inclination would be to run away or even to kill it. So why would the Buddha compare the dharma to something people would instinctively avoid? For what possible purpose would someone *need* a snake and then set out to find and catch one?

In fifth century BCE India, one of the few people who might have been interested in capturing a poisonous snake would have been a doctor. We know that cobra venom was used in traditional Ayurvedic medicine, specifically as an ingredient in the treatment of arthritis. Recent clinical experiments on arthritic rats have confirmed that small doses of venom might indeed be an effective remedy.[2] We also know that the Buddha frequently compared himself to a physician and the dharma to a course of medical treatment. With Sunakkhatta, we saw that Gotama likened reactivity to a poisoned arrow that had pierced a person's body, and presented the "probe" of mindfulness and the "knife" of understanding as effective ways to extract the "arrow" of reactivity and the "poison" of ignorance so that the man, provided he took good care of the wound, could resume a healthy life. The account indicates that Gotama possessed a knowledge of contemporary medical practice that we would not normally associate with a wandering "monk" intent on founding a "religion."

Whether or not snake venom was actually used in Gotama's time to treat arthritis, it would be fitting for a disease that results in joint pain, swelling, stiffness, and limited movement to be thought of as a metaphor for reactivity, which is likewise painful and causes swelling and stiffening: it "swells" one's sense of self, "stiffens" habitual views and behaviors, and inhibits momentum toward and along the eightfold path. Just as there is something "arthritic" about cleaving fiercely to one's "place," so there is a creative, mobile quality about seeing and awakening to one's "ground."

This way of thinking about the parable leads to the possibility that the dharma contains within it a "toxin" of some kind that has to be skillfully extracted and then applied in tiny, measured doses to cure the "sickness" of reactivity. If speaking about the dharma of conditioned arising is a way of talking about the vital sublimity of life, then a snake serves as one of its preeminent symbols. The practitioner would thus be like a man who is quick and adept enough to seize a cobra by the back of its neck, encourage it to inject its venom into a container, then prepare the venom for use in medical treatment. But if the snake symbolizes "life" in all its glory and danger, what does its "venom" stand for?

As in the case of Mahānāma, it is entirely feasible for someone to be overwhelmed by sensual desire while still being inclined toward nirvana. Tempting as it may be to try, we cannot neatly divide human experience into one part that is "good" and another part that is "bad." Human beings are far more complex and ambiguous than such a crude division allows. A perennial question asked of Buddhist teachers is "How is wanting to become enlightened different from wanting anything else? Surely it, too, is just another kind of greed?" Typically, the teacher elaborates on the subtle distinctions between different modalities of desire in Buddhism and concludes that some of these, such as aspiration (*chanda*), are perfectly acceptable, whereas others, such as craving (*taṇhā*), are to be avoided at all costs. Exactly how to make this distinction in practice, however, is far from clear.

No matter what you call them, all forms of desire are rooted in the wish to replace an unsatisfactory state of affairs with an improvement. The improvement can be anything from longer orgasms to the end of suffering. At one extreme are the most trivial and petty desires, and at the other, the most noble and selfless desires. Whether your desire is brute lust or spiritual aspiration, it remains desire.

Śāntideva, in his *Guide to the Bodhisattva's Way of Life,* declares that vanquishing afflictions (Sanskrit: *kleśa;* Pali: *kilesa*) such as greed and hatred will be his "sole obsession," that he bears a "strong grudge" against them and will "meet them in battle." Then he realizes that he might be contradicting himself: he seems to have endorsed resorting to certain afflictions (obsession, aggressive confrontation, grudge bearing) as a means to overcome others. But "afflictions such as these," he reflects, "destroy afflictions and are not to be relinquished."[3]

I admire Śāntideva's honesty in acknowledging the presence of paradox, struggle, and conflict at the heart of dharma practice. Logically, it might appear contradictory to "crave the end of craving" or "hate the hatred inside me," but in practice this is what we find ourselves doing once we embark on such a path. We may disguise what we are doing with various semantic tricks—by saying "aspire to" rather than "crave," or "renounce" rather than "hate"—but Śāntideva admits the blunt truth: that as conflicted humans we cannot help but engage self-interested wants and aversions in order to overcome self-interested wants and aversions. The parable of the snake is making much the same point. The "venom" that the Buddha extracts from the "cobra" has to be just the right homeopathic dose of want, aversion, and self-interest to motivate a person to undertake the fourfold task. Too small a dose would risk leaving the patient listless and complacent; too large a dose might inflate the patient's ego and prevent the patient from experiencing "the good for the sake of which (the patient) learned the dharma."

"Want, aversion, and self-interest" is a paraphrase of the more usual "greed, hatred, and confusion," which the Buddha calls the "three fires" but which later became more widely known as the "three poisons." While poison is clearly a property of snakes, what possible connection might there be between snakes and fire?

According to my reconstruction of the chronology of events in chapter 3, Gotama spent the first Rains after the awakening with his former companions in Uruvelā. During this time he taught his first two discourses: *The Four Tasks* and *On Not-Self.* Once the monsoon was over, he and his ragtag band of followers set off in the direction of the city of Gayā, probably along the bank of the Nerañjarā River.

Somewhere on this route they encounter three matted-haired ascetics, all of whom are fire worshippers called "Kassapa." Gotama asks one of them whether he can spend the night in the fire room. The ascetic tries to dissuade him by saying that a poisonous snake lives there. The Buddha is undeterred. He enters the room, lays out a grass mat, sits cross-legged, and enters into mindful contemplation. When the snake notices him, it becomes angry and exhales smoke. In return, Gotama exhales smoke. The duel escalates until the snake, the Buddha, and the room are all ablaze with flames. The next morning the Buddha shows his host the snake, which is now peacefully curled up in his begging bowl. "Here, Kassapa," he says, "is your serpent. His heat was mastered by my heat."[4]

In addition to scoring propaganda points by showing the Buddha trouncing the local gurus at their own game, this strange episode highlights the control the Buddha was able to exercise over fire, which in this instance is clearly an internal, symbolic heat. Whereas the snake's heat is associated with the flaring up of instinctive anger, the Buddha's heat seems to arise from his mastery over the workings of his own psyche. We might have expected him to deal with the snake by not reacting at all, by remaining in meditative equanimity—nirvana, after all, is often thought of as the extinguishing of the three fires. But here he responds to the snake in kind and overwhelms it with his superior power. The principle is homeopathic: treating like with like.

The problem with the three fires of greed, hatred, and confusion does not lie in their being hot but in the havoc they cause when they get out of control. The tiniest spark can ignite one of these fires: an unkind remark, a depressing thought, an erotic image. Before we realize it, our minds and bodies are burning with revenge, self-pity, or lust. The parable of the snake might suggest that these fires are not to be extinguished but regulated. Since emotions appear to be rooted deep in our limbic system as the legacy of biological evolution, regulation might be all that is possible and feasible. Rather than suffer fires that erupt and engulf us, we might learn how to adjust our inner airflow to enable them to become like the steady blue flame of a Bunsen burner. In this way, perhaps, we could discover how to burn like miniature suns.

Having converted the three Kassapas and a "thousand" (a great number) of their matted-haired, fire-worshipping followers to the dharma, Gotama made his way to Gayā Head, a steep hill near Gayā, a city a few miles downstream from Uruvelā. And it is here that he delivers his third discourse: *On Fire*. Just as he reimagined the sun, the object of sun worship, as a symbol for nirvana, here he reimagines fire, the object of fire worship, as a symbol for reactivity. Rather than treating fire as an object of devotion, a medium of sacrifice, or a vehicle for performing miracles, he turns it into a metaphor for greed, hatred, and confusion. He thus represents a cultural shift away from externalized rites to internalized contemplation, away from ritual objects to mental symbols. "*Everything*," Gotama tells his audience of fire worshippers, "is burning." One's entire sensorium is on fire: eyes, ears, nose, tongue, body, and mind as well as the sights, sounds, smells, tastes, sensations, and ideas by coming into contact with which, consciousness is generated. "Burning with what?" he asks. "I say the world is burning with the fire of greed, the fire of hatred, the fire of confusion, it is burning because of birth, aging, dying, grief, sorrow, suffering, lamentation, and despair."[5]

To realize how life flares up, blazes, and overheats in this way is the first step in a process of mindful disengagement, which leads to non-reactivity, which in turn leads to the awareness that "I am freed."[6] Understood in the framework of the fourfold task, nirvanic freedom is not the goal of the eightfold path but its beginning. Detaching oneself from the burning world is not an end in itself, but it affords the possibility of letting those flames die down of their own accord so that one can respond to the world from the solar perspective of nirvana, unconditioned by the reactivity and pain that are consuming it.

Just as the controlling of fire is a skill mastered by potters and welders, and the extraction and administering of snake venom is an acquired accomplishment for a physician, the training of a student on the path requires instructional abilities in a teacher. In all cases the forces of Māra, the archetypal trickster, are liable to subvert whatever one sets out to achieve. It is no accident that we find Māra depicted as a cobra. A discourse reports that "on a gloomy night drizzling with rain" the Buddha was sitting in the Bamboo Grove at Rājagaha:

> Then Māra manifested himself in the form of a giant king serpent and approached the Teacher, . . . its tongue darting

> out from its mouth, like flashes of lightning; the sound of its breath, like the noise of a smith's bellows filling the air.[7]

Such imagery exposes the menacing, destructive side of the natural world, its ability to terrify us, to wipe us out at any moment. The sheer contingency of the world may constitute the ground of life to which Gotama awoke, but this ground can also be unsettling, untrustworthy, and unpredictable. But the Buddha remains equanimous and "stirs not a hair" before this terrifying apparition. [8]

Rather than fight like with like, here he responds by not reacting at all.

(3)

On one occasion, the wanderer "Topknot" Sīvaka asks the Buddha what he thinks of those wanderers and brahmins who regard everything we experience—pleasant, painful, or neither—as the result of actions committed in the past. Gotama replies:

> Some experiences are caused by bile, some by phlegm, some by wind, some by all three together. Some experiences are caused by the change of seasons, some by poor care, some by sudden assault, and some are the fruit of one's actions.[9]

Not only does this answer contradict the widely accepted Buddhist view that all feelings (*vedanā*) are the "ripening effects" of past actions; it provides further confirmation that Gotama was familiar with the principles of the regional medical tradition.[10] Illness was regarded as a consequence of disturbance in the three "bodily humors" (*dosa*) of phlegm, bile, and wind. In this passage he recognizes that one's previous actions are only one factor among many that contribute to one's well-being or suffering at a given time.

This commonsense approach likewise challenges another central dogma of Buddhism: that all suffering originates in craving. The

Buddha's pragmatism appears to be based on close observation of how human beings live and feel, not on metaphysical beliefs such as the all-explaining theory of karma. Anyone who makes such sweeping claims as "everything is caused by previous actions" surpasses both what can be known by themselves and what is accepted as true in the world.[11] Here, as elsewhere, the Buddha's analysis of the human condition is closer to that of a physician who seeks to understand the exact causes of a specific malady than to that of an "enlightened" sage who makes generalized truth-claims about human nature.

Where might Gotama have acquired detailed knowledge of the medical traditions and practices of his day? And why did he model his approach to teaching the dharma on the way a doctor treats a patient? Although the canon abounds in medical imagery, it is silent on these points. But we do know that one of the Buddha's friends and adherents was the royal physician of Rājagaha, a man called Jīvaka, one of the twenty-one householders who are praised for "having found fulfillment in the *tathāgata,* having become seers of the deathless, and going about having beheld the deathless."[12]

Jīvaka is said to have been an illegitimate son of King Bimbisāra ("a man who was always longing after other women") with the wife of a merchant from Rājagaha. Ashamed of the affair, the mother placed the newly born infant in a winnowing basket and instructed a slave woman to discard it on a pile of refuse. On seeing crows hovering over the basket, Prince Abhaya, an illegitimate son of King Bimbisāra by the Vesālī courtesan Ambapālī, inquired what was inside. Some townsfolk had a look and announced, "It's alive (*jīvati*)!" which gave the baby its name, "Jīvaka." Abhaya—the child's half-brother, though he may not have known it—placed the little boy in the care of foster mothers. As the two boys grew older, they realized that they needed to learn a trade in order to prosper. Abhaya chose to become a carriage maker. Jīvaka set off to study medicine with a renowned physician called Atraya who was teaching at the university in Taxilā.[13]

Given that this story is recounted in the Vinaya—the section of the canon that broadly deals with monastic training, it is perhaps surprising to learn that Jīvaka did not consider becoming a mendicant. His half-brother Abhaya was a follower of the Jain teacher the Nigaṇṭha Nātaputta (Mahāvīra) and may have brought him up in that tradition. Whatever the case, the story of Jīvaka is an account of someone who exemplifies Buddhist virtues but did not join, or apparently want to join, the community of mendicants.

At the Buddha's time, Taxilā was the capital of Gandhāra, in the Indus River valley. Today, the ruins of Taxilā are in Pakistan, twenty-two miles northwest of Rawalpindi. To travel there from Rājagaha, an arduous journey westward of some eight hundred miles along "wilderness roads with little water and little food," would have taken Jīvaka two to three months.[14] On arriving, he would have entered the household of his teacher at the university, from whom he would have received both theoretical and practical instruction. Although tuition was free, as a poor student, he probably had to work in some menial capacity for his board and lodging. It is said that he was a gifted student who learned quickly, thought deeply about the subject matter, and did not forget what he studied. After seven years, his teacher told him to take a spade and walk all around the city of Taxilā to a radius of ten miles and bring back to him any plant that had no medicinal value. On his return, Jīvaka announced that he could not find a single thing without any medical use. "Then you are well trained, good Jīvaka," declared his teacher.[15]

During his seven years in Taxilā, Jīvaka would have been exposed to a bustling cosmopolitan culture. While Rājagaha may have been emerging as an important center of power in northeast India, citizens of Taxilā would have regarded the Magadhan capital (had they heard of it at all) as a distant, provincial town far removed from the civilized world. In the university itself, he would have encountered students from elsewhere in the subcontinent and beyond, engaged in mastering subjects as diverse as military science, archery, elephant training, law, philosophy, and sorcery. His studies in medicine would have included herbalism, diagnostics, and surgery. To be educated at Taxilā meant more than acquiring expertise in a specific subject. It would have provided a young man from the provinces with a far richer culture than he could possibly have acquired had he stayed at home.

In 518 BCE, almost forty years before Gotama was born, the Persian emperor Darius I invaded Gandharā and incorporated it as a satrapy (province) of the Achaemenid empire, the most extensive political entity the world had known up until then. Connected by an extensive system of roads and an efficient postal service, Achaemenid territory extended from Thrace (a region straddling present-day Greece, Turkey, and Bulgaria) and Egypt in the west to Armenia and Georgia in the north, Arabia in the south, and Bactria (Afghanistan) and Gandhāra in the east. Its population has been estimated at around fifty million, approximately 44 percent of the world's inhabitants. Although its ceremonial capital was Persepolis, during the probable time of Jīvaka's stay at Taxilā, Darius's grandson Artaxerxes I ruled the empire from Babylon.

Physicians were in much demand at the Persian court. Yet they would have been regarded very differently from how we see practitioners of medicine today. "The specialized profession of 'physician,'" writes Thomas McEvilley, "had not yet separated itself out from the larger profession of shaman or 'medicine man,' which included functions of magic, mythmaking, protophilosophy, and song or poetry, along with healing."[16] Although there are no extant records of Indian physicians at the Persian court, we know that the Greek Democedes spent two years as the personal physician to Darius I, and another Greek, a certain Apollonides of Kos, became physician to Artaxerxes I, the ruler during Jīvaka's stay at Taxilā.

The physicians were as much philosophers, sages, and miracle workers as "doctors." That philosophy was a way of healing the soul and that the philosopher was a physician were ideas the ancient Greeks took for granted. The philosopher Empedocles, a contemporary of Gotama's renowned today for developing the idea of the four classical elements, said that some approached him "seeking prophecies, while others, for many a day stabbed by grievous pains, beg[ged] to hear the word that heals all manner of illness." He followed Pythagoras in believing in reincarnation and maintained that the soul, in its last incarnation, is born as "a prophet, a poet, a physician or a prince."[17]

Jīvaka could conceivably have encountered the Greek philosopher Democritus (c. 460–c. 370 BCE), a native of Abdera in Thrace. According to the third century CE biographer Diogenes Laertius, Democritus set out for Egypt "to see the priests there, and to learn mathematics from them; and proceeded further to the Chaldeans [in modern Iraq], penetrated into Persia, and went as far as the Persian Gulf. Some also say that he made acquaintance with the 'naked sages' in India."[18] If Democritus did reach India, Taxilā would probably have been his first port of call.

In the account of Jīvaka's return journey from Taxilā to Rājagaha, he cures a merchant's wife of a head ailment in Sāketa (modern Ayodhya), in return for which he is offered the huge sum of sixteen thousand *kahāpanas* (for comparison: the courtesan Ambapālī charged fifty *kahāpanas* a night for her services), a male and a female slave, and a horse-drawn chariot. When he arrives in Rājagaha, Jīvaka offers these earnings to Abhaya out of gratitude for his having raised him. But Abhaya refuses and tells him to build a house for himself in the palace grounds instead.[19] It seems likely that this house would have come to serve as a clinic and perhaps a small hospital.

Jīvaka is summoned to treat King Bimbisāra (whom he may or may not have known was his father) for an embarrassing anal fistula, which had led to an in-house joke among the ladies that he had started menstruating. Having cured the king of Magadha of the fistula, he is appointed physician to the royal court and instructed to minister to "the order of mendicants with the Buddha at its head."[20] Since Bimbisāra is likely to have sponsored teachers from different schools, the doctor was probably charged with offering his services more widely than just to the Buddhists. As was the custom with rulers elsewhere at the time, Bimbisāra appears to have valued Jīvaka but to have regarded him as an indentured retainer, someone who would do his bidding and who was forbidden to leave Rājagaha without permission. When we read of his going elsewhere, it is always on Bimbisāra's orders. On one occasion he is sent by the king to Benares to cure the son of a wealthy merchant of a twisted bowel (for which he performs surgery), and on another he is sent west to the neighboring land of Avantī to treat its ruler, King Pajjota, for jaundice.[21]

The first time we hear of the Buddha receiving medical treatment from Jīvaka is when he is suffering from "a disturbance of the bodily humors." It is impossible to know precisely what this means, since all illness was understood to result from disturbances of the humors. Jīvaka tells Ānanda to rub the Buddha's body with fat for several days. He instructs Gotama to inhale a medical infusion of lotuses as a purgative, to follow that by a hot bath, and to drink juices until he is fully recovered. After the treatment is successful, Jīvaka requests the Buddha to allow his mendicants permission to wear the good-quality cloth offered by householders instead of rags, to which Gotama agrees.[22]

The Pali Vinaya tells of a time in Magadha when so many people were suffering from leprosy, boils, eczema, tuberculosis, and epilepsy that Jīvaka was too busy to receive them and had to turn them away from his clinic. Some of these desperate people decided to be ordained as mendicants in order to receive treatment from him. Once they were cured, though, they gave back their vows and returned to their families. When Jīvaka realized what was going on, he was furious and criticized them publicly for their behavior (whether because they had deceived him or because they had abused the privileged position of a mendicant is unclear). In any case, he told the Buddha that he should no longer allow a person afflicted with one of these diseases to be accepted into the community of mendicants. Gotama agreed.[23] On another occasion, this time in Vesālī, Jīvaka observed that the mendicants were eating too much rich food, and told the Buddha that this was bad for their health.

He suggested providing them with a "place for pacing up and down and a room for a steam bath." Again Gotama agreed.[24]

In all these instances, Jīvaka does not hesitate to place demands on the Buddha, who accepts them without demur. Jīvaka carries an authority, which may have accrued to him purely on account of his medical skills but may have been augmented by the prestige of his having studied and lived at Taxilā. A widely traveled self-made man, he could have been the most learned, cultivated, and cosmopolitan figure in Rājagaha.

These passages present Jīvaka as someone who does not defer to Gotama in the way an ordinary adherent would. He offers medical treatment to him and his mendicants because he has been ordered to do so by the king, not necessarily out of devotion as a practitioner of the dharma. It is possible that he formally embraced Buddhism relatively late in the Buddha's life. Gotama seems to have regarded Jīvaka as an equal and perhaps admired him as a model of the kind of person who embodied the virtues of an adherent. He describes him in one short discourse as the foremost among his adherents "who was loved by the people," as G. P. Malalasekara puts it, or "in displaying confidence in persons," as Bhikkhu Bodhi prefers to translate *puggalappasannāna*.[25] Jīvaka may have naturally radiated warmth, care, and trust toward others, which led to their affection.

(4)

When Gotama was seventy-two years old, a crisis erupted in Rājagaha. In conspiracy with Bimbisāra's son Ajātasattu, Gotama's cousin Devadatta proposed that he himself be placed in charge of the community of mendicants so that Gotama could retire and spend the rest of his days in quiet retreat. Gotama rejected this offer out of hand, dismissing Devadatta as a "lick-spittle" and reminding him that he had no intention of placing anyone in charge of the order after his death. In addition, the Buddha had Sāriputta denounce Devadatta in public, declaring that he no longer be considered worthy of respect. This eventually led to a schism in the community, with Devadatta breaking away with his followers to establish a more ascetic, vegetarian community at Gayā Head, where forty years earlier Gotama had preached the discourse *On Fire*. Prince Ajātasattu, meanwhile, succeeded in forcing his father to abdicate, whom he then imprisoned and starved to death.

News of Gotama's condemnation of Devadatta soon found its way to the Buddha's principal rival, the Nigaṇṭha Nātaputta (Mahāvīra). The discourse *To Prince Abhaya* recounts how Jīvaka's half-brother Abhaya, who by now was a man in his sixties or seventies, "went to the Nigaṇṭha Nātaputta, who said to him: 'Come, prince, refute the wanderer Gotama's teaching, and people will speak highly of you.'" Nātaputta sees this as an excellent opportunity to damage further the reputation of Gotama. He tells Abhaya to ask Gotama whether he (Gotama) would ever utter speech that would harm others. If Gotama answers yes, say to him: "Then what difference is there between you and an ordinary person?" And if he answers no, say to him: "Then why did you say that Devadatta is incorrigible and going to hell? For these words have made Devadatta angry and upset." Nātaputta believed that "were Gotama posed this two-horned question, then, like an iron spike stuck in a man's throat, he will be unable either to gulp it down or throw it up."[26]

Abhaya invites the Buddha to his home for a meal. After they have eaten, he poses Nātaputta's question: "Would you ever say anything that would be unwelcome and disagreeable to others?" Gotama replies: "There is no simple answer to that question, prince." "In that case," remarks Abhaya, "the Nigaṇṭhas have lost in this."[27]

This (admittedly polemical) Buddhist discourse reveals Nātaputta as still dependent on the duality of "it is" and "it is not," on yes and no, whereas the Buddha "avoids these dead-ends and teaches the dharma by the middle."[28] Gotama recognizes that language can easily trick one into expecting a simple answer for any question, whereas life can be far more ambiguous and complicated than the law of the excluded middle allows.

Throughout their discussion, Abhaya is cradling a baby on his lap. The Buddha asks him what he would do if the baby put a stick or stone into its mouth. The prince says that he would "take the child's head in my left hand, crook a finger of my right hand, and remove the object even if it meant drawing blood, because I have compassion for the child." Gotama explains that his words to Devadatta were spoken because he, too, was moved by his compassion for others. He lists all the variables that had to be taken into account before he uttered what he said to his cousin. As with the example of the baby, he also had to act in a way that was swift, timely, and appropriate to the situation at hand. In his case, he had to say something that would be beneficial but also disagreeable.

Abhaya inquires whether the Buddha has a preformulated response for when someone poses a question, or whether he answers spontaneously. In reply, Gotama asks the prince how he responds when someone asks the name of an obscure part of a chariot. "As an accomplished chariot maker," says the prince, "I am familiar with all the parts of a chariot. So the answer would occur to me on the spot." In the same way, continues Gotama, when people come to me with a question, "the answer also occurs to me on the spot." The reason, he explains, is because he has "penetrated into 'what goes on in people's minds' (*dhammadhātu*)." His understanding of human beings is as thorough as Abhaya's knowledge of chariots; people and their motives have become transparent to him. He responds immediately and intuitively, surprising, perhaps, even himself.

Impressed by the way Gotama dealt with Nātaputta's challenge, Abhaya declares: "You have made the dharma clear in many ways. Henceforth, please consider me an adherent who has gone for refuge for life."[29] In other words, the prince renounces his faith in Jainism and converts to Buddhism.

It may have been around this time that Jīvaka also chooses to become a committed follower of the Buddha. The eponymous discourse *To Jīvaka* tells that Gotama was staying at the doctor's Mango Grove, which lay outside the city of Rājagaha on the road to Vulture's Peak. Possibly this grove served as a place for convalescence, in which case the Buddha might have been there for reasons of injury or ill health. In any case, Jīvaka comes to see Gotama and tells him that people are saying that animals are being killed for the Buddha and he eats their meat in full knowledge of its provenance.[30] This is exactly the sort of rumor that supporters of Devadatta would have spread through Rājagaha to discredit the Buddha. If Jīvaka had been raised, like Abhaya, to follow Nātaputta, who taught that one should not harm even the tiniest insect, it could have been personally troubling for him to learn of the accusation against Gotama.

The Buddha replies that he is being misrepresented by these people. He then explains that meat may be eaten only in three instances: "when it is not seen, not heard and not suspected" that the animal has been slaughtered for one's sake.[31] This is his standard position, repeated throughout the canon, on the topic of eating meat. It is what he had said to Devadatta in reply to his cousin's proposal that the community of mendicants be vegetarian.

Many modern readers find this stance disingenuous. How, they ask, can someone whose teaching is founded on the principles of conditionality and harmlessness fail to understand that animals are killed for food because a market exists for their meat? Becoming a vegetarian diminishes the market's demand for meat and thereby spares the lives of fish, birds, and animals who otherwise would have ended up in the kitchen. The cause and effect in this case is obvious, so why does Gotama—whose awakening is supposedly based on his insights into the workings of causality—not pay heed to it? To say that you must never eat the meat of an animal that you suspect was killed for you personally, but can eat as much of its meat as you want so long as the animal was killed for sale on the open market, is a self-serving morality, which gives no guidance at all as to how a society should address the issue of violence against animals.

This could well have been the sort of well-reasoned argument that Devadatta himself employed in persuading his followers to become vegetarian. It would be in keeping with his idea that moral rules are formulated in the abstract and then applied across the board. The Buddha's approach to ethics was entirely different; today we would call it "situational." This is an ethics that starts by recognizing the complexity and uniqueness of every moral situation and recognizing, too, that no Torah-like book of rules is capable of providing a definitive, a priori solution. In facing a moral dilemma, one does not ask "What is the right thing to do?" as though the answer to the question already exists in an ideal metaphysical space, but rather "What is the most wise and loving thing to do in this specific instance?" For that question, no answer in the abstract is even conceivable.

When the Buddha founded his community of mendicants, there were no rules whatsoever. Only if mendicants committed specific deeds that led to specific consequences was a rule devised to prohibit such behavior. But toward the end of his life, Gotama told Ānanda that after his death the community could "discard the minor rules."[32] All this suggests that the rules he formulated were responses to the particular social and historical context in which he lived. So when Jīvaka insisted that the mendicants be allowed to accept good-quality cloth, the Buddha instituted a rule—presumably on grounds of health. He also recognized that as times and situations changed, rules may become anachronistic or redundant and therefore no longer applicable.

That a situational ethics focuses on specific, unrepeatable dilemmas does not mean that it lacks guiding values. Having explained his position on eating meat to Jīvaka, Gotama identifies the core principles that underpin an ethical life. "Here, Jīvaka, a mendicant lives in dependence upon a certain village or town. He lives pervading the world with a mind imbued with loving kindness, compassion, sympathetic joy and equanimity."[33] That is to say, irrespective of the community in which you live, with its unique mix of persons caught up in their highly specific dramas, you seek to maintain a radiant, generous, open-hearted equanimity in your interactions. Whatever you find yourself saying and doing in those circumstances is not primarily determined by a list of rules or laws but by your concern and care for the particular people with whom you are engaged.

In the case of eating meat, a situational approach would first take into consideration as many factors involved as possible: the use of the land on which the animals are raised, how the animal is treated, the degree of pain involved in its death, the extent to which animal protein is necessary for one's health, the views and practices of one's religion or culture, one's moral concerns about taking life, and so on. The stance the Buddha took on this issue was, I suspect, informed by a comparable evaluation of the many conflicting needs and perceptions that were current. To accept Gotama's view on the matter as being the official "Buddhist" position on eating meat, valid for all time, would be to contradict precisely what was distinctive in his approach to ethics. Likewise, to insist, with Devadatta, that all Buddhists should be vegetarians would endorse the sort of dogmatism from which the Buddha encouraged his followers to break free.

To Jīvaka concludes with the same pericope that appears at the end of the discourse *To Prince Abhaya*. Jīvaka praises the Buddha's words and says: "Henceforth, please consider me an adherent who has gone for refuge for life."

(5)

According to the Pali commentaries, Abhaya was so shocked by Prince Ajātasattu's murder of King Bimbisāra by starvation that he renounced the household life to join Gotama's order of mendicants. By inflicting a slow and agonizing death on Bimbisāra, Ajātasattu killed the father of his half-brothers Abhaya and Jīvaka. We have no idea how close these illegitimate sons were to their father, but since Abhaya was titled "prince," it is likely that he was accepted within the royal household. After entering the community, Abhaya became a stream entrant on hearing the Buddha deliver the parable of the blind turtle, which illustrates that to be born as a human being is as unlikely as it is for a blind turtle rising to the surface of the ocean once in a hundred years to put its neck through a golden yoke tossing about on the waves.[34] Jīvaka, meanwhile, continued as physician to the court—as an indentured retainer he may have had little choice—and as personal doctor to the new king, who was both his half-brother and his father's murderer.

Abhaya and Jīvaka were not the only ones to be troubled by the death of Bimbisāra. The *Sāmaññaphala Sutta* describes an occasion after this tragic event when King Ajātasattu was relaxing on the roof of his palace with his ministers and advisors on a full-moon night. Yet the king was troubled by what he had done and asks whether anyone could recommend a wanderer or brahmin they could visit who could "bring peace to my heart."[35]

The ministers suggest that he could go and see any one of a number of saintly figures, such as the revered Nigaṇṭha Nātaputta, currently residing in Rājagaha. But Ajātasattu is unmoved and does not respond. Then he turns to his half-brother, who is seated beside him, and says: "You, friend Jīvaka, why are you silent?" The doctor proposes that the king pay a visit to the wanderer Gotama, who happens to be staying in Jīvaka's mango grove with a large contingent of mendicants. The implication seems to be that the king's guilt and anguish are such that they are beyond the reach of conventional medical treatment and require the skills of a physician of the human soul.

Thereupon the king and his entourage proceeded by elephant to the doctor's mango grove. But when they approached the grove, "the king felt fear and terror, and his hair stood on end. And feeling this fear, he said to Jīvaka: 'Friend Jīvaka, you are not tricking me? Are you not handing me over to an enemy? How is it that from this great number of mendicants not a sneeze, a cough, or a shout is to be heard?'" Jīvaka reassures Ajātasattu that he is perfectly safe. They then dismount and head toward a round pavilion in which lamps can be seen to be burning. The king looks anxiously inside the building and whispers to Jīvaka: "Where is the Teacher?" Jīvaka explains that the Teacher is the one sitting against the middle column with the mendicants in front of him.

Unless this passage is intended for dramatic effect, it would appear that Ajātasattu has neither seen Gotama before nor is able to pick him out from among the assembled mendicants. He walks over to the Buddha and stands beside him. Surveying the mendicants seated in silence, he remarks: "If only Prince Udāyabhadda were possessed of such calm." "Your thoughts go out to the one you love?" asks Gotama. "Yes," says the king. "Prince Udāyabhadda is very dear to me. But if only he could be as quiet as your mendicants."[36]

Is this curious exchange a way of illustrating the king's own nervous and unquiet state of mind? Or does it capture the awkward interaction between two men at their first meeting, who would have known of but would have been unlikely have trusted each other? At this point, in response to a formulaic question from the king about the benefits of leading a wanderer's life, we read a lengthy, polemical digression, at the conclusion of which Ajātasattu praises the Buddha's discourse and declares, in exactly the same words that Abhaya and Jīvaka used: "Henceforth, please consider me an adherent who has gone for refuge for life." Once this formal bond of trust is established, the king summons up the courage to admit what is tormenting him. "Transgression overcame me," he says. "Foolish, erring and wicked as I was, for the sake of the throne I deprived my father, that good man and just king, of his life. May the Teacher accept my confession of this evil deed that I may restrain myself in the future!"[37]

Although Buddhist tradition considers patricide a deed—along with murdering one's mother, killing an arahant, drawing the blood of a *tathāgata,* and causing a schism in the community—whose result is immediate and inexpiable (*ānantarikakamma*), Gotama says to Ajātasattu: "Since you have acknowledged your transgression and confessed it as is right, we will accept it. For he who acknowledges his transgression as such and confesses it for betterment in the future will grow in the noble discipline."[38] While this statement might give the impression that the king's sins have been forgiven, it does no such thing. The Buddha is a doctor of the soul, not a priest who dispenses absolution. There is nothing he can do about the inevitable consequences that will unfold from what the king has done. All he can do is affirm that public acknowledgment of the act may ease Ajātasattu's psychological trauma and that in due time he may find himself in a fit state of mind to proceed on the eightfold path.

These subtleties seem to have been lost on Ajātasattu. Presumably under the impression that he has been absolved of his crime, "rejoicing and delighting at these words," the king "rose from his seat, saluted the Teacher, and departed with his right side towards him." Once he was gone, Gotama turned to his mendicants and declared: "The king is done for, his fate is sealed." Had he not been so tormented with the guilt and remorse of having killed his father, "The pure and spotless dharma eye would have arisen in him as he sat here" listening to the discourse.[39]

Gotama and Ajātasattu are not recorded as ever seeing each other again. Jīvaka, too, now vanishes from the narrative of the Buddha's life. Even the commentaries, whose authors generally like to tie up such loose ends, tell us nothing of what became of him after this meeting.

(6)

The Pali Vinaya recounts a moving story about how Gotama and his attendant Ānanda visited a community of mendicants, one of whom was suffering from dysentery but lay uncared for in a pool of his own excrement. When the Buddha asked why no one was tending him, the man replied that because of his illness he was of no use to the community. Gotama instructs Ānanda to go and fetch some water so that they can bathe him. Once they cleaned him, they laid him on a couch and went to find the other mendicants. The Buddha berated them for ignoring their sick brethren, then said:

> Bhikkhus, you have not a father, you have not a mother, who might tend you. If you do not tend to each other, then who is there who will tend to you? Whoever would tend to me, he should tend to the sick.[40]

This remarkable passage shows us three things: Gotama takes it upon himself to offer nursing care to a sick mendicant who has been rejected by his community, identifies himself with those who are sick, and declares that those who care for him, that is, what he embodies, should care for the sick. This passage goes much further than simply *comparing* the Buddha to a physician and his dharma to a course of medical treatment, which has become a Buddhist commonplace. Here we find Gotama non-metaphorically getting his hands dirty by caring for a sick person. It raises the possibility that Gotama actively encouraged his followers to serve as doctors and nurses, that his early community was not concerned solely with spiritual well-being but also with attending to the very real sufferings caused by birth, illness, aging, and death. That mendicants were regarded as physicians is reinforced by a passage in the Mūlasarvāstavāda Vinaya, which tells how King Pasenadi "several times mistook doctors for Buddhist mendicants on account of their similar costumes."[41]

The episode likewise offers another perspective on the first of the four tasks. To comprehend suffering means to embrace concretely the condition of those who are unwell by regarding them in the same way as one would regard the Buddha. The helpless newborn, the person tormented by disease, the elderly man who can no longer take care of himself, the terminally ill woman aware that her life is drawing to an end—these people reveal the dharma to us as effectively as the Buddha himself. In the presence of such suffering, there is no room to ponder the meaning of the term *dukkha* or to speculate about what its end might be. We are challenged to respond to the immediacy of the situation in a way that is not determined by our habitual reactivity. There is no correct "Buddhist" way of speaking or behaving in such cases. We are called upon to say or do something without hesitation—just as Gotama and Ānanda immediately attended to the sick mendicant's needs.

That more and more people encounter the dharma today through their firsthand experience of the effectiveness of mindfulness in treating a medical condition points to the centrality of this kind of care and healing in Gotama's dharma. Such people are not drawn to this practice because of an interest in Buddhist philosophy or doctrines. The idea of becoming a Buddhist might be the last thing on their minds. They have found a meditative strategy that works in coming to terms with specific physical or mental ailments. Yet rather than dismissing their experience as the result of a secularized practice of mindfulness from which the rich philosophical and ethical context of Buddhism has been removed, I would prefer to think that they have experienced the living heart of the dharma, around which, over the centuries, numerous layers of religiosity, morals, and belief have been superimposed.

The only other canonical text to mention Jīvaka is a sutta in the *Numerical Discourses,* where the doctor is included (together with Mahānāma) in the list of twenty-one realized householders and adherents:

> Possessing six qualities, the householder Jīvaka has found fulfillment in the *tathāgata,* has become a seer of the deathless, and goes about having beheld the deathless. What six? Lucid confidence in the buddha, lucid confidence in the dharma, lucid confidence in the sangha, noble virtue, noble understanding, and noble liberation.[42]

This passage affirms unambiguously that Jīvaka and these other householders were leading fulfilled lives grounded in the deepest insights of the dharma. The addition of "noble understanding" and "noble liberation" to the standard definition of stream entry suggests that fulfillment like this entails more than adopting the commitments and ethics of the eightfold path. In utilizing the language of the fourfold task, the passage shows that the householder sees the "deathless" (the third task) and, further, by living a life rooted in and inspired by that experience, is also fully engaged in the cultivation of the eightfold path (the fourth task). Such an existence, infused with understanding and freedom, leads to what the text describes as "fulfillment in the *tathāgata*."

If I am correct in assuming that Jīvaka became a formal adherent in the wake of Devadatta's rebellion, when Gotama was seventy-two years old, then he would have reached fulfillment during the final eight years of the Buddha's life. This chronology implies that his fulfillment, grounded in awareness of the deathless, was achieved in the context of his daily work as a physician attending to the suffering of his patients. In following the Buddha's injunction that those who would tend to him "should tend to the sick," Jīvaka serves as an example of someone who has experienced nirvana, but rather than turning his back on the world, embraces it fully.

9

The Everyday Sublime

Good snowflakes. They don't fall anywhere else.
—LAYMAN PANG (740–808)

(1)

Meditation originates and culminates in the everyday sublime. I have little interest in achieving states of sustained concentration in which the sensory richness of experience is replaced by pure introspective rapture. I have no interest in reciting mantras, visualizing Buddhas or mandalas, gaining out-of-body experiences, reading other people's thoughts, practicing lucid dreaming, or channeling psychic energies through chakras, let alone letting my consciousness be absorbed in the transcendent perfection of the Unconditioned. Meditation is about embracing what is happening to this organism as it touches its environment in this moment. I do not reject the experience of the mystical. I reject only the view that the mystical is concealed behind what is merely apparent, that it is anything other than what is occurring in time and space right now. The mystical does not transcend the world but saturates it. "The mystical is not how the world is," noted Ludwig Wittgenstein in 1921, "but that it is."[1]

As understood by Edmund Burke and the Romantic poets, the

sublime exceeds our capacity for representation. The world is excessive: every blade of grass, every ray of sun, every falling leaf is excessive. None of these things can be adequately captured in concepts, images, or words. They overreach us, spilling beyond the boundaries of thought. Their sublimity brings the thinking, calculating mind to a stop, leaving one speechless, overwhelmed with either wonder or terror. Yet for we human animals who delight and revel in our place, who crave security, certainty, and consolation, the sublime is banished and forgotten. As a result, life is rendered opaque and flat. Each day is reduced to the repetition of familiar actions and events, which are blandly comforting but devoid of an intensity we both yearn for and fear.

To experience the everyday sublime requires that we dismantle the perceptual conditioning that insists on seeing ourselves and the world as essentially comfortable, permanent, solid, and "mine." It means to embrace suffering and conflict rather than to shy away from them, to cultivate the embodied attention that contemplates the tragic, changing, empty, and impersonal dimensions of life, rather than succumbing to fantasies of self-glorification or self-loathing. This takes time. It is a lifelong practice.

The everyday sublime is our ordinary life experienced from the perspective of the fourfold task. As we have seen, this entails (1) an openhearted embrace of the totality of one's existential situation, (2) a letting go of the habitual reactive patterns of thought and behavior triggered by that situation, (3) a conscious valorization of those moments in which such reactive patterns have stilled, and (4) a commitment to a way of life that emerges from such stillness and responds empathetically, ethically, and creatively to the situation at hand.

Understood in this way, meditation is not about gaining proficiency in technical procedures claimed to guarantee attainments that correspond to the dogmas of a particular religious orthodoxy. Nor is its goal to achieve a privileged, transcendent insight into the ultimate nature of reality, mind, or God. In the light of the fourfold task, meditation is the ongoing cultivation of a sensibility, a way of attending to every aspect of experience within a framework of ethical values and goals.

Over the course of history monks and yogins in Buddhist cultures have developed spiritual technologies to a high degree, resulting in levels of mental refinement, control, and absorption that may seem incredible to modern Westerners. Yet from a dharmic perspective the value of these attainments lies not in their being humanly possible but in their contribution to the practice of the fourfold task. It is not hard to imagine being highly accomplished in certain meditative techniques, yet still failing to embrace wholeheartedly the condition of *dukkha* that pervades the life of oneself and others, still failing to let go of self-centered reactions to *dukkha,* still failing to behold the stopping of such reactivity, and still failing to cultivate a radically different way of being in this world.

As a sensibility, meditation enables us to cultivate an understanding of moment-to-moment experience much as we develop an appreciation of art or poetry or nature. Grounded in the body and the senses, we value an open-mindedness to what is unfamiliar, probe our sensorium with relentless curiosity, listen attentively to what others have to say, are willing to suspend habitual attitudes and opinions, and question what is going on instead of simply taking things for granted. The disengagement of meditation is not an aloof regard (or disregard) but a perspective that engenders another kind of response to what is happening. And it begins with the breath, our primordial relationship to the fabric of the world in which we are embedded.

(2)

In Gotama's time, it was impossible to wander through the countryside of north India during the three months of monsoon because the rivers flooded and the paths and roads became muddy torrents. The Buddha and his followers would settle in a park or grove, dedicating themselves to discussion and contemplation. Inevitably, people became curious as to what this man did during these retreats. "Why," they may have asked, "did this person known as the 'Awakened One' have to practice meditation at all?" Here is the answer Gotama told his followers to give such people: "During the Rains' residence, friend, the Teacher generally dwells in concentration through mindfulness of breathing. . . . [For] if one could say of anything: 'this is a noble dwelling, this is a sacred dwelling, this is a *tathāgata*'s dwelling,' it is of concentration through mindfulness of breathing that one could truly say this."[2]

This passage shows that awareness grounded in the breath is the foundation of all the contemplative tasks taught by Gotama and his followers. At its core, meditation is an existential "dwelling" within the primary rhythms of the body that link one seamlessly to the biosphere. As a discipline, it involves constant vigilance against getting "eaten up" by the rush of thoughts in one's head and to instead keep returning to the felt embodiment of experience that is so easily forgotten. By calling it a "noble dwelling" Gotama suggests that it is more than just a psychological skill in controlling one's thoughts. It encourages a moral stance of dignity. Settling into the rhythm of breathing leads to a balanced and upright physical posture as well as a dignified and sensitized relation to others and the world.

By calling it not just a "noble dwelling" but a "sacred dwelling" (*brahmavihāra*), Gotama employs a term commonly used to refer to a god (Brahma) in a non-theistic context. Here, "sacred" denotes, not a supramundane deity, but the everyday sublime that is revealed when the mind becomes still and focused through settling into the rhythm of breathing. The sacred is not found in a transcendent realm beyond oneself or the world; it is disclosed here and now once the mind relaxes, quietens, and becomes clearer and sharper as attention stabilizes on the breath. The "sacred" dimension of experience opens up as one lets go of the constrictive, obsessive concern with "me" and "mine," thereby allowing a return to a world that transcends one's petty interests and reflects one's ultimate concerns. Such a world is excessive; it is not manageable. It pours forth relentlessly, voluptuously, but is gone by the time one reaches out to seize and control it.

In considering mindfulness of breathing as a sacred dwelling, Gotama places it in the company of the better-known "sacred dwellings" of loving-kindness, compassion, sympathetic joy, and equanimity, four qualities of mind that are celebrated throughout the canon. Since focusing on the breath grounds one in the very rhythm of life, it allows one to feel the same rhythm that animates other sentient creatures and realize an empathetic rapport with all that breathes. Such openhearted equanimity provides the foundation for wishing all others to be well (loving-kindness), wishing them not to suffer (compassion), and rejoicing in their good fortune (sympathetic joy). Wishing all others—a potentially infinite number of creatures—to be well and not suffer means that these wishes likewise partake of the thought-exceeding dimension of sublimity. They are not calculated desires whose fulfillment is judged in terms of achieving a satisfactory result; rather, they are the yearnings of a sensibility that cannot hold itself back any more than the sun can restrain itself from radiating light and heat.

To practice such meditative dwelling, you need to find a quiet place, such as a woodland or an empty chapel, sit down with a straight back beneath a tree or on a pew, and turn your attention to what it feels like to be breathing in and out. You should let the breath arise and be released without any conscious interference. You will learn to anchor your attention in its natural rhythm, without drifting off into trains of thought or succumbing to drowsiness.

Yet as soon as you become conscious of your breathing, the breath tends to feel forced and deliberate. You start to think of it as "mine" rather than an impersonal process. Instead of the body just breathing in and out unprompted, which it does as long as you are *not* attending to it, you assume control of the process. Now you have to relax your attention but without losing your heightened awareness of the breath. Pretend that you are waiting, as a disinterested observer, to catch the body in the act of inhaling and exhaling of its own accord. Then suddenly, perhaps with a shock, you will notice the breath just happening.

When asked by Mahā Koṭṭhita about "freedom of mind through emptiness," Sāriputta replied: "When one has gone to the forest or to the root of a tree or an empty hut, one reflects: 'All this is empty of a self or what belongs to a self.' This is the freedom of mind through emptiness."[3] One retreats to the wilderness in order to dwell in a region that is free from human ownership and control. In the absence of anyone else to impress or flatter, one is able to recover a natural dignity based on one's awed participation in and indebtedness to life itself. The natural world thus becomes a metaphor for emptiness, a sublime revelation of what is not self, an abode of freedom and ease.

Like birds and deer, a meditator who dwells in such emptiness does not intend to breathe in any particular way. The discourses do not prescribe a right or approved way of breathing. If your breath is shallow and unsteady, then it is shallow and unsteady. You just let the body be the body, let the breathing happen, while remaining fully aware. As you settle into this practice, not only does your mind gradually become more focused and calm, but you notice how the experience of breathing is not limited to the nostrils, windpipe, lungs, and diaphragm. The breath rises and falls as a tidal rhythm throughout the entire body. "I shall breathe in experiencing the whole body; I shall breathe out experiencing the whole body. I shall breathe in and out calming the body's inclination (to breathe)."[4]

Gotama compares a meditator who dwells on the breath to a skilled woodturner, who understands the effect of the slightest movement the hands and fingers will have on the wood being worked on the lathe. This analogy illustrates how mindfulness is not just about stepping back and passively noticing what is passing before the inner eye. It involves an exploratory and potentially transformative relationship with the pulsing, sensitive, and conscious "material" of life itself. Such embodied attention heightens mindful awareness, intensifies curiosity about and investigation of what is unfolding, stimulates an energetic application to the task, induces a sense of delight in what one is doing, and leads to tranquillity, concentration, and equanimity.[5]

Nor is such meditation confined to what you do in a formal seated posture. "When walking, one understands: 'I am walking'; when standing, one understands: 'I am standing'; when lying down, one understands: 'I am lying down.'" The practice extends to everything you do. To associate mindfulness primarily with sitting on a cushion for a prescribed length of time is to limit its effectiveness. The aim is to integrate mindful attention into the totality of your conscious life. This is clear from the following passage, which is repeated throughout the canon (I have secularized the terminology):

> They are ones who act with full awareness when leaving and returning, when looking ahead and looking back, when flexing and extending their limbs, when wearing their clothes and carrying their bags, when eating, drinking, consuming, and tasting, when shitting and pissing, when walking, standing, sitting, falling asleep, waking up, talking, and keeping silent.[6]

Such meditation is also not restricted to awareness of your own body but includes awareness of others' bodies, too. You attend to their poignant physical presence, the way they inhabit and move their bodies, the way their bodies interact with yours, the way their eyes and mouths signal emotion, pleasure, pain, fear, longing, love, hate, the way their hand squeezes yours, the way you press against each other as you embrace.

Those who practice embodied meditation do not shy away from imaginatively peeling off the skin and considering what lies inside the body, either. They scan the body "up from the soles of the feet and down from the top of the head," recollecting "the head-hairs, body-hairs, nails, teeth, skin, flesh, sinews, bones, bone-marrow, kidneys, heart, liver, diaphragm, spleen, lungs, intestines, stomach contents, feces, bile, phlegm, pus, blood, sweat, fat, tears, grease, spittle, snot, oil of the joints, and urine." In Gotama's day, wanderers would meditate in charnel grounds, observing corpses as they became "bloated, livid and oozing matter," as they were torn apart and devoured by crows, jackals, and worms. "This body too," they would reflect, "is of the same nature, it will be like that, it is not exempt from that fate."[7] To be mindful of the body involves honesty and the courage to go beyond the revulsion one may feel about its constituent parts and the terror invoked by anticipation of its death and disintegration.

(3)

Gotama's teaching originates in opening one's heart and mind unconditionally to the everyday sublime. One starts with what is most close and intimate: the body itself. Then one turns this attention to the hedonic tonality of one's experience, the entire spectrum of how one feels in a given situation at a given moment. These feelings, too, are initially registered in the flesh: an uneasiness in the stomach, a warmth and openness in the chest, a constriction in the throat, a stirring in the genitals. At this point the affective dimension of meditation comes into play. While mindfulness entails a degree of detachment and equanimity, it is not a cold, disinterested state of mind. To know fully the shades and nuances of feelings, one needs first to quieten the inner turmoil so often provoked by them in order to establish a clear, penetrating attention.

Cultivating an awareness of feelings is crucial because many habitual reactive patterns are triggered as much by these subjective bodily affects as by the objects or persons we believe to be responsible for them. I might react with fear to another person's threat of violence, but that instinctive reaction is prompted by the way I feel about what has been said, which is registered somewhere in my body. Mindfulness allows us to open up a gap between the person's angry words and my feelings about them, which usually appear so intertwined that they are hard to disentangle. In cultivating this gap, one learns how to dwell calmly and vividly in its empty space, which is the "clearly visible, immediate, inviting" space of nirvana itself.

Buddhist tradition presents the cultivation of mindfulness along a spectrum that starts with attention to one's breath and extends to a comprehensive awareness of whatever is occurring in one's body, mind, and environment. In the discourse *The Grounding of Mindfulness,* this practice culminates in the fourfold task itself. It would be a mistake, however, to think that one should meditate on this task in the same way as one would pay attention to the breath or the body. Here, *sati* should be understood in its more literal meaning of "recollection" instead of its broader meaning of "mindfulness." This means that the practice of mindfulness includes *recollecting* the core vision of the dharma as a way of further refining one's awareness of experience as a whole.

"What is the power of mindfulness?" asks Gotama in another discourse. "Here a disciple is mindful; he is equipped with the keenest mindfulness and awareness; he recollects well and keeps in mind *what has been said and done in the past*" (my italics).[8] To be mindful of the breath, for example, means you recollect an instruction heard in the past—whether ten minutes or ten years ago—and then apply it by sustaining your attention on the breath. If your attention wanders,you have forgotten what you were supposed to be doing and need to remind yourself again. This kind of awareness is not dissimilar to the kind you have of being married, which, though largely unconscious, will prompt a recollection of your marriage vows as soon as your thoughts stray to doing something in conflict with them. This "recollective" aspect is obscured as soon as mindfulness is understood as simply being fully attentive in the present moment or remaining in a state of nonjudgmental awareness, neither of which would seem to have much to do with remembering something said or done in the past.

To ground mindfulness in the fourfold task means to keep these ideas in mind and apply them to illuminate whatever is taking place in our experience at a given time and place. In this way, the fourfold task serves as a framing device that provides meditation with its raison d'être. When *The Grounding of Mindfulness* describes mindfulness as the "direct path to nirvana," it affirms that paying embodied attention to life leads to a falling away of habitual patterns, which leads to nirvanic moments when we realize the freedom to respond to life unconditioned by our longings and fears, which opens up the possibility of living sanely in this world. Nirvana is reached by paying close, uncompromising attention to our fluctuating, anguished bodies and minds and the physical, social, and cultural environments in which we are embedded.

(4)

The Noble Quest describes conditioned arising and nirvana, the two grounds of the dharma that constituted Gotama's awakening, as being "difficult to see" (*dudaso*) and "difficult to awaken to" (*duranubodho*).[9] There are at least three ways in which something could be "difficult" to see: as a topic that is intellectually hard to grasp, as a scene that is painful or upsetting to observe, and as an object that is obscured or hidden from view. Since Gotama describes his awakening as a radical shift in perspective from a "place" to a "ground," the experience was more than just arriving at the solution to an intellectually challenging problem. It is true that Buddhist orthodoxies often present "conditioned arising" and "nirvana" as subtle and difficult concepts to grasp, yet their definitions in the Pali discourses are not that hard to understand. "Conditioned arising" boils down to the underlying principle of contingency, whereas "nirvana" is simply the ending (for shorter or longer durations) of reactivity. Any difficulty we might have in seeing or awakening to them is not primarily conceptual but existential.

That the difficulty is existential is suggested by the prefix *du* (difficult) that precedes both—*daso* ("see") and *anubodho* ("awaken"). This *du* is the same as the prefix found in another key term: *dukkha*. So *dudaso* might be translated as "painful to see," and *duranubodho* as "painful to awaken to." Conditioned arising and nirvana are not difficult to see and awaken to because they are tricky to grasp with the intellect. They are difficult to see and awaken to because they confront us with a groundless ground that can be overwhelming and terrifying. Conditioned arising entails that life is endlessly fluid, contingent, and unpredictable; nirvana implies that in the absence of our default reactions we find ourselves facing moral dilemmas that require us to risk a response that might make things worse.

By contrast, to "love, delight, and revel" in one's place seems a more attractive option. We persuade ourselves that all is well, that we are secure in our certainties and conceits, that nothing can threaten us. Illusory as this stance may be, it offers at least a degree of comfort. It can be deeply disturbing to acknowledge that every "place" (a house, a job, a marriage, a self) that we cling to is entirely contingent on a delicate balancing act of conditions and could vanish as soon as any one of those conditions fails. Equally disturbing is to confront the bewildering number of possible ways to think, act, and respond to the circumstances of our existence. How much easier it is to rely on a familiar set of fixed reactive patterns. When the "dharma eye" opens, if only for a moment, what is revealed might seem almost unbearable in its complexity, its tragedy, and the moral demands it imposes upon a frail creature.

The third sense of being "difficult to see"—because an object is obscured or hidden from view—is also the case here. Clinging to the perspective of one's place obscures and hides one's contingent and nirvanic ground. But once one abandons this stance, even for a moment, then conditioned arising and nirvana are no longer so difficult to see.

In chapter 3 we saw how Gotama dealt with Sīvaka's question about the meaning of "clearly visible" by having his interlocuter acknowledge how he recognized when the three fires were flaring up within him and when they were not.[10] In the maieutic style of a Socratic dialogue, Gotama drew out the answer to Sīvaka's question by having him probe into his own firsthand experience. The dharma was accessible to Sīvaka as soon as he recognized the presence or absence of reactivity within his own mind. In the discourse, the figure of Sīvaka stands for the puzzled everyman; he is no different from you and me.

As soon as we start considering meditation from an ethical and existential perspective, we realize the inadequacy of thinking of it as primarily a cognitive process directed toward realizing the "truth." We recognize how untenable it is to think of awakening as just an enhanced kind of knowing. That mindfulness includes a cognitive dimension, however, is quite clear: meditators systematically focus their attention on features of experience that are habitually overlooked or denied, thus cultivating a cognition of impermanence, for example, rather than persisting in a longing for permanence. Yet in coming to know intimately the impermanent, tragic, and empty aspects of life, one opens oneself to unsuspected affective and aesthetic possibilities of experience as well.

In addition to paying refined attention to the spectrum of feelings and mental states that arise "inside" (*ajjhatta*) oneself, meditators pay attention to feelings and mental states that occur "outside" (*bahiddhā*) themselves as well, as *The Grounding of Mindfulness* states. The cultivation of mindfulness extends beyond the boundaries of one's own skin to the feelings and mental states of other people and other living organisms. The development of awareness in the context of the fourfold task thus entails a fundamental realignment of one's sensitivity to the feelings, needs, longings, and fears of others. Rather than being a supersensory capacity to "read" other people's minds, mindfulness means empathizing with the condition and plight of others as revealed through an enhanced "reading" of their bodies, which comes from the stilling and brightening of one's own awareness through meditative discipline. Making mindfulness other-centered disrupts the innate tendencies of egoism and thus contributes to the second task: letting go of self-interested reactivity.

(5)

The Sŏn (Chan/Zen) school of Buddhism has a long tradition of valuing aesthetic experience and the arts, including architecture, sculpture, poetry, calligraphy, pottery, painting, martial arts, and gardening, as integral parts of dharma practice. By contrast, the Indian-based schools of Southeast and Central Asia have tended to be suspicious of art, treating it as a distraction from realizing the contemplative states of mind required for enlightenment and liberation. They consider the production of art to be largely a responsibility of the laity and limit its use to devotional and religious purposes. As a result, artistic practice is generally discouraged in their monastic communities.

At first glance, this difference would seem to be due to the cultural values of East Asia that influenced the understanding and practice of Buddhism after it was introduced from India. When Buddhism came to China around the first century CE, it encountered a culture with strong artistic and literary traditions and a keen appreciation of the beauty of the natural world. As the dharma assumed indigenous Chinese forms, it inevitably adopted many of the cultural traits of its new host, including its aesthetic sensibility. Yet, we might ask, does the source of this disparity lie in cultural differences alone? Could it reflect a difference in the underlying orientation to the practice of the dharma? While Sŏn Buddhism emphasizes the centrality of doubt (*ŭisim*) in the practice, the Indian-based traditions tend to stress the importance of belief. Might there be a connection between doubt and encouragement of the imagination, on the one hand, and belief and suspicion of the imagination, on the other?

I was drawn to the practice of Sŏn for two reasons. The first was because of its positive emphasis on doubt, the second because of its valuing of the imagination. These two elements of the practice coalesce around the core idea of the *hwadu,* which is introduced by Kusan Sunim as follows:

> In all four postures of walking, standing, sitting, and lying, in speaking and being silent, in activity and stillness, the doubt-mass must appear clearly by itself. If the Doubt remains unalloyed and unobscured during all activity, the practice will ripen naturally. At that time, although we do

> not try to cut off mental fantasizing, it is naturally removed; and although we do not try to progress towards Bodhi (awakening), naturally we progress and reach it. From then on we can taste the rare flavor of the *hwadu*.[11]

The most widely practiced *hwadu* in modern Korea is the question "What is this?" (*Imoko*). *Hwadu* (Chinese: *huatou*) is a Chinese literary term that refers to the "gist" of a textual passage. In the context of Sŏn practice, the *hwadu* is understood as the "gist" of a *kungan* (Japanese: *kōan*). A *kungan* means a "public case." This juridical term refers to a past legal decision that serves as a precedent and guide in making subsequent judgments.

The "public case" of which "What is this?" is the *hwadu,* or "gist," concerns the encounter between two monks at the beginning of the eighth century in China. One of these was Huineng (638–713), the esteemed Sixth Patriarch of the Chan school, while the other was his less-known disciple Huairang (677–744). According to tradition, Huairang traveled by foot from Mount Song in north China to Nanhuasi, a monastery in the far south of the country, to receive instruction in meditation from Huineng. This is the record of their first exchange:

> HUINENG: Where have you come from?
> HUAIRANG: I've come from Mount Song.
> HUINENG: But what is this thing, and how did it get here?
> Huairang was speechless.

Huineng opens the exchange with a polite inquiry and then subverts it. Without warning, he shifts from conventional chitchat to an existential challenge, which undermines Huairang's complacency and leaves him exposed, vulnerable, and dumbstruck. The text continues with the terse comment "Huairang spent eight years in the monastery." At the end of this period, he returns to the Patriarch and announces that he has an answer:

> HUINENG: What is this?
> HUAIRANG: To say it is like something misses the point.[12]

The entire exchange boils down to the simple question "What is this?" As is clear from the dialogue, the question is not about Huairang's "place" but about his "ground." Huineng has little, if any, interest in learning facts or details about his interlocutor's *place* in the world: where he lives, where he has traveled from, where he is going. He directs his questioning to Huairang's *ground:* to the sheer contingency of the young monk's being there at all: "What is this thing, and how did it get here?"

Such questioning provides another perspective on the practice of the fourfold task. To embrace *dukkha* entails letting go of one's views about suffering in order to open oneself to the mystery of suffering. Since *dukkha* is shorthand for one's life in its totality, "What is this?" becomes an uncompromising inquiry into what is going on at any given moment. This kind of embodied attention entails the suspension of all views, including Buddhist views. In posing this question, it is irrelevant whether things are impermanent, suffering, not-self, or empty. One ponders the mystery that life is occurring at all. As Huairang's answer ("To say it is like something misses the point") suggests, any account of what is going on will be inadequate. The aim of the practice of the *hwadu* is not to arrive at a satisfactory solution to a problem but to achieve a sensibility from which one's response to the exigencies of life is not determined by the influence of fixed opinions.

The paradoxical teachings of Sŏn are very different from the logical and rational teachings of Indian Buddhism. The Pali tradition does not grant doubt anything like the same centrality and importance as it is given in Sŏn. The term "doubt" (*vicikicchā*) generally refers to one of the five hindrances (*nīvarana*). This doubt is something to be overcome and abandoned, not a quality to be assiduously cultivated. The closest one comes to a positive sense of doubt may be in the notion of the "investigation of dhamma" (*dhammavicaya*), one of the seven factors of awakening, which refers to the contemplative inquiry into whatever presents itself in one's phenomenal experience of life. The aim of such questioning is not to develop perplexity but to impel one to achieve unambiguous, affirmative insight into life's impermanent, tragic, and not-self nature.

The concept of doubt in the Tibetan Geluk tradition allows for a degree of ambiguity not found in the Pali Canon. Following Dharmakīrti, the textbooks of the Gelukpa distinguish between doubt that inclines to a correct conclusion (*don 'gyur the tshom*) and doubt that inclines to an incorrect conclusion (*don mi 'gyur the tshom*). Doubt can serve as the hinge on which the mind turns away from wrong views (*log lta*) toward belief (*yid dpyod*), which is seen as the necessary basis from which to reach valid cognition (*tsad ma;* Sanskrit: *pramāṇa*). To illustrate this point, Geluk lamas are fond of quoting a verse from Āryadeva's *Four Hundred* (*Catuḥśataka*): "Even when one of little merit becomes uncertain whether things are empty or not, this doubt undermines saṃsāra."[13]

While doubt may no longer be exclusively thought of as a hindrance, its value nonetheless resides in its ability to take you beyond the condition of vacillation toward one of belief and certainty. This doubt is treated at best with caution, as a phase that you have to go through as a benighted soul of little merit until you become convinced of the truth of Buddhist teaching.

The kind of doubt spoken of in Sŏn is existential rather than epistemological in nature. Such doubt is far from being part of an intellectual inquiry, even if that inquiry has as its goal a non-discursive state of awakening. It should be thought of as a psychosomatic condition of astonishment and bafflement rather than as a discursive mental process.

Perhaps the only passage in the Pali discourses to describe awakening as the resolution of existential questions comes when Gotama recalls how he was motivated as a young man by the questions "What is the delight of life? What is the tragedy of life? What is the emancipation of life?"[14] While the text goes on to say how Gotama regarded his awakening as the discovery of an authentic response to these fundamental questions, it says nothing at all about how he came to this response. Sŏn Buddhists, however, would recognize the emergence of these questions as the first stirrings of the "great doubt," and the questions themselves as Gotama's *hwadu*. By focusing his total psychosomatic attention upon them over a number of years, they finally triggered an awakening as he sat beneath the bodhi tree.

"Great doubt" is comparable to the shock that the Buddha-to-be is said to have experienced on encountering, for the first time, a sick person, an aging person, and a corpse, which prompted him to leave Kapilavatthu in search of enlightenment. Yet nowhere in the discourses does this famous account of the renunciation refer to Gotama himself. It occurs as part of a story told by the Buddha about a distant, legendary predecessor called Vipassī.[15] We should therefore treat it as a mythical rather than historical way of describing the existential process of waking up. Its power lies in the way it addresses the human condition as such, thereby offering a template for every human being to use in coming to terms with the great matter of birth and death.

The Indian Buddhist schools interpret this story as an account of how Gotama became disenchanted with a life that was "subject to birth, aging, sickness, death, sorrow, and defilement" and was motivated to achieve "the unaging, unailing, deathless, sorrowless, and undefiled supreme security from bondage, nirvana."[16] Although this language suits the prevailing asceticism of the Indian renunciant tradition by emphasizing that the sights of mortality led to an aversion to mortal existence, it fails to capture the existential shock that comes when the realization dawns that *I* will get sick, *I* will grow old, and *I* will die. In the myth, Gotama turns to his charioteer and asks him: "Is this what happens to everyone?" At that moment, we glimpse his initial reaction, which is not one of disgust but of bewilderment. His life ceased at that moment to be a collection of more or less interesting facts and became an urgent question for him. The question forced him to relinquish his attachment to his "place" and confront the sublimity of his "ground." And the fourth sight, that of a wanderer, gave him a clue as to how he might pursue such existential questions.

Since Chan was an indigenous Chinese response to Buddhism,

inflected by a Daoist sensibility, the Sŏn reading of the legend would also be in keeping with the tradition's move to achieve a critical distance from the world-denying and metaphysical concerns of Indian Buddhism in order to recover the primary questions that prompted Gotama to seek awakening in the first place. Alternatively, we could interpret this move as a more general revolt against dogmatism, with its insistence on cognitive certainty, and a return to the disquieting and uncanny experience of living in an ephemeral, finite, and highly contingent world that seems incapable of ever being pinned down by oppositional concepts like "it is" and "it is not."

(6)

This anti-dogmatic perspective of Sŏn echoes the deep suspicion of views and opinions that we find in the *Chapter of Eights*. The following verses capture the non-oppositional, non-dogmatic perspective of the sage (*muni*):

> He does not elaborate a view
> on the grounds of knowledge or morals—
> he neither claims to be equal
> nor thinks of himself as better or worse.
>
> He lets go of one position without taking another—
> he's not defined by what he knows.
> Nor does he join a dissenting faction—
> he assumes no view at all.
>
> He's not lured into the blind alleys
> of *it is* and *it is not, this world* and *the next*—
> for he lacks those commitments
> that make people ponder and seize hold of teachings.[17]

These verses do not point to a distant state of enlightenment that one might realize after years and lifetimes of gradual practice. They point to a possibility of being in this world here and now, freed from any entanglement in views and opinions. The "sage" is a metaphor for being optimally human: totally detached but totally alert to whatever is occurring. One "who takes no issue with things"

> sees what's before his eyes, is open to what is said,
> acts in tune with what he senses.[18]

In both the poetic style of the verses and the message they convey, Sŏn Buddhists will recognize an ideal to which their tradition likewise aspires. The sage of the *Chapter of Eights* is reminiscent of the "true person of no rank" extolled by Linji Yixuan (d. 866). "Here in this lump of red flesh," says Linji to his audience, "there is a true person of no rank."

> "Constantly he goes in and out of the gates of your face. If there are any of you who don't know this for a fact, then look! Look!"
>
> A monk came forward and asked, "What is he like—the true person of no rank?"
>
> The master got down from his chair, seized hold of the monk, and said: "Speak! Speak!"
>
> The monk hesitated, whereupon the master let go of him, shoved him away, and said, "True person of no rank—what a dried-up piece of shit!"[19]

To have "no rank" means that the true person is no longer concerned about his or her "place" or standing in the world. This frees them to act spontaneously from their "ground" in ways that may be unconventional and shocking. In this case, Linji urges his followers to "look," to behold, the nirvanic freedom within them. The monk who hesitates to respond from this ground—out of his reactive worry about what the right thing to say is or what others might think of him—is dismissed as a dried-up turd or "toilet stick" (depending on how you interpret the Chinese).

It would be hard to find a better metaphor for aridity (*khila*) than Linji's expression "a dried-up piece of shit." When the *Chapter of Eights* says "there is nothing arid about the sage," in the light of Sŏn we can understand this as showing that the sage responds spontaneously to life from the perspective of his ground rather than the hesitant standpoint of his place.[20] While there is no specific term in the *Chapter of Eights* that is equivalent to "doubt" in Sŏn, the text's repeated use of the polarity "it is" and "it is not" (*bhava vibhava* and *bhavābhava*) points to the sage's commitment to not taking a stand, which is comparable to the not-knowing of Sŏn.

The flip side of the *hwadu* "What is this?" is "I don't know." Such not-knowing is far removed from the dull, foggy confusion of ignorance. It is a vivid alertness that avoids being drawn into any position at all. As such, it hovers on the cusp between "it is" and "it is not," resisting the seductive lure of certainty. This is true of any genuine doubt. If I sincerely ask my wife, "Do you love me?" I am implicitly acknowledging that I do not know. Such doubt is difficult to sustain because human beings seem primed as language users to prefer an answer—even a negative one—to resting in the disquieting perplexity of not-knowing. In the *Chapter of Eights,* this preference for "it is" or "it is not" (yes or no) is precisely what the sage has overcome.

Despite the presence of the verb "is" in "What is this?," the question is not an ontological inquiry, which seeks to ascertain the essential "being" or "nature" of what is being examined. As Huairang remarked: "To say it is like something misses the point." Likewise, the Chan master Deshan Xuanjian (819–914) would ask his monks a question, then warn them: "If you speak, you get thirty blows. If you don't speak, you get thirty blows."[21] To ask such questions with embodied attention requires that one abandon any attempt to affirm or deny anything. Again this points to the excessive nature of life itself, to the way the everyday sublime outstrips our capacity for representation, whether in positive ("it is") or negative ("it is not") terms.

As we have seen, Gotama's discourse *To Kaccānagotta* presents complete vision (*sammā diṭṭhi*), the first step on the eightfold path, as a perspective on life that no longer relies on the duality of "it is" and "it is not."[22] As in Sŏn, the Buddha understands that the key to arriving at such a perspective is paying close attention to the flux of experience. The more clearly you understand how things endlessly rise and pass away, the more fully you come to realize that the fundamental categories of thought and language are incapable of pinning down the fluid, contingent, and tragic nature of life. The apophatic language of the discourse fails, however, to spell out in more positive terms what it would be like for a person with complete vision to experience the world once he or she no longer relies on this duality. Linji likewise affirms that such a person is "born from the realm that leans on nothing," but elaborates:

> If you want to be free to be born or die, to go or stay as one would put on or take off a garment, then you must understand right now that the person here listening to the dharma has no form, no characteristics, no root, no beginning, no place he abides, *yet he is vibrantly alive.*[23]

The absence of reactivity leads to a spontaneous vitality in which the world is revealed as questionable, mysterious, and radiant. It is the *hwadu* itself. Kusan Sunim describes the Sŏn meditator as one who considers the *hwadu* "as his very life":

> When going, the *hwadu* goes; when coming, the *hwadu* comes; when eating, the *hwadu* eats; when sleeping, the *hwadu* sleeps. Even when shitting you must investigate earnestly, never letting the *hwadu* out of your mind, to the point where it seems that the *hwadu* is shitting.[24]

At this point, the *hwadu* ceases to be a purely subjective disposition of doubt, a question one poses in the privacy of one's mind. It embraces the totality of what is taking place at any given moment. The division between "meditator," "meditation" and "what is meditated upon" collapses. Instead, the totality of experience becomes the *hwadu*. As one rests in that vulnerable and centered space, life is revealed as profoundly unknowable and strange but uncannily familiar. Deshan puts it like this: "What is known as 'realizing the mystery' is nothing but breaking through to grab an ordinary person's life."[25]

Gotama concludes *To Kaccānagotta* with these words: "'Everything is' is the first dead end. 'Everything is not' is the second dead end. The *tathāgata* reveals the dharma from a center that avoids both dead ends."[26] This center (*majjhama*) is the "emptiness" of the Buddhist philosopher Nāgārjuna, who cites *To Kaccānagotta* as the source for his philosophy of the center (*Madhyamaka*).[27] A person who "dwells" in such emptiness leads a balanced life that is open to the ineffability of experience, and is constantly poised to respond to circumstances in ways not determined by any prior ideological or psycho-emotional convictions.

As scholars such as Luis Gómez have argued, there is a compelling link between the "proto-Madhyamaka" of the *Chapter of Eights* and the philosophy of Nāgārjuna and his followers.[28] Can we detect a further continuity with the stance of not-knowing and doubt as found in Sŏn Buddhist practice? Although the language of Sŏn differs considerably from that of its Indian precursors, the radical suspension of judgment found in the *Chapter of Eights, To Kaccānagotta,* and Nāgārjuna's philosophy could be thought of as the flip side of the intense Sŏn questioning found in the *hwadu* "What is this?"

By returning to the sources of Buddhist tradition, whether in the myth of Prince Siddhartha or proto-Madhyamaka philosophy, we recover a dimension of human experience that goes beyond anything specific to Buddhism. We touch on the core, imponderable questions that are the source of all contemplative traditions. The *Song of Creation* in the ancient Rig Veda declares:

> Who really knows? Who will proclaim it? Whence was
> it produced? Whence is the creation? The gods came

> afterwards, with the creation of this universe. Who then knows whence it has arisen?
> Whence this creation has arisen—perhaps it formed itself, or perhaps it did not—the one who looks down on it, in the highest heaven, only he knows—or perhaps he does not know.[29]

This passage acknowledges a shocking degree of uncertainty for a foundational text of Hinduism. Rather than providing a sound basis for theistic belief, as one might expect, it affirms the awed humility of one who can do nothing but open up to the extraordinary fact that there is anything at all rather than nothing.

The same sort of relentless questioning runs through the texts attributed to the Daoist sage Zhuangzi (369–286 BCE), for whom "a state in which 'this' and 'that' no longer find their opposites is called the hinge of the Way."[30] Here, too, the writer struggles, albeit playfully, with the same antinomies of language that engaged the author of the *Chapter of Eights* and Nāgārjuna. He famously illustrates his sense of puzzlement with the following example:

> Once Zhuang Zhou dreamt he was a butterfly, a butterfly flitting and fluttering around, happy with himself and doing as he pleased. He didn't know he was Zhuang Zhou. Suddenly, he woke up and there he was, solid and unmistakably Zhuang Zhou. But he didn't know if he was Zhuang Zhou who had dreamt he was a butterfly, or a butterfly dreaming he was Zhuang Zhou. Between Zhuang Zhou and a butterfly there must be *some* distinction! This is called the Transformation of Things.[31]

Since Sŏn Buddhism finds its origins both in India and in China, it represents a synthesis of two great traditions of philosophical skepticism in Asia. Still, we need to recognize that such questioning is not the preserve of Asian religions. It points to the intrinsic limits of thought and language whenever human beings are confronted with the puzzle of being here at all. All people, whether devoutly religious or avowedly secular, share this unknowing and perplexity.

Pyrrho of Elis, the ancient Greek founder of the Western tradition of skepticism, was born about forty years after the Buddha died. He also based his philosophy on uncertainty and doubt. According to the third century CE Greek biographer Diogenes Laertius, Pyrrho "seems to have practiced philosophy in a most noble way, introducing that form of it which consists in non-cognition and suspension of judgement."[32] Pyrrho accompanied Alexander the Great to India in the fourth century BCE and studied with "naked philosophers" there.

Here is a passage recorded by the early Christian historian and bishop Eusebius, who quotes a now-lost Greek text by Aristocles:

> According to [his disciple] Timon, Pyrrho declared that things are equally in-different, un-measurable and un-decidable. Therefore, neither our sensations nor our opinions tell us truths or falsehoods.
>
> Therefore, we should not put the slightest trust in them, but be without judgement, without preference, and unwavering, saying about each thing that it no more is than is not, or both is and is not, or neither is or is not.
>
> The result for those who adopt this attitude, says Timon, will first be speechlessness (*aphatos*), then untroubledness (*ataraxia*).[33]

For Pyrrho, like other thinkers in Greece and India at the time, philosophy was first and foremost a practice. It was only by applying such ideas in one's life that their value was realized. The aim was not intellectual knowledge but a radical transformation of one's entire outlook on oneself and the world.

By not trusting the evidence of either one's senses or reason, the Pyrrhonist skeptic refuses to take a stand on whether things "are" or "are not," much in the same way as we have seen in the *Chapter of*

Eights, Nāgārjuna's thinking, and Sŏn. This practice results in speechlessness, which may refer both to a recognition of the inadequacy of language and to a stunned sense of wonder at the sublime excess of life itself. And it culminates in the untroubledness of *ataraxia,* a state akin to nirvana, which was sought by Pyrrhonists and subsequently by Epicureans as well.

Ataraxia, however, is not mere passivity and resignation in the face of life's challenges. This point is illustrated by a story about the Greek painter Apelles, who was once trying to paint the foamy saliva of a horse. Apelles was so unsuccessful that, in a rage, he gave up and threw the sponge with which he was cleaning his brushes at the canvas, thus spontaneously producing the effect of the horse's foam. The skeptic philosopher Sextus Empiricus explains that Apelles was able to achieve this effect because he was abiding in the non-stance of *ataraxia.*[34]

(7)

Meditation is an integral part of a caring/care-full relationship to oneself and the world. As such, it forms a crucial dimension of each aspect of the fourfold task. It is involved in the cultivation of the eightfold path, which requires fully embracing the conditions of one's life, letting go of habitual reactivity, and beholding the ceasing of that reactivity. Such a meditative sensibility allows one to flourish by leading a life of ethical commitment, contemplative attention, philosophical reflection, and aesthetic appreciation.

A secular approach to Buddhism could unwittingly encourage the tendency to regard meditation as simply a method for solving problems. By instrumentalizing mindfulness, for example, one could end up rejecting any sense of sublimity, mystery, awe, or wonder from the practice. This tendency is reinforced when meditation is presented as a "science of the mind," when people are routinely wired up to fMRI scans to take detailed readings of brain function while meditating, and government-sponsored studies are conducted on volunteers over long periods in order to understand the "effectiveness" of meditation.

Treating meditation as a technique for solving the problem of human suffering, however, is nothing new. Buddhism itself has frequently lapsed into this way of thinking and, in some schools, uncritically endorses such an approach. Take, for example, the concluding section of *The Grounding of Mindfulness*. "Bhikkhus," declares Gotama, "if anyone should develop these four groundings of mindfulness in such a way for seven years, one of two fruits could be expected for him: either final knowledge here and now, or if there is a trace of clinging left, non-return" (non-return is the penultimate state prior to becoming an arahant). In other words, if you undertake this practice correctly, the final result is guaranteed. This is no different from a sales pitch for an effective diet: if you follow this regime for X amount of time, it is certain that you will lose X amount of weight. The hyperbole continues to mount: "Let alone seven years, bhikkhus, if anyone should develop these four groundings of mindfulness for six years, . . . five years, . . . four years, . . ." they can expect such fruits. And finally: "Let alone half a month, bhikkhus. If anyone were to develop these four foundations of mindfulness for seven days, one of two fruits could be expected for him."[35]

Even if we regard such passages as later additions designed to give Buddhism an edge in the competitive world of Indian religions, the rhetoric seems out of place in a foundational text of the canon. Human beings are treated as meditating machines, not as mysterious creatures who can only stammer the question "What is this?" in shocked response to the everyday sublime. In practice, however, we need to recognize that meditation includes a technical *as well as* a meta-technical dimension. It is forged out of the tension between both. There are meditation techniques that, having been learned and cultivated, lead to predictable results. If you train yourself in concentration exercises, for example, there is a good chance that you will become more focused and less distracted. Clinical studies of those who practice mindfulness have likewise suggested that a significant percentage of practitioners will experience specific effects as a result of their efforts. Yet there are also meta-technical virtues, such as wisdom, compassion, and imagination, that are indispensable for the practice of the fourfold task but that no amount of technical skill in meditation can guarantee.

Meditation is more usefully compared to the ongoing practice of an art than the development of a technical ability. Just as a painter or a musician needs to develop a certain range of technical skills in order to flourish as an accomplished artist, so a meditator needs to be adept at a number of technical skills to flourish as a practitioner of life. There will, in either case, be a spectrum of individuals ranging from those who are naturally gifted but technically incompetent to those who are technically competent but lacking in vision, spontaneity, and imagination. The aim of a fully realized practice of the dharma is to find a balance between the two.

The Sŏn tradition has its origins in a revolt against the institutional and doctrinal formalism that had come to characterize much of Indian Buddhism. It consistently maintains that external authority, scripture, and lofty ideas alone are incapable of conveying the living heartbeat of what Gotama taught. As Deshan says:

> Here there are no ancestors and no buddhas. Bodhidharma is a stinking foreigner. Shakyamuni is a dried-up piece of shit. "Awakening" and "nirvana" are posts to tether donkeys. The scriptural canon was written by devils; it's just paper for wiping infected skin boils. None of these things will save you.[36]

A similar revolt against established Buddhism was taking place in India around the same time (from around the eighth century CE). This involved the rejection of monasticism and a recognition that the practice of the dharma was entirely compatible with a life embedded in the everyday messiness of the world. The leaders of the revolt came to be known as the *mahāsiddhas* (great adepts). Like their contemporaries in

China, they lived unconventional lives and articulated their vision in poetry and song rather than densely argued prose.

A similar rupture with Buddhism's past may be under way today. As participants in this process, we will find it difficult to appreciate or even notice the broad historical currents of change as they unfold. A person committed in good faith to the preservation of a revered Asian form of Buddhism might well find that the tumult and pace of change threaten the very foundations of Buddhist tradition. The tide of secularization that has swept up mindfulness and turned it into a therapeutic technique is unlikely to subside. The tide need not be viewed as a threat. Rather, it is an extraordinary opportunity for the dharma to be reimagined from the ground up in such a way that it speaks more clearly and directly to the condition of men and women confronting the challenges of today's world.

An oft-heard complaint among traditional Buddhists is that the mindfulness movement is a "dumbing down" of the dharma. This elitist objection fails to recognize that Buddhism has been dumbing itself down ever since it began. It is doubtful that those who condemn the mindfulness movement on such grounds would likewise condemn the practice of millions of Buddhists that consists in repeating over and over again the name of the mythical Buddha Amitabha or the title of the *Lotus Sutra*. Mindfulness is becoming the *Om Mani Padme Hum* of secular Buddhism. Instead of mumbling a mantra while spinning a prayer wheel and once a week going to the monastery to light butter lamps, modern practitioners may sit on a cushion for twenty minutes a day observing their breathing and once a week attend a "sitting group" in a friend's living room. In both cases, those involved may have little understanding of Buddhist philosophy or doctrine but find these simple exercises rewarding in helping them live balanced and meaningful lives.

In retrospect, the widespread adoption of mindfulness in diverse areas of contemporary life may come to be seen as part of the longer historical process of Buddhism's adaptation to modernity. It could mark a key moment in the acceptance of contemplative disciplines in a secular context, when the public perception of meditation as an exotic, alien, and marginal practice is transformed and it is accepted as an unexceptional and mainstream activity. If this turns out to be the case, then rather than complain about the "dumbing down" of the dharma, Buddhists need to rise to the challenge of articulating a philosophically coherent and ethically integrated vision of life that is no longer tied to the religious dogmas and institutions of Asian Buddhism. In this way, perhaps, they might help encourage the dawning of a culture of awakening, which may or may not call itself "Buddhist."

10

Ānanda: The Attendant

Pasenadi: "What is this mendicant's name?"
Gotama: "His name is Ānanda, your majesty."
Pasenadi: "He is joyful (*ānanda*) indeed, and so he appears."
—Kaṇṇakatthala Sutta

Ānanda: "The Teacher's complexion is no longer pure and bright, his limbs are all flaccid and wrinkled, his body is stooped, and some alteration is seen in his faculties."
—Indriyasaṃyutta

All directions are obscure,
Nothing is clear to me anymore;
With our good friend departed,
It seems as if all is darkness.
—Ānanda, *Theragāthā*

(1)

The world that gradually emerges out of the mass of incidental detail contained in the discourses and the Vinaya turns out to be much like our own quirky, complex, conflicted, and uncertain world. It has little in common with the mythic worlds evoked by such great Indian epics as the *Mahābhārata* or grandiloquent Mahāyāna Buddhist works like the *Lotus Sutra*. Although gods and demons occasionally appear in the early canon, they function as a supporting cast or Greek chorus for the all-too-human protagonists. In the discourses King Pasenadi, for example, is one of the two most powerful rulers of the day. But he is a far cry from the heroic king of Indian epics. Pasenadi is an overweight and tragic man, internally conflicted, who struggles to cope with the challenges and threats to his power and ends up dying ignominiously in exile after gorging himself on turnip leaves. Rather than leading his army into mighty battles, he engages in inconclusive border skirmishes. Instead of ruling with pomp over an awed populace, he complains that his equerries do not respect him and that his ministers interrupt and ignore him. This sort of tawdry, fraught political reality is all too familiar from the media coverage of current affairs today.

For the first time in the history of Indian literature, the texts of early Buddhism opened a window onto an unapologetically human world. Take the twenty-one householders and adherents who are said to have found fulfillment in the *tathāgata,* to have become seers of the deathless, and to go about having beheld the deathless.[1] Out of these twenty-one, only four are mentioned with any frequency in the discourses—Anāthapiṇḍika, Citta, Mahānāma, and Jīvaka—while four do not appear anywhere in the canon apart from this passage. Of those about whom we have information, seven were from Kosala, four from the Vajjian Confederacy, and two each from Magadha, Anga, and Ukala (the last two countries are east of Magadha). In terms of their social positions, eight were merchants or financiers, four were chiefs or government officials, and one was a doctor. From this rare snapshot of a group of Gotama's principal lay followers, we can infer that his teaching attracted men from the emerging mercantile and ruling classes who were actively involved in establishing the new urban societies that were springing up in northeast India. For them, the dharma was an eminently practical way of life that sustained their demanding work in the world.

Did these men actually live and breathe and walk the earth? Although it would be rash on the basis of one obscure passage in the *Numerical Discourses* to state with certainty that they did, it is hard to imagine circumstances under which such a motley group would have been invented at a later date and then praised for their attainments in a nonstandard phrase that occurs only once in the canon. This difficult and discontinuous text about householders is another example of a passage that could lay a strong claim to describing events that occurred during Gotama's lifetime. That the twenty-one have been almost entirely forgotten by Buddhist tradition may be indicative of how the collective memory of the community began to be biased in favor of the notable mendicants of the Buddha's time—toward celebrating them while marginalizing the householders and adherents. The discourses give a clear and consistent impression that Gotama was primarily concerned with establishing a proto-monastic community of renunciants. But such an impression needs to be treated with caution precisely because it serves to legitimize the later monastic communities who happened to be responsible for memorizing and transmitting the discourses.

I focus on the lives of a chief (Mahānāma), a king (Pasenadi), a failed mendicant (Sunakkhatta), a doctor (Jīvaka), and, in this chapter, a mendicant derided as a "boy" (Ānanda) in order to counterbalance the traditional emphasis on the revered arahants who supposedly abounded in Gotama's time. The advantage of concentrating on such figures is that we are immediately exposed to ambitions and anxieties being played out in a complex, precarious world rather than confronted by the serene detachment of depersonalized saints. At the same time, we can catch fleeting images of the Buddha reflected in their dialogues with him. Tentative though the composite portrait might be, we are afforded an alternative view of the man: instead of the perfect arahant who never makes a wrong move, we encounter a person who does his best to realize his goals within the same imperfect world as his interlocuters.

Fortunately, we have two independent versions of the story of Gotama's life. One is based on texts scattered throughout the Pali Canon, the other on a Tibetan translation of a lost Sanskrit original belonging to the Vinaya of the Mūlasarvāstavāda school. Certain details differ in the two accounts, but the core narrative is identical, which strongly suggests that both draw on a common source, which is no longer extant. Since the dharma is known from epigraphic sources to have spread throughout the subcontinent during the reign of Emperor Aśoka in the third century BCE, it seems likely that Gotama's story was disseminated in different dialects to various parts of India and Sri Lanka by wandering groups of mendicants around this time, a hundred and fifty years after his death.

As an illustration of how the two versions differ, here are the passages that recount the death of Mahānāma. Both were discussed in chapter 2. The text in Pali, first written down in Sri Lanka, reads (in Burlingame's translation):

> Mahānāma thought to himself, "if I refuse to eat with [Viḍūḍabha], he will kill me. That being the case, it is better for me to die by my own hand." So taking down his hair, he knotted it at the end, thrust his great toes into his hair, and plunged into the water.[2]

The text that found its way into Tibet as a translation of a lost Sanskrit version in north India reads (in Rockhill's translation):

> Filled with anguish for his people, Mahānāma went down into the water of a pool. On the edge of the pool grew a sal tree, the branches of which fell into the water; they got entwined in his hair-knot, so that he was pulled under and drowned.[3]

The reasons for Mahānāma's death are explained differently in the two versions, but both agree that he drowned in a pool in a way that somehow involved his long hair, after being taken prisoner by Viḍūḍabha during the invasion of Sakiya. Although it is impossible to know exactly what happened, the two accounts confirm the same basic facts.

The agreement on such minor details as these, of which there are numerous other examples, in two textual traditions that had no contact with each other for hundreds of years and were separated by the entire length of the Indian subcontinent, is an indication that the underlying story may well be founded on historical events. True, the account may be a fabrication concocted for unknown reasons in the century and a half after Gotama's death. But I find it hard to imagine how the invention of such inconsequential details as the role of Mahānāma's hairknot in his suicide could have served to promote the interests of unknown persons in the early Buddhist community. Far more plausible, it seems to me, is to take the common elements of this story as surviving fragments of an oral tradition that goes back to the time of Gotama himself.

(2)

Ānanda was the younger son of Suddhodana's brother Amitodana, making him a first cousin of both Gotama and Mahānāma. His elder brother, Devadatta, was among the first group of Sakiyan nobles to join the order of mendicants but became, in Buddhist legend, the traitor and renegade who sought to usurp the Buddha's role. Since Ānanda is said to have been born in the same year as Gotama's son Rāhula, he would have been around thirty years younger than his cousin. If Devadatta was roughly the same age as Gotama, then Ānanda would have been born to a younger wife, possibly a woman from Videha, making him Devadatta's half-brother.[4] Ānanda is the only major figure in the canon who belongs to that younger generation. He probably entered the order when he reached twenty—the youngest permissible age. He was appointed as the Buddha's attendant five years later and remained in the post until Gotama died at the age of eighty, when Ānanda would have been fifty.

Since Amitodana is said to have tried to prevent the young Ānanda from having contact with the Buddha, going as far as taking him to Vesālī whenever Gotama stayed in Kapilavatthu, it seems that even as a child Ānanda was fascinated by his renowned cousin and his teaching. Gotama likewise seems to have regarded Ānanda as a gifted young man with great promise and may have encouraged him to become a mendicant. In the end, Amitodana relented and allowed his son to leave Kapilavatthu to join the Buddha's community.[5]

The person whose instructions led Ānanda to his first insight into the dharma was not Gotama but a mendicant called Puṇṇa Mantāniputta, who, according to Pali sources, was the nephew of Koṇḍañña, the leader of the five ascetics to whom the Buddha delivered his first teachings. In a text in the *Connected Discourses,* Ānanda recalls how Puṇṇa encouraged him with the following exhortation:

> It is by clinging, Ānanda, that "I am" occurs, not without clinging. And by clinging to what does "I am" occur? It is by clinging to forms, feelings, perceptions, inclinations, and consciousness that "I am" occurs, not without clinging. Suppose a vain young person would examine his face in a mirror or bowl filled with pure, clean water: he would look at it with clinging, not without clinging. Likewise, by clinging to form, feelings, perceptions, inclinations, and consciousness does "I am" occur, not without clinging.[6]

Since Ānanda would have been in his early twenties and is said to have been physically beautiful, Puṇṇa may have chosen this image of a vain young person to focus Ānanda's attention on his tendency toward narcissism. By encouraging his student to consider the physical and mental elements of his experience unsentimentally and impersonally, Puṇṇa enables him to see through his love of his own appearance and to reflect on what constitutes his sense of self. Having settled Ānanda's attention on the raw constituents of his experience, Puṇṇa asks a series of probing questions: "Are your form, feelings, and so on, permanent or impermanent?" "Is what is impermanent satisfying or unsatisfying?" "Is what is impermanent and unsatisfying fit to be regarded thus: 'this is mine, this I am, this is my self'?"

As a result of inquiring into his felt experience in this way, Ānanda concludes: "I made a breakthrough to the dharma."[7] By liberating him from a compulsive fascination with his own appearance, this insight led (according to the commentaries) to his becoming a stream entrant. Rather than seeing a reflection of himself in everything that he perceived in the world, he came to see things impersonally as they rise and fall, which allowed him to let go of his habitual reactivity and gain a direct experience of nirvana, which in turn opened up the possibility of his living in the world from a perspective no longer governed by reactivity.

Yet Ānanda's breakthrough did not inspire him to retire to the forest and devote himself to intense meditation in order to become a liberated saint. Rather, it led him to take on one of the most challenging roles in the community: personal attendant to Gotama.

During the first twenty years of his ministry, the Buddha was served by a number of attendants, including Sunakkhatta. None of them appears to have lasted very long in the post. Some of them did not obey his orders; others simply found the role too demanding and left. When Gotama reached his mid-fifties, he declared that he was not well, that he was feeling his age, that he was worn out from his duties as a teacher. He formally requested his mendicants to appoint someone to serve him who could be relied upon to attend to his needs. Those who initially volunteered were refused the position on account of their age. So Moggallāna and Sāriputta approached Ānanda to take on the job. "Just as it is difficult to approach a mighty sixty-year-old elephant in the forest," the young man replied, "strong, with great curved tusks and deep-set chest, reveling in the fight when he is ready for the fray, so it is difficult to serve the Teacher and attend to him."[8] Gotama may have complained of weariness and age, but Ānanda was under no illusions as to what would be involved in serving someone who still appeared to be full of vitality and urgency, and eager to engage with opposition and conflict to realize his goals.

Ānanda finally accepted the role on three conditions: (1) that he would not have to share the Buddha's food or clothing; (2) that he would not have to accompany him when he visited an adherent's house; and (3) that he would have free and complete access to him. Evidently, it was not only the heavy workload and responsibility that had led others to abandon this role but also the criticism and backbiting from those who envied the attendant's proximity to Gotama. By insisting on these conditions, Ānanda demonstrated that he was not interested in personal gain but was motivated by his devotion to the Buddha.

Remember that this is a young man in his mid-twenties, a mendicant of only five years' standing, taking on a key position in a movement that has been steadily growing in size and influence for the past twenty years. His "employer" is not only a man at the height of his powers but an intimate of kings, generals, and leading merchants. Gotama's acknowledgment of his failing health and increasing age suggests that he was aware that his time on earth was running out. He had reached a crucial juncture in his life and realized that he needed someone with managerial and interpersonal skills to establish his dharma and the community. Ānanda's job would have entailed far more than just "bringing him his water and toothpick, washing his feet and sweeping his cell," as G. P. Malalasekera quaintly describes it.[9] He would have been personal assistant, butler, chief of staff, secretary, minder, fixer, and masseur all rolled into one.

He may well have been chosen because of his youth. Ānanda represented the future, someone who could keep the torch of the dharma burning after Gotama and the other senior disciples had died. The Buddha could have seen him as an ally, a young, bright, and dynamic aide who could help combat the creeping conservatism of the old guard that might already have started to make itself felt. Yet since the Buddha intended the dharma alone—an impersonal body of ideas, values, and practices—to be his legacy, he would not have considered Ānanda his heir apparent. He would have seen him as an able administrator who could oversee the affairs of the community after his death and, more important, as the preserver of the teaching of the dharma, someone who had acquired an encyclopedic knowledge of his teaching as well as the ability to communicate it clearly and sensitively. Ānanda, who was renowned for both his prodigious memory and his pedagogical skills, would have fit this role perfectly.

Ānanda is known by all traditions for having recited from memory the entirety of the Buddha's discourses at the council convened in Rājagaha some months after Gotama's death. Yet Ānanda joined the order twenty years into Gotama's teaching career, so he could not have been present at every discourse he had memorized. The discourses themselves show us that memorization was practiced as a means of recording the dharma, both for one's own purposes and for the purpose of teaching others. Gotama sometimes asks a mendicant to recite a discourse to him to ascertain his credentials and his understanding; on other occasions, a mendicant recites a passage from memory and asks Gotama to explain its meaning. Ānanda's role, therefore, would have been to collate what others remembered, to memorize what he himself heard from the lips of Gotama and other senior mendicants, and to organize the material into some kind of coherent corpus. Exactly how this was done, and what form the canon reached during the Buddha's lifetime, we do not know. It seems likely, though, that Ānanda would not have undertaken the task by himself. He undoubtedly sought the collaboration of others, particularly Sāriputta, who was regarded as the community's foremost intellectual.

(3)

When Gotama was seventy-two and Ānanda was forty-two, the cohesion of the community was seriously threatened in Rājagaha. The person responsible was Ānanda's older brother, Devadatta. As the Judas

Iscariot figure in Buddhist legend, it is almost impossible to find an image of Devadatta in the canon as anything but a weak, conniving, self-serving villain. Yet during the thirty-seven years before he proposed the Buddha's retirement in his own favor, he seems to have been held in high regard. A passage in the *Udāna* includes Devadatta among eleven senior mendicants singled out by the Buddha as ones who "have expelled evil states, fare ever mindful, and have destroyed the fetters."[10] Elsewhere, Sāriputta recalls having spoken in praise of Devadatta as one of "great psychic power and majesty."[11] Given cousinship with Gotama, as well as his inclusion among the first group of Sakiyan nobles to join the community, Devadatta was probably in the Buddha's core group of senior disciples.

The occasion that triggered the crisis was a public teaching at which the elderly King Bimbisāra was present. Devadatta stands up, comes forward, bows respectfully, and says to Gotama: "Sir, you are old now. You have lived out the span of your life. May you now be content to dwell in ease here and now, and hand over the community of mendicants to me." But Gotama has no intention of handing over control of the community to anyone: "not even to Sāriputta or Moggallāna, let alone a lick-spittle like you."[12] Humiliated in the presence of the king, Devadatta leaves.

If Devadatta had been part of the Buddha's entourage for the previous thirty-seven years, he was surely aware that there was no plan to appoint a successor to Gotama. His plea, therefore, may have been intended to persuade his cousin to drop his idealistic vision of a leaderless community governed solely by the principles of the dharma and instead to empower someone like himself to take on the job of heading the order of mendicants. Devadatta may have seen himself as a realist, as one with a sincere concern for the survival of the community once its wise and charismatic founder was no longer around to settle disputes and lay down rules. Others, for all we know, may have seen him in that light, too.

Gotama's response to Devadatta's proposal is swift and harsh. He persuades the mendicants that an official statement should be made throughout Rājagaha denouncing Devadatta as one "whose nature was formerly of one kind, but now is of another kind," and adding that whatever Devadatta says or does should no longer be regarded as having the sanction of either himself, the dharma, or the community. Gotama does not present Devadatta as an evil person, but as someone who has departed so radically from Gotama's guiding vision as to be no longer trustworthy. When Sāriputta and others publicize the official statement, it creates an uproar, splitting the people of Rājagaha into opposing camps: some insist that Gotama must be jealous of the success of his cousin, and others consider that it must have been a very serious matter indeed for Gotama to respond in such a way.

The Buddha knows exactly what he wants and does not want to happen to his community after his death and is willing to do whatever is necessary to realize that goal. His desires are in conflict with Devadatta's desires. He counters Devadatta with a public display of scorn, abuse ("lick-spittle"), and humiliation, forcing his perceived adversary to retreat. This is not the Buddha of popular imagination: the serene, faintly smiling sage dwelling in the peace of nirvana. This is a fierce and uncompromising figure, in full "mighty elephant" mode, who will broach no dissent.

Devadatta does not give up. Stung by his rejection, angry perhaps that his plans to ensure the survival of the community were thwarted, he adopts a different strategy. Together with a group of followers, he approaches the Buddha and makes another proposal. "Sir, you speak frequently in praise of desiring little, of being contented. Would it not then be good if all mendicants, for the rest of their lives, remain as forest-dwellers who never settle in towns or villages, as beggars who subsist entirely from alms and refuse invitations to eat indoors, as wearers of discarded rags who take no cloth offered them by householders, as people who sleep only at the feet of trees and accept no shelter, and as vegetarians who eat neither fish nor meat?"[13]

The Buddha insists that it is up to mendicants to decide for themselves whether they live in a forest or settle in a village, live entirely by begging or eat in the homes of supporters, wear robes made of rags or of fine cloth offered by a householder. Provided that mendicants seek proper shelter during the monsoon, he has no objection to their living under the branches of a tree for the rest of the year, and unless they learn that an animal has been killed specifically for them, he sees no reason why they should not eat meat. In rejecting Devadatta's proposal, Gotama affirms the mendicants' freedom to choose their own lifestyle and refuses to place any further limits on their freedom to interact with society. Implicitly, he also rejects the idea that rules should be imposed on the basis of an abstract principle (such as contentment with little). They should emerge as a response to harmful deeds committed in concrete situations.

Devadatta and his followers go into Rājagaha and announce to the people that although Gotama refuses to live by these five rules, they have decided to do so. When the Buddha learns from Ānanda that Devadatta has gone ahead and established a separate community of mendicants under his new rules, he chastises him for creating a schism, which is such a serious matter that the perpetrator will be "boil[ed] in hell for an aeon."[14] Devadatta's new order, however, attracts a large number of fervent young monks. Rather than stay in Rājagaha, they leave the city and base themselves at Gayā Head, the hill on which Gotama delivered his discourse *On Fire* nearly forty years earlier.

Devadatta's rebellion had a further, political dimension. The traditional account presents it as part of a conspiracy with Prince Ajātasattu, the heir to King Bimbisāra's throne. To gain the prince's support, Devadatta appeared on Ajātasattu's lap in the form of a young boy wearing a girdle of snakes. Having impressed the prince by this display of magical power, Devadatta encourages him to assassinate his father, Bimbisāra, and seize control of the kingdom. Devadatta promises Ajātasattu that he, for his part, will "kill the Teacher and become the Buddha."[15] Although Devadatta fails in his comical attempts to kill Gotama (assassins who lose their nerve at the last minute, a boulder pushed off the top of a cliff or fired from a giant catapault, the release of a crazed elephant), Ajātasattu—as we saw in chapter 8—forces Bimbisāra to abdicate in his favor, then imprisons him and starves him to death.

When the Chinese pilgrim Faxian (337–c. 422) visited India seven centuries after the Buddha's death, he describes encountering a community of mendicants near Sāvatthi who still followed Devadatta's five rules. Though revering three mythical Buddhas of the distant past, the group refused to honor the historical Gotama. Two hundred years later, another Chinese monk, Xuanzang (c. 602–64), describes three monasteries in Bengal where "in accordance with the teaching of Devadatta, milk products were not taken as food."[16] These reports cast doubt on the canonical versions of Devadatta's rebellion, which triumphantly conclude with Sāriputta and Moggallāna traveling to Gāya Head and convincing Devadatta's disciples to return to the fold.

In other words, Devadatta's rebellion may not have been a dismal failure but a resounding success. In standing up to Gotama and his lax ways, Devadatta appealed to those mendicants—possibly the majority—who saw the renunciant life as an uncompromising rejection of the world and its affairs. Scholars have argued that the canonical story of Devadatta that has come down to us was invented at a later date by a faction that sought to restore Gotama's authority.[17]

(4)

Devadatta's rebellion is but one instance of how Gotama's world started to fall apart as he approached the end of his life. The Buddha may have been spared the tragedy of being crucified early in his teaching career, but his last years were marked by a series of calamities both within and outside his community. They describe an extended passion of sorts that culminates in his death in a sal grove in Kusinārā. We have already seen that the armies of Viḍūḍabha annihilated his homeland of Sakiya. His cousin Mahānāma and his benefactor and friend King Pasenadi died, and he himself had to flee Sakiya for Vesālī, only to discover on his arrival that his former attendant Sunakkhatta had denounced him to the Vajjian assembly. When he fled to Rājagaha, King Ajātasattu cynically used him as a sounding board for his war plans. During his stay in Rājagaha, his two main disciples, Sāriputta and Moggallāna, died within a short time of each other, leaving a void in the leadership of the community.

Gotama's last months and the events that followed his death are recorded chronologically in considerable detail, enabling us to construct what might be the most reliable portion of biographical narrative to be found in the canon. Much of this information is presented in the *Great Discourse on the Passing,* parallel versions of which are found in Pali, Sanskrit, Chinese, and Tibetan. Further details are scattered in the Pali discourses as well as in the accounts of the events leading up to the First Council, which are provided by the Vinayas of the different schools.

After leaving Rājagaha for the last time, Gotama and his remaining followers cross the Ganges and return to Vesālī, where they lodge in the mango grove of the courtesan Ambapālī. Gotama decides to spend the coming Rains at the small village of Beluva, with Ānanda as his sole companion. He tells the other mendicants to go anywhere in Vesālī where they have supporters and spend the Rains there.[18]

During the Rains, however, the Buddha falls seriously ill and nearly dies. When he had recovered and was well enough to sit outside, Ānanda came to him and said: "I have seen you in comfort, and I have seen you patiently endure pain. Sir, my body was like a drunkard's. I lost my bearings and things were unclear to me because of your sickness. The only thing that was of some comfort to me was the thought: 'the Teacher will not attain final nirvana until he has made some statement about the community of mendicants.'"[19]

Ānanda is torn between his anguished response to the suffering of a man to whom he is profoundly devoted and his urgent sense of duty. He wanted to help realize the Buddha's goal of ensuring the survival of his dharma and community, but, given the perilous conditions of the time, he must have wondered whether Gotama's enterprise would either fizzle out and be forgotten after his death or else be turned into another life-denying ascetic movement led by someone like Devadatta. Unlike Sāriputta, who, as a liberated arahant, is never shown displaying a hint of emotion, Ānanda gives free rein to his feelings. It is this capacity—which, from the point of view of orthodoxy, is a sign of unenlightened weakness—that renders him fully human and sympathetic. In some ways, Ānanda prefigures the later Mahāyāna ideal of the bodhisatta, one who rejects the transcendent peace of nirvana in order to respond to the suffering of myriad others in the world.

Gotama's response would have exacerbated his attendant's concerns. "But Ānanda," he says, "what does the community of mendicants expect of me? I have taught the dharma without making any distinction between 'inner' and 'outer' teachings. I have no 'teacher's fist' in regard to doctrines. If there is someone who thinks, 'I shall take charge of the community,' or 'the community should refer to me,' let him make some statement about it, but I do not think in these terms."[20] With these words, Gotama appears to relinquish control over the movement to which he had dedicated the past forty-five years of his life. From now on, the dharma will have to suffice in regulating the affairs of the community. There is no secret teaching or instruction that he has held back to pass on to an anointed successor. He has completed his work. He has taught everything he deems important. And he seems indifferent to what will happen next. He has no doubt that someone is waiting in the wings, eager to take control of the community and have it do his bidding.

"Ānanda," he goes on. "I am old now and worn out. Just as an old cart is made to go by being held together with straps, so my body is kept going by being strapped up. It is only when I withdraw my attention from the world and enter into the signless concentration of mind that my body knows comfort."[21] He knows that his life is over, that he will soon leave the world. The only relief he can find from his bodily pains is to enter into deep meditative absorption. Yet instead of issuing orders, he exhorts his followers to be independent of him and work things out for themselves.

"Therefore, Ānanda, you should live as islands unto yourselves, being your own refuge, with no other refuge, with the dharma as an island, with the dharma as your refuge, with no other refuge."[22] This famous last testament is succinct, but its meaning complex. It seems to involve a contradiction: after declaring oneself to be one's sole refuge, Gotama claims the dharma to be one's sole refuge. How can a person have two *sole* refuges? The sense of the passage turns on how one resolves this puzzle.

I take this statement to be the Buddha's final word on self-reliance, a core feature that distinguishes his dharma from other doctrines of the day. The kind of self-reliance he advocates is in no way akin to naive self-interest, or unthinkingly putting the fulfillment of one's desires above all other considerations. His emphasis on self (*atta*) underlines the importance of becoming "independent of others" in the dharma, which is a characteristic of stream entry. Such independence is not the freedom just to do what you want but the freedom to lead a life framed by the ethos of the dharma, where you respond to your own and others' suffering in a way that is not conditioned by reactivity. Gotama encourages a caring and care-full life, founded on personal responsibility and autonomy rather than on a set of rules or precepts to be applied irrespective of circumstance. The seemingly double character of refuge is thereby resolved into one: it is to be grounded in the dharma, which you have integrated into your own life.

After urging independence, Gotama poses a rhetorical question: How do you go about living as an island unto yourself, with the dharma you have integrated into your person as your sole refuge? "Here, Ānanda," he answers himself, "a mendicant abides contemplating the body as body, clearly aware, mindful, having relinquished attachment to the world, and likewise with regard to feelings, mind, and ideas." In other words: comprehend and embrace your existence, thereby undermining your habitual reactivity and opening yourself to the vision of nirvana, that non-reactive space whence you can respond freely, in ways not determined by self-interest alone. "And those who now in my time or afterward live thus," he concludes, "they will become the highest if they are desirous of learning."[23]

Once the monsoon is over, Gotama leaves Vesālī for the last time. The *Great Discourse on the Passing* is curiously silent about why a terminally ill old man would set out on a journey and where he intended to go. It is generally assumed that he decided to return to Kapilavatthu to die. This hypothesis is supported by the route he takes, which heads northwest to the republic of Mallā, through which he would have had to pass en route to Sakiya. But if he knew that Kapilavatthu was being laid waste by the armies of Viḍūḍabha, why would he head there? Gotama would not have embarked on a journey of nearly two hundred miles for purely sentimental reasons. He repeatedly states that his only goal in life is to establish his dharma and his community, so presumably he would have set out on the journey with that aim in mind. Kapilavatthu may not have been his destination after all.

The *Great Discourse on the Passing* says that Gotama left Vesālī "with a large company of mendicants," but the phrase is probably just a formula. In addition to Ānanda, only three other mendicants (Anuruddha—the brother of Mahānāma and thus another cousin of Gotama's—Cundaka and Upavāṇa) are mentioned during the course of this journey, giving the impression that the group was small. Because of the Buddha's age and health, it is probable that he did not walk the whole way but was carried, at least for part of the time, on a stretcher.

The travelers pass through a number of villages and towns: Bhaṇḍagāma, Hatthigāma, Ambagāma, Jambugāma, and Bhoganagara, in each of which Gotama instructs his listeners to adhere to four principles: noble ethics, noble meditation, noble understanding, and noble liberation. As his life ebbs away, Gotama seems intent on identifying the key elements of the dharma that free one from a life of meaningless repetition. Eventually—we do not know how long it took—they reach the Mallān town of Pāvā and settle in the mango grove of a smith called Cunda.

The next day, the group of mendicants go to Cunda's home to receive their midday meal. Cunda had prepared for them "a fine meal of hard and soft food with an abundance of *sūkara maddava,*" or "soft pig." In the account preserved in the Tibetan translation from Sanskrit, this dish is not mentioned. Whether *sūkara maddava* was cured pork or the soft truffles that pigs enjoy or something else altogether, Gotama asks Cunda to serve it to him and only him. Once he has eaten it, he tells Cunda to bury the leftovers in a pit. He then delivers an inspiring talk and takes his leave of Cunda. At some point after this, he "was attacked by a severe sickness with bloody diarrhoea." He bore with the pain, then said to Ānanda: "Let us go to Kusinārā."[24]

Dr. Mettanando Bhikkhu offers an interpretation of this text from the perspective of modern medicine. He argues that Gotama did not, as is generally supposed, die of food poisoning as a result of eating *sūkara maddava,* but of a mesenteric infarction—a gangrenous condition of the tissue of the intestinal wall caused by a loss of blood supply. He points out that food poisoning caused by bacteria not only takes between two and twelve hours to manifest but is *not* accompanied by "bloody diarrhoea." Since Gotama believes that something is wrong with the *sūkara maddava* while he is still eating it, the food may have provoked a reaction in him owing to a preexisting medical condition. That he had some such condition is clear from the account of his illness at Beluva during the Rains retreat. Mettanando concludes that "a disease that matches the described symptoms—accompanied by acute abdominal pain and the passage of blood, commonly found among elderly people, and triggered by a meal—is mesenteric infarction, caused by an obstruction of the blood vessels of the mesentery. It is lethal."[25] His thesis is further supported by Gotama's repeated requests to Ānanda to bring him water to quench his thirst, another symptom of such an infarction.

When the group reaches Kusinārā, about ten miles from Pāvā, the exhausted Gotama asks Ānanda to prepare a bed for him between two sal trees. He lies down on his right side with his head to the north and instructs Ānanda on how to wrap his corpse, prepare his funeral pyre, and enshrine his remains in a stupa erected at a crossroads. Ānanda goes to his lodging nearby, leans against a wall, and breaks down. On hearing his distress, Gotama summons him back to his side. "Enough," he says. "Do not weep and wail. Have I not told you that all pleasant things are changeable, subject to separation, and become something else? So how could it be that I should not pass away? For a long time, you have been in my presence, showing me kindness wholeheartedly. You have achieved much good. Make the effort, and in a short time you will be free from the effluences."[26] He turns to the other mendicants and praises Ānanda as one who is pleasing to the sight of those who come into his presence, delights them when he talks about the dharma, and disappoints them when he remains silent.

But Ānanda is not placated by these words of praise. He pleads with the Buddha not to pass away in this "miserable little town of wattle-and-daub, in the jungle in the back of beyond" but to go to one of the great cities of the day—Campā, Rājagaha, Sāvatthi, Sāketa, Kosambī, or Benares—where his followers would provide a proper funeral.[27] Gotama berates him for portraying Kusinārā in such a dismissive way and tells him that in the distant past it was once a great city called Kusāvati, the seat of an empire ruled over by a mighty king called Mahāsudassana.

This passage makes no sense. Ānanda, of all people, would have known that this elderly, terminally ill man could not possibly have travelled to any of those distant cities. Moreover, the existence of an ancient, imperial city called Kusāvati on the site of Kusinārā is clearly a myth with no historical foundation. For what reasons, then, might this episode have been introduced into the narrative?

The story makes two points: (1) Kusinārā is a "miserable" and obscure little place and thus unfit to be the final resting place of the Buddha, but (2) it was a fit place for him to die after all, since it had been an imperial city.

The first point is refuted by evidence within the *Greater Discourse on the Passing* itself. A few pages later, when describing the funeral procession, we read that the Buddha's body is carried "through the north gate of the city, the city centre and out through the east gate," which suggests something far grander than a rundown collection of shacks in the jungle. [28]

Kusinārā may not have been a city on the scale of Rājagaha or Sāvatthi, but it was still the capital of the powerful Mallān republic and a place where Gotama is reported to have had a following and to have delivered discourses. Moreover, Kusinārā was the birthplace and fief of Bandhula, the Mallān chief and old friend of King Pasenadi's who had served as commander of the Kosalan army until Pasenadi had him murdered on suspicion of mounting a coup. To absolve his grief, Pasenadi allowed Bandhula's wife, also called Mallikā, to return to Kusinārā and appointed Bandhula's nephew Dīgha Kārāyaṇa as head of the military in his place. Dīgha Kārāyaṇa, as we have seen, gained revenge for his uncle's death by deposing Pasenadi and crowning Viḍūḍabha king, then letting him embark on the rape of Sakiya. According to the *Dhammapada Commentary,* Viḍūḍabha was killed in a flashflood when he returned home to Sāvatthi in triumph. He drowned in the Aciravatī River and became "food for fish and turtles."[29] Whether the story is the narrator's way of meting out well-deserved karmic justice on the man who attacked the Buddha's homeland or whether it reflects a historical event is impossible to know. In either case, Dīgha Kārāyaṇa, as kingmaker and commander of the Kosalan military, would have become one of the most powerful figures north of the Ganges. And his family home was in the Mallān capital of Kusinārā.

Far from being "a miserable little town of wattle-and-daub" at the time of Gotama's last journey, Kusinārā was very likely becoming a new center of power in north India as the capital city of the rising dynasty of the Mallāns. Although the *Great Discourse on the Passing* gives the impression that Gotama's death in this jungle backwater was entirely accidental, Kusinārā might in fact have been the destination to which the Buddha was deliberately heading when he left Vesālī. Since he no longer seems to have been welcome at Sāvatthi, Rājagaha, or Vesālī, he may have considered Kusinārā the best place to regroup his community and establish its base before he died. He would have had wealthy supporters there, principal among whom would have been Mallikā, the widow of Bandhula, as well as the security of being under the protection of a powerful military chief: the very conditions he had required when founding the Jeta Grove at Sāvatthi and the Bamboo Grove in Rājagaha.

Yet someone or some faction, for unknown reasons, sought at a later date to downplay the importance of Kusinārā and concoct the myth of Kusāvati, making Gotama's journey conclude with a whimper. We could see it, however, as a triumphant arrival at his destination just as his life draws to a close.

Gotama instructs Ānanda to go into Kusinārā and announce to the Mallāns that tonight, in the last watch, he will die. When Ānanda makes his way to the assembly hall and tells them the news, they are "overwhelmed by sorrow, their minds tormented by grief," so that they are "all weeping and tearing their hair."[30] Because so many of them wish to pay their last respects, Ānanda groups them by household for the final visit. This language might reflect the pious enthusiasm of later editors rather than describe actual events. It nonetheless supports the possibility that Gotama was not just passing through town on the way to somewhere else but was highly regarded and would have been welcome to stay in Kusinārā.

During what may have been the final hours of his life, Gotama is recorded to have made three important statements about his dharma.

One: Asked by the renunciant Subhadda (who shows up at the sal grove as Gotama lies dying) whether the other teachers of the day have gained enlightenment, Gotama replies: "Enough, Subhadda. Never mind whether all, or none, or some of them have gained enlightenment. In whatever dharma and discipline that the noble eightfold path is not found, there you will not find any realized wanderers. Yet wherever the noble eightfold path is found, there you will find realized wanderers."[31] Subhadda provides Gotama with another opportunity to identify what is essential about his teaching. The answer is unambiguous. What constitutes the core of the dharma is the cultivation of a comprehensive middle way that embraces the entirety of one's humanity. The core is not a simple subjective state of insight or enlightenment.

Two: Immediately after the episode with Subhadda, Gotama says to Ānanda: "It may be that you will think: 'the Buddha's instruction has ceased, now we have no teacher!' It should not be seen like this, Ānanda, for what I have taught and explained to you as dharma and discipline will, at my passing, be your teacher."[32] This equally unambiguous statement affirms that Gotama has no intention of appointing a successor to be the teacher of the community. He insists one last time that his dharma and discipline will provide adequate direction for his followers.

Three: Having discussed the way mendicants should address each other after his death, Gotama adds: "If it wishes, the community may abolish the minor rules after my passing."[33] What he understands, therefore, as the basis of "discipline" (*vinaya*) is not for practitioners to blindly follow every rule and precept that he formulated on a case-by-case basis during his lifetime. Instead, he hopes they will have the wisdom and maturity to pursue an ethics founded on the principles of his dharma that responds and adapts to the changing conditions of the world.

As with his injunction at Vesālī to live "like islands unto yourselves," here, too, Gotama emphasizes the importance of leading a life of self-reliance based on the ideas and values of the dharma rather than uncritically trusting in another person's "enlightenment," uncritically obeying the authority of an appointed teacher, and uncritically adhering to a set of time-honored rules. Shortly after making these points, the Buddha utters his very last words: "Well now, bhikkhus, I say to you: things fall apart, tread the path with care."[34]

(5)

The morning after the Buddha's death, Ānanda returns to the assembly hall and asks the Mallāns to cremate the body according to their customs. So the Mallāns gather perfume and wreaths and hire musicians. Then they all go to the sal grove where Gotama's body is lying and honor his memory with dance and song and music.[35] After seven days of mourning, the Mallāns carry the body in procession through the north gate of Kusinārā into the center of the city, then leave by the east gate, continuing until they reach the Makuṭa Bandhana shrine, where the cremation was to be held. According to the commentaries, Mallikā, the elderly widow of Bandhula, placed her most prized jewelery on the bier to accompany the body.

Just as four Mallān chiefs are preparing to light the pyre, a group of mendicants arrive at the shrine from the direction of Pāvā. At their head is the arahant Mahākassapa, who, "covering his shoulder with his robe, joined his hands in salutation, circumambulated the pyre three times and, uncovering the Teacher's feet, paid homage with his head to them." Once he concluded his devotions, the funeral pyre spontaneously burst into flame.[36]

Mahākassapa (Kassapa the Great) plays a marginal role in the story of Gotama's life, only rising to prominence once the Buddha is dead. His arrival at Kusinārā introduces an abrupt shift in register. We move from the rituals of the Mallāns, who honor the memory of Gotama with song, dance, and music, to find ourselves in the presence of a stern, intimidating ascetic who immediately imposes his authority on the proceedings. He seems to embody everything that Gotama warned against as he lay dying. Mahākassapa is regarded as "chief among those who expound the ascetic practices," does not hesitate to declare how enlightened he is and takes it for granted that he is the Buddha's appointed successor.[37] He is the very antithesis of Ānanda, but Ānanda seems powerless to resist him.

The *Connected Discourses with Kassapa* consists of thirteen discourses that together paint a vivid and unapologetic portrait of the man. We learn that after renouncing the household life to become a wandering mendicant, he encountered the Buddha at the Bahuputta shrine on the road between Rājagaha and Nālandā. After receiving instruction, he spent a week in meditation, at the conclusion of which, he says, "final knowledge arose." When he next meets Gotama, he offers to exchange his "soft patchwork robe" for Gotama's robe of "worn-out hempen rags." The Pali commentary to this passage explains that the Buddha gave him his robe "because he wished to appoint the elder to his own position."[38] Taking this gesture to be a symbol of transmission, Mahākassapa continues: "If one speaking rightly could say of anyone: 'He is a son of the Teacher, born of his breast, born of his mouth, born of the dharma, a receiver of worn-out hempen rag-robes,' it is of me that one could rightly say this." Then he praises his own attainments: "By the destruction of the effluences, in this very life I enter and dwell in the pure liberation of mind, realizing it for myself with direct knowledge. One might just as well think that a bull elephant seven cubits high could be concealed by a palm leaf as think that my direct knowledge could be concealed."[39]

That such a self-serving speech can coexist with Gotama's self-effacing last testament in Vesālī again illustrates that the early canon is a patchwork stitched together from the narratives of various factions within the community who held conflicting views of what constituted the dharma. The arrival of Mahākassapa at Kusinārā marks the beginning of a protracted struggle to determine the nature of orthodoxy, on the one hand, and ecclesiastical authority, on the other, that continues to exercise Buddhists of all schools to this day.

When Gotama said: "If there is someone who thinks, 'I shall take charge of the community,' or 'the community should refer to me,' let him make some statement about it, but I do not think in these terms," we can wonder whether he had Mahākassapa in mind. Gotama accepts that such thinking is intrinsic to the power politics of human institutions, but he neither endorses nor encourages it. When he left Vesālī on his last grueling journey to Kusinārā, might he have been trying to create as much distance as possible from Mahākassapa and his followers in Rājagaha? If so, he does not seem to have counted on Mahākassapa's dogged pursuit. Given the miles involved, once Mahākassapa received word of Gotama's severe illness at the end of the Rains, he would have had to set out immediately from Rājagaha in order to reach Kusinārā only seven days after the Buddha's death.

As soon as the cremation is over and the relics from the pyre have been distributed, the *Great Discourse on the Passing* comes to an end. The story is picked up at this point in the Vinaya texts of the different schools.

Rather than stay at Kusinārā, Mahākassapa proposes that the community convene a council in Rājagaha under the auspices of the "devout" king Ajātasattu, "who will provide it with all its necessities." One of the assembled mendicants asks whether Ānanda, who is not yet an arahant, will be permitted to attend the council. Mahākassapa replies that making an exception for Ānanda would anger unenlightened mendicants who had a connection with Gotama but were not allowed to participate. He suggests a compromise. If Ānanda agrees to be the water provider for the council, he can attend. Mahākassapa puts the proposal to a vote:

> The venerable Ānanda, the Teacher's attendant, who stayed near his person, and to whom the Teacher delivered several discourses, has for these reasons been appointed to supply the assembly with water. If the assembly requires water, then the venerable Ānanda, having been appointed to the office of serving water, must supply it with water.[40]

By remaining silent, the gathered arahants accept the proposal.

It is hard not to see this proposal as a way of humiliating Ānanda by making him little more than a servant. I think it goes further than this. The episode is a critique not only of Ānanda as a spiritual failure but of all that he stands for. This and similar passages imply that Mahākassapa and his clique—like Devadatta before them—disapproved of what they regarded as Gotama's lax style of teaching and leadership. On three occasions, Gotama is said to have requested Mahākassapa to teach the community. And on each occasion Mahākassapa refused, on the grounds that "the mendicants are difficult to admonish now, they are impatient and do not accept instruction respectfully." He haughtily dismissed them as having "no faith in regard to wholesome states, no sense of shame, no fear of wrongdoing, no energy and no understanding."[41] By exposing the poor morals of those under Gotama's guidance, these texts seem to elevate Mahākassapa above the Buddha himself. Gotama may have prepared the ground, but the world had to wait until his death before Mahākassapa could step in and organize things in a correct and proper way.

On Mahākassapa's return to Rājagaha in preparation for the council, we learn that "when King Ajātusattu first saw him, the recollection of an awakened one made him fall senseless to the ground."[42] Remember, this is the same Ajātasattu who was impressed by Devadatta's magical powers, colluded with Devadatta in his plan to take over leadership of the community of mendicants, murdered his own father, was dismissed by Gotama, then cynically used Gotama as a sounding board before launching a war. None of this seems to trouble Mahākassapa, who does not stint in his praise of his sponsor.

Once in Rājagaha, Mahākassapa settles in the Bamboo Grove, while Ānanda goes on a walking tour in a place called the "Southern Hills" together with a large group of mendicants. During their time together, thirty of these mendicants, all of whom are young students of Ānanda, disrobe and return to being adherents. Not surprisingly, when Ānanda gets back to the Bamboo Grove, Mahākassapa verbally attacks him for wasting his time wandering about in the hills with his undisciplined followers. "One would think that you were trampling on crops, destroying families. Your retinue is breaking apart. Your young disciples are slipping away. You do not know your measure, boy!"[43]

Ānanda draws to him those who are powerless in the community: women and now a group of young men. By the customs of orthodoxy, to be party to another's disrobing is shameful. So the accusations might constitute a smear campaign by supporters of Mahākassapa's hard-line faction to destroy Ānanda's reputation. On the other hand, it could indicate a split in the community after Gotama's death between what we would today call liberal and conservative wings. With power concentrated in the hands of the aging conservatives under Mahākassapa, some junior mendicants may well have reconsidered their future in such an organization.

"Are these not gray hairs growing on my head?" retorts Ānanda in response to Mahākassapa's jibe. "Can't you stop calling me a 'boy'?" Mahākassapa repeats what he has already said and refuses to withdraw the insult. When word of this exchange gets out, the *bhikkhuni* "Fat" Nandā comes to Ānanda's defense: "How can Mahākassapa, who was formerly a member of another sect, think to disparage Ānanda, the Videhan sage, by calling him a 'boy'?" When Mahākassapa hears of this, he says to Ānanda: "Surely, Fat Nandā made that statement rashly. For since I shaved off my hair and beard, put on saffron robes, and went forth from home to homelessness, I do not recall ever having acknowledged any other teacher except the completely awakened one."[44] In saying this, he does not deny the accusation that he formerly belonged to another order. Yet the comment rankles with him, and he launches into a self-serving defense of his impeccable devotion and enlightenment. For Nandā, Mahākassapa's loyalty is questionable. She regards him as an interloper who seeks to impose the norms of another ascetic order on Gotama's community. Predictably, the discourse concludes with Fat Nandā disrobing and leaving the community.

I find it hard to see Mahākassapa as anything but an insufferable prig. If an arahant, who is supposedly liberated from any trace of greed, hatred, and egotistic delusion, can behave in such a manner, what, we might ask, is gained by becoming an arahant? Yet these detailed passages have been preserved in the canon, implying that people in the past experienced no cognitive or moral dissonance in reading or hearing of Mahākassapa's conduct. The way he treated Ānanda must have seemed appropriate and praiseworthy to them.

The discourse *To Gopaka Moggallāna* illuminates the tensions within the community in the build-up to the council. It tells of how Ānanda was staying at Rājagaha in the Bamboo Grove not long after the Buddha had died. At this time, King Ajātasattu was afraid of being attacked by King Pajjota and was having Rājagaha fortified.[45] The king's suspicions probably tell us more about the paranoia of Ajātasattu than about any actual threat to the city. Pajjota, known as Pajjota the Cruel, was ruler of Avanti, a country whose capital of Ujjenī was about five hundred miles to the southwest of Rājagaha. The commentaries explain that Pajjota sought to avenge the murder of his friend Bimbisāra at the hands of Ajātasattu, but do not say whether any such attack ever materialized.

One morning, before going on his daily alms round, Ānanda is invited to visit the brahmin Gopaka Moggallāna, who seems to have been a government official. Gopaka asks: "Ānanda, is there any mendicant who possesses in each and every way all those qualities that were possessed by Mr. Gotama?" Ānanda replies that there is no such mendicant. Their discussion is interrupted by the arrival of the chief minister, brahmin Vassakāra. Having been told what they are talking about, the minister asks: "Is there any mendicant who was appointed by the Teacher thus: 'He will be your refuge when I am gone'?" Ānanda replies that there is no such mendicant. So Vassakāra asks: "But is there any mendicant who has been chosen by the community and appointed by a number of elders thus: 'He will be our refuge after the Teacher is gone'?" Ānanda says no. "But," Vassakāra persists, "if you have no refuge, Ānanda, then how do you maintain harmony?" Ānanda replies: "We are not without a refuge, brahmin. We have the dharma as our refuge."[46]

If the passages cited before this one represent the view of the faction associated with Mahākassapa, the current text would appear to represent the position of those who supported Ānanda. Indeed, the discourse drives home this point. Although Mahākassapa is not mentioned by name, it seems likely that this discussion concerns his status. Neither of these government officials are recorded as being Buddhists, but both appear concerned about what is going on at the Bamboo Grove, which suggests that the turmoil over leadership may have spilled out into the wider community of supporters in Rājagaha. But then there is a twist. Having reflected on Ānanda's response, the chief minister asks: "Is there any mendicant whom you now honor, respect, revere, and venerate, and on whom you live in dependence?" To this, Ānanda unequivocally answers: "Yes, there is such a mendicant."[47]

When asked to explain what he means, Ānanda enumerates the Buddha's list of "ten qualities that inspire confidence." These include being virtuous in following the rule, being learned in the doctrine, being content with little, and being able to enter into the four meditative absorptions at will, as well as abiding in the pure liberation of mind. "When these qualities are found in anyone among us," explains Ānanda, "we honor, respect, revere, and venerate him, and live in dependence on him."[48] While this list of criteria would not exclude Mahākassapa from being such a mendicant, it shifts the emphasis away from privileging one specific individual and places it on an impersonal set of moral and spiritual qualities that anyone can achieve. What one relies upon is not the person but the dharma that the person has internalized and embodies.

That "such a mendicant" can be the person one reveres, respects, and trusts shows that Ānanda's vision of Gotama's community is one of democratic equality. "Such a mendicant" is Everyman. If we extend this description from mendicants to adherents like Mahānāma and Jīvaka, who are said to be "seers of the deathless," then householders would be included as well.[49] In this community the dharma becomes manifest through individual human lives, irrespective of their rank or gender. Each person learns its significance by listening to, reflecting on, and practicing its teachings and, further, by forming relationships with and coming to know those who embody it. Herein lies the sense of true friendship, which Gotama said constituted the "entirety of the spiritual life."

(6)

As the time for the council in Rājagaha grew near, Mahākassapa and the elders sought to further impose their authority on Ānanda by forcing him to confess all the mistakes he had made while serving as Gotama's attendant. The first issue on which they take him to task is his failure to ask Gotama to specify what he meant when he said: "If it wishes, the community may abolish the minor rules after my passing." Since the legalistically minded elders are unable to agree on what constituted a minor rule, Mahākassapa makes a proposal:

> If it seems right to the community, we should not lay down anything that has not already been laid down, nor should we abolish what has been laid down. We should proceed in conformity with and according to the rules of training that have been laid down. [50]

In adopting this resolution, the community endorses a rigid morality, allowing no possibility for either innovation or change. Even today, Buddhist monks adhere to a set of rules laid down on a case-by-case basis to address specific issues in north India twenty-five hundred years ago.

When asked to admit his error in this case, Ānanda agrees that he did not ask the Buddha to be more specific, but he denies that he made a mistake. As a sign of respect to his elders, however, he agrees to confess it as a wrongdoing, thus capitulating before the majority opinion. He may have decided not to sow discord in the community by insisting on a dissident view. Four other charges are laid against him: stepping on the patches for the Buddha's robe before sewing them together; letting the Buddha's body be defiled by women's tears; failing to ask the Buddha to remain on earth for an aeon; and endorsing women's ordination as *bhikkhunis*. In each case, Ānanda gives the elders the same reply. His capitulation is complete.[51]

How did Ānanda feel about his treatment at the hands of the arahants? We find three stanzas attributed to him that are preserved among the *Verses of the Male Elders* (in Caroline Rhys Davids's translation):

All directions are obscure,
Nothing is clear to me anymore;
With our good friend departed,
It seems as if all is darkness.

For one whose friend has passed away,
Whose teacher has gone forever,
There is no friend that can compare
With mindfulness of the body.

They of old have passed away,
The new men suit me not at all.
Alone today this child does ponder,
Like nesting bird when rain does fall.[52]

The candor of these verses is startling, and it is surprising that the editors of the canon did not suppress them. The "new men" who succeeded Gotama do not appear in a flattering light. Such moving and heartfelt words testify to the sense of abandonment and isolation that Ānanda felt after his teacher's death. In keeping with Gotama's final testament at Vesālī, Ānanda turns away from dependence on people and devotes himself to living as "an island," starting with the cultivation of mindful attention to his own body.

On the evening before the council convenes, Ānanda is said to have made one last effort to become an arahant in order that he would be deemed worthy to participate. He spends much of the night practicing mindfulness of the body, but to no avail. So, just before dawn, he decides to lie down and rest. "But before his head had touched the pillow and while his feet were off the ground—in that interval his mind was freed from the effluences with no residue remaining."[53] It is difficult to know what to make of this odd story, which depicts Ānanda's final liberation as taking place in a liminal zone, as he is suspended between all normal physical postures. It may suggest that Ānanda was such a spiritual lost cause (from the perspective of the followers of Mahākassapa) that no matter how much he persevered in practicing mindfulness of the body while standing, sitting, walking, and lying down, he would never achieve the desired goal. Alternately, it could show that Ānanda was different from all those others who had become arahants before him, thus raising him (in the eyes of *his* followers) and making him an exceptional figure in the community—a kind of super saint.

At the council, held in the Seven Leaf Cave, high in the hills above Rājagaha, Mahākassapa invites Ānanda to sit on the "lion's seat" and recite to the assembled elders all the discourses that he has memorized. He intones *The Four Tasks,* followed by *On Not-Self,* and continues until he has recited every discourse that he knows.[54]

Since the council meeting concludes the account of the Buddha's life and teaching, the canonical record is silent as to the fate of Ānanda and the other participants. Traditional Buddhist sources, however, preserve a broadly similar account of Ānanda's death. He is believed to have lived to a very advanced age. Aware that death was approaching, he headed from Magadha to Vesālī, where he intended to die. Once his followers realized what was happening, his Magadhan followers gathered on the south bank of the Ganges to bid him farewell, and his Vajjian followers lined up on the north bank to greet him. Not wishing to incur the displeasure of either party by not achieving his final nirvana in their country, he entered the contemplation on fire (*tejokasiṇa*) when he was midway across the river, and his body spontaneously burst into flames.

Sŏn Buddhists remember Ānanda as the second patriarch of their lineage, who succeeded his nemesis Mahākassapa, who, as we saw, believed Gotama had appointed him as his successor when he was presented with the symbolic gift of Gotama's "worn-out hempen robe." The Sŏn tradition further maintains that Mahākassapa received a direct "mind-to-mind" transmission from the Buddha on Vulture's Peak when Gotama held up a flower and Mahākassapa smiled. This famous episode, however, is not recorded in the Pali or other early canonical sources.

II

A Culture of Awakening

Bhikkhus, I do not dispute with the world; rather, it is the world that disputes with me. A proponent of the dharma does not dispute with anyone in the world. Of that which the wise (*paṇḍitā*) in the world agree upon as not existing, I too say that it does not exist. And of that which the wise in the world agree upon as existing, I too say that it exists.

—KHANDHASAṂYUTTA

(1)

As human beings, we grow up embedded in a specific culture, society, and language. Since we have no say as to where and when we are born, we can do nothing about this. It is the ineluctable background to our lives. A great deal of what we come to take for granted about ourselves and the world is the result of such embeddedness. Everything from our gender identity to our beliefs about the origin of the universe is to a considerable degree linguistically and socially constructed. It is not as though we can change our minds about such things on a whim. If—despite direct sensory evidence to the contrary—we are convinced that the earth circles the sun, we are embedded in the worldview of naturalistic science. That view is not self-evident: the majority of human beings who have ever lived were just as convinced of the opposite.

For people who were born into and grew up in a culture in which classical Indian cosmology was accepted without question, the law of karma and the reality of reincarnation were as self-evidently true as the worldview of modern science is to most people today. The former no more had to struggle to believe in karma and rebirth than the latter have to struggle to believe in the Big Bang and evolution by natural selection. In both cases, people would be hard pressed to demonstrate their picture of the world to be true to anyone who did not accept it. Yet the picture is so self-evident to them that it would require a determined, conscious effort to abandon and replace it with something else.

Since Buddhism developed in cultures where the worldview of classical India either already prevailed or had come to be accepted over a number of generations, its teachings take for granted the law of karma as a cosmogonic explanation for how things are the way they are, and multiple lifetimes as the medium within which acts (*karma*) are committed and come to fruition (*vipāka*). Accepting the truth of these doctrines is considered necessary for Buddhist teaching to make any sense. To challenge them is not simply objectionable but unintelligible. The doctrines are so deeply rooted in Buddhism that it seems no more conceivable that one could become a Buddhist without accepting them than that one could become a Christian or Muslim without believing in a version of the Abrahamic God.

To say that such beliefs are *embedded* in Buddhist culture is not the same as saying that people are convinced that they are true. Most Buddhists throughout history have probably spent little time worrying about such matters. The embeddedness of these beliefs extends far beyond their privately held religious opinions into their emotional, social, economic, and political life.

Take, for example, the death ceremonies (*chesa*) performed in a Korean Sŏn monastery. When a parishioner dies, the monks perform a series of rituals once a week for forty-nine days to guide the departed person through an intermediate zone to a Pure Land ("Heaven") or a favorable rebirth. As Buddhists, the monks accept without question the value of what they are doing, but as Sŏn practitioners, they may have little understanding of or interest in the doctrinal intricacies of the theory of reincarnation. Yet the monastery depends on these ceremonies for a significant portion of its yearly income. At the same time, the family and friends of the deceased, irrespective of whether they believe in karma or rebirth, are comforted by a solemn ritual framework that helps them come to terms with their grief and loss. To reject these time-honored practices because the theory of reincarnation appears to be incompatible with a scientific worldview would largely miss the point. People participate in these rites for a range of reasons that has nothing to do with the underlying theology that legitimates them.

Or imagine you have been recognized as the fourteenth reincarnation of the Tibetan teacher Gendun Drup (1391–1474), who came to be known as the first Dalai Lama. In the sociopolitical context of Tibet, your upbringing, education, authority, and charisma are inextricably tied to your having been identified with this line of reincarnating lamas when you were two years old. As the figurehead of an endangered culture in exile, you work tirelessly to uphold the teachings of Tibetan Buddhism and achieve political autonomy for your six million fellow Tibetans. You also have a passionate interest in the natural sciences and have spent many years in discussion with leading scientists from a variety of disciplines. Yet it would be absurd for you to question belief in reincarnation because of something you have learned from neuroscience, since it would threaten to undermine everything you have spent your life working for. Not only would you risk destabilizing the faith of your followers, but you would cast doubt on the authority of every reincarnate lama within the schools of your own tradition. Here, too, the theoretical validity of the doctrines of karma and rebirth turns out to be subordinate to the practical role they play in the historical, social, and political life of a culture.

For a Western convert to Buddhism, reincarnation is an alien concept, decoupled from any underlying social or cultural function, that you are nonetheless required to adopt as part of your new-found Buddhist identity. Unless you are one of those spiritual souls who is already intuitively convinced of the idea, it might take you a great deal of time and anguish to persuade yourself through reasoned argument of its truth. It is a foreign religious belief that you struggle to embrace in the context of an unaccommodating culture and in the face of skeptical bemusement from your peers. You are likely to take it far more seriously than your Asian co-religionists but feel much less secure in its validity because, unlike them, you are incapable of taking it for granted.

For the majority of Buddhists over time, belief in reincarnation has served as a pragmatic, rather than dogmatic, way of understanding oneself and the world. As a functional belief embedded within their culture and society, it works well enough for it not to be seriously doubted. Whether exposure to a modern secular worldview will, over generations, compromise that functionality and alienate Asian Buddhists from their traditional beliefs and practices remains to be seen. And it is equally uncertain whether the dogmatic belief of converts will ever become sufficiently naturalized for the idea of rebirth to function in a pragmatic, unselfconscious way in environments that are not traditionally Buddhist.

(2)

When Western Buddhists seek to defend their belief in rebirth, they cite traditional arguments found in the works of commentators such as Dharmakīrti, but they also look to the empirical evidence of researchers who have studied cases of young children who claim to remember a previous existence. Having grown up embedded in secular modernity, such converts intuitively appeal to the authority of scientific research even while, in other contexts, criticizing it as materialistic and reductive.

Foremost among the researchers into rebirth was the late Dr. Ian Stevenson, a psychiatrist at the University of Virginia, who investigated around three thousand cases of children from all over the world who claimed to recall a past existence, and published numerous articles and books based on his work.[1] Certain of these children seemed able to provide detailed information about their former lives as well as the circumstances of their deaths, which, in some cases, was reportedly corroborated by others who knew them in their earlier incarnation. A number of the children also bore birthmarks that seemed to correspond to wounds incurred through a violent death in a past life. The response to Stevenson's findings was mixed: some considered the work groundbreaking, and others dismissed him as gullible and his work as bad science. For the most part, the scientific community has ignored his research—possibly because of its own ideological commitment to an inflexibly materialist view of the world.

Instead of discussing the merits and weaknesses of Stevenson's work, I would like to conduct a thought experiment. Let us imagine that the scientific community comes to accept his findings and to view his cases not merely as "suggestive" (Stevenson's word) of reincarnation but as compelling evidence for it. Although Hindu and Buddhist proponents of rebirth would doubtless hail scientific acceptance as a resounding confirmation of their beliefs, would they be justified? The evidence might indicate the possibility of some as-yet-unknown means of acquiring information, but it would entirely fail to account for the complex metaphysics that underpins the traditional doctrine of rebirth.

At first glance, the evidence presented in the case studies seems to endorse the Buddhist belief in rebirth. Yet it says nothing whatsoever about the law of karma that is integral to this belief. A child's recollection of a detail from a past life does not establish moral causation between an act committed in the past and the quality of the child's present existence. The doctrine of karma is a theory of cosmic justice. Rebirth is simply the medium within which such justice plays itself out: those who do good in this life will be rewarded in a future life, whereas those who commit evil in this life will be punished in one of the numerous Buddhist hells or will be reborn as a ghost or an animal.

Rebirth is seen as a necessary condition for the law of karma to operate. In the absence of such an underlying theory of cosmic justice, however, the phenomenon of rebirth would be meaningless.

Buddhists habitually speak of karma and rebirth as though it were a single process without seeming to notice that two entirely distinct claims are being made. While belief in rebirth maintains that something—usually a subtle form of consciousness—survives physical death and transfers itself across time and space into a fertilized ovum, belief in the law of karma maintains that a person's current experience is determined by past behavior, and that actions commited now will have consequences in the future, even after death. Logically, therefore, anyone could accept the karmic law of cosmic justice while rejecting belief in reincarnation (and vice versa).

What matters for secular Buddhists is to live life in such a way that it results in a better world for those who will inhabit this earth after their death. They understand how both their personal actions and the deeds of a society or state that they endorse will have consequences long after their death. In accepting degrees of responsibility for these acts, they affirm a belief in natural justice, but they can do so without ever entertaining the idea that they will survive in any form to experience the results of those acts themselves.

While such a secular interpretation may be unacceptable to many Buddhists, it is entirely congruent with Gotama's reply to Topknot Sīvaka's question. Sīvaka asks:

> There are some wanderers and brahmins who voice the opinion and hold the view that whatever a person experiences—be it pleasant, painful, or neither—is caused by what was done in the past. What do you say about this?[2]

Ironically, the view that Sīvaka describes is identical to that of much current Buddhist orthodoxy. As a Gelukpa monk, I was taught that all feelings (*tshor ba*) of pleasure and pain are by definition the ripening effects (*rnam smin gyi 'bras bu*) of previously committed actions. The fourth-century Indian scholar Vasubandhu, in his famous *Abhidharmakośa,* goes further still. "The various worlds," he writes, "are born from actions (*karma*)."[3] By Vasubandhu's time, Indian Buddhists had adopted the view that everything from subjective states of mind to the most distant galaxies were the product of the actions of the sentient beings who experienced them.

Gotama, however, takes a completely different approach. While not denying that certain aspects of one's experience result from one's past behavior, he recognizes that a wide range of conditions, including physical health (the humors of phlegm, bile, and wind) and external circumstances, equally contribute to how one feels at any given time. His response is based on a matter-of-fact assessment of how life unfolds, not on metaphysical beliefs. "Sīvaka," he says, "you can know for yourself how such experiences occur. And people in the world agree upon how such experiences occur."[4]

In keeping with his insistence on self-reliance, Gotama throws the question back to Sīvaka. He refuses to act as a quasi-omniscient authority who delivers ex cathedra opinions on the big questions of human life. He wants Sīvaka to think for himself and engage in discussion with others to resolve such matters. And he is scathing about those who claim to answer such questions by piously repeating a dogma that neither they nor anyone else can either validate or invalidate: "Those who believe that all experience is caused by what was done in the past, Sīvaka, surpass what can be known by themselves and what is accepted as true in the world. Therefore, I say that those wanderers and brahmins are mistaken."

A child's first-person account of a previous life, corroborated by witnesses, could suggest that that child underwent reincarnation. But in itself, the account offers no evidence as to whether that child will be reincarnated again. It would be reasonable to conclude from such an account that a person's life is split into two parts, as with a chrysalis (life 1) and a butterfly (life 2). There is no basis to assume either that the person of the previous life had been born before or that the present child will be reborn after its death. Nor are there any grounds for inductively assuming that anyone else either has been or ever will be reincarnated. Traditional Buddhist metaphysics, however, maintains that *all sentient beings* have undergone a "beginningless" sequence of past lives and will potentially undergo an endless sequence of future lives. Without this assertion, there is no rationale for becoming an arahant—for striving to attain permanent liberation from the cycle of rebirth.

A further key objection to these reports about recollecting a previous life concerns the status of whatever is reborn. If the transmigrating entity is an immaterial mind, how is it able to interact with a material body and brain? This vexed question is a latter-day variant on one of the metaphysical questions that Gotama refused to address. He said that knowing whether the animating spirit (*jīva*) and bodily matter (*sarira*) are identical or different would not be an aid in practicing the fourfold task. Buddhist proponents of rebirth tend to ignore this oft-repeated injunction and opt for a body-mind dualism. They maintain that mind and matter are ontologically separate "substances" (Sanskrit: *dravya*) and thus fundamentally incommensurable. For thinkers like Dharmakīrti, mind is invisible, inaudible, unsmellable, untastable, and untouchable, for it has no shape, color, sound, scent, flavor, or tactility. It is just "luminous and knowing" (*gsal zhing rig pa*). But if mind cannot be touched, how can it "touch"—that is, contact or connect with—a neuron? And if it exists as a non-sense-based knowing, why does it require sense organs and a brain to know anything? On the other hand, if mind must be physical in some sense, then it is even more difficult to explain how it can survive the complete destruction of the body and the brain at death.

(3)

A common Buddhist tactical move at this point in the argument is to shift course and appeal to the authority of scripture. In the discourse *On Fear and Dread,* Gotama provides one of the most detailed accounts of his awakening. Having overcome the fear and dread of living in a jungle retreat, he describes how he then entered successively into the four absorptions (*jhāna*). "When my concentrated mind was thus purified, bright, and unblemished," he says, "I directed it to knowledge of the recollection of past lives."

> I recollected my manifold past lives, that is, one birth, two births, three births, . . . a hundred thousand births, many aeons of world expansion and contraction: "There I was so named, of such a clan, with such an appearance, such was my experience of pleasure and pain, such my life-term; and passing away from there, I reappeared elsewhere . . ." This was the first true knowledge attained by me in the first watch of the night.[5]

The difficulty with this much-cited passage is that it does not describe the awakening itself but a spiritual power (*iddhi*) that even unawakened people are said to be able to achieve. We sometimes find the Buddha speaking in general terms of "those wanderers and brahmins who recollect their manifold past abodes" or declaring that a mendicant who has attained the four bases of spiritual power (i.e., specific levels of deep concentration) "recollects his manifold past lives," and in these instances he uses exactly the same terms with which he describes his own memory of them.[6] Recollection of one's past lives is traditionally believed to be attainable by anyone who has mastered the fourth absorption, a refined state of concentration that experiences neither-pain-nor-pleasure and is settled in total equanimity.

After recalling his past lives, Gotama describes how he directed his mind "to knowledge of the passing away and reappearance of beings":

> With the divine eye, I saw beings passing away and reappearing, inferior and superior, fair and ugly, fortunate and unfortunate. I understood how beings pass on according to their

> actions. . . . This was the second true knowledge attained by me in the second watch of the night.[7]

Thus Gotama came to understand how the law of karma plays out in the lives of sentient beings. But even this insight is not equivalent to the experience of awakening; it, too, according to the discourses, is a spiritual power available to those who have mastered the fourth absorption.

On Fear and Dread demonstrated to an Indian audience of believers that Gotama gained direct insight into rebirth and karma, thereby confirming the twin pillars of Indian cosmology, *before* he achieved his own distinctive awakening. As Johannes Bronkhorst points out, these insights "have no obvious and intrinsic connection with liberation." Their presence in the text serves as "a confirmation that the doctrine of rebirth and karmic retribution is true, and provides this doctrine with the highest seal of approval imaginable for a believing Buddhist."[8] Only then, in the third watch of the night, does Gotama direct his mind to "knowledge of destruction of the effluences," which enables him to understand *dukkha,* arising, cessation, and the path. It is this, rather than any knowledge of rebirth or the law of karma, that is unique to him and constitutes his awakening.

While *On Fear and Dread* presents mastery of the four absorptions as a precursor to the attainment of awakening, the account in *The Noble Quest,* which scholars believe to be earlier, makes no mention at all of the absorptions, let alone the spiritual powers to remember past lives and to understand the law of karma.[9] By locating this central experience of Buddhism within the context of Indian asceticism and cosmology, *On Fear and Dread* fits it into the metaphysical framework of the culture of the Buddha's time. It likewise represents Gotama as having attained what is tantamount to the mind of God: he gained first-hand knowledge of what makes the universe tick. For him to have attained this knowledge served the purpose of those who sought to raise him beyond merely human to quasi-divine status.

(4)

This critical assessment of the doctrines of rebirth and karma risks overlooking a crucially important role that they have played in historical Buddhist cultures. To dismiss them as unverifiable metaphysical beliefs of a former age fails to recognize how they served to situate human life within a vision of the cosmos. Rather than conceiving of one's life as a brief flicker of self-interested consciousness on the surface of the earth, people with these beliefs could see, in the mythic language of the time, how all living beings are intimately connected to a complex series of causal conditions that preceded their existence, as well as to a seemingly infinite unfolding of future consequences for which each was in some small way responsible. In providing a sense of humility, connectedness, and responsibility, this worldview encouraged people to consider the significance of their existence in the selfless context of the immensity of life itself, not reduce it to the service of their egotistical greed and hatred.

Imagining thus, we can begin to appreciate the grandeur of these beliefs. To speak of recalling "one birth, two births, three births, . . . a hundred thousand births, many aeons of world expansion and contraction" and seeing "with the divine eye . . . beings passing away and reappearing, inferior and superior, fair and ugly, fortunate and unfortunate" evokes a vision that is both magnificent and tragic. There is poetry in this cosmic dance: beings emerge and disappear infinitely, linked together in an infinite web of interactions. The vision takes the believer out of petty concerns into an astonished fascination with the sheer play of life. The vision is mind-stopping, excessive, sublime. There is no need to validate it as true or reject it as false. To do so would be as absurd as dismissing Hieronymus Bosch's depictions of heaven and hell because they do not correspond to any empirically observable reality.

A sense of the sublimity and interconnectedness of life does not require retaining or reverting to the cosmological beliefs of ancient India. Secular modernity provides an entirely adequate alternative. The vision of life that has been revealed during the past two centuries by the natural sciences more than compensates for the loss of premodern religious worldviews. Compared with the finely detailed descriptions of the emergence of life from the singularity of the Big Bang, the mind-boggling extent of the galaxies in this expanding universe, the extraordinary unfolding of myriad life-forms from single-celled organisms, and the sublime complexity of the human brain, the theories of rebirth and karma appear crude and simplistic.

At the conclusion of *On the Origin of Species,* Charles Darwin declared: "There is grandeur in this view of life, with its several powers, having been originally breathed into a few forms or into one; and that, whilst this planet has gone cycling on according to the fixed law of gravity, from so simple a beginning endless forms most beautiful and most wonderful have been, and are being, evolved." If we take seriously the Buddha's remark at the head of this chapter—"And of that which the wise in the world agree upon as existing, I too say that it exists"—it is hard to conclude that he would have rejected the work of Darwin and his followers ("the wise of the world") simply because it conflicted with the opinions current in Kosala and Magadha in the fifth century BCE. As a pragmatist, what ultimately mattered to Gotama was not whether this or that opinion about reality was true or false but whether the opinion supported or impeded the practice of the fourfold task. Far from impeding the practice of the task, the worldview of modern science provides it with a sound and fertile foundation. The practice of mindfulness, for example, is liberated from the dogmatic constraints of Indian metaphysics and afforded new possibilities that extend its benefits beyond the narrow context of the Buddhist religion.

If evolution by natural selection offers a compelling account of the physical dimension of conditioned arising, the study of human history provides vivid lessons in moral and ethical contingency. That our thoughts, words, and deeds can continue to have powerful effects after our death is no better illustrated than by examining the lives of individuals who have influenced the course of human history. Whether we consider Shakespeare, Darwin, or Hitler, our historical understanding enables us to see how their actions have borne fruit—both for good and for bad—in the kind of world we inhabit today. Likewise, sociology has made us far more aware of the consequences of our collective behavior in a culture or society, while, on a more personal level, psychology and psychotherapy have enabled each of us to penetrate the history of our own childhood to arrive at insights into how our sense of self has been formed by the ways we have been treated by others and by our reactions and choices.

And thanks to the work of ecologists and environmentalists, when we turn our attention to the future, we are increasingly conscious of how our individual and collective actions today will bear fruit long after we have turned to dust and been forgotten. Far more than the generalized speculations of karma theory, this knowledge provides a sobering vision of a degraded future world that is being shaped by how we lead our lives now. Rather than concern ourselves with our own hypothetical rebirth, we are challenged to assume a heightened responsibility for this planet and the continued flourishing of its inhabitants, human, animal, and vegetable, as we live our lives now.

This secular vision teases out the intuitions of the doctrines of karma and rebirth in vivid and compelling detail. Biology, physics, ecology, psychology, and history provide boundless illustrations of conditioned arising made flesh, from the most intimate details of our own mental states to the most devastating accounts of melting polar ice caps. This vision is likewise able to awaken and fine-tune our moral sense. It brings the dharma firmly down to earth. Before our stunned gaze, the *dukkha* of which Gotama spoke is rendered more immediate, palpable, and extensive than ever before. The need to respond to it unconditioned by the instincts of reactive egotistic greed has reached a point where the very survival of life on earth may be at stake. This vision does not, however, constitute a plea for a "socially engaged" Buddhism. It is a plea to recover what the dharma has always been about: embracing the suffering of the world, letting go of reactivity, and experiencing that still, clear center from which we respond to the world in ways no longer determined by self-interest alone.

(5)

The real problem with rebirth is not suffering periodic hellish torments or other forms of acute pain in different realms of existence but undergoing the same cycle of birth and death again and again for eternity (unless one does something about it). Rebirth is a metaphor for hell. If we remove the metaphysical carapace and strip the concept down to its psychological-existential core, we arrive at *repetition*. This is explicit in the Pali term *punabbhava,* usually translated as "rebirth," which literally means "again-becoming." A modern translation might be "repetitive existence," which highlights how a life conditioned by reactivity is one that goes round and round in circles. You may expend a great deal of energy and time on many different things, but at the end of the day, you find yourself back in the same state of bored restlessness whence you set out. You realize, with a sinking feeling, that existentially you have achieved nothing. It is as though you have been running on the spot, like a hamster on its wheel, a dog chasing its tail, without getting anywhere.

If we take the idea of rebirth literally, then the only way out of its eternal cycle is to overcome the forces of reactivity that drive the process of *saṃsāra,* so that after death we will not be born again. From this orthodox perspective, the goal of our practice is the attainment of a final, transcendent nirvana. A secular reading, however, treats rebirth as a metaphor for a repetitive existence in which we remain locked into cycles of reactive behavior. In this case, the goal of the practice is to stop thinking, speaking, and acting reactively, thereby liberating ourselves to respond to life unconditioned by such impulses. Instead of lying beyond the transient, suffering world, nirvana is revealed to lie in the very heart of our own sentient experience here and now.

These two conflicting interpretations of nirvana yield very different understandings of what constitutes the good. For an orthodox Buddhist, the highest good is a transcendent state of nirvana located beyond the conditioned world; for a non-orthodox, secular practitioner, the highest good is an eightfold path of human flourishing that springs from an immanent condition of nirvana. In the language of the four tasks, a dharma of transcendence emphasizes the experience of stopping reactivity (third task), whereas a dharma of immanence emphasizes the cultivation of a way of life (fourth task). Whatever one's outlook, one still needs to perform both tasks; the difference lies in how one understands the relationship between them. Transcendentalists regard the cultivation of the path as a precondition for the attainment of nirvana; secularists regard the experience of nirvana as a precondition for cultivating the path.

A particular thread running through the Pali Canon provides valuable endorsement for this secular interpretation. It is found in those discourses scattered through the canon where the Buddha is depicted in conversation with his nemesis, the "demon" Māra. These texts employ a symbolic, mythic language to convey an understanding of the perennial human struggle between good and evil. Gotama's encounters with Māra illustrate how the good is conceived: a life unconstrained by those forces that impede it from flourishing. Māra is sometimes referred to as the *antaka:* the one who imposes dead ends (*anta*), which, by keeping one caught in cycles of reactive behavior, limit the ability to respond to life with care. The word *māra* literally means "the killer" and is thus equivalent to *pamāda*—carelessness, which, in the words of the *Dhammapada,* is "the path to death."[10]

The discourses that show Gotama in dialogue with Māra are composed in a very different language from those that report Gotama's discussions with contemporaries like Mahānāma, Pasenadi, and Ānanda. Although Māra is presented as if he were an autonomous quasi-human individual, he is not in any sense a historical figure but a mythic personification of evil. Unless we think of Māra as a talking apparition, it is difficult to treat him as anything other than a symbolic way of representing something about the Buddha himself. As Gotama became elevated to increasingly inhuman degrees of perfection, it became correspondingly difficult to accommodate the conflicted humanity of a man who had to deal with crises and betrayals, as well as his own sickness, aging, and death. The problem was solved by splitting him into two: the all-good Buddha, versus the all-bad Māra. Suppressing every trace of ordinary humanity in the figure of Gotama perhaps made it inevitable that an autonomous counterfigure would come to function as his shadow.

A central paradox in the life of Gotama is that of a man who famously conquered the forces of Māra on the night of the awakening only to continue for the remaining forty-five years of his life to have intimate dealings with the very same forces. Clearly, then, he did not successfully delete reactivity from his experience; it was not, as the discourses say, "cut off like a palm stump, never to arise again." Rather, he had discovered a radically new way of coming to terms with reactivity.

In other words, Gotama has not eliminated the forces of Māra but become immune to them.[11] If reactivity arises in his mind, it can no longer gain any purchase. He neither assents to nor struggles against it. When regarded with mindful awareness, greed and hatred are seen for what they are: impermanent emotions that, when left to their own devices, will fizzle out. Realizing that they are conditioned processes and not essentially "me" or "mine" takes away their power—hence the phrase that occurs at the conclusion of many of the dialogues: "I know you, Māra." Nirvanic freedom is the result of understanding how reactivity works. It is not the result of uprooting reactivity.

In the traditional doctrines of karma and rebirth, the three fires of greed, hatred, and confusion are seen as nonphysical mental states that accompany the reincarnating consciousness from life to life until they are eventually eliminated and the consciousness is born no more. From the perspective of modern biology, greed and hatred are a legacy of our evolutionary past. They are physical drives rooted in our limbic system, which still possess such potency because of the exceptional survival advantages the drives conferred on humans as a species. However effective the practice of mindfulness might be in training us not to assent to the demands of our basic drives, it seems naive to think that meditation could permanently delete them from our limbic system. Their force may be diminished by not acting on them, but their underlying presence will persist. This scientific perspective helps us understand how Gotama conquered Māra by no longer assenting to him but was still subject to Māra's promptings.

Māra is far more than just the reactivity triggered in response to the impact of the world. The "evil" he personifies extends to the very structure of contingent existence. If Māra is whatever imposes constraints and limits upon us, then we need to consider how our very being-in-the-world is permeated by the demonic. On one occasion, Māra approaches Gotama "in the form of a farmer, carrying a large plow on his shoulder, holding a long goad stick, his hair disheveled, wearing hempen garments, his feet smeared with mud." He asks: "Have you seen my oxen, wanderer?" Gotama replies: "what are oxen to you, evil one?" Māra declares:

> The eye is mine, forms are mine, eye-contact and its base of consciousness are mine. The ear . . . , the nose . . . , the tongue . . . , the body . . . , the mind, mental contact and its base of consciousness . . . , are mine. Where can you go to escape me?[12]

Limitation is built into a world that is parsed into separate, independently existent parts that we identify as "me" or "mine." As long as we are unselfconsciously locked into such a naive (farmer-like) sense of the world, we are prone to being trapped by Māra's "snares," caught on one of his "barbed hooks," seduced by his "daughters." Gotama replies: "Where there is no eye, no ear, no nose, no tongue, no body, no mind—there is no place for you there, evil one." As soon as we begin to loosen the cognitive-affective grip of exclusive self-concern, we discover the first inklings of a freedom to respond to life situations from a more selfless perspective.

Māra's snares amplify the meaning of *dukkha*. Birth, sickness, aging, and death are *dukkha* not just because they are painful but because they limit our capacity to realize our possibilities. Māra is whatever impedes human flourishing. Psychologically Māra may refer to our habitual reactivity, but existentially Māra refers to any physical, social, political, or economic impediment to our practice of the four tasks. A debilitating stroke, a patriarchal culture, a despotic government, an oppressive religion, grinding poverty: these can prevent our flourishing just as effectively as our own greed and hatred.

Ultimately, Māra refers to the sheer unreliability and unpredictability of this world into which we were thrown at birth and from which we will be evicted at death. In an impermanent and contingent world, where life depends on a single heartbeat, there are no guarantees that Māra will not cut us down, bringing to an abrupt end whatever aspirations we might cherish.

To embrace suffering means to embrace Māra. To let go of reactivity means to let go of Māra. Letting go entails facing up to the condition we find ourselves in without bitterness or despair while being acutely aware of the first stirrings of reactivity that prompt us to think, speak, or act in ways we subsequently regret. To adopt such a stance vis-à-vis Māra offers a way of living in this world that is premised on the still, radiant equanimity symbolized by the figure of the Buddha. We suddenly see two faces in profile rather than a vase. In a gestalt switch, Māra *becomes* Buddha. A closed mind becomes an open mind. Carelessness becomes care. Death becomes the deathless. "Mine" becomes "not-mine."

But the opposite is true as well. A Buddha-perspective can just as easily switch back into a Māra-perspective. This ambivalence is captured in a saying by Huineng, the sixth Sŏn patriarch:

> Therefore, we know that, unawakened, even a Buddha is a sentient being, and that even a sentient being, if he is awakened in an instant of thought, is a Buddha.[13]

We might be uncomfortable with splitting Gotama into two—good Buddha and evil Māra—but in practice this conception proves instructive. The Buddha-Māra paradigm enables us to see that the fourfold task entails not only a sequence of actions but a radical perceptual shift that is constantly under threat. This realization undermines any wishful notion that the cultivation of the path will unfold along a steady gradient of self-improvement. Thinking so requires an ironic self-regard constantly alert to the possibility that one may be deceiving oneself.

If "Māra" is a way of describing a repetitive existence that goes nowhere, then "Buddha" describes a way of being-in-the-world that unfolds as human flourishing. If Māra is a metaphor for death, then Buddha is a metaphor for life. We can no more make sense of Buddha without Māra than we can make sense of life without death. The performance of the fourfold task is impossible without the resistance of Māra, just as lighting a wooden match is impossible without resistance that generates friction. It is here, I believe, that we start to discern the unsteady heartbeat of a culture of awakening.

(6)

In the parable of the city, Gotama compares himself to a man wandering through a forest who chances upon an ancient road. Following it, he reaches the ruins of a city.[14] On leaving the forest, he reports this discovery to the local king and urges him to rebuild the city, which once again becomes "prosperous, well-populated, attained to growth and expansion." This story is one of the few occasions in the canon that provides a clue as to how the Buddha saw his dharma enacted through the structures of the world. By comparing the ancient road in the forest to the noble eightfold path, he implies that the goal of the path is not the transcendent experience of nirvana, achieved through the cessation of death and rebirth, but the building of another kind of society, based on understanding the four great tasks as a function of the principle of conditionality. Although the redactors of the canon struggled to make this parable fit with the orthodox goal of bringing existence to an end, its guiding metaphor of a thriving, bustling city strongly resists such an interpretation.

Gotama depicts the city as a space that encourages human flourishing through the provision of economic opportunity ("prosperity"), security ("ramparts"), family life ("well populated"), and leisure ("parks, groves, ponds"). A city is a civic space where individuals can live in close proximity as "rational, sociable agents who are meant to collaborate in peace to their mutual benefit."[15] Since the dharma has no place for either the providential designs of a Creator or a divinely ordained social hierarchy, the realization of the city's potential lies squarely in the hands of human beings who enjoy equality. In this sense, the practice of the fourfold task becomes more than just a template for personal flourishing. When practiced with others who share one's ultimate concerns, the four tasks become acts of solidarity working together as residents build a communal and social future based on an understanding of a naturalistic causality.

In urging the king to *rebuild* the ancient city, Gotama seems to be making three separate but related points. First, he does not want to be considered exceptional. Anyone who has penetrated the principle of conditionality and the practice of the middle way will arrive, he suggests, at the same sort of conclusions that he did. In principle at least, there was no reason why dharma-centered cities would not have been built in the past (perhaps he had in mind the ruined cities of the Indus Valley or, closer to home, those of Indraprasta). Second, he does not wish to present his project as utopian. In keeping with his understanding of the pervasive nature of impermanence and tragedy, he recognizes that, like everything else, civilizations rise and fall. And third, he does not conceive of the rebuilding of the city as a hubristic endeavor. To rebuild a city is not the same as founding a city. Although a king or a minister would have been needed to fund, recruit labor for, and oversee the task, the rebuilding would have been essentially a communal activity of a society devoted to recovering its past glory rather than feeding the ego of a monarch.

When considered communally, the fourth task of cultivating the path can be understood as an activity that lays the foundations for a culture. In English, "cultivate" and "culture" are cognates: a cultivated person is a cultured person. A culture is a set of shared values that have been cultivated by those who are dedicated to a life of the mind. A Buddhist culture, therefore, is one that embodies the values of the dharma as realized over generations by people who have practiced it. Yet, as with cities, cultures undergo periods of creativity and growth, stagnation and decline, even disappearance, leaving only archaeological and textual remains. The challenge facing those today who seek to give form to a secular dharma (or a Buddhist secularity) is similar to that of the man in the forest who stumbles across the ruins of an ancient city and aspires to rebuild it.

From a modern perspective, many of the traditional forms of Buddhism inherited from Asia appear to be stagnating. They seem primarily intent on preserving time-honored doctrines and practices by endlessly repeating past teachings and instructions. Although gifted individual teachers might seek to break out of this mold, they tend to be restrained by the forces of tradition, on which they are ultimately dependent for their authority and legitimacy. After the death of a radical teacher, it is often difficult for his or her followers to resist the pull of orthodoxy that seeks to rein them back into the fold. Any serious reconsideration of doctrines such as reincarnation makes little headway. Religious institutions that have survived for hundreds of years tend to regard even minor modifications of views or behavior as anathema.

A contemporary culture of awakening is unlikely to emerge from the traditional schools of Buddhism without outside impetus. For a stagnant culture to flower will require a return to the often ignored or forgotten sources of the tradition, a systematic unlearning of outdated Buddhist dogma, a radical transformation of institutions, and a concerted effort to rethink the dharma from the ground up. The primary and crucial question for those who are drawn to the possibility of such a culture will be how to create, sustain, and develop a Buddhist community based on the principle of conditionality and the practice of the four tasks.

Over the centuries the term "community" (*sangha*) has tended to be monopolized by monastic institutions. In fifth-century BCE India, by contrast, the word *sangha* denoted republican societies (such as Mallā and the Vajjian Confederacy) that were governed by assemblies rather than monarchies (such as Magadha and Kosala) that were ruled by a sovereign lord. Not only did Gotama explicitly model his community on that of a republican society, but he repeatedly stated that the assembly of his followers was fourfold: it consisted of *bhikkhus* and *bhikkhunis*, male adherents and female adherents. Moreover, this community was to govern itself by adhering to an impersonal body of laws (dharma) rather than deferring to the will of a senior mendicant (like Mahākassapa). And, crucially, membership of the noble community (*ariyasangha*) was to be determined not by social status but by stream entry—not by whether one was a renunciant or a householder but by whether one had made the eightfold path one's own.[16]

We have already seen how adherents such as Mahānāma, Jīvaka, and even the drunkard Sarakāni were regarded as stream entrants and thereby formed part of the noble community. The *Connected Discourses* also includes a section devoted to the adherent Citta, a householder from the town of Macchikāsanda in Kāsi, who is shown explaining the dharma to mendicants and praised as one who possesses "the eye of understanding that penetrates the profound buddha-word."[17] In the *Greater Discourse to Vacchagotta,* the Teacher declares to his inquisitive but suspicious interlocuter:

> There are not only one hundred, or five hundred, but far more men and women adherents, my disciples, clothed in white, enjoying sensuality, who carry out my instruction, re-

> spond to my advice, have gone beyond doubt, become free from perplexity, gained intrepidity, and become independent of others in my teaching.[18]

The picture that emerges from these and other passages is of a diverse community of self-reliant individuals who mutually support one another, yet without compromising their independence in terms of their understanding and practice of the dharma.

The dispute between Ānanda and Mahākassapa that took place after the Buddha's death boils down to a struggle between conflicting ideas of what would constitute an effective sangha. That Mahākassapa's vision of a top-down hierarchy prevailed over Ānanda's vision of a more inclusive and pluralistic community might, as far as we know, have enabled the dharma to survive under the fraught conditions of the time. But it also set the stage for the eventual separation of the mendicants into monastic institutions, whose economic and political vulnerability was partly responsible for the disappearance of Buddhism in India fifteen centuries after the Buddha's death.

In a secular age like our own, it is difficult to imagine the standard Asian model of Buddhist monasticism taking root outside either Buddhist communities or small groups of traditional-minded converts. To imagine a secular sangha begins by posing the fundamental question of where authority lies. If we follow the earliest sources, we learn that authority lies in the dharma. By restoring this key but often forgotten principle, monastics and householders, men and women alike, are seen to be beholden to a law that supersedes whatever institutional power someone might have acquired in the course of a career in a Buddhist hierarchy. A secular sangha, therefore, allows for the empowerment of those who were previously marginalized and disempowered. This does not mean, however, that adherents should now replace mendicants at the top of the hierarchy. To put authority in the dharma entails abandoning any hierarchy and replacing it with a model that functions (like that of the Quakers) through consensus among spiritual equals.

A secular sangha is a community of like-minded, self-reliant individuals, united by friendship, who work to mutually support each other in their own flourishing. Such a community is an ongoing *practice;* it requires commitment and action. As a *living* community, where all members regard themselves as works in progress, it is an unfinished project. Martin Buber makes a useful distinction here between a *community* and a *collective*. Whereas members of a collective surrender their autonomy to achieve a common goal, the members of a community create a network of friendships that support and celebrate the individuation of each member within the context of a shared set of values.[19]

Might such a conception of sangha be just another utopian ideal with little bearing on what human beings might realistically be able to achieve? If we adopt such an ideal, might we be in danger of rejecting a model of community that, whatever its imperfections, has proven itself to be viable over many centuries? The Buddhist order of mendicants is, after all, one of the most enduring human institutions the world has ever known. So how are secular Buddhists to create, sustain, and develop a sangha based on communal, dharma-oriented principles? How are they to find a middle way between autocratic and hierarchical religious institutions, on the one hand, and isolated, alienated individualism, on the other? This is the challenge.

(7)

There are records of a Greek becoming a Buddhist mendicant—called Dharmarakshita—less than two centuries after Gotama's death. In modern times the first Westerner to take this step, as far as we currently know, was an itinerant Irish laborer, atheist freethinker, and political agitator born as Laurence Carroll (or O'Rourke) around 1856 and ordained in Rangoon as U Dhammaloka in 1900. Details of this remarkable man's life have only recently come to light through the dogged research of three scholars: Brian Bocking, Alicia Turner, and

Laurence Cox.[20] The picture of Dhammaloka is still incomplete—there are long gaps in his biography, and the date and place of his death remain a mystery—but enough is known to allow this long-forgotten radical to upset much received opinion about the nature of early Western converts to Buddhism.

Carroll/O'Rourke emigrated to the United States sometime in the 1870s or 1880s, crossed the continent, and made his way by ship to Japan. He eventually arrived in Burma, where he found employment as a tally clerk for a logging company. He may have become a novice monk as early as the mid-1880s; he received full ordination in July 1900. From this time until his disappearance from the public record fourteen years later, he was a temperance advocate and a vociferous opponent of Christianity and colonialism. For Dhammaloka, "a bottle of 'Guiding Star Brandy,' a 'Holy Bible' and a 'Gatling Gun'" served as interconnected symbols of the British attempt to undermine the traditional values of Burma in order to bring the country firmly under colonial rule.[21] Found guilty of sedition in 1910, he received a light sentence. His preaching activities led him far afield: to Japan, Siam, Singapore, Ceylon, and Cambodia, even Australia. In 1914 a Christian missionary report has him directing the Siam Buddhist Freethought Association in Bangkok, which is the last we hear of him.

As a working-class itinerant who takes the outrageous step of adopting the beliefs and garb of a colonized people and then publicly denounces the religion and culture into which he was born, Dhammaloka stands in stark contrast to the cultured, bookish figures of Allan Bennett (Ananda Metteyya) and Anton Gueth (Nyanatiloka), who have, until now, been regarded as the first Western Buddhist monks.[22] Bennett (1872–1923) was a frail British intellectual, trained as a chemist, who became an enthusiastic occultist and close friend of Aleister Crowley. Gueth (1878–1957) was born in Wiesbaden, privately trained as a classical musician and composer, and became an avid reader of Arthur Schopenhauer before becoming interested in Buddhism. Both men were ordained in Burma shortly after Dhammaloka, but there is no record that either of these middle-class Europeans met or had anything to do with the fiery Irish vagabond.

For Dhammaloka, homelessness was not the idealized gesture of renunciation made by cultured men living in simple but comfortable hermitages but a harsh, uncertain lifestyle of which he had firsthand experience. He was not the only poor white man who drifted through Asia at the end of the nineteenth century, eking out a living on the periphery of empire. It would have been entirely natural for itinerants to seek hospitality in Buddhist monasteries, where they would have been provided with food and shelter without charge. Possibly, some of them also were ordained as monks for shorter or longer periods. But since the lives of such men were rarely documented, by either themselves or others, they tend to leave no trace. Today we might see them as forerunners of the Beats and hippies who also wandered through Asia on a shoestring budget and likewise often ended up in Buddhist monasteries.

Even today, the fragments we know of Dhammaloka's life challenge the widely held view of Buddhism as a tradition grounded in scholarship, meditation, and retreat from the affairs of the world. Here we find a man who lived outside the norms of polite Western society, a *bhikkhu* who engaged in passionate rhetoric, a radical who embraced the suffering of the oppressed. In addition to being the first Western *bhikkhu*, Dhammaloka was also the first Westerner to practice a Buddhism that was vitally engaged with the challenges of secularization.

Dharma practice takes place on the very ground on which you stand, as the life of U Dhammaloka shows. It is your most caring/care-full response to the conditions you face here and now. There is no ideal form or model of practice, perfect for all time, to seek to conform to. Although Dhammaloka founded a Buddhist Tract Society in Rangoon in 1907, which published, among other things, Thomas Paine's *Rights of Man* and *The Age of Reason*, his dharma finds its most compelling expression not in what he wrote or printed but in his public, bodily acts.

We may need to unlearn Buddhist dogma to discover the dharma afresh, but we may also need to unlearn the stories that Buddhism has constructed about its own past if we are to gain a three-dimensional and nuanced account of its history. Rather than think of Dhammaloka as exceptional (thereby tacitly reinforcing the colonial assumption that it took a European to shake up the passive Burmese), we need to consider that the picture of Buddhism presented by its apologists—as a religion of nirvanic tranquillity and enlightenment—may be just a pious caricature that fails to account for how most Buddhists in history actually lived. As the lives of Mahānāma, Pasenadi, Sunakkhatta, Jīvaka, and Ānanda illustrate, the early canon reveals a community composed of imperfect people who struggled to apply the dharma in their very different lives. As Gregory Schopen's studies of epigraphical and archaeological evidence show, Buddhist monasteries in ancient India commonly engaged in commercial and other activities that are at odds with the idealistic representations of monasticism found in the texts.[23] The work of the scholar Jacques Gernet similarly reveals that the large Buddhist monastic institutions in China were enfolded in the mechanisms of the state and owned granaries, treasuries, and slaves.[24]

As Buddhism finds itself subject to the gaze of the intrusive media of modernity, held to account by its followers, and judged according to the standards of transparency, we have an unprecedented opportunity to observe what actually goes on in its name. Buddhist centers turn out to be just as prone to power struggles, sexual scandals, and misuse of funds as any other human institution, and Buddhist "masters" are routinely exposed as possessing restless libidos and feet of clay. If we are shocked and disappointed by such revelations, we entertained an idealistic view of Buddhism to begin with. In accepting Buddhism's unselfconscious rhetoric about its awakened teachers, pure lineages, and meditations that guarantee enlightenment, we are in danger of setting ourselves up either for painful disillusionment or increasingly elaborate forms of justification and denial.

I do not propose cynicism. All I wish to point out is that Buddhist institutions and teachers are human and subject to human failings. In this regard, Buddhism is no different from any other religion. But it can trick Westerners, bemused by its novelty and unfamiliarity, into thinking that it might have avoided the ossification and corruption that tend to seep unnoticed into any establishment that has come to take its authority for granted. Only by taking Buddhism off its romantic pedestal and bringing it down to earth gives us a chance to imagine what kind of culture the dharma might be capable of engendering in a secular world grown wary of charismatic priests and inflexible dogmas.

(8)

One recent consequence of modernity's encounter with the dharma is that secular Buddhist spaces have sprung up in various parts of the world. Scattered individuals and groups are committed to a practice of the dharma but have no affiliation with a traditional school of Buddhism. These spiritual nomads tend to be informed more by writings and podcasts from across the Buddhist spectrum than by a teacher of any particular lineage. Their sense of belonging to a community may be more virtual than actual. When they meet together in person, the location is as likely to be the living room of a city apartment as a Buddhist center. Though wary of the inflexible beliefs, uncritical devotion, and patriarchal institutions of the Buddhist religion, they may nonetheless value the facilities of and benefit from the training offered by more traditional groups. Some are refugees from such organizations. They have have devoted many years to a specific Buddhist lineage, only to leave because they can no longer in good faith accept its doctrines, endorse its polemics of exceptionalism, or submit to the authority of its leaders. Others continue happily to identify themselves as Christians, Jews, or nonbelievers while pursuing a heartfelt practice of the dharma.

In 2005 I started to formulate a series of theses to define the kind of secular Buddhist space in which I found myself then and continue to find myself today—the kind of space I have been writing about in this book. I offer a revised version of them here:

Ten Theses of Secular Dharma

1. A secular Buddhist is one who is committed to the practice of the dharma for the sake of this world alone.

2. The practice of the dharma consists of four tasks: to embrace suffering, to let go of reactivity, to behold the ceasing of reactivity, and to cultivate an integrated way of life.

3. All human beings, irrespective of gender, race, sexual orientation, disability, nationality, and religion, can practice these four tasks. Each person, in each moment, has the potential to be more awake, responsive, and free.

4. The practice of the dharma is as much concerned with how one speaks, acts, and works in the public realm as with how one performs spiritual exercises in private.

5. The dharma serves the needs of people at specific times and places. Each form the dharma assumes is a transient human creation, contingent upon the historical, cultural, social, and economic conditions that generated it.

6. The practitioner honors the dharma teachings that have been passed down through different traditions while seeking to enact them creatively in ways appropriate to the world as it is now.

7. The community of practitioners is formed of autonomous persons who mutually support each other in the cultivation of their paths. In this network of like-minded individuals, members respect the equality of all members while honoring the specific knowledge and expertise each person brings.

8. A practitioner is committed to an ethics of care, founded on empathy, compassion, and love for all creatures who have evolved on this earth.

9. Practitioners seek to understand and diminish the structural violence of societies and institutions as well as the roots of violence that are present in themselves.

10. A practitioner of the dharma aspires to nurture a culture of awakening that finds its inspiration in Buddhist and non-Buddhist, religious and secular sources alike.

Afterword

The Pali Canon effectively concludes with an account of the first council in Rājagaha, about nine months after Gotama's death. However, a final chapter in the Vinaya jumps ahead one hundred years (to c. 300 BCE) to give an account of a second council that took place in Vesālī.[1] It appears that Vajjian mendicants had introduced ten modifications to the training rule, which relaxed some of the strictures concerning food and drink and allowed the handling of money. When an elder called Yasa learned of the modifications, he consulted widely with other mendicants from as far afield as Avanti and Pāvā and organized an assembly in Vesālī to settle the issue. The result was a unanimous rejection of the modified rule. Apart from an insightful glimpse into how conservatives in the order reacted to an attempt to liberalize the rule, we learn nothing further about what had become of the Buddhist community since Gotama died. At this point, the canonical narrative comes to an abrupt halt, and the door that had been opened onto the human world of ancient northeastern India is closed.

So we are never told whether King Ajātasattu of Magadha succeeded in his ambition to destroy the Vajjian republic or what happened to the kingdom of Kosala after the overthrow and death of King Pasenadi. Nor do we learn whether Sakiya managed to recover from the Kosalan invasion under Viḍūḍabha. To find out what happened during the century after the Buddha's death, we need to turn to Brahmanic and Greek sources, both of which are fragmentary and provide little more than tantalizing glimpses.

The Brahmanic *Purāṇas* say that a low-caste soldier called Mahāpadma Nanda overthrew the rulers of Magadha about fifty years after Gotama's passing to establish the Nanda dynasty. Apart from a list of ten kings, who together ruled for only twenty or so years, very little is known about the Nandas. They are believed to have built up a powerful army and expanded the territory of Magadha, although exactly how far is uncertain. Because none of these kings can have ruled for very long, the Nandas must have suffered from considerable infighting and instability. Dhana Nanda (known to the Greeks as Agrammes) was the last of their kings. He was overthrown by Chandragupta, founder of the Mauryan empire and grandfather of Aśoka, in 322 BCE.[2]

The defining historical event of the century that followed Gotama's death was the invasion of India by Alexander the Great in 326 BCE. Fired by his initial victories in Gandhāra, Alexander wanted to press on eastwards into the Gangetic basin. But his exhausted army rebelled upon reaching the Beas River, in modern-day Himachal Pradesh. Unwilling to confront the forces of the Nandas, they turned back and headed south down the Hydaspes River (a tributary of the Indus) toward the Arabian Sea. Two powerful tribes in the region, the Mallians and the Oxydracians, decided to form an alliance to prevent Alexander's army from crossing their territory. Alexander moved swiftly to prevent their troops from joining forces. After the alliance crumbled, Alexander launched a series of brutal offensives against the Mallians. At the final battle, in the citadel of Multan, Alexander killed the Mallian chief but was himself badly wounded by an arrow. Four days later, he had recovered sufficiently to receive the final submission of the Mallians.

In the entry on the republic of Mallā in the *Dictionary of Pāli Proper Names*, G. P. Malalasekera claims that "the Mallāns are generally identified with the Malloi (= Mallians) mentioned in the Greek accounts of Alexander's invasion of India."[3] This intriguing suggestion provides a tentative answer to what happened to the kingdom of Kosala after the deaths of Pasenadi and Viḍūḍabha. As we have seen, Mallā was a close ally of Kosala and provided the generals for the Kosalan army: initially Bandhula, then, after Bandhula's murder by Pasenadi, his nephew Dīgha Kārāyaṇa. Gotama's final journey ended in the Mallān town of Kusinārā, the fief of Bandhula, possibly because he recognized it as a secure base for his community and a future center of power. We also know that Dīgha Kārāyaṇa conspired with Viḍūḍabha to overthrow Pasenadi. Once Viḍūḍabha and his retinue were conveniently washed away in a flash flood, Kārāyaṇa, the commander of the army, would have been in a very strong position—particularly since Viḍūḍabha appears to have left no heir. It is possible, therefore, that Kārāyaṇa seized this opportunity to establish a Mallān dynasty in Kosala with himself at its head. This could, in fact, have been his plan all along.

If Malalasekera is correct in identifying the Mallāns with the Malloi who fought Alexander, then in the seventy-five years after Gotama's death the descendents of Bandhula and Kārāyaṇa must have expanded their territory considerably farther westward across the northern Gangetic plain, at least as far as Multan (now just inside Pakistan), the site of their defeat by Alexander. In this scenario, the Nanda dynasty would have been successor to the Magadhan, controlling the lands to the south of the Ganges, while Mallā would have ruled over the territories north of the river that formerly were part of Kosala. The primary concern of Alexander's forces was the Nandas, which might indicate that the Nandas had already overrun parts of the northeastern Gangetic basin and had forced the Mallāns westward. Whatever the case, the memory of a powerful Mallā empire in India was kept alive by the Mallā dynasty that ruled in the Kathmandu valley of Nepal from 1201 to 1769, whose founders claimed to be descendents of the Mallāns of the Buddha's time.

After Alexander's conquest of the Persian empire, it was divided up among his generals and gradually Hellenized. The general who gained control of the eastern part of the former Achaemenid territory, including Gandhāra, was Seleucus I Nicator (c. 358–281 BCE). In 305 BCE he was forced to cede these easternmost territories to Chandragupta, the founder of the Mauryan empire. The two leaders concluded a treaty in which Seleucus received five hundred (that is, many) war elephants from Chandragupta in exchange for Gandhāra. To seal the agreement, Seleucus presented Chandragupta with a Greek bride, so perhaps his famous Buddhist grandson Aśoka was one quarter Greek.

Seleucus subsequently dispatched an ambassador to Chandragupta's capital of Pāṭaliputta, at the confluence of the Ganges, Son, and Gandak Rivers. The man he chose for the mission was a Greek from Asia Minor called Megasthenes, who was to spend ten years in the heart of the region where the Buddha had lived and taught less than a century before. Fortunately for us, Megasthenes wrote a book called *Indika* (India) in which he gave the first detailed account of the country and its people. Although the work is now lost, it survives in many fragments quoted in other Greek sources.

In describing the "philosophers" he encountered during his stay, Megasthenes distinguishes between two primary types: the *brachmanes* and the *sarmanes,* familiar from early Buddhist texts in the common phrase "brahmins and wanderers (*samaṇa*)." The *brachmanes,* he says,

> are best esteemed for they are more consistent in their opinions. They live in simple style, and lie on beds of rushes or skins. They abstain from animal food and sexual pleasures, and spend their time listening to serious discourses, and in imparting their knowledge.[4]

This non-Indian and thus independent source tells us that within the century after Gotama's death, the brahmins had clearly succeeded in consolidating their authority in the region.

Among the *sarmanes,* Megasthenes says, "those who are held in most honor are called the Hylobioi." He describes them as much like any group of forest-dwelling ascetics of the time:

> They live in the woods, where they subsist on leaves of trees and wild fruits, and wear garments made from the bark of trees. They abstain from sexual intercourse and from wine. They communicate with the kings, who consult them by messengers regarding the causes of things, and who through them worship and supplicate the deity.[5]

While some scholars believe he is referring to brahmin ascetics, Megasthenes could conceivably have had Devadatta's order of mendicants in mind. As we saw, these men broke away from Gotama's community and vowed to "remain as forest-dwellers who never settle in towns or villages, as beggars who subsist entirely from alms and refuse invitations to eat indoors, as wearers of discarded rags who take no cloth offered them by householders, as people who sleep only at the feet of trees and accept no shelter, and as vegetarians who eat neither meat nor fish." If the Hylobioi were Devadatta's followers, it would support the contention made in chapter 10 that Devadatta's community did indeed flourish after the Buddha's death. Whoever the Hylobioi were, at the time of Megasthenes' stay in Pāṭaliputta one particular forest-dwelling ascetic group had come to stand out above the others.

"Next in honor to the Hylobioi," says Megasthenes, "are the Physicians, since they are engaged in the study of the nature of man."

> They are simple in their habits, but do not live in the fields. Their food consists of rice and barley-meal, which they can always get for the mere asking, or receive from those who entertain them as guests in their houses. By their knowledge of pharmacy they can make marriages fruitful, and determine the sex of the offspring. They effect cures rather by regulating diet than by the use of medicines. The remedies most esteemed are ointments and plasters. All others they consider to be in a great measure pernicious in their nature. This class and the other class [i.e. the Hylobioi] practice fortitude, both by undergoing active toil, and by the endurance

> of pain, so that they remain for a whole day motionless in one fixed attitude.[6]

Since this is all that Megasthenes has to say about the communities of wanderers (*sarmanes*) he observed in and around Pāṭaliputta, scholars have concluded that he cannot have encountered any Buddhist monks. Buddhism at the time of Chandragupta, they infer, must have been a small and inconsequential movement that would rise to prominence some forty years later once it had been embraced by Chandragupta's grandson Aśoka.[7] Yet as we have seen, Buddhists had extensive communication networks, the collective will to resolve their internal differences, and sufficient resources to convene a second council at Vesālī (across the river from Pāṭaliputta), which would have taken place around the very time Megasthenes was living in the Mauryan capital. The account of the council conflicts with the notion that Buddhist mendicants would have formed such a tiny group of *sarmanes* that they escaped the notice of a curious Greek diplomat.

When scholars conclude on the basis of Megasthenes' memoir that he did not encounter any Buddhist mendicants, what they imply is that he did not encounter any group that we would recognize *today* as Buddhist monks. Had he seen any *bhikkhus* in Pāṭaliputta, we assume he would have described silent, shaven-headed, saffron-robed men with downcast eyes going from house to house in search of alms much like those we might now observe in Bangkok, Rangoon, or Colombo. As Gregory Schopen has shown, actual Buddhist practices that can be inferred from epigraphic and archaeological evidence often conflict with the idealized picture of monastic life recorded in the writings of the Vinaya. The descriptions that *bhikkhus* preserved of themselves in their texts may not correspond, then, to their actual behavior.

Might Megasthenes' account of the "Physicians" have referred to the followers of Gotama? After all, these mendicants were wanderers (*sarmanes*) who engaged in the study of human beings, were simple in their habits, did not live in the countryside, begged for their food, and were entertained as guests in people's homes. Indeed, these are some of the things that the Buddha allowed and Devadatta wished to forbid. Like the Hylobioi, the Physicians also spent long periods of time sitting "motionless in one fixed attitude." The part of Megasthenes' description that is most at odds with our usual understanding of Buddhist monastic behavior has to do with the practice of medicine. The idea of mendicants "making marriages fruitful, and determining the sex of the offspring" clashes with the monastic rule as it has come down to us today, which forbids monks from engaging in such activities.

We saw earlier that Gotama was familiar with both the medical theory and practices of his time and frequently employed them as metaphors for his teaching. He often compared himself to a physician and his dharma to a form of medical therapy. We know that on at least one occasion he personally took care of a mendicant suffering from dysentery, declaring that "whoever would tend to me, he should tend to the sick." At other times, he reportedly emerged "from seclusion" and went to the sick ward to attend to the patients.[8] Moreover, the sort of treatment the Physicians are said to have practiced broadly corresponds to the way Jīvaka healed Gotama's "disturbance of the bodily humors" with ointment, a hot bath, and diet.

Was the most visible group of Buddhist mendicants around Pāṭaliputta serving as a guild of wandering doctors or therapists, much as Megasthenes described them? Might they have been the ones whose liberal interpretation of the rule led to the second council at Vesālī, where conservative mendicants like Yasa formally condemned such laxity? It is unlikely that Yasa and his colleagues would have undertaken the complex and time-consuming preparations for a council were they concerned only with the behavior of a handful of miscreants. The possibility that mendicants were regarded as doctors is reinforced by a passage in the Mūlasarvāstavāda Vinaya, which tells us that King Pasenadi "several times mistook doctors for Buddhist mendicants on account of their similar costumes."[9] Although Megasthenes recognized this particular group to be composed of *sarmanes,* we can assume that its members must have either called themselves or been known by others as "Physicians." We cannot be certain that they were Buddhists, but of the *samaṇa* groups we know to have existed at Megasthenes' time, the Buddhists would best fit the description he gives.

Some of Gotama's ideas may have influenced the skeptical philosophy of Pyrrho, who traveled in Alexander's train with his mentor Anaxarchus to India, where he reportedly studied with "gymnosophists." The first explicit mention of the Buddha in Western sources is found, however, in the *Stromata* of the church father Clement of Alexandria (c. 150–c. 215). In his account of the origins of philosophy—which "flourished in antiquity among the barbarians, shedding light over the nations and afterwards came to Greece"—Clement talks of the *brachmanes* and the *sarmanes* as described by Megasthenes, then adds: "Some, too, of the Indians obey the precepts of Boutta; whom, on account of his extraordinary sanctity, they have raised to divine honors."[10]

As Christendom established its dominion over Europe, Asia Minor, and the Middle East, the Greek philosophical schools were shut down and "paganism" was vigorously suppressed. This "closing of the Western mind" meant that no further contact with Buddhist cultures took place until a Franciscan friar called William of Rubruck (c. 1220–c. 1293) was sent by Louis IX of France on a mission to convert the Mongol emperor Möngke to Christianity in 1253. During his eight-month stay in Karakoram, William debated with Buddhist monks, but he showed no interest in what they taught. His sole concern was to convince them of the one true faith. He was eventually expelled by the khan and made his way back to Europe, where he wrote a detailed report of his journey.

With the rise of Spanish and Portuguese colonial ambitions in the sixteenth century, a number of Jesuit missionaries were dispatched to Asia in a more concerted attempt to convert Hindus, Buddhists, and Confucians to Christian teaching. Principal among these were the Spanish co-founder of the order, Francis Xavier (1506–52), and the Italians Matteo Ricci (1552–1610) and Ippolito Desideri (1684–1733). From

Xavier, Europe received its first accounts of Japanese Buddhism, including a sympathetic description of a Zen monastery and its training methods. From Ricci, who spent the final twenty-seven years of his life in China and immersed himself in its language and culture, Europe learned that Buddhism was "a Babylon of doctrines so intricate that no one can understand it properly, or describe it." From Desideri, who lived in Lhasa from 1716 to 1721, Europe learned little, at least immediately. He composed a memoir on his return to Italy, but it, as well as the polemical texts he wrote in Tibetan, languished forgotten on library shelves until the end of the nineteenth century.[11]

Although well-educated missionaries provided Europe with detailed accounts of the Buddhist cultures they observed in different parts of Asia, it took a long time before anyone realized that all these diverse ideas and practices shared a common origin in the teachings of a historical figure called Gotama. This commonality did not become fully apparent until the nineteenth century, when such pioneering scholars as Eugène Burnouf (1801–52) and T. W. Rhys Davids (1843–1922) began the systematic study and translation of Buddhist texts in Sanskrit and Pali. "One only has to admire," wrote a certain Abbé Deschamps in 1860, "with what speed, through its first contact with the spirit of investigation that characterizes our age, Buddhism has emerged from its profound obscurity and its long silence." Yet this news of a unitary Buddhism was also unsettling. "The appearance of this little known religion," wrote another *abbé,* Paul de Broglie, in 1886, "has produced profound surprise. It seems to destroy the entire basis of Christian apologetics and even some of the proofs for the existence of God."[12]

Buddhism soon found its own apologists and enthusiasts. As early as 1844, the philosopher Arthur Schopenhauer wrote that he was gratified "to see my doctrine in such close agreement with a religion that the majority of men on earth hold as their own."[13] The founders of the Theosophical Society, Helena Blavatsky (1831–91) and Colonel Henry Steel Olcott (1832–1907), went further still and formally received the lay Buddhist precepts from a *bhikkhu* in Galle, Ceylon, in

1880. Despite some fanciful esoteric doctrines, Theosophists held Buddhism in high esteem and were highly influential in introducing the West to a socially acceptable non-Christian spirituality. This open cultural environment was a key factor in enabling the first Europeans to ordain as Buddhist monks in Asia in the first years of the twentieth century.

Interest in and knowledge of Buddhism grew slowly but steadily in the West through the first half of the twentieth century. Classical texts were translated, learned studies were written, Buddhist associations were established, but few Westerners did much more than dabble in the dharma. When the Jesuit scholar Henri de Lubac (1896–1991) published his survey of encounters between Buddhism and the West (*La rencontre du bouddhisme et de l'occident*) in 1952, he seemed to be writing the closing chapter of an episode of purely historical interest. He had no inkling that Buddhism would spread rapidly throughout Europe and the Americas in the following decades.

In 1959, Tenzin Gyatso, the fourteenth Dalai Lama of Tibet (b. 1935), fled his homeland and sought refuge across the Himalayas in India. He was joined by a hundred thousand or so of his followers, including a considerable number of educated lamas. Buoyed by the optimism and affluence of the 1960s, waves of young Europeans and Americans traveled to Asia to study Buddhism over the next couple of decades. Some trained with Tibetan teachers in India and Nepal, some settled in Theravāda monasteries and retreat centers in Sri Lanka, Thailand, and Burma, and others found their way to Zen monasteries in Japan and Korea. These encounters gave rise to the first generation of Western men and women who had received formal Buddhist training in the East. On returning to their home countries they established meditation centers and communities, earned doctorates in Buddhist studies, invited Asian teachers to the West, and translated and wrote books. All these activities initiated an unprecedented interest in the dharma across the Western world and laid the foundation for a community of practitioners. The growth of this nascent community shows little sign of abating.

Selected Discourses from the Pali Canon

In translating these discourses, I abbreviated and paraphrased to make them more accessible to a modern reader. For more literal and traditional interpretations, please consult the translations cited in the notes.

(1) Three Questions

"When I was still a bodhisatta, it occurred to me to ask: 'What is the delight (*assādo*) of life? What is the tragedy (*ādhinavo*) of life? What is the emancipation (*nissaraṇa*) of life?' Then, *bhikkhus*, it occurred to me to answer: 'The happiness and joy that arise conditioned by life, that is the delight of life; that life is impermanent, difficult (*dukkha*), and changing, that is the tragedy of life; the removal and abandonment of grasping (*chandarāga*) for life, that is the emancipation of life.'"[1]

(2) Awakening

"This dharma I have reached is deep, hard to see, difficult to awaken to, quiet and excellent, not confined by thought, subtle, sensed by the wise. But people love their place (*ālaya*): they delight and revel in their place. It is hard for people who love, delight, and revel in their place to see this ground (*ṭhāna*): 'because-of-this' conditionality (*idap-*

paccayatā), conditioned arising (*paṭiccasamuppāda*). And also hard to see this ground: the stilling of inclinations, the relinquishing of bases, the fading away of reactivity, desirelessness, ceasing, nirvana."[2]

(3) The Four Tasks

This is what I heard. The Teacher was staying at Benares in the Deer Park at Isipatana. Then he addressed the group of five mendicants.

"There are, *bhikkhus*, two dead ends which should not be pursued by one who has gone forth. Which two? Addiction to pleasure through indulging in sensuality, which is low, village-like, pertaining to the unawake person, undignified, and unfulfilling; and addiction to self-punishment, which is painful, undignified, and unfulfilling.

"The middle way, *bhikkhus*, awakened to by the *tathāgata,* does not lead to these two dead ends, but makes for vision and knowledge and is conducive to calming, lucid understanding, awakening, and nirvana.

"And what, *bhikkhus*, is this middle way . . . ? It is just this noble eightfold path—that is, complete vision, thought, speech, action, livelihood, effort, mindfulness, and concentration. . . ."

"This is *dukkha:* birth is *dukkha,* aging is *dukkha,* sickness is *dukkha,* death is *dukkha,* encountering what is not dear is *dukkha,* separation from what is dear is *dukkha,* not getting what one wants is *dukkha.* In short, the five bundles of clinging are *dukkha.*

"This is the arising (*samudaya*): it is craving (*taṇhā*), which is repetitive, wallows in attachment and greed, obsessively indulges in this and that—craving for stimulation, craving for existence, craving for non-existence.

"This is the ceasing: the traceless fading away and ceasing of that craving (*taṇhā*), the letting go and abandoning of it, freedom and independence from it.

"And this is the path: the path with eight branches—complete vision, complete thought, complete speech, complete action, complete livelihood, complete effort, complete mindfulness, complete concentration.

"Such is *dukkha*. It can be comprehended. It has been comprehended.

"Such is the arising. It can be let go of. It has been let go of.

"Such is the ceasing. It can be beheld. It has been beheld.

"Such is the path. It can be cultivated. It has been cultivated.

"So there arose in me illumination about things previously unknown.

"As long as my knowledge and vision were not entirely clear about the twelve aspects of these four, I did not claim to have had a peerless awakening in this world with its humans and celestials, its gods and devils, its wanderers and brahmins. Only when my knowledge and vision were clear in all these ways did I claim to have had such awakening.

"The freedom of my mind is unshakable. Birth is overcome; the spiritual life has been lived; what is to be done has been done; there will be no more repetitive existence."

This is what he said. Inspired, the five delighted in his words. While he was speaking, the dispassionate, stainless dharma eye arose in Koṇḍañña: "Whatever is subject to arising is subject to ceasing."[3]

(4) On Fire

On one occasion the Teacher was staying near Gayā at Gayā Head, together with a thousand mendicants, who had formerly been matted-hair fire worshippers. He addressed them:

"*Bhikkhus*, everything is burning. And what is it that is burning?

"The eye is burning, forms are burning, eye-consciousness is burning, eye-contact is burning, whatever is felt as pleasant or painful or neither that arises with eye-contact as its condition, that too is burning. Burning with what? Burning with the fire of greed, with the fire of hatred, with the fire of delusion. . . .

"The ear is burning, sounds are burning. . . .

"The nose is burning, smells are burning. . . .

"The tongue is burning, tastes are burning. . . .

"The body is burning, sensations are burning. . . .

"The mind is burning, ideas are burning. . . .

"*Bhikkhus*, when a learned noble follower sees thus, he disengages from the eye, from forms, from eye-consciousness, from eye--contact, from whatever is felt as pleasant or painful or neither that arises with eye-contact as its condition, from that too he disengages.

"He disengages from the ear, from sounds . . . ; from the nose, from smells . . . ; from the tongue, from tastes . . . ; from the body, from sensations . . . ; from the mind, from ideas . . . .

"Disengaging, he becomes dispassionate; through dispassion he is freed; he knows: 'I am free.' He understands: 'Birth is overcome; the spiritual life has been lived; what is to be done has been done; there will be no more repetitive existence.'"

And while this discourse was being spoken, the minds of the thousand were, through non-clinging, freed from effluences.[4]

(5) The All

"*Bhikkhus*, I will teach you the all. Listen to this.

"And what, *bhikkhus*, is the all? The eye and forms, the ear and sounds, the nose and smells, the tongue and tastes, the body and sensations, the mind and its contents. That is called the all.

"If anyone, *bhikkhus*, should say—'Having rejected this all, I shall make known another all'—that would be a mere empty boast on his part. If he were questioned, he would not be able to reply, and, further, he would end up frustrated. Why? Because, *bhikkhus*, *that* all would not be within his domain."[5]

(6) To Kaccānagotta

The Teacher was living at Sāvatthi. Then the good Kaccānagotta approached him, greeted him, sat down to one side, and said: "You say 'complete vision,' sir. In what respects is vision complete?"

"By and large, Kaccāna, this world relies on the duality of 'it is' and 'it is not.' But one who sees the arising of the world as it happens with complete understanding has no sense of 'it is not' about the world. And one who sees the ceasing of the world as it happens with complete understanding has no sense of 'it is' about the world.

"By and large, this world is bound to its prejudices and habits. But such a one does not get caught up in the habits, fixations, prejudices, or biases of the mind. He is not fixated on 'my self.' He does not doubt that when something is occurring, it is occurring, and when it has come to an end, it has come to an end. His knowledge is independent of others'.

"In these respects his vision is complete.

"'Everything is' is one dead end. 'Everything is not' is the other dead end. The *tathāgata* reveals the dharma from a middle that avoids both dead ends."[6]

(7) On Emptiness

The Teacher was once living at Sāvatthi in the eastern garden of Migāra's mother's villa. As evening fell, the good Ānanda emerged from seclusion and approached him. He greeted him, sat down to one side, and said:

"You were once living in Sakiya, sir, among your kinsfolk in the town of Nāgaraka. It was there that I heard you say from your own lips: 'Now I mainly live by dwelling in emptiness.' Did I hear that correctly?"

"Yes. Then, as now, do I mainly live by dwelling in emptiness.

"In being empty of elephants, cattle, and horses, gold and silver, crowds of women and men, there is one thing alone due to which this villa is not empty: this group of mendicants.

"So, too, in not being aware of villages or people, there is one thing alone due to which a mendicant focuses his mind: awareness of wilderness.

"His heart rejoices in that awareness of wilderness, is made radiant and calm by it, is dedicated to it. He knows: 'With none of the anxieties due to being aware of villages or people, there is one thing alone due to which I am prone to a degree of anxiety: awareness of wilderness.'

"'This state of awareness is empty of any awareness of villages and people. There is one thing alone due to which it is not empty: awareness of wilderness.'

"Thus he regards it as empty of what is not there. And of what remains, he knows: 'This is what's here.' So is this entry into emptiness in accordance with what happens, undistorted, and pure.

"Then, no longer aware of wilderness, one thing alone focuses that mendicant's mind: awareness of the earth's expanse.

"Just as a bull's hide loses its wrinkles when stretched by numerous pegs, so, too, by ignoring all the hills and valleys, rivers and ravines, lands covered with tree stumps and thorns, the jagged lines of hills, one thing alone focuses that mendicant's mind: awareness of the earth's expanse.

"No longer aware of the earth's expanse, one thing alone focuses that mendicant's mind: awareness of unbounded space.

"No longer aware of unbounded space, one thing alone focuses that mendicant's mind: awareness of unbounded consciousness.

"No longer aware of unbounded consciousness, one thing alone focuses that mendicant's mind: awareness of nothing.

"No longer aware of nothing, one thing alone focuses that mendicant's mind: awareness of neither being aware nor unaware.

"No longer aware of neither being aware nor unaware, one thing alone focuses that mendicant's mind: an unthemed meditation of the heart.

"His heart rejoices in that unthemed meditation, is made radiant and calm by it, is dedicated to it. He knows: 'With none of the anxieties due to being aware of neither being aware nor unaware, I am prone to the amount of anxiety that comes from having the six sense fields of a living body.'

"Then he realizes: 'An unthemed meditation of the heart is conditioned and contrived, and whatever is conditioned and contrived is impermanent and subject to cessation.'

"In knowing and seeing thus, his heart is freed from the effluences of cupidity, becoming, and ignorance. In this freedom, an insight dawns: 'This is freedom.' He knows: 'Birth is overcome; the spiritual life has been lived; what is to be done has been done; there will be no more repetitive existence.'

"'With none of the anxieties due to those effluences, I am prone to the amount of anxiety that comes from having the six sense fields of a living body.'

"'This state of awareness is empty of those effluences. That which is not empty is this: the six sense fields of a living body.'

"So he regards it as empty of what is not there. And of what remains, he knows: 'This is what's here.' So is this entry into emptiness in accordance with what happens, undistorted, and pure.

"Those wanderers and priests of the past, present, or future who have dwelt, are dwelling, or will dwell in pure, unsurpassed emptiness, all of them have dwelt, are dwelling, or will dwell in this very emptiness. So should you train yourselves: 'Let us live in this emptiness.'"

This is what the Teacher said. Delighted, the good Ānanda rejoiced in his words.[7]

(8) To Sīvaka I

The Teacher was once staying at the squirrels' feeding ground in the Bamboo Grove at Rājagaha. Then the wanderer Topknot Sīvaka approached and exchanged greetings with him. After a pleasant and courteous conversation, he sat down to one side and said:

"Mr. Gotama, there are some wanderers and brahmins who voice the opinion and hold the view that whatever a person experiences—be it pleasant, painful, or neither—is caused by what was done in the past. What do you say about this?"

"Some experiences are caused by bile, some by phlegm, some by wind, some by all three together. Some experiences are caused by the change of seasons, some by poor care, some by sudden assault, and some are the fruit of one's actions.

"You can know for yourself how such experiences occur.

"People in the world agree on how such experiences occur.

"Those who believe that all experience is caused by what was done in the past overestimate what can be known by themselves and what is accepted as true in the world. Therefore, I say that those wanderers and brahmins are mistaken."[8]

(9) To Sīvaka 2

Again the wanderer Topknot Sīvaka approached and exchanged greetings with the Teacher. After a pleasant and courteous conversation, he sat down to one side and said:

"You talk of a 'clearly visible dharma,' sir. In what respects is the dharma clearly visible, immediate, inviting, uplifting, to be personally experienced by the wise?"

"Let me ask you a question about this. Respond as you see fit. What do you think: When there is greed within you, do you know 'there's greed within me,' and when there is no greed within you, do you know 'there's no greed within me'?"

"Yes."

"With hatred, delusion, and those qualities of mind associated with greed, hatred, and delusion, when they are within you, do you know they are present? And when they are not within you, do you know they are absent?"

"Yes."

"It is in this way that the dharma is clearly visible, immediate, inviting, uplifting, to be personally experienced by the wise."

Sīvaka said to the Teacher:

"Excellent, sir. From now on regard me as an adherent who goes for refuge as long as he draws breath."[9]

(10) The Twenty-One

"*Bhikkhus*, possessing six qualities, the householder Mahānāma has found fulfillment in the *tathāgata*, has become a seer of the deathless, and goes about having beheld the deathless. What six? Lucid confidence in the Buddha, lucid confidence in the dharma, lucid confidence in the sangha, noble virtue, noble understanding, and noble liberation."[10]

(11) From the *Dhammapada*

Just as a farmer irrigates his field,
Just as a fletcher fashions an arrow,
Just as a carpenter shapes a piece of wood,
So the sage tames the self.[11]

Care is the path to the deathless;
Carelessness the path to death.
The caring do not die;
The uncaring are as if already dead.[12]

The sage moves through a village
Just as the bee gathers pollen
And flies off without harming
The flower, its color, or its fragrance.[13]

Notes

In referring to Pali canonical sources in these notes, I provide the title and location of the work in Pali, followed by the page reference in a currently available English translation. I have not provided the pagination of the Pali Text Society's edition of the Pali Canon. My source for the Pali-language texts is SuttaCentral: Early Buddhist Texts, Translations, and Parallels, https://suttacentral.net.

I cross-checked the passages translated here against other available English translations. Rather than present word-for-word literal translations, I often modified the passages by removing repetition and employing an abbreviated and idiomatic style. My translations of those Pali texts that are frequently cited here and serve as the basis for my interpretation of the Buddha's teaching are included in "Selected Discourses from the Pali Canon," the appendix to this book, cited below as "Selected Discourses."

(1) After Buddhism

Epigraph: *Udāna* 1:10, Ireland (1997), p. 21.

1. *Udāna* 6:4, Ireland (1997), p. 86. For a discussion of the meaning of the term *tathāgata*, see chapter 5, section 9.
2. *Udāna* 6:4, Ireland (1997), p. 87.
3. *Saṃyutta Nikāya* 22:94, Bodhi (2000), p. 949.
4. *Udāna* 6:4, Ireland (1997), p. 88.
5. *Saṃyutta Nikāya* 22:94, Bodhi (2000), p. 949.
6. *Blue Cliff Record*, case 14, Cleary and Cleary (1977), p. 46.

7. *Majjhima Nikāya* 121, Ñāṇamoli and Bodhi (1995), p. 965. See *On Emptiness* in "Selected Discourses."
8. *Majjhima Nikāya* 151, Ñāṇamoli and Bodhi (1995), p. 1143.
9. *Majjhima Nikāya* 121, Ñāṇamoli and Bodhi (1995), pp. 965–66. See *On Emptiness* in "Selected Discourses."
10. *Majjhima Nikāya* 121, Ñāṇamoli and Bodhi (1995), p. 969. See *On Emptiness* in "Selected Discourses."
11. *Majjhima Nikāya* 121, Ñāṇamoli and Bodhi (1995), p. 970. See *On Emptiness* in "Selected Discourses."
12. *Udāna* 1:10, Ireland (1997), p. 21.
13. For further details on this practice, see Kusan (2009); Batchelor (2015).
14. *The Gateless Gate,* case 1, Yamada (2004), p. 11.
15. *Saṃyutta Nikāya* 12:15, Bodhi (2000), p. 544. See *To Kaccānagotta* in "Selected Discourses."
16. Rockhill (1884), p. 34. I have cited the passage as it appears in *Dīgha Nikāya* 16, Walshe (1995), pp. 246–47.
17. See Mohr and Tsedroen (2010).
18. *Cullavagga* X, Horner (1952), pp. 354–56.
19. See Nongbri (2013).
20. See Tillich (1958).
21. Quoted in Metaxas (2010), p. 466.
22. This tension is sensitively explored in Wakoh Shannon Hickey, "Two Buddhisms, Three Buddhisms, and Racism," *Journal of Global Buddhism* 11 (2010).
23. Slavoj Žižek has suggested that Western Buddhism is in danger of becoming the opium of the bourgeoisie. See Žižek's essay "From Western Buddhism to Western Marxism," *Cabinet* (Spring 2001), http://www.cabinetmagazine.org/issues/2/western.php.
24. See McMahan (2008).
25. MacIntyre (1981), p. 222.
26. Ibid., p. 146.
27. *Sutta-Nipāta* 780, 786, 796, Norman (2001), pp. 104–6.
28. *Aṅguttara Nikāya* III:65, Bodhi (2012), p. 280.
29. *Aṅguttara Nikāya* III:65, Bodhi (2012), p. 280.
30. *Aṅguttara Nikāya* III:65, Bodhi (2012), p. 282.
31. *Majjhima Nikāya* 63, Ñāṇamoli and Bodhi (1995), p. 535.

32. *The Gateless Gate,* case 18, Yamada (2004), p. 89.
33. *The Gateless Gate,* case 37, Yamada (2004), p. 177.
34. *Udāna 8:3* and *Itivuttaka* 43, Ireland (1997), pp. 103, 180. This translation is from Walshe (1995), p. 29. See chapter 5, sections 6–8, for a detailed analysis of this text.
35. See Ling (1973).

(2) Mahānāma: The Convert

Epigraph: *Saṃyutta Nikāya* 55:22, Bodhi (2000), p. 1809.

1. Rockhill (1884), p. 119.
2. See Bronkhorst (2007).
3. *Bṛhadāraṇyaka Upaniṣad* III.1, Radhakrishnan (1994), p. 211.
4. McCrindle (1877), p. 98.
5. Dhammika (1994).
6. *Majjhima Nikāya* 4, Ñāṇamoli and Bodhi (1995), p. 104.
7. Rockhill (1884), p. 25.
8. Ibid., p. 50.
9. *Cullavagga* VII, Horner (1952), pp. 253–54. Cf. Rockhill (1884), pp. 53–54.
10. *Cullavagga* VII, Horner (1952), pp. 253–54.
11. *Cullavagga* VII, Horner (1952), pp. 253–54.
12. *Cullavagga* VII, Horner (1952), p. 255.
13. *Cullavagga* VII, Horner (1952), pp. 257–59.
14. *Majjhima Nikāya* 53, Ñāṇamoli and Bodhi (1995), p. 460.
15. *Majjhima Nikāya* 53, Ñāṇamoli and Bodhi (1995), pp. 460–61.
16. *Sutta-Nipāta* 422–23, Norman (2001), p. 51.
17. *Saṃyutta Nikāya* 45:49, Bodhi (2000), p. 1543.
18. *Majjhima Nikāya* 53, Ñāṇamoli and Bodhi (1995), p. 461.
19. *Dīgha Nikāya* 27, Walshe (1995), p. 409.
20. *Aṅguttara Nikāya* III. 70, Bodhi (2012), p. 300.
21. Burlingame (1995), vol. 2, pp. 291–93.
22. Cf. Rockhill (1884), p. 54.
23. *Aṅguttara Nikāya* III:126, Bodhi (2012), pp. 356–57.
24. *Saṃyutta Nikāya* 55:5, Bodhi (2000), p. 1792.
25. *Saṃyutta Nikāya* 38:1, Bodhi (2000), p. 1294.

26. *Saṃyutta Nikāya* 55:22, Bodhi (2000), p. 1809.
27. *Majjhima Nikāya* 73, Ñāṇamoli and Bodhi (1995), pp. 596–97.
28. *Aṅguttara Nikāya* 11:12, Bodhi (2012), p. 1568; *Udāna* 5.5; Ireland (1997), pp. 69–74.
29. *Saṃyutta Nikāya* 55:2, Bodhi (2000), p. 1789.
30. *Saṃyutta Nikāya* 55:21–25, Bodhi (2000), pp. 1808–16.
31. *Saṃyutta Nikāya* 55:24, Bodhi (2000), p. 1811.
32. *Saṃyutta Nikāya* 55:24, Bodhi (2000), p. 1813.
33. *Saṃyutta Nikāya* 55:23, Bodhi (2000), pp. 1809–11.
34. *Majjhima Nikāya* 14, Ñāṇamoli and Bodhi (1995), p. 186.
35. *Majjhima Nikāya* 14, Ñāṇamoli and Bodhi (1995), p. 186.
36. Rig Veda X.129. I am grateful to John Peacock for alerting me to this passage. The translation is his.
37. *Majjhima Nikāya* 26, Ñāṇamoli and Bodhi (1995), p. 260. See *Awakening* in the "Selected Discourses."
38. *Majjhima Nikāya* 14, Ñāṇamoli and Bodhi (1995), p. 187.
39. *Saṃyutta Nikāya* 55:21, Bodhi (2000), p. 1808.
40. *Aṅguttara Nikāya* VI:128, Bodhi (2012), p. 989. See *The Twenty-One* in "Selected Discourses."
41. *Saṃyutta Nikāya* 55:37, Bodhi (2000), pp. 1824–25.
42. Rockhill (1884), p. 58.
43. Finnegan (2009), p. 130.
44. Ibid.
45. Rockhill (1884), pp. 74–77.
46. Ibid., pp. 11–12.
47. Ibid., p. 77.
48. Ibid., p. 116.
49. Ibid., p. 119.
50. Burlingame (1995), vol. 2, p. 45.

(3) A Fourfold Task

Epigraphs: (1) *Saṃyutta Nikāya* 56:11, Bodhi (2000), p. 1846. See *The Four Tasks* in "Selected Discourses." (2) *Saṃyutta Nikāya* 56:19, Bodhi (2000), p. 1851.

1. *Majjhima Nikāya* 26, Ñāṇamoli and Bodhi (1995), p. 256.
2. *Saṃyutta Nikāya* 35:13, Bodhi (2000), p. 1136. See *Three Questions* in "Selected Discourses."
3. *Sutta-Nipāta* 406, Norman (2001), p. 50.
4. *Saṃyutta Nikāya* 35:13, Bodhi (2000), p. 1137.
5. See Wynne (2007).
6. *Majjhima Nikāya* 26, Ñāṇamoli and Bodhi (1995), p. 260. See *Awakening* in "Selected Discourses."
7. *Majjhima Nikāya* 28, Ñāṇamoli and Bodhi (1995), p. 283.
8. *Majjhima Nikāya* 79, Ñāṇamoli and Bodhi (1995), p. 655.
9. *Dhammapada* 80 (cf. 145), Fronsdal (2005), p. 21. See *From the "Dhammapada"* in "Selected Discourses."
10. *Dīgha Nikāya* 16, Walshe (1995), p. 245.
11. *Dhammapada* 183, Fronsdal (2005), p. 49.
12. Rhys Davids and Stede, *Pali-English Dictionary*, p. 289.
13. *Saṃyutta Nikāya* 38:1, Bodhi (2000), p. 1294.
14. *Aṅguttara Nikāya* III:55, Bodhi (2012), p. 253.
15. *Aṅguttara Nikāya* VI:47, Bodhi (2012), p. 919. See *To Sīvaka 2* in "Selected Discourses."
16. *Aṅguttara Nikāya* III:55, Bodhi (2012), p. 253.
17. Wittgenstein (1958), II:xi.
18. *Majjhima Nikāya* 26, Ñāṇamoli and Bodhi (1995), p. 260.
19. *Sutta-Nipāta* 436–38, Norman (2001), p. 52.
20. *Sutta-Nipāta* 443–44, Norman (2001), p. 53.
21. *Sutta-Nipāta* 447–48, in Norman (2001), p. 53.
22. *Majjhima Nikāya* 26, Ñāṇamoli and Bodhi (1995), p. 260.
23. See chapter 1, section 5.
24. *Majjhima Nikāya* 26, Ñāṇamoli and Bodhi (1995), p. 261.
25. Ñāṇamoli and Bodhi (1995), p. 1217 n. 307.
26. *Majjhima Nikāya* 26, Ñāṇamoli and Bodhi (1995), p. 265.
27. *Majjhima Nikāya* 26, Ñāṇamoli and Bodhi (1995), pp. 263–64.
28. Radiocarbon dating reveals that the city of Benares was not established until sometime between 460–440 BCE—that is, during the lifetime of the Buddha. See Bronkhorst (2007), p. 249.
29. *Majjhima Nikāya* 26, Ñāṇamoli and Bodhi (1995), p. 263.

30. *Mahāvagga* I. Horner (1951), p. 54.
31. Rhys Davids and Stede, *Pali-English Dictionary*, p. 421.
32. See *The Four Tasks* in "Selected Discourses," Bodhi (2000), p. 1844.
33. The five bundles will be examined at length in chapter 7.
34. *Saṃyutta Nikāya* 22:60, Bodhi (2000), p. 903.
35. *Dhammapada* 80 (cf. 145), Fronsdal (2005), p. 21. See *From the "Dhammapada"* in "Selected Discourses."
36. *Aṅguttara Nikāya* III:102, Bodhi (2012), p. 338.
37. *Majjhima Nikāya* 10, Ñāṇamoli and Bodhi (1995), p. 146.
38. *Majjhima Nikāya* 10, Ñāṇamoli and Bodhi (1995), p. 148.
39. *Aṅguttara Nikāya* III:126, Bodhi (2012), pp. 356–57.
40. *Saṃyutta Nikāya* 22:23, Bodhi (2000), p. 872.
41. *Saṃyutta Nikāya* 38:1, Bodhi (2000), p. 1294.
42. *Dhammapada* 49, Fronsdal (2005), p. 13. See *From the "Dhammapada"* in "Selected Discourses."
43. *Saṃyutta Nikāya* 56: 11, Bodhi (2000), p. 1844. See *The Four Tasks* in "Selected Discourses."
44. *Saṃyutta Nikāya* 36:6, Bodhi (2000), pp. 1263–65.
45. *Majjhima Nikāya* 18, Ñāṇamoli and Bodhi (1995), p. 202.
46. *Saṃyutta Nikāya* 4:2, Bodhi (2000), p. 196.
47. *Dīgha Nikāya* 15, Walshe (1995), p. 223.
48. *Saṃyutta Nikāya* 22:83, Bodhi (2000), p. 928.
49. *Majjhima Nikāya* 16, Ñāṇamoli and Bodhi (1995), pp. 194–97.
50. *Saṃyutta Nikāya* 45:166, Bodhi (2000), p. 1561.
51. *Saṃyutta Nikāya* 4:9, Bodhi (2000), p. 201.
52. *Saṃyutta Nikāya* 56: 11, Bodhi (2000), p. 1844. See *The Four Tasks* in "Selected Discourses."
53. *Aṅguttara Nikāya* III:55, Bodhi (2012), p. 253.
54. *Aṅguttara Nikāya* VI:47, Bodhi (2012), p. 919. See *To Sīvaka 2* in "Selected Discourses."
55. *Aṅguttara Nikāya* VI:119–39, Bodhi (2012), p. 989.
56. *Saṃyutta Nikāya* 45:7, Bodhi (2000), p. 1528.
57. *Majjhima Nikāya* 121, Ñāṇamoli and Bodhi (1995), pp. 969–70. See *On Emptiness* in "Selected Discourses."
58. *Majjhima Nikāya* 151, Ñāṇamoli and Bodhi (1995), p. 1143.

59. *Sutta-Nipāta* 780, Norman (2001), p. 104.
60. Wittgenstein (1958), I.115.
61. *Saṃyutta Nikāya* 56: 11, Bodhi (2000), p. 1844. See *The Four Tasks* in "Selected Discourses."
62. *Saṃyutta Nikāya* 12:15, Bodhi (2000), p. 544. See *To Kaccānagotta* in "Selected Discourses."
63. *Saṃyutta Nikāya* 12:15, Bodhi (2000), p. 544.
64. An early source is *Sutta-Nipāta* 231, Norman (2001), p. 29.
65. *Saṃyutta Nikāya* 12:65, Bodhi (2000), p. 603.
66. *Saṃyutta Nikāya* 12:65, Bodhi (2000), p. 603.

(4) Pasenadi: The King

Epigraph: *Dīgha Nikāya* 27, Walshe (1995), p. 409.

1. *Majjhima Nikāya* 35, Ñāṇamoli and Bodhi (1995), pp. 325–26.
2. *Majjhima Nikāya* 35, Ñāṇamoli and Bodhi (1995), pp. 325–26.
3. *Majjhima Nikāya* 35, Ñāṇamoli and Bodhi (1995), pp. 325–26.
4. *Saṃyutta Nikāya* 22:59, Bodhi (2000), pp. 901–3.
5. *Majjhima Nikāya* 35, Ñāṇamoli and Bodhi (1995), p. 328.
6. *Saṃyutta Nikāya* 3:11, Bodhi (2000), p. 173.
7. *Saṃyutta Nikāya* 3:11, Bodhi (2000), p. 173.
8. *Saṃyutta Nikāya* 3:6, Bodhi (2000), pp. 169–70.
9. *Dīgha Nikāya* 27, Walshe (1995), p. 409.
10. *Saṃyutta Nikāya* 3:5, Bodhi (2000), p. 169.
11. *Saṃyutta Nikāya* 3:13, Bodhi (2000), pp. 176–77.
12. *Majjhima Nikāya* 87, Ñāṇamoli and Bodhi (1995), pp. 718–22.
13. *Saṃyutta Nikāya* 3:8, Bodhi (2000), pp. 170–71.
14. *Bṛhadāraṇyaka Upaniṣad* I:4, 8, Radhakrishnan (1994), pp. 167–68.
15. *Sutta-Nipāta* 705, Norman (2001), p. 92; cf. *Dhammapada* 130; Matthew 7:12.
16. Śāntideva, *Bodhicaryāvatāra* 8:95–96, Batchelor (1979); cf. Crosby and Skilton (1996).
17. Burlingame (1995), vol. 3, p. 340.
18. *Aṅguttara Nikāya* V:49, Bodhi (2012), p. 676.
19. *Saṃyutta Nikāya* 3:17, Bodhi (2000), p. 179.
20. *Saṃyutta Nikāya* 45:140, Bodhi (2000), p. 1551.

21. Heidegger (1962), pp. 237–38. For the German text see p. 193.
22. Steinkellner (1981), pp. 42–49.
23. Romans 7:15–24 (New International Version of the Bible).
24. Śāntideva, *Bodhicaryāvatāra* I:28, in Batchelor (1979); cf. Crosby and Skilton (1996).
25. *Majjhima Nikāya* 28, Ñāṇamoli and Bodhi (1995), p. 278.
26. *Aṅguttara Nikāya* 10:15, Bodhi (2012), p. 1354.
27. *Dhammapada* 21, Fronsdal (2005), p. 6.
28. Rabten (1992), p. 133.
29. *Saṃyutta Nikāya* 3:18, Bodhi (2000), pp. 180–81.
30. *Saṃyutta Nikāya* 3:18, Bodhi (2000), pp. 180–81.
31. *Saṃyutta Nikāya* 3:18, Bodhi (2000), pp. 180–81.
32. *Saṃyutta Nikāya* 3:4, Bodhi (2000), p. 168.
33. *Saṃyutta Nikāya* 3:5, Bodhi (2000), p. 169.
34. *Saṃyutta Nikāya* 3:19, Bodhi (2000), p. 182.
35. *Saṃyutta Nikāya* 3:10, Bodhi (2000), p. 172.
36. *Saṃyutta Nikāya* 3:9, Bodhi (2000), p. 171.
37. *Saṃyutta Nikāya* 3:25, Bodhi (2000), p. 192.
38. Bodhi (2000), pp. 410–11 n. 257.
39. *Saṃyutta Nikāya* 3:25, Bodhi (2000), p. 192.
40. See Batchelor (2010), pp. 245–51.
41. *Saṃyutta Nikāya* 3:7, Bodhi (2000), p. 170.
42. Burlingame (1995), vol. 2, pp. 41–46.
43. *Majjhima Nikāya* 89, Ñāṇamoli and Bodhi (1995), pp. 728–33. The same story is told in Rockhill (1884), pp. 112–13.
44. *Saṃyutta Nikāya* 3:18, Bodhi (2000), p. 180.
45. *Majjhima Nikāya* 121, Ñāṇamoli and Bodhi (1995), p. 965. See *On Emptiness* in "Selected Discourses."
46. *Majjhima Nikāya* 89, Ñāṇamoli and Bodhi (1995), p. 729.
47. Burlingame (1995), vol. 2, pp. 42–48.
48. *Majjhima Nikāya* 89, Ñāṇamoli and Bodhi (1995), p. 730.
49. *Majjhima Nikāya* 89, Ñāṇamoli and Bodhi (1995), p. 731.
50. *Majjhima Nikāya* 89, Ñāṇamoli and Bodhi (1995), p. 733.
51. Rockhill (1884), p. 77n. Since Varshikā does not appear in the Pali account, I have left her name in the Sanskrit spelling.

52. *Saṃyutta Nikāya* 3:14–15, Bodhi (2000), pp. 177–78.
53. Burlingame (1995), vol. 3, p. 77.
54. Rockhill (1884), p. 115.

(5) Letting Go of Truth

Epigraphs: (1) *Sutta-Nipāta* 882, Norman (2001), p. 116; (2) *Majjhima Nikāya* 140, Ñāṇamoli and Bodhi (1995), p. 1093.

1. My distinction between "engaged agency" and a "theorizing stance" draws from Charles Taylor's essay "Engaged Agency and Background in Heidegger," in Guignon (2006).
2. *Majjhima Nikāya* 141, Ñāṇamoli and Bodhi (1995), p. 1097.
3. Bronkhorst (2011), p. 77.
4. See Nagel (1986).
5. Aśoka's second pillar edict, in Dhammika (1994).
6. Rorty (2007), p. 89.
7. Ibid.
8. Vattimo (2011), p. 77.
9. Bodhi (2000), pp. 32–33.
10. Rahula (1967), pp. 92–94.
11. "Dhamma" (Ed. Access to Insight), *Access to Insight (Legacy Edition)*, 30 November 2013, http://www.accesstoinsight.org/ptf/dhamma/index.html.
12. *Majjhima Nikāya* 26, Ñāṇamoli and Bodhi (1995), p. 260.
13. *Saṃyutta Nikāya* 56:11, Bodhi (2000), p. 1845.
14. Woodward (1993), p. 358n.
15. Norman (2003), p. 223.
16. *Dīgha Nikāya* 12, Walshe (1995), p. 182.
17. *Majjhima Nikāya* 141, Ñāṇamoli and Bodhi (1995), p. 1101.
18. *Majjhima Nikāya* 71, Ñāṇamoli and Bodhi (1995), p. 588.
19. *Majjhima Nikāya* 140, Ñāṇamoli and Bodhi (1995), p. 1093.
20. *Majjhima Nikāya* 70, 95; *Aṅguttara Nikāya* IV:113.
21. Newland (1999), p. 7.
22. Nāgārjuna, *Mūlamadhyamaka-kārikā* 24:9, Garfield (1995), p. 68.
23. Walshe (1995), Introduction, p. 31.

24. Jayatilleke (1963), pp. 363–64. My adapted translation.
25. *Sutta-Nipāta* 795–96, Norman (2001), p. 106.
26. Hopkins (1983), p. 302.
27. *Udāna* 8:3; *Utivuttaka* 43. The translation is from Walshe (1995), Introduction, p. 29.
28. *Dhammapada* 204, Fronsdal (2005), p. 54.
29. Walshe (1995), Introduction, p. 29.
30. *Saṃyutta Nikāya* 35:23, Bodhi (2000), p. 1140. See *The All* in "Selected Discourses." Cf. *Saṃyutta Nikāya* 35:92; Bodhi (2000), pp. 1171–72.
31. Walshe (1995), p. 30.
32. *Dīgha Nikāya* 11, Walshe (1995), p. 179.
33. *Saṃyutta Nikāya* 12:15, Bodhi (2000), p. 544. See *To Kaccānagotta* in "Selected Discourses."
34. Woodward (1948), p. 98.
35. Ibid., p. xiii.
36. *Saṃyutta Nikāya* 43:1, Bodhi (2000), p. 1372.
37. *Saṃyutta Nikāya* 38:1, Bodhi (2000), p. 1294.
38. *Saṃyutta Nikāya* 45:7, Bodhi (2000), p. 1528.
39. *Saṃyutta Nikāya* 22:23, Bodhi (2000), p. 872.
40. *Saṃyutta Nikāya* 22:23, Bodhi (2000), p. 872.
41. Conze (1954), p. 95.
42. *Saṃyutta Nikāya* 35:13, Bodhi (2000), pp. 1136–37. See *Three Questions* in "Selected Discourses."
43. *Aṅguttara Nikāya* IV:23, Bodhi (2012), p. 410.
44. Rhys Davids and Stede, *Pali-English Dictionary*, p. 296.
45. Gombrich (2009), p. 151.
46. *Majjhima Nikāya* 22, Ñāṇamoli and Bodhi (1995), p. 234.
47. *Aṅguttara Nikāya* VI:128, Bodhi (2012), p. 989. See *The Twenty-One* in "Selected Discourses."

(6) Sunakkhatta: The Traitor

Epigraph: *Majjhima Nikāya* 12, Ñāṇamoli and Bodhi (1995), p. 164.

1. For example, *Dīgha Nikāya* 14, Walshe (1995), pp. 205–6.
2. *Majjhima Nikāya* 140, Ñāṇamoli and Bodhi (1995), p. 1087.

3. *Majjhima Nikāya* 140, Ñāṇamoli and Bodhi (1995), p. 1087.
4. Ñāṇamoli and Bodhi (1995), p. 1345 n. 1246.
5. Ñāṇamoli and Bodhi (1995), p. 1345 n. 1246.
6. *Sutta-Nipāta,* Norman (2001), pp. 69–73. The identical text is found in *Majjhima Nikāya* 92, Ñāṇamoli and Bodhi (1995), 755–62.
7. *Majjhima Nikāya* 12, 105; *Dīgha Nikāya* 6, 24.
8. *Aṅguttara Nikāya* V:58, Bodhi (2012), p. 690.
9. Cited in Malalasekera (1997), vol. 1, p. 780.
10. *Saṃyutta Nikāya* 20:8, Bodhi (2000), p. 709.
11. *Dīgha Nikāya* 29, Walshe (1995), p. 427.
12. See the Jain *Ākārāṅga Sūtra,* in Jacobi (1884). Since the earliest Jain texts are believed to postdate the earliest Buddhist texts, it is possible that the Jains drew on Buddhist sources for these doctrines.
13. *Majjhima Nikāya* 35, Ñāṇamoli and Bodhi (1995), p. 322.
14. *Majjhima Nikāya* 36, Ñāṇamoli and Bodhi (1995), p. 343.
15. *Mahāvagga* VI:31, Horner (1951), p. 323.
16. *Majjhima Nikāya* 105, Ñāṇamoli and Bodhi (1995), p. 861.
17. *Majjhima Nikāya* 105, Ñāṇamoli and Bodhi (1995), p. 862.
18. *Majjhima Nikāya* 105, Ñāṇamoli and Bodhi (1995), p. 863.
19. Ñāṇamoli and Bodhi (1995), p. 1309 n. 1000.
20. *Majjhima Nikāya* 26, Ñāṇamoli and Bodhi (1995), p. 258.
21. *Majjhima Nikāya* 4, Ñāṇamoli and Bodhi (1995), p. 105.
22. For examples of passages where the practice is considered praiseworthy see *Saṃyutta Nikāya* 40:1–8, Bodhi (2000), pp. 1302–8.
23. *Majjhima Nikāya* 105, Ñāṇamoli and Bodhi (1995), p. 864.
24. *Majjhima Nikāya* 105, Ñāṇamoli and Bodhi (1995), p. 864.
25. *Majjhima Nikāya* 105, Ñāṇamoli and Bodhi (1995), p. 865. Cf. *Majjhima Nikāya* 63.
26. *Majjhima Nikāya* 105, Ñāṇamoli and Bodhi (1995), p. 865.
27. *Majjhima Nikāya* 105, Ñāṇamoli and Bodhi (1995), p. 866.
28. *Majjhima Nikāya* 105, Ñāṇamoli and Bodhi (1995), p. 868.
29. *Dīgha Nikāya* 6, Walshe (1995), p. 145.
30. *Dīgha Nikāya* 24, Walshe (1995), p. 373.
31. *Dīgha Nikāya* 24, Walshe (1995), pp. 371–72.
32. *Dīgha Nikāya* 11, Walshe (1995), p. 176.

33. *Dīgha Nikāya* 11, Walshe (1995), p. 176.
34. *Aṅguttara Nikāya* III:60, Bodhi (2012), pp. 264–65.
35. *Majjhima Nikāya* 63, Ñāṇamoli and Bodhi (1995), pp. 533–35.
36. *Dīgha Nikāya* 24, Walshe (1995), pp. 372–73.
37. Malalasekera (1997), vol. 2, p. 1206.
38. *Saṃyutta Nikāya* 56:11, Bodhi (2000), p. 1844. See *The Four Tasks* in "Selected Discourses."
39. *Majjhima Nikāya* 76, Ñāṇamoli and Bodhi (1995), pp. 624–25.
40. *Majjhima Nikāya* 12, Ñāṇamoli and Bodhi (1995), pp. 164–65.
41. *Majjhima Nikāya* 12, Ñāṇamoli and Bodhi (1995), p. 177.
42. The five discourses are *Majjhima Nikāya* 12 and 89; *Dīgha Nikāya* 16 and 24; *Saṃyutta Nikāya* 47:14.
43. *Dīgha Nikāya* 24, Walshe (1995), p. 371.
44. *Majjhima Nikāya* 12, Ñāṇamoli and Bodhi (1995), p. 164.
45. *Dīgha Nikāya* 24, Walshe (1995), p. 371.
46. *Dīgha Nikāya* 16, Walshe (1995), p. 231.
47. *Dīgha Nikāya* 16, Walshe (1995), p. 232.
48. *Dīgha Nikāya* 2, Walshe (1995), p. 108.
49. *Dīgha Nikāya* 16, Walshe (1995), p. 231. The remark "*tathāgatas* never lie" further supports the claim in chapter 5, section 9, that the *tathāgata* is "one who is just so," who does not dissimulate or pretend.
50. *Dīgha Nikāya* 16, Walshe (1995), p. 239.
51. *Saṃyutta Nikāya* 47:14, Bodhi (2000), p. 1644.
52. *Dīgha Nikāya* 16, Walshe (1995), p. 243.
53. *Mahāvagga* VI:30, Horner (1951), p. 316.
54. *Dīgha Nikāya* 16, Walshe (1995), p. 244. Following Tibetan sources, W. Woodville Rockhill states that the lack of any support for the Buddha and his mendicants during the Rains was due to a famine. Rockhill (1884), p. 130.

(7) Experience

Epigraph: Nāgārjuna, *Mūlamadhyamaka-kārikā* 18.1, Batchelor (2000), p. 114.

1. *Saṃyutta Nikāya* 35:23, Bodhi (2000), p. 1140. See *The All* in "Selected Discourses."

2. *Dīgha Nikāya* 13, Walshe (1995), pp. 187–95 for the Buddha's views on theism.
3. *Saṃyutta Nikāya* 2:26, Bodhi (2000), p. 158.
4. *Saṃyutta Nikāya* 35:82, Bodhi (2000), p. 1162.
5. See Robert H. Scharf's essay "Experience" in Taylor (1998), pp. 94–116.
6. "Definition of Sensorium," MedTerms Medical Dictionary, MedicineNet .com, http://www.medterms.com/script/main/art.asp?articlekey=15732.
7. Rhys Davids and Stede, *Pali-English Dictionary*, pp. 232–33.
8. *Saṃyutta Nikāya* 22:56, Bodhi (2000), p. 895.
9. *Saṃyutta Nikāya* 24:1, Bodhi (2000), p. 992.
10. *Saṃyutta Nikāya* 22:23, Bodhi (2000), p. 872.
11. *Saṃyutta Nikāya* 22:55, Bodhi (2000), p. 894. Ironically, this is said in the context of people who remember their past lives.
12. *Saṃyutta Nikāya* 22:79, Bodhi (2000), p. 915. See translator's footnote, p. 1070.
13. *Saṃyutta Nikāya* 22:79, Bodhi (2000), p. 915.
14. *Saṃyutta Nikāya* 22:79, Bodhi (2000), p. 915.
15. See Sacks (1995), chapter 4.
16. *Saṃyutta Nikāya* 22:79, Bodhi (2000), p. 915.
17. *Saṃyutta Nikāya* 22:56, Bodhi (2000), p. 896.
18. On karma see *Aṅguttara Nikāya* VI:63, Bodhi (2012), p. 963.
19. *Majjhima Nikāya* 44, Ñāṇamoli and Bodhi (1995), p. 399. Cf. *Saṃyutta Nikāya* 41:6.
20. *Majjhima Nikāya* 44, Ñāṇamoli and Bodhi (1995), p. 399.
21. *Saṃyutta Nikāya* 22:79, Bodhi (2000), p. 915.
22. *Majjhima Nikāya* 43, Ñāṇamoli and Bodhi (1995), p. 388.
23. *Saṃyutta Nikāya* 12:2, Bodhi (2000), p. 535.
24. For example, Tsong-kha-pa, in his fourteenth-century work the *Lam rim chen mo,* states that *rūpa* is the first of the five bundles (form), whereas *nāma* corresponds to the other four (feeling, perception, inclination, and consciousness). See Tsong-kha-pa (2000), vol. 1, p. 317.
25. *Bṛhadāraṇyaka Upaniṣad* 1.4.7, Radhakrishnan (1994), p. 166.
26. *Saṃyutta Nikāya* 12:2, Bodhi (2000), p. 535.
27. This idea resonates with the later ideas of Maurice Merleau-Ponty, who also struggled to find a language to evoke the profoundly embodied

nature of experience. He uses the term "flesh" (*le chair*) to convey the world's sensuous fabric in and of which our bodies are intimately woven, intertwined, and "in-touch." For a good summary of this aspect of Merleau-Ponty's thought, see Carman (2008), chap. 3.

28. *Saṃyutta Nikāya* 22:56, Bodhi (2000), p. 896.
29. *Saṃyutta Nikāya* 22:56, Bodhi (2000), p. 897.
30. *Majjhima Nikāya* 38, Ñāṇamoli and Bodhi (1995), p. 351.
31. *Majjhima Nikāya* 38, Ñāṇamoli and Bodhi (1995), p. 351.
32. *Majjhima Nikāya* 43, Ñāṇamoli and Bodhi (1995), p. 388.
33. *Saṃyutta Nikāya* 12:65, Bodhi (2000), pp. 601–2. Cf. *Dīgha Nikāya* 14, Walshe (1995), p. 211.
34. *Saṃyutta Nikāya* 12:65, Bodhi (2000), pp. 601–2.
35. *Saṃyutta Nikāya* 12:67, Bodhi (2000), p. 608.
36. *Saṃyutta Nikāya* 9:11, Bodhi (2000), p. 301.
37. Rhys Davids and Stede, *Pali-English Dictionary*, p. 560.
38. *Saṃyutta Nikāya* 22:122, Bodhi (2000), p. 971.
39. *Saṃyutta Nikāya* 55:5, Bodhi (2000), p. 1792.
40. *Bṛhadāraṇyaka Upaniṣad* 1.4.7, Radhakrishnan (1994), p. 166.
41. *Saṃyutta Nikāya* 22:22, Bodhi (2000), pp. 871–72.
42. *Dhammapada* 80, Fronsdal (2005), p. 21. See *From the "Dhammapada"* in "Selected Discourses."
43. *Saṃyutta Nikāya* 22:59, Bodhi (2000), p. 901.
44. *Bṛhadāraṇyaka Upaniṣad* 3.7.3, Radhakrishnan (1994), p. 225.
45. *Saṃyutta Nikāya* 44:10, Bodhi (2000), pp. 1393–94.
46. *Saṃyutta Nikāya* 22:59, Bodhi (2000), p. 903.
47. *Bṛhadāraṇyaka Upaniṣad* 2.3.6, Radhakrishnan (1994), p. 194.
48. *Saṃyutta Nikāya* 22:86, Bodhi (2000), p. 937. Cf. *Majjhima Nikāya* 22.
49. Nāgārjuna, *Mūlamadhyamaka-kārikā* 18:1, Garfield (1995), p. 48. A freer translation of this verse appears as the epigraph of this chapter.
50. *Saṃyutta Nikāya* 12:65, Bodhi (2000), pp. 601–2. My italics.
51. *Dīgha Nikāya* 16, Walshe (1995), p. 245.
52. *Sutta-Nipāta* 651–53, Norman (2001), p. 84.
53. *Saṃyutta Nikāya* 22:59, Bodhi (2000), p. 901.
54. *Muṇḍaka Upaniṣad*. 3.2.8, Radhakrishnan (1994), p. 691.
55. *Udāna* 5.5, Ireland (1997), p. 73.

(8) Jīvaka: The Doctor

Epigraph: *Majjhima Nikāya* 22, Ñāṇamoli and Bodhi (1995), p. 227.

1. *Majjhima Nikāya* 26, Ñāṇamoli and Bodhi (1995), p. 260.
2. On snake venom to cure arthritis see A. Gomes, "Snake Venom—An Anti-Arthritis Natural Product," *Al Ameen Journal of Medical Science* (2010): 176, http://ajms.alameenmedical.org/ArticlePDFs/AJMS.3.3.2010.176.pdf. I am grateful to Dr. Graham Meadows for pointing out the possibility that a man in search of a snake in this context could be a doctor.
3. Śāntideva, *Bodhicaryāvatāra* IV:43, Batchelor (1979), p. 42.
4. *Mahāvagga* I:15, Horner (1951), p. 35.
5. *Mahāvagga* I:21, Horner (1951), p. 45. See *On Fire* in "Selected Discourses."
6. *Mahāvagga* I:21, Horner (1951), p. 45.
7. *Saṃyutta Nikāya* 4:6, Bodhi (2000), p. 199.
8. *Saṃyutta Nikāya* 4:6, Bodhi (2000), p. 199.
9. *Saṃyutta Nikāya* 36:21, Bodhi (2000), p. 1279. See *To Sīvaka 1* in "Selected Discourses."
10. Bronkhorst maintains that the three humors are not derived from Vedic medical tradition but were features of the local medical theory of Greater Magadha. Bronkhorst (2007), p. 60.
11. *Saṃyutta Nikāya* 36:21, Bodhi (2000), p. 1279. See *To Sīvaka 1* in "Selected Discourses."
12. *Aṅguttara Nikāya* VI:128, Bodhi (2012), p. 989. See *The Twenty-One* in "Selected Discourses."
13. Rockhill (1884), pp. 64–65. Cf. the Pali version: *Mahāvagga* VIII:1, Horner (1951), pp. 380–97.
14. *Mahāvagga* VII:1.8, Horner (1951), p. 382.
15. *Mahāvagga* VII:1.8, Horner (1951), p. 382.
16. McEvilley (2002), p. 15.
17. Ibid.
18. Laertius (1853), IX:35.
19. *Mahāvagga* VIII: 1.13, Horner (1951), p. 385.
20. *Mahāvagga* VIII: 1.13, Horner (1951), p. 386.
21. *Mahāvagga* VIII: 1.13, Horner (1951), pp. 390–94.

22. *Mahāvagga* VIII: 1.13, Horner (1951), p. 394.
23. *Mahāvagga* I:39, Horner (1951), p. 89.
24. *Cullavagga* V:14, Horner (1952), p. 164.
25. *Aṅguttara Nikāya* 1:256, Bodhi (2012), p. 112.
26. *Majjhima Nikāya* 58, Ñāṇamoli and Bodhi (1995), p. 498.
27. *Majjhima Nikāya* 58, Ñāṇamoli and Bodhi (1995), p. 499.
28. *Saṃyutta Nikāya* 12:15, Bodhi (2000), p. 544. See *To Kaccānagotta* in "Selected Discourses."
29. *Majjhima Nikāya* 58, Ñāṇamoli and Bodhi (1995), p. 501.
30. *Majjhima Nikāya* 55, Ñāṇamoli and Bodhi (1958), p. 474.
31. *Majjhima Nikāya* 55, Ñāṇamoli and Bodhi (1958), p. 474.
32. *Dīgha Nikāya* 16, Walshe (1995), p. 270.
33. *Dīgha Nikāya* 16, Walshe (1995), p. 270.
34. *Majjhima Nikāya* 129, Ñāṇamoli and Bodhi (1958), p. 1021.
35. *Dīgha Nikāya* 2, Walshe (1995), p. 91.
36. *Dīgha Nikāya* 2, Walshe (1995), pp. 91–93.
37. *Dīgha Nikāya* 2, Walshe (1995), p. 108.
38. *Dīgha Nikāya* 2, Walshe (1995), p. 108.
39. *Dīgha Nikāya* 2, Walshe (1995), p. 108.
40. *Mahāvagga* XXVI:1–3, Horner (1951), pp. 431–32. Cf. Matthew 25:35–36.
41. Rockhill (1884), p. 50.
42. *Aṅguttara Nikāya* VI:128, Bodhi (2012), p. 989. See *The Twenty-One* in "Selected Discourses."

(9) The Everyday Sublime

Epigraph: Ferguson (2000), p. 96.

1. Wittgenstein (1961), 6.44.
2. *Saṃyutta Nikāya* 54:11, Bodhi (2000), p. 1778.
3. *Majjhima Nikāya* 43, Ñāṇamoli and Bodhi (1995), p. 394.
4. *Majjhima Nikāya* 10, Ñāṇamoli and Bodhi (1995), p. 146.
5. These are traditionally known as the seven "factors of awakening" (*sambojjhanga*).
6. *Majjhima Nikāya* 10, Ñāṇamoli and Bodhi (1995), p. 147.
7. *Majjhima Nikāya* 10, Ñāṇamoli and Bodhi (1995), p. 148.

8. *Aṅguttara Nikāya* V:14, Bodhi (2012), p. 637.
9. *Majjhima Nikāya* 26, Ñāṇamoli and Bodhi (1995), p. 260. See *Awakening* in "Selected Discourses."
10. *Aṅguttara Nikāya* VI:47, Bodhi (2012), p. 919. See *To Sīvaka 2* in "Selected Discourses."
11. Kusan (1978), p. 52.
12. Cited in Buswell (1983), p. 335. The wording is my own.
13. Rabten (1992), pp. 79–81.
14. *Saṃyutta Nikāya* 35:13, Bodhi (2000), pp. 1136–37. See *Three Questions* in "Selected Discourses."
15. *Dīgha Nikāya* 14, Walshe (1995), pp. 207–10.
16. *Majjhima Nikāya* 26, Ñāṇamoli and Bodhi (1995), p. 259.
17. *Sutta-Nipāta* 800–802, Norman (2001), p. 107.
18. *Sutta-Nipāta* 793, Norman (2001), p. 106.
19. Watson (1993), p. 13.
20. *Sutta-Nipāta* 780, Norman (2001), p. 104.
21. Ferguson (2000), p. 199.
22. *Saṃyutta Nikāya* 12:15, Bodhi (2000), p. 544. See *To Kaccānagotta* in "Selected Discourses."
23. Watson (1993), p. 36. My italics.
24. Kusan (2009), p. 76.
25. Ferguson (2000), pp. 198–99.
26. *Saṃyutta Nikāya* 12:15, Bodhi (2000), p. 544. See *To Kaccānagotta* in "Selected Discourses."
27. Nāgārjuna, *Mūlamadhyamaka-kārikā* 15:6–7, Garfield (1995), p. 40.
28. Gómez (1976), pp. 137–65.
29. Rig Veda, 10.129, O'Flaherty (1981), pp. 25–26.
30. Watson (1964), p. 35.
31. Ibid., p. 45.
32. Long and Sedley (1987), p. 13.
33. Ibid., pp. 14–15.
34. Sextus Empiricus (1933), p. 19.
35. *Majjhima Nikāya* 10, Ñāṇamoli and Bodhi (1995), p. 155.
36. Ferguson (2000), 199.

(10) Ānanda: The Attendant

Epigraphs: (1) *Majjhima Nikāya* 90, Ñāṇamoli and Bodhi (1995), p. 739; (2) *Saṃyutta Nikāya* 48:41, Bodhi (2000), p. 1686; (3) *Theragāthā* 1034, C. Rhys Davids (1980).

1. *Aṅguttara Nikāya* VI:119–39, Bodhi (2012), p. 989. See *The Twenty-One* in "Selected Discourses."
2. Burlingame (1995), vol. 2, p. 45.
3. Rockhill (1884), p. 119.
4. Bodhi (2000), p. 802 n. 288.
5. Rockhill (1884), p. 57.
6. *Saṃyutta Nikāya* 22:83, Bodhi (2000), p. 928.
7. *Saṃyutta Nikāya* 22:83, Bodhi (2000), p. 928.
8. Rockhill (1884), p. 88.
9. Malalsekera (1997), pp. 250–51.
10. *Udāna* 1.5, Ireland (1997), p. 16. Ireland omits Devadatta from the list on the grounds that "this hardly makes sense, as Devadatta was the Buddha's evil-minded, ambitious cousin" (p. 118). He thereby uncritically follows the orthodox view. He points out that while Devadatta appears in the Pali Text Society's edition of the Pali text, his name is absent in the Singhalese and Burmese editions of the canon.
11. *Cullavagga* VII, Horner (1952), p. 265.
12. *Cullavagga* VII, Horner (1952), p. 264.
13. *Cullavagga* VII, Horner (1952), p. 276. Rockhill (1884), p. 87, gives a different list.
14. *Cullavagga* VII, Horner (1952), p. 278.
15. *Cullavagga* VII, Horner (1952), p. 260.
16. Ray (1994), p. 172; this accords with the prohibitions listed in the Tibetan Vinaya, translated in Rockhill (1884), p. 87.
17. Ray (1994), pp. 162–73.
18. *Dīgha Nikāya* 16, Walshe (1995), p. 244.
19. *Dīgha Nikāya* 16, Walshe (1995), pp. 244–45.
20. *Dīgha Nikāya* 16, Walshe (1995), p. 245.
21. *Dīgha Nikāya* 16, Walshe (1995), p. 245.

22. *Dīgha Nikāya* 16, Walshe (1995), p. 245.
23. *Dīgha Nikāya* 16, Walshe (1995), p. 245.
24. *Dīgha Nikāya* 16, Walshe (1995), p. 257.
25. Mettanando (2000).
26. *Dīgha Nikāya* 16, Walshe (1995), p. 265.
27. *Dīgha Nikāya* 16, Walshe (1995), p. 266.
28. *Dīgha Nikāya* 16, Walshe (1995), p. 273.
29. Burlingame (1995), vol. 2, p. 45.
30. *Dīgha Nikāya* 16, Walshe (1995), p. 272.
31. *Dīgha Nikāya* 16, Walshe (1995), p. 268.
32. *Dīgha Nikāya* 16, Walshe (1995), pp. 269–70.
33. *Dīgha Nikāya* 16, Walshe (1995), p. 270.
34. *Dīgha Nikāya* 16, Walshe (1995), p. 270.
35. *Dīgha Nikāya* 16, Walshe (1995), p. 273.
36. *Dīgha Nikāya* 16, Walshe (1995), p. 275.
37. *Aṅguttara Nikāya* I:191, Bodhi (2012), p. 109.
38. Bodhi (2000), p. 806 n. 307.
39. *Saṃyutta Nikāya* 16:11, Bodhi (2000), p. 679.
40. Rockhill (1884), pp. 150–51.
41. *Saṃyutta Nikāya* 16:6–8, Bodhi (2000), pp. 667–71.
42. Rockhill (1884), 151.
43. *Saṃyutta Nikāya* 16:11, Bodhi (2000), p. 677.
44. *Saṃyutta Nikāya* 16:11, Bodhi (2000), p. 677.
45. *Majjhima Nikāya* 108, Ñāṇamoli and Bodhi (1995), p. 880.
46. *Majjhima Nikāya* 108, Ñāṇamoli and Bodhi (1995), pp. 881–82.
47. *Majjhima Nikāya* 108, Ñāṇamoli and Bodhi (1995), pp. 882–83.
48. *Majjhima Nikāya* 108, Ñāṇamoli and Bodhi (1995), p. 883.
49. *Aṅguttara Nikāya* VI:128, Bodhi (2012), p. 989. See *The Twenty-One* in "Selected Discourses."
50. *Cullavagga* XI, Horner (1952), p. 399.
51. I follow the Pali here. Cf. Rockhill (1884), p. 154.
52. *Theragāthā* 1034–36, C. Rhys Davids (1980).
53. *Cullavagga* XI, Horner (1952), p. 396.
54. The Pali Vinaya has him start his recitation with the *Brahmajāla Sutta*

(*Dīgha Nikāya* 1). Scholars disagree as to whether this council actually took place, let alone in which sequence the texts were recited.

(11) A Culture of Awakening

Epigraph: *Saṃyutta Nikāya* 22:94, Bodhi (2000), p. 949.

1. Stevenson's best-known work is *Twenty Cases Suggestive of Reincarnation* (1966).
2. *Saṃyutta Nikāya* 36:21, Bodhi (2000), p. 1279. See *To Sīvaka 1* in "Selected Discourses."
3. Vasubandhu, *Abhidharmakośa* 3:1, Vallée Poussin (1923–31), vol. 3.
4. *Saṃyutta Nikāya* 36:21, Bodhi (2000), p. 1279. See *To Sīvaka 1* in "Selected Discourses."
5. *Majjhima Nikāya* 4, Ñāṇamoli and Bodhi (1995), p. 105.
6. *Saṃyutta Nikāya* 51:11, Bodhi (2000), pp. 1726–29. For an example of his speaking in general terms see *Saṃyutta Nikāya* 22:79, Bodhi (2000), p. 914.
7. *Majjhima Nikāya* 4, Ñāṇamoli and Bodhi (1995), pp. 105–6.
8. Bronkhorst (2007), p. 144.
9. *Majjhima Nikāya* 26, Ñāṇamoli and Bodhi (1995), pp. 259–60. See *Awakening* in "Selected Discourses."
10. *Dhammapada* 21, Fronsdal (2005), p. 6.
11. Cf. *Sutta-Nipāta* 446–48, Norman (2001), p. 53.
12. *Saṃyutta Nikāya* 4:19, Bodhi (2000), p. 208.
13. Yampolsky (1967), p. 151.
14. *Saṃyutta Nikāya* 12:65, Bodhi (2000), p. 601. See chapter 3, section 8, for a longer discussion of this parable.
15. Taylor (2007), p. 159.
16. *Saṃyutta Nikāya* 55:2, Bodhi (2000), p. 1789.
17. *Saṃyutta Nikāya* 41:1, 5, 7, Bodhi (2000), pp. 1314–26.
18. *Majjhima Nikāya* 73, Ñāṇamoli and Bodhi (1995), p. 597.
19. Buber (1979), pp. 50–52.
20. See the special issue of *Contemporary Buddhism*, 14, no. 1 (2013), which contains articles by these authors on the life of U Dhammaloka.
21. Turner (2013), p. 70.

22. See Batchelor (2011), pp. 41, 307–8.
23. See Schopen (1997).
24. See Gernet (1995).

Afterword

1. *Cullavagga* XII, Horner (1952), pp. 407–30.
2. See Lamotte (1988), pp. 96–100, for details on the Nanda dynasty.
3. Malalasekara (1997), vol. 1, p. 454.
4. McCrindle (1877), pp. 98–99.
5. Ibid., pp. 101–2.
6. Ibid., p. 102.
7. Lamotte (1988), p. 416.
8. *Saṃyutta Nikāya* 36.7, Bodhi (2000), p. 1266. The Pali commentary (p. 1434 n. 237) says that he did this in order to set an example to the other *bhikkhus* to attend to the sick.
9. Rockhill (1884), p. 50.
10. Batchelor (2011), p. 28.
11. Ibid., pp. 161–69, 171, 190–95.
12. Ibid., pp. 242, 243–44.
13. Ibid., pp. 256–57.

Selected Discourses from the Pali Canon

1. *Saṃyutta Nikāya* 35:13, Bodhi (2000), p. 1136.
2. *Majjhima Nikāya* 26, Ñāṇamoli and Bodhi (1995), p. 260.
3. *Mahāvagga* I:6.16–28, in Horner (1951), pp. 15–17; *Saṃyutta Nikāya* 56:11; Bodhi (2000), pp. 1843–46.
4. *Mahāvagga* I: 21.1–4, in Horner (1951), pp. 45–46; *Saṃyutta Nikāya* 35:28; Bodhi (2000), p. 1143.
5. *Saṃyutta Nikāya* 35.23, Bodhi (2000), p. 1140.
6. *Saṃyutta Nikāya* 12:15, Bodhi (2000), p. 544.
7. *Majjhima Nikāya* 121, Ñāṇamoli and Bodhi (1995), pp. 965–70.
8. *Saṃyutta Nikāya* 36:21, Bodhi (2000), pp. 1278–79.
9. *Aṅguttara Nikāya* 6:47, Bodhi (2012), pp. 919–20.

10. *Aṅguttara Nikāya* 6:119–39, Bodhi (2012), pp. 989–90. In addition to Mahānāma and Jīvaka, nineteen other householders are described in the same way, making a total of twenty-one.
11. *Dhammapada* 80, Fronsdal (2005), p. 6.
12. *Dhammapada* 21, Fronsdal (2005), p. 21.
13. *Dhammapada* 49, Fronsdal (2005), p. 13.

Bibliography

Allchin, F. R. *The Archaeology of Early Historic South Asia: The Emergence of Cities and States*. Cambridge: Cambridge University Press, 1995.

Bailey, Greg, and Mabbett, Ian. *The Sociology of Early Buddhism*. Cambridge: Cambridge University Press, 2003.

Batchelor, Stephen. *Alone with Others: An Existential Approach to Buddhism*. New York: Grove, 1983.

———. *The Awakening of the West: The Encounter of Buddhism and Western Culture*. Brattleboro, VT: Echo Point Press, 2011 (first published 1994).

———. *Buddhism without Beliefs: A Contemporary Guide to Awakening*. New York: Riverhead, 1997.

———. *Confession of a Buddhist Atheist*. New York: Spiegel and Grau, 2010.

———. *The Faith to Doubt: Glimpses of Buddhist Uncertainty*. Berkeley: Counterpoint, 2015 (first published 1990).

———. *Living with the Devil: A Meditation on Good and Evil*. New York: Riverhead, 2004.

———. "A Secular Buddhism." *Journal of Global Buddhism*, 13 (2012): 87–107, http://www.globalbuddhism.org/13/batchelor12.pdf.

———. *Verses from the Center: A Buddhist Vision of the Sublime*. New York: Riverhead, 2000.

Bodhi, Bhikkhu (Trans.). *The Connected Discourses of the Buddha: A New Translation of the Saṃyutta Nikāya*. Somerville, MA: Wisdom Publications, 2000.

——— (Trans.). *The Numerical Discourses of the Buddha: A Translation of the Aṅguttara Nikāya.* Somerville, MA: Wisdom Publications, 2012.

Boep Jeong (Trans.). *The Mirror of Zen: The Classic Guide to Buddhist Practice by Zen Master So Sahn.* Boston: Shambhala, 2006.

Bronkhorst, Johannes. *Buddhism in the Shadow of Brahmanism.* Leiden: Brill, 2011.

———. *Greater Magadha: Studies in the Culture of Early India.* Leiden: Brill, 2007.

Buber, Martin. *Between Man and Man.* Glasgow: Collins, 1979 (first published 1947).

Burlingame, Eugene Watson (Trans.). *Buddhist Legends (Dhammapada Commentary).* 3 volumes. Oxford, UK: Pali Text Society, 1995 (first published 1921).

Buswell, Robert E. *The Korean Approach to Zen: The Collected Works of Chinul.* Honolulu: University of Hawaii Press, 1983.

Carman, Taylor. *Merleau-Ponty.* New York: Routledge, 2008.

Cleary, Thomas, and Cleary, J. C. *The Blue Cliff Record.* Boulder, CO: Shambhala, 1997.

Conze, Edward (Ed. with I. B. Horner, D. Snellgrove, and A. Waley). *Buddhist Texts through the Ages.* Oxford, UK: Bruno Cassirer, 1954.

Cupitt, Don. *After God: The Future of Religion.* London: Weidenfeld and Nicholson, 1997.

Darwin, Charles. *On the Origin of Species; or, The Preservation of Favoured Races in the Struggle for Life.* Cambridge: Harvard University Press, 1964 (first published 1859).

Dhammika, Ven. S. (Trans.). *The Edicts of King Asoka.* Kandy: Buddhist Publication Society, 1994. www.accesstoinsight.org/lib/authors/dhammika/wheel386.html.

Ferguson, Andy. *Zen's Chinese Heritage: The Masters and Their Teachings.* Boston: Wisdom Publications, 2000.

Finnegan, Damchö Diana. "'For the Sake of Women, Too': Ethics and Gender in the Narratives of the Mūlasarvāstivāda Vinaya." Ph.D. dissertation, University of Wisconsin-Madison, 2009.

Fronsdal, Gil (Trans.). *The Dhammapada.* Boston: Shambhala, 2005.

Garfield, Jay L. (Trans.). *The Fundamental Wisdom of the Middle Way: Nāgār-*

juna's "Mūlamadhyamakakārikā." New York: Oxford University Press, 1995.

Gernet, Jacques. *Buddhism in Chinese Society: An Economic History from the Fifth to the Tenth Centuries.* New York: Columbia University Press, 1995.

Gombrich, Richard F. *How Buddhism Began: The Conditioned Genesis of the Early Teachings.* London: Athlone, 1996.

———. *What the Buddha Thought.* London: Equinox, 2009.

Gómez, Luis O. "Proto-Mādhyamika in the Pāli Canon." *Philosophy East and West,* 26 (1976): 137–65.

Guignon, Charles B. (Ed.). *The Cambridge Companion to Heidegger.* 2nd edition. Cambridge: Cambridge University Press, 2006.

Jacobi, Hermann (Trans.). *Jaina Sutras.* Part 1, *The Ākārāṅga Sūtra and the Kalpa Sūtra.* Oxford: Clarendon Press, 1884.

Heidegger, Martin. (Trans. John Macquarrie and Edward Robinson.) *Being and Time.* Oxford, UK: Basil Blackwell, 1962.

Hopkins, Jeffrey. *Meditation on Emptiness.* London: Wisdom Publications, 1983.

Horner, I. B. (Trans.). *The Book of the Discipline.* Vol. IV, *Mahāvagga.* Oxford, UK: Pali Text Society, 1951.

——— (Trans.). *The Book of the Discipline.* Vol. V, *Cullavagga.* Oxford, UK: Pali Text Society, 1952.

Ireland, John D. (Trans.). *The Udāna and the Itivuttaka.* Kandy: Buddhist Publication Society, 1997.

Jayatilleke, K. N. *Early Buddhist Theory of Knowledge.* Delhi: Motilal Banarsidass, 1963.

Kusan Sunim. *Nine Mountains: Dharma Lectures of the Korean Meditation Master Ku San.* Song Kwang Sa Monastery, Suncheon, South Korea: International Meditation Center, 1978.

———. *The Way of Korean Zen.* Boston: Weatherhill, 2009 (first published 1985).

Laertius, Diogenes. (Trans. C. D. Yonge.) *The Lives of Eminent Philosophers.* London: Henry G. Bohn, 1853.

Lamotte, Étienne. (Trans. Sara Webb-Boin.) *History of Indian Buddhism: From the Origins to the Śaka Era.* Louvain, Belgium: Peeters Press, 1988.

Ling, Trevor. *The Buddha: Buddhist Civilisation in India and Ceylon.* London: Temple Smith, 1973.

Long, A. A., and Sedley, D. (Trans. and ed.). *The Hellenistic Philosophers.* Volume I. Cambridge: Cambridge University Press, 1987.

MacIntyre, Alasdair. *After Virtue: A Study in Moral Theory.* Notre Dame: University of Notre Dame Press, 1981.

Malalasekera, G. P. *Dictionary of Pāli Proper Names.* 3 volumes. Oxford, UK: Pali Text Society, 1997 (first published 1938).

McCrindle, J. W. *Ancient India as Described by Megasthenes and Arrian.* London: Trübner, 1877.

McEvilley, Thomas. *The Shape of Ancient Thought: Comparative Studies in Greek and Indian Philosophy.* New York: Allworth, 2002.

McMahan, David L. *The Making of Buddhist Modernism.* New York: Oxford University Press, 2008.

Metaxas, Eric. *Bonhoeffer: Pastor, Martyr, Prophet, Spy.* Nashville, TN: Thomas Nelson, 2010.

Mettanando Bhikkhu, Dr. "Did Buddha Die of Mesenteric Infarction?" *Bangkok Post,* 17 May 2000. http://www.lankalibrary.com/Bud/buddha_death.htm.

Mohr, Thea, and Tsedroen, Jampa (Eds.). *Dignity and Discipline: Reviving Full Ordination for Buddhist Nuns.* Somerville, MA: Wisdom Publications, 2010.

Montaigne, Michel de. (Trans. and ed. M. A. Screech.) *The Complete Essays.* London: Penguin, 2003.

Nagel, Thomas. *The View from Nowhere.* New York: Oxford University Press, 1986.

Ñāṇamoli, Bhikkhu, and Bodhi, Bhikkhu. (Trans.) *The Middle Length Discourses of the Buddha: A Translation of the Majjhima Nikāya.* Boston: Wisdom Publications, 1995.

Newland, Guy. *Appearance and Reality: The Two Truths in the Four Buddhist Tenet Systems.* Ithaca, NY: Snow Lion, 1999.

Norman, K. R. *Collected Papers.* Vol. II. Oxford, UK: Pali Text Society, 2003.

——— (Trans.). *The Group of Discourses (Sutta-Nipāta).* Oxford, UK: Pali Text Society, 2001.

———. *A Philological Approach to Buddhism.* Lancaster, UK: Pali Text Society, 2006.

Nongbri, Brent. *Before Religion: A History of a Modern Concept.* New Haven: Yale University Press, 2013.

Nyanaponika, Thera, and Hecker, Hellmuth. (Ed. Bhikkhu Bodhi.) *Great Disciples of the Buddha: Their Lives, Their Works, Their Legacy.* Boston: Wisdom Publications, 2003.

O'Flaherty, Wendy Doniger. *The Rig Veda: An Anthology.* Harmondsworth: Penguin, 1981.

Parks, Tim. *Teach Us to Sit Still: A Sceptic's Search for Health and Healing.* London: Harvill Secker, 2010.

Rabten, Geshe. (Trans. and ed. Stephen Batchelor.) *The Mind and Its Functions.* Le Mont-Pèlerin, Switzerland: Editions Rabten Choeling, 1992 (first published 1978).

Radhakrishnan, S. *The Principal Upaniṣads.* New Delhi: HarperCollins, 1994.

Rahula, Walpola. *What the Buddha Taught.* Bedford, UK: Gordon Fraser, 1967.

Ray, Reginald A. *Buddhist Saints in India: A Study in Buddhist Values and Orientations.* New York: Oxford University Press, 1994.

Rhys Davids, Caroline A. F. (Trans.). *Psalms of the Early Buddhists.* Oxford, UK: Pali Text Society, 1980. (Includes the *Theragāthā*, first published 1909, and the *Therigāthā*, first published 1937.)

Rhys Davids, T. W., and Stede, William. *The Pali Text Society's Pali-English Dictionary.* London: Pali Text Society, 1979 (first published 1921–25).

Rockhill, W. Woodville (Trans.). *The Life of the Buddha and the Early History of His Order: Derived from Tibetan Works in the Bkah-hgyur and Bstan-hgyur.* London: Trübner, 1884.

Rorty, Richard. *Contingency, Irony and Solidarity.* New York: Cambridge University Press, 1989.

———. *Philosophy as Cultural Politics.* Volume 4 of *Philosophical Papers.* Cambridge: Cambridge University Press, 2007.

Rorty, Richard, and Vattimo, Gianni. *The Future of Religion.* New York: Columbia University Press, 2005.

Sacks, Oliver. *An Anthropologist on Mars: Seven Paradoxical Tales.* London: Picador, 1995.

Śāntideva. (Translated from the Sanskrit by Kate Crosby and Andrew Skilton.) *The Bodhicaryāvatāra.* Oxford, UK: Oxford University Press, 1996.

———. (Translated from the Tibetan by Stephen Batchelor.) *A Guide to the Bodhisattva's Way of Life.* Dharamsala, India: Library of Tibetan Works and Archives, 1979.

Schopen, Gregory. *Bones, Stones, and Buddhist Monks: Collected Papers on the Archaeology, Epigraphy, and Texts of Monastic Buddhism in India*. Honolulu: University of Hawai'i Press, 1997.

Schumann, H. W. *The Historical Buddha: The Times, Life and Teachings of the Founder of Buddhism*. London: Arkana, 1989.

Sextus Empiricus. (Trans. R. G. Bury.) *Outlines of Pyrrhonism*. Cambridge: Harvard University Press, 1933.

Steinkellner, Ernst. *Śāntideva: Eintritt in das Leben zur Erleuchtung* (*Bodhicaryāvatāra*). Düsseldorf: Diederichs, 1981.

Stevenson, Ian. *Twenty Cases Suggestive of Reincarnation*. Charlottesville: University of Virginia Press, 1966.

Sujato, Bhikkhu, and Brahmali, Bhikkhu. "The Authenticity of Early Buddhist Texts." *Journal of the Oxford Centre for Buddhist Studies*, 5 (2014): supplement.

SuttaCentral: Early Buddhist Texts, Translations, and Parallels, https://suttacentral.net.

Taylor, Charles. *A Secular Age*. Cambridge, MA: Belknap, 2007.

Tillich, Paul. *The Dynamics of Faith*. New York: Harper and Row, 1958.

Tsong-kha-pa. (Trans. The Lamrim Chenmo Translation Committee.) *The Great Treatise on the Stages of the Path to Enlightenment*. 3 volumes. Ithaca, NY: Snow Lion, 2000, 2002, 2004.

Turner, Alicia. "The Bible, the Bottle and the Knife: Religion as a Mode of Resisting Colonialism for U Dhammaloka." *Contemporary Buddhism*, 14 (2013): 66–77.

Vallée Poussin, Louis de la (Trans.). *L'Abhidharmakosa de Vasubhandu*. 6 volumes. Paris: Paul Geuthner, 1923–31.

Vattimo, Gianni. *After Christianity*. New York: Columbia University Press, 2002.

———. *A Farewell to Truth*. New York: Columbia University Press, 2011.

Walshe, Maurice (Trans.). *The Long Discourses of the Buddha: A Translation of the Dīgha Nikāya*. Boston: Wisdom Publications, 1995.

Watson, Burton. *Chuang Tzu: The Inner Chapters*. New York: Columbia University Press, 1964.

———. *The Zen Teachings of Master Lin-chi: A Translation of the Lin-chi-lu*. New York: Columbia University Press, 1993.

Wittgenstein, Ludwig. (Trans. G. E. M. Anscombe.) *Philosophical Investigations.* Oxford, UK: Basil Blackwell, 1958.

———. (Trans. David Pears and Brian McGuinness). *Tractatus Logico—Philosophicus.* London: Routledge, 1961 (first published 1921).

Woodward, F. L. (Trans.). (Ed. and with an introduction by Caroline Rhys Davids.) *The Book of Kindred Sayings (Sanyutta Nikāya), Part IV.* Oxford, UK: Pali Text Society, 1993 (first published 1930).

——— (Trans.). (With an introduction by Caroline Rhys Davids.) *The Minor Anthologies of the Pāli Canon.* Part II: *Udāna.* London: Geoffrey Cumberlege / Oxford University Press, 1948 (first published 1935).

Wynne, Alexander. *The Origin of Buddhist Meditation.* London: Routledge, 2007.

Yamada, Kōun (Trans.). *The Gateless Gate: The Classic Book of Zen Koans.* Somerville, MA: Wisdom Publications, 2004.

Yampolsky, Philip B. (Trans.). *The Platform Sutra of the Sixth Patriarch.* New York: Columbia University Press, 1967.

Index